Property & Peace:
Insurgency, Strategy and the Statute of Frauds

by Geoffrey Demarest

Published by Books Express Publishing
Copyright © Books Express, 2011
ISBN 978-1-780390-46-8

Books Express publications are available from all good retail
and online booksellers. For publishing proposals and direct
ordering please contact us at: info@books-express.com

Abstract

The success of a society depends on construction of formal, liberal property regimes. The United States and other Western countries waste billions of development dollars every year on programs that have not been built on firm property systems.

The West's property regimes are successful because of the high quality of the evidence of everyday rights, the capacity of the citizenry and governments to implement the meaning of that evidence, and because the basic rules which determine what can be owned and who can be owners are liberal in measure appropriate to the common understanding of justice.

Formalized property information feeds conflict resolution mechanisms by clearly identifying owners, claimants, rights and duties so that disagreements can be more peaceably reconciled; creates confident stakeholders willing to support the rule of law; helps create and expose capital, which ameliorates negative socio-economic conditions that fuel internal conflict; produces landowners who are less inclined to engage in illegal behavior because they risk forfeiture; and the records associated with formal property provide a powerful forensic tool with which to support peaceful conflict resolution processes, restitution programs, and bring violators of basic human rights to justice.

The condition in which humans are secure in their possessions is in-and-of-itself a happiness. Nevertheless, the principle assertion of this book is not that building property systems will lead to peace. The assertion has been in the negative. In countries where informal property regimes are allowed to continue, there will not be peace. Outside the lines of formal property lies possession by force. The gamut of societal choices is narrow, the choices few – formal property, internal violence, or tyranny. People should not be led to choose tyranny over violence because the condition of formal property has not been offered.

ii

Property & Peace:
Insurgency, Strategy and the Statute of Frauds

Contents

Acknowledgements

The number of individuals that deserve my thanks is so great I will undoubtedly forget to include important names if I attempt to list each of them. Among the organizations that contributed most to completion of this project I want to highlight our Foreign Military Studies Office, the members of which have suffered me in this matter far longer than humanity dictates. Their assistance and guidance is always insightful, informed, positive, enthusiastic, useful and creative. Of special help from outside the Office were the Mercatus Center at George Mason University, the Department of Geography at the University of Kansas, and the Consortium for the Study of Intelligence in Washington, D.C. I also wish to thank my family for their patient support.

Author's note regarding the subtitle

In 1677 the English Parliament passed what would survive as one of the most durable instruments in English-speaking law, the Statute of Frauds. More than just a convenience for the court, it was a moment of recognition that physical technologies, and persons who could put them to use, were available in sufficient quantity to be applied to ameliorate the human tendency to lie, cheat and steal. From that point on, any important agreement in the realm (anything dealing with land was considered important) would have to be in writing if it were to be recognized and enforced by the State. Later, agreements would have to be signed, then witnessed, then notarized, then copied, photocopied, distributed and even put on the Internet. All of the requirements go to the same end – to make evidence more reliable and court decisions more effective. Subornation, perjury, contempt and vigilantism are more likely contained, and systems of commitments can span beyond human memory and familial control. The jurisprudential event of 1677 was a milestone in the evolution of an innovative discipline that had not been not so formally appreciated since the time of the Romans. The Statute of Frauds is mentioned in the title to this book to acknowledge that the rejection of oral evidence became a competitive advantage of Western civilization. The West systematically prepared the legal environment for conflict resolution. That the pen is mightier than the sword is more than shibboleth. The importance of this cultural inheritance may have been overlooked, forgotten or taken for granted, but it is a quotidian key to peace. The requirement that the evidence of human agreements be precise, comprehensive and transparent is much of what makes life in your county peaceable. It is what puts so many of today's practical geographers to work at the county courthouse or office of the city manager. There they maintain ownership maps, land-use plans and the like. If not for such records, their maintenance and the courts and markets that apply them, we would live in a world of possession by force -- a continual physical struggle -- the kind of constant violent contest in which we find much of the rest of the world.

Concepts Summary

1. Why Property?

Property is an elemental approach to conflict resolution.

> -- Property is not touchable things, but things along with sets of rights and duties associating people with things.
> -- Property is a social contract - an agreement about who has what, and about enforcing agreements.
> -- The alternative to property is 'possession by force.'

2. Globalization of trespass

Power, property and wealth can be the same.

> -- Insurgents reject the social contract, criminals simply break it. Both can use terror. There are plenty of combinations.
> -- Globalization includes expanding civil law and social contracts.
> -- Globalization also means diffusion of the power to reject social contracts, or to break them.
> -- Some of the most pressing national security issues, like changes coming to Cuba, are best considered in property terms.

3. The Colombia Case

Colombia has suffered violent organized insurgents and criminals more than most countries. A democracy, property is the key to both victory and lasting peace.

4. Hohfeld versus Haushofer

US strategy was built on obsolete, big-space geopolitics.

> -- We can improve the way we measure power.
> -- We can apply property analysis to internal armed
> conflicts that geopolitics does not help us understand.
> -- Property analysis starts with the rights and duties at
> issue, identifies owner and claimant identities, their
> objectives and their resources.
> -- Formalized property causes wealth and power to leave
> tracks that can be found and followed. The most
> important tracks are not physical, but cultural.
> -- We can measure the likelihood that societies will
> harbor smugglers and murderers.

5. What is to be done?

Study social contracts, improve property.

> -- Learn geography at the local level and at the contract
> level.
> -- Seek knowledge about property rights and duties.
> -- Prepare environments for conflict resolution and
> victory.
> -- Fix a bad social contract, defend a good one.

Chapter One: Why "Property"?

Chapter One: Why "Property"?

Dosn't thou 'ear my 'erse's legs, as they canters awaäy,
Proputty, proputty, proputty--that's what I 'ears 'em saäy.
Proputty, proputty, proputty--Sam, thou's an ass for thy paaïns;
Theer's moor sense i' one o' 'is legs, nor in all thy braaïns.[1]
Alfred Lord Tennyson from "The Northern Farmer"

---

[1] Alfred Tennyson, Alfred Tennyson Selected Poetry: Edited, with an Introduction by Douglas Smith (New York: Random House, 1951), p. 307. See also, Tennyson's *Lady Godiva*, perhaps the best rendition of the legend, which relates her ride as a property tax protest.

Purpose and assertions

"How could something so important have slipped our minds?"[2]
Hernando De Soto

Places with informal property are doomed to violence. No formal property, no peace.[3]

This book argues that the quality of foreign real property systems be made a priority issue in US diplomatic, military and intelligence thinking and strategy. The text does not argue that creating better land records will assure peaceful coexistence. Formal real property record systems correlate with peaceful societies, but the principle assertion here is in the negative. Even with formal records, functioning property courts, and a free and fluid market in land a place may still suffer violent dissention. However, a polity that does not formalize ownership rights and duties, especially rights and duties related to land, will not enjoy peace. Comprehensive, precise, transparent expression of real property is a necessary precondition of peace; places outside the lines of formal property necessarily slump toward possession by force. From this assertion others follow that bear on the way global security is pursued…

In lands where property has not been formalized, most other developmental efforts will be a waste of time and

---

[2] Hernando De Soto, The Mystery of Capital: Why Capitalism Triumphs in the West and Fails Everywhere Else. New York,: Basic Books, 2000, p. 8. Mr. De Soto is one of the leading proponents of property formalization as a cornerstone of equitable development.

[3] In some social contexts and on small scale humans live harmoniously without the necessity of a local courthouse filled with property plats and their keepers. But the author's assertion is made in a world of large polities and desperate conflicts. In this context, the assertion is absolute: there cannot be a liberal polity, free and peaceful, without formal property.

2

money, since they will ultimately succumb to violence and tyranny.

Human rights prosecutions are usually a chase after the ultimate symptoms of a society's failure to create and respect formalized property.

The above statements imply a prescription that property systems be strengthened or "formalized" -- a word that will be given its required explanation a bit later, but which in shorthand means that agreements about rights and duties be accurate, comprehensive, and easily available for inspection, so that they may be given meaning through some predictable enforcement mechanism. Formal is not the same as liberal, also an important quality ultimately likely to promote social peace. Liberality concerns the variety of identities that can successfully claim ownership, as well as the gamut of rights that can be successfully claimed. The revolutionary or the insurgent, for the purposes of this text, rejects the overall system of ownership -- the basic rules regarding who can own what and how. The pure criminal just breaks the rules.

As to some countries of the world where political violence is the norm, or armed conflict is underway, an argument may arise that formalized property is a luxury attainable only after security and peace are achieved. This may be true in the most immediate sense of active combat, however, the more consequential truth is the opposite. <u>First there must be formal property, *and then* there can be security and peace.</u> A final assertion, leading from those just made, regards what we know and what we don't know about the world, and about conflict. We do not know enough about who owns what in the world. Hence, the last of the series of secondary assertions, touched on repeatedly throughout the book, is as follows:

Those who deal with issues of peace and violence, or of economic development and social justice, or of threats to security, should demand to know who owns what, and

3

where. A democratic society must know in detail who owns the land and how much it is.

The above point, about what leaders should demand to know, does not exclude military commanders, and especially those facing an intelligent enemy in situations where maneuver combat of heavily equipped forces is the exception. In 'low intensity' combat situations, property information may fuel the most powerful kind of intelligence able to uncover enemy whereabouts, associations, wealth and lines of communication.

A purpose of this book, then, is to convince, on both the theoretical and practical levels, why property creation and formalization should be raised as a principal column of plans for a peaceful world. As a virtue of "nation-building," "stabilizing" or "democratizing," the formalization of property deserves mental, emotional and practical weight equal to that of human rights prosecutions, fair elections or satellite images.[4] Foreign diplomacy, security strategy, intelligence planning and developmental efforts would do well to incorporate the spread and growth of formal, if not liberal, property regimes.

Let there be no doubt as to the relationship of this argument to national security, beginning with that of the United States. The United States' national security goals for places like Iraq, Afghanistan or Colombia are that they not be cradles, harbors or facilitators of smuggling and murder. Whether the specific object of contraband is

---

[4] That property creation and formalization would be as important as elections in aiding the cause of liberty is a point eloquently made by Richard Pipes in Property and Freedom (New York: Vintage Books, 2000); "Democratic procedures in electing governments do not automatically ensure respect for the civil rights of citizens. If proof is required, one need only recall the reign of Napoleon III, who used his lawfully obtained mandate to suppress freedom of the press, to arrest and exile citizens without due process, and altogether to arrogate to himself dictatorial powers. Democracy, indeed, can be "illiberal"." Ibid., p. 280. We can recall with this master historian the reign of Napoleon III, or we can watch Venezuela's Hugo Chavez doing the same now.

4

drugs, people or plutonium; or if murder is perpetrated by suicide, landmines or something bigger, our best understanding holds some places more likely than others to be source-grounds of dangerous behavior. The United States has apparently determined that peaceful measures cannot timely deter some smugglers and murderers from doing it grave harm, and considers itself within its right to label them enemies, and to visit preemptive violence on them. The nature of things thus stated (and regardless of the validity of the posture in any given case) the national strategy documents of the United States express an observation that underlying social, economic and cultural conditions help determine if a foreign place will birth or aid the intolerable.

The United States has proposed a goal: to protect itself, and a corollary hypothesis: that to do so it must destroy an identified enemy, and at the same time ameliorate conditions that create enemies. Whether or not it is succeeding in the latter is for the reader to decide and is not the point of this work. However, restating the upshot -- efforts to ameliorate the conditions that create enemies will fail if they are not founded on the improvement of property systems, *whatever else is or is not done*. The social contract is the property system and vice-versa. To the extent the property regime in Haiti is better now than it was a decade ago Haiti will proceed away from the kinds of behaviors that are dangerous both to Haitians and to others. This will be correspondingly true for Iraq ten years into the future. Unfortunately, despite all the foreign developmental and security resources expended on Haiti, too little was directed at building the social contract as evidenced in a functioning property system -- and the disheartening result is patent. The same may be true of Iraq.

American strategic and military thinking has evolved in the context of state-on-state concepts, which are obsolescing. With so many non-state entities able to enter lethal competitions, it can be clumsy and misleading to define conflicts according to large physical spaces. The new power entities, whether dangerous in the context of some apparently localized contest over control of valuable resources, or because of a demonstrated ability to apply force in distant corners of the world, rarely act out of pure spirituality. They act according to a plan to take or maintain power -- to change, preserve or violate a social contract -- to gain, protect or ignore some set of preferential rights and duties. The complexity of some of these violent enterprises can be better understood through the kind of analysis that a property lawyer might apply. While such an approach may sound legalistic, it is based on an idea of flexibility and cost-benefit, seeking first to understand the rights and duties at issue, the rules that might apply, the identities of interested parties, their objectives, resources and vulnerabilities. It is a method not so distant from military strategy. It is very cognizant of physical geography, but in terms of the many overlapping sets of rights and duties associated with space, and of the many possible identities and alliances that pertain. There exists a tradition of analysis of property not well known to the military and intelligence communities, but to Americans in general, litigious bunch that we are.

To begin the argument, this first chapter examines property theory and its place in questions of human rights and organized violence. It asserts the relation of formal property to peace as a matter of economic and legal logic, common sense and universal experience. Chapter Two applies the theme and its pieces to worldwide security concerns. Chapter Three uses the context of a real place suffering a virulent armed conflict to repeat the same arguments in greater depth. Chapter Four moves back in the direction of theory, exposing an essential flaw in American strategic writing. It prescribes insertion of property-based strategic theory, property intelligence and property-directed courses of action. It proposes that the timely improvement of property regimes can improve prospects for military and police success. The last chapter, Chapter Five, restates the consequences of failure to insert property toward the center of foreign policy, and re-asserts the opportunity. Finally, *Caveat Lector*:

> Property is a bore. It rarely contributes meaningfully to a
> conversation. It's an annoying old idea that, given half
> the chance, will sit down beside you and maunder on

about its past glory, its veneration by Locke and
Blackstone, or its running battles with Marx and
Proudhon … Mention something topical though, and
property will be at a loss…[5]

The topic here is not an abstract peace, however. The topic is catching
kidnappers and bombers, stopping drug dealers and poachers,
ameliorating conditions that invite rebellion, subversion and
insurgency, and winning wars.. It is about creating safe, prosperous
and free societies. Still, you have to want to read about property. If it
were not so important, I would advise reading something else.

What is it?

> *"That low, bestial instinct…."*[6]
> Leo Tolstoy

The rub is in the definitions, naturally, so some pedantry in
defining the word *property* is necessary, a chore to be completed
immediately and, I hope, painlessly.

**Property is a contract among society and owners that
recognizes preferential rights and correlated duties. The strength
of the social contract can be judged by the quality of its
observance, which depends on the quality of the evidence of
ownership and on the capacity of both owners and the society
(usually by way of some government) to act on conclusions logically
drawn from the evidence.**

The mental exercise to be mastered in understanding *property*
as used here requires adopting the idea that property is not a tangible

---

[5] J.E. Penner, The Idea of Property in Law, (Oxford: Clarendon Press, 1997), p. 1.
[6] Simon James, A Dictionary of Economic Quotations, Second Edition, (Totowa,
New Jersey: Barnes & Noble: 1984) p. 25.

7

object, but a set of recognized rights and duties associating a tangible item (perhaps a place) with an owner-identity. Although the term *property* denotes a broader set of preferential interests than just those associated directly with real estate, we are most immediately concerned with struggles relating to real property, and it is in the context of rights and obligations related to land that most of the examples in this book reside.[7] Those rights and obligations constitute the details of a contract between society and its members. The 'social contract' is an agreement to peaceably enforce lesser agreements (and to resolve disagreements) regarding advantages and disadvantages. If politics is the allocation of scarce resources, then the property regime is the pacification by law of that allocation. So the definitional starting point is that property is not so much about locations and dirt (although these are important), but rather about the mix of rights and obligations that someone or some group claims, and that the society (generally by way of government) affirms. Therefore, "creating property" means the entire process of establishing and solidifying an *agreement about agreements* regarding rights and duties associated with places and objects. The creation of property is a process of institution building.[8] A property regime is *formal* to the degree that documentation regarding ownership and tenancy is accurate, comprehensive and transparent.

A column of Western cultural progress is the use of technology

---

[7] We can go further to say that a useful idea is 'tangible' and that intellectual property is a growing source of conflict. On this point and on the relation of innovation to national security see, Robert J. Shapiro and Kevin A. Hassett, The Economic Value of Intellectual Property, Washington, D.C: USA for Innovation, 2005 online at < http://www.usaforinnovation.org/news/ip_master.pdf; See also, Geoffrey Demarest, "Patent Earnings and Military Power," Arms Control, Vol. 14, No. 3, December 1993, pp.440-450.

[8] Reinold Noyes, The Institution of Property (New York: Longmans, Green and Co., 1936). "[T]he idea of the right of property--the central concept of the legal institution, grew out of the right of action...In early law, property was the legal means of securing it. Only later did it come to be conceived as something which existed independently of the action or transaction and which the law merely confirmed." Ibid. p. 159.

to improve the faithfulness of evidence regarding everyday rights and duties, including the duties of government. (Formalizing real estate records can involve considerable technical effort --interviewing, surveying, monumenting, mapping, registering, filing, digitizing, web-mounting and so-on). Much of the success of Western societies, and much of what is often alluded to as the American Way, is bound to the systemic creation of irrefutable evidence regarding rights and duties related to things, and particularly to real estate. However good the evidence, however, rights remain inchoate unless they can be exercised. This exercise of rights usually requires that an authoritative body can consider and act upon the evidence, or that a functioning market exists within which rights and duties can be traded. That is why we judge the strength of the social contract according to its *observance*, by which we mean to tie the evidence together with its practicable consequence. This observance of the social contract (the combination of solid evidence and the realistic possibility of doing something with it) gives the contract strength within its basic rules. These basic rules, however, may still be unjust according to one perspective or another. For instance, we may be easily able to determine what varying rights and duties pertain to owners within an area, and all of those owners may have quick access to enforcement mechanisms that operate smoothly and according to set procedures and standards; but if an appreciable claimant identity lives within the population, but is excluded from participation as owners, there still exists great potential for conflict.

Some readers may be immediately stressed by the word *property*, or challenged; preoccupied that it is synonymous with "private property" and a tattoo of capitalism and Western cultural arrogance. Indeed, formalized property is a hallmark of Western culture and a basic institution in most materially successful economies, if not all. The most defensible goals of human development: freedom of expression, association, movement, worship, material prosperity, and non-violent resolution of conflict, are more likely achieved where rights and duties associated with land are formalized -- regardless of the name given the overall system. The question of cultural variation, and the attendant possibility of outright rejection of private land ownership as an element in the social contract, is addressed later in this chapter, and so the reader is asked to suspend judgment on that point for a bit longer. It *is* argued, however, that private property and semi-private property exist everywhere, whatever the nature of a property regime's broad outlines. These property preferences can be made explicit and protected wherever the social contract agrees to their existence.

By *government* we do not mean to imply 'big,' 'federal,' 'national' or even 'county' government, but rather any organizational construct imbued with the authority to judge evidence, resolve disputes, limit the exercise of rights, and probably tax. We call the property system an *agreement about agreements* or a *contract regarding contracts*, but we suppose contracts are best made freely among parties somehow capable of negotiating terms, albeit at times indirectly. To the extent fewer-and-fewer individuals exercise more-and-more of the rights we associate with real estate (access and exclusion, profit, safe enjoyment, alienation, preservation, collection of rents, etc.) a property system tends toward tyranny. The tyrannies of a property regime may grow from the cultural fabric as much as from political formulae. Matrimony is a contract involving property, a contract type that almost all human societies recognize and underwrite in some form or another. Many societies enforce uneven rights between spouses, and it could be fairly said that by way of this institution alone the number of potential owners can be cut almost in half.[9] A piece of land may be the subject of many contracts and many levels of government expression beyond matrimony… to include neighborhood covenants, municipal codes, county zoning, school district levies, and so on. Furthermore, governments are so often themselves owner identities that, while

---

[9] For instance, from a 2005 report from the Nepal Section of the Women's League for Peace and Freedom comes the following: "In September 2001, the parliament of Nepal passed a bill accepting, though mainly in principle, an equal inheritance right for females and males. The bill says that a female child is equally entitled to paternal property as a male child but the girl must leave her share of paternal property to her parent family after her marriage. Though it still retains the age –old discrimination between males and females in the society, the bill is progressive in many respects. It is a victory of progressive people, especially that of progressive women of Nepal." See http://www.wilpf.int.ch/world/windex.htm.

distinction between government and owner is often clear, it is as often not.

The word *liberal* adds difficulty to our assertion about property and peace. *Liberal* and *formal* are not the same qualities. Formal property ownership entails comprehensive, precise and transparent evidence of ownership, the logic of which can be duly enforced. *Liberal*, meanwhile, refers to the most basic rules delimiting the distribution of rights, however evidenced. A property regime is more or less liberal to the extent different categories of person are admitted as owners and a broader array of rights can be had. This text does not stay completely clear of the debate over the relative advantages of private as opposed to common ownership, but that debate itself can be a fetter. The ultimate expression of private ownership -- total, independent, unencumbered and uncompromised individual exercise of rights in land -- may not constitute property ownership at all. Such a condition is sovereign lordship, which must be defended by unyielding force. It is only when lords reach agreement with their neighbors that property is created. That is to say, in order to speak of property at all an agreement must exist regarding conflict resolution – which leads inexorably to the recognition of a role for government. Mundane facts of ownership show how complex and subtle the lines between private and common ownership rights actually are. So, rather than focusing solely on owner rights, we want also to underline duties, and especially those of government in the social contract. We see that where the State fails to shoulder its immediate duties (conflict resolution and prevention or amelioration of trespass), the property regime is less likely to promote human flourishing, and that the reverse is true also: to the extent governments *do* shoulder duties; the balance in the social contract favors the prospects of peace, prosperity and freedom. Rather than claim that this or that balance between individual and communal ownership is best, the argument herein favors liberal property regimes that feature fluidity, divisibility, precision and transparency in determining the balance.

There are, then, two broad qualities that this book advocates

11

regarding property systems as they relate to the cause of peace: formality and liberality. The principle argument is about formality, however, because without precise, clear, stable evidence regarding who claims what, any question of how to divide the pie is subject to corruption, deceit and extortion. Likewise, clear evidence makes the observance of contracts far more likely and peaceable. There is almost no practical amount of additional formality in a property system that would be detrimental to the cause of peace, and without formality no long-term peace is likely. A liberal property regime is one that broadens the range of potential owner-identities and allows these identities to own the fullest range of rights. If a property regime encourages flexible, rapid and precise markets for rights in real estate, it may be more conducive to peace than one in which decisions are made more centrally or by political processes. In this, however, there reside questions of balance and timing, the optimal measure of liberalness being susceptible to specific cultural and political details. As we tinker with who is allowed to own what in a society foreign to our own, we can directly threaten cultural basics. The property rules related to gender that the West confronts in Islamic lands present an interesting example. As a property regime becomes more liberal it may become more conducive to social peace, but disclaimers and exceptions are obviously required. To the extent a system of ownership is informal, however, liberality is an empty notion and the prospects of peace dim.

Believing that to identify a problem without stating a solution is only to depress, this book makes several recommendations about what to do and about who should do it. Western powers will continue to insert themselves into the fates of a number of less fortunate countries, often on the back of good intentions. (By *Western* I mean the *have* countries, *first-world*, *developed*, the *North*, etc. The author doesn't buy in happily to any of these terms.[10] All, including *Western*, are

---

[10] Regarding this point see Bauer, Peter. The Development Frontier: Essays in Applied Economics. Cambridge, Massachusetts: Harvard University Press, 1991. Bauer is thoughtfully unrelenting in his destruction of popular developmental categorizations. "Discussion on foreign aid envisages the world as being one-third

stylizations and relative ones at that. Japan is in the *West* and Chile in the *North*. I use *West* and *Western* in this book as admittedly lazy shorthand.) This book says flatly that unless this one area of Western success -- formalized property -- is actively exported, the West's good intentions will be paid in disappointment.

On occasion, as in Iraq after the takedown of the Hussein regime, a window of opportunity presents itself during which the old status quo of ownership is weak, when basic changes in a property regime can be more speedily implemented. At such times, property can be formalized and liberalized by external influence and action.[11] If in Iraq, Haiti, or places like them, the property regime is not formalized while the opportunity presents itself, there will be less likelihood of success in setting those societies on a path toward whatever goals of societal engineering the West might wish for them. There exists a more aggressive aspect as well, a Big Brother aspect that must be weighed carefully for better and worse. Formal records – transparent, comprehensive and accurate – allow for control, for enforcement, for punishment. At best they represent the ability of the public to ensure tax equity, environmental protection, debt responsibility, forensic efficiency and government accountability. At worst, and especially when the quality of transparency is missing, precise records are another tool in the service of repression and tyranny, exposing individual wealth and whereabouts to government abuse.

---

rich (the West) and two-thirds poor (the Third World or South). In this picture, extreme poverty is the common and distinguishing characteristic of the Third World. But there is a continuous range in the per capita incomes of countries. The absence of a distinct break in the series undermines the concept of a Third World demarcated from the West on the basis of per capita incomes. The line of division between rich and poor countries is quite arbitrary. One could equally well say that the world is two-thirds rich and one-third poor." Ibid at p. 40.

[11] Meanwhile, we should recover Geography itself as a lead discipline for matters of state, because the object of ownership, and of most armed struggles is, after all, a place. Property, as a subject of study, provides a link between law and geography. It is simultaneously the link between economics and strategy in assessing and addressing internal conflicts, allowing precise assignment of relative value to territory.

There is one more disclaimer and one more admission to be made at the outset. It is a disclaimer demanded by the semantic muddle: Peace to me is not the absence of violence, but rather the absence of both violence and its impending threat.[12] What constitutes "impending" and "violence" is left for the reader to decide, and there exists considerable logic in the supposition that at some point all ownership is backed by force. So when does law become tyranny? This is a subjective question that could take the wind out of any idea if it were pressed home. The author trusts that he and the reader share some common understanding about the difference, about the conditions under which we would flourish and under which we would not. Maybe there are property systems that make active physical violence a rare occurrence, where private real property is all but non-existent, and where listings of rights and duties are not easily recognizable as property records. North Korea might be one of these places, but the author does not suppose it to enjoy peace. For the logical integrity of this book, places such as North Korea, Syria or Cuba are tyrannies. To the extent a reader disagrees, gives these countries a bye and calls them peaceful, then the cause of this book becomes equivalently difficult to share with that reader.

As for the admission, it is about the impertinence of saying the emperor has no clothes. Does this book say, "You missed this, and if you do not change you will continue to fail."? Yes, the book does in fact have that in it. The admission is made up front so that the reader might regard the claim and overlook the insolence. To the extent the claim is valid, however, it calls for a sea change in developmental aid expenditure, intelligence spending, and diplomatic focus. It is an expensive observation. It says no less than the following: The West, and especially the United States, does not export quite the right thing,

---

[12] In this I defer to British historian Sir Michael Howard, who notes "peace implies a social and political ordering of society that is generally accepted as just." See Michael Howard, The Invention of Peace: Reflections on War and International Order, (New Haven: Yale University Press, 2000), p. 2. Moreover, Howard observes that peace is a recent invention, not the historically natural state of human politics.

or search for quite the right knowledge. Elections are a useful tool in the service of liberty, but their implementation is chimera when done in the absence of a formal property regime. America is not just about elections. It is about property -- that is, the systemic creation of irrefutable evidence regarding who has what rights, the enforcement of logical conclusions drawn from that evidence, and liberal interpretations regarding who can own what. The ability of the US citizen to go to the polls and vote his or her individual conscious is a good thing. The ability to go to the county seat and pull out a plat map showing the exact boundaries of his or her rights in land is, too. The former is publicly extravagant and contested. The latter is taken for granted, but it is just as much an indispensable ingredient of a peaceful and prosperous social order.

The United States will be more successful in whatever expeditions it takes to guide the prospects other lands if it focuses a little less on the election of leaders and a lot more on the creation of peaceful property systems.

Quality of the evidence

> *"When we say that a man owns a thing, we affirm directly that he has the benefit of the consequences attached to a certain group of facts, and, by implication, that the facts are true of him."*[13]
>
> Oliver Wendell Holmes, Jr.

Rights and duties written down

The first stream of inquiry into the quality of a property regime regards the quality of evidence. When we in the West examine the

---

[13] Oliver Wendell Holmes, Jr. "A Legal Right is Nothing But…" in Edward Allen Kent, editor. Law and Philosophy: Readings in Legal Philosophy, (New York, Appleton-Century-Crofts, 1970), p. 125.

improvisational and unregulated circumstances of many less-developed parts of the world, we generally neglect to consider the informality of land records. For that matter, most of us don't think about land records at all, ever. Still, property records are integral to our political heritage and success as a society -- as much as elections, about which we think obsessively. Particularly when the United States has attempted to export liberty, it has stressed fair and open elections, but it is only just beginning to sense the superficiality of democratic edifices constructed to pacify the way leaders are picked, but uninformed by the architecture used to stabilize rights and duties in everyday life. As the developing world perfects its property records, markets and enforcement of real property rights, its prospects for peace and prosperity will increase. Nevertheless, the assertion here is not so much that real estate maps, registries and property courts will bring peace to violent lands. Again, the assertion is inverse: If developing countries in conflict do not formalize property, electoral democracy will not be sufficient to provide long periods of internal peace. The options are few: formalized property, violent internal competition, or tyranny.

Figure 1 below is a cadastral map showing what was, at the time of writing, a nice corner lot owned at one time by Horace Demarest just outside the western boundary of Fort Leavenworth, Kansas. (A *cadastre* is an inventory of land information, usually based on the parcel lot, and matched to a registry of ownership interests.) The lot is at 159th Street and Fort Riley Road. The map is a copy of the subdivision plat from county records. Any of the readers of this book can go to the Leavenworth County courthouse and obtain all this same information and more to see if Horace still owns the lot, if he paid his taxes, if the area has been changed in some way, what zoning laws apply, how much it costs to buy a building permit, etc. (the records in Leavenworth County are *transparent*)[14] All the land has some owner of record; there isn't any "no man's land" (the records in Leavenworth County are *comprehensive*). Everyone knows pretty much who owns

---

[14] Leavenworth County has a modernization project underway with which it hopes to eventually digitize all the county map data and mount it on the Internet.

what, although the details are forever being re-considered, as the market for land is fluid. The lines on the plat map shows easements for utilities of various types, including a natural gas pipeline, setbacks delimiting permissible building areas and so on. Visible on the aerial photo is a burden not recorded on the plat; the Department of Agriculture did some terracing as a conservation measure, and may require that it not be substantially undone. Other local owners got the county to disallow overweight vehicles on 159th Street, which might pass the property going north toward the military prison. The surveyors who created the subdivision plat map are licensed and bonded, and Horace bought title insurance (the records in Leavenworth County are *precise*). The chances he would ever have had to defend his rights with physical force are remote. He was confident that the law enforcement and justice systems in the county were sufficiently aware of the meaning of the evidence, sufficiently secure against bribery and sufficiently accessible that he could obtain relief in a peaceable way from any potential trespasses (*the social contract is observed*).

Figure 1. Horace's Old Lot

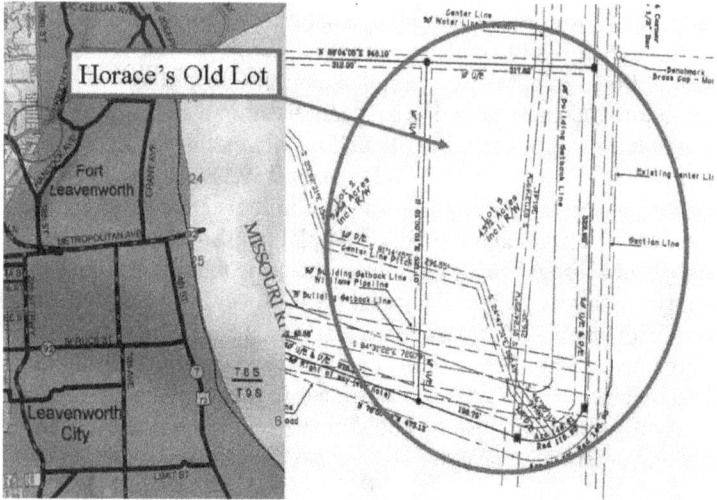

From the Leavenworth County GIS Department and the County Registrar's Office

It is unlikely that the political or managerial leaders in Leavenworth would make a decision to pave the road, change zoning or garbage collection without considering the properties affected. This isn't to say local leaders would never violate citizens' rights if they thought they could get away with it on occasion, but the system makes it difficult. Horace's property is a complicated set of rights tied to a precisely demarked place on the earth, those rights protected by an extensive edifice of laws, regulations and contracts, almost all of which are evidenced in written, signed and witnessed documents. Even if the federal government wished to expand Fort Leavenworth to the west, it

18

would have to hurdle a number of legal and political barriers.[15]

Regarding the "rule of law," it bears repeating that Horace's rights were evidenced in written, signed and witnessed documents. Kansas, like all of the United States, has a Statue of Frauds. A jurisprudential inheritance coming from 17th century England, the statutes require that in order to be enforced, important agreements must be in writing, and that all agreements involving an interest in land are important. In other words, if the State is to hold up society's end of the social contract we call property (that is to say, enforce the alleged rights of an owner or claimant against some trespass, infringement or denial), the agent of the State (perhaps the court) must be shown a written document. Acceptance of this standard is so broadly internalized that we refer to the document itself as the contract (or maybe we say, "Who has the deed to the ranch?") – no document, no agreement, nothing to enforce. In almost every dispute regarding an interest in land, the defense lawyer will at the outset invoke the protection of the Statute of Frauds when there is no instrument (acceptable writing).

The purpose of statutes of fraud may be variously stated – to avoid a fraud on the court, or to protect people from false allegations of having entered into a binding agreement. The aggregate historical purpose, however, and what makes the Statutes of Frauds a gem of the English-speaking jurisprudential heritage, is broad practical rejection of oral evidence of important contracts. This rejection of oral evidence serves justice in several ways. For one thing it protects the judicial system. To put a court in such a position that it must choose among contending stories is to assure that on occasion the party telling the truth will loose in spite of the best efforts of judge and jury. In such a case, the righteousness of the truth lies with the loser, thus engendering

---

[15] The positive scenario does not deny the worrisome drama of federal "takings" issues, usually appearing in environmental cases that have raised the question of property out of its century-long slumber. Perhaps best among the readings that put US property rights in historical, philosophical and international context is Tom Bethel, The Noblest Triumph: Property and Prosperity through the Ages, New York: St. Martin's Press, 1998.

disrespect for the court as well as vigilantism. Moreover, to not establish a system that rejects oral evidence is to encourage subornation, perjury, bribery, blackmail and extortion. If a system of jurisprudence does not generally reject oral evidence, that system necessarily fosters dissipation of whatever standard of honest dealing the society might otherwise hope to maintain. Perhaps there exist societies in which witnesses never lie under oath, and judges are wise to all the subtleties of differing stories. Those societies do not need our help.

Broad rejection of oral evidence was a possibility that presented itself on the attainment of specific technologies. The written contract becomes a norm because of writing, obviously, but also because of paper, ink, printing presses, formal education, signatures, notaries, etc. The phenomenon of written contracts is not jurisprudential alone -- an observation which brings us to yet another useful term, *transparency*. Transparency, as a valued aspect of democratic governance, has gained force and favor in recent decades, but it is the same quality as embodied in the Statute of Frauds. Transparency evokes the idea that government debates, records, decisions and agreements should be apparent, visible, available for inspection and so on. Transparency is a better word than 'visible' in this context because transparency carries with it not just a sense of exposure, but of seeing through the evidence to the truth of the matter at hand, and it carries as well the notion that things be visible not just to a select group, but to everyone. The technologies of writing allow that an agreement be manifested in visible form. Throw in a photocopier and agreements are made more transparent. As each party keeps a copy, another goes to a neutral office, and notice is published in the local newspaper, etc. The whole effect is to better reject the loss of trust and credit that a system that accepts oral evidence can suffer.[16]

---

[16] This is not to suggest that there could ever be an all-or-nothing, oral-vice-written evidentiary world divide. The author worked a case involving a forged mortgage document, and to prove the document was a forgery had to hire a handwriting expert – whose testimony was oral.

Society's effort to limit fraud is an uphill struggle against a clever enemy, but now the Internet offers the latest contribution to transparency and to the construction of social trust. Web-based or web-available records make tampering more easily detectable. Requiring that a set of land records be made permanently available on the Internet is an extension of the same public policy thinking that led to the original Statue of Frauds in the 17th century. It is not just a rejection of oral evidence; it is a purposeful march against a human tendency toward dishonest dealing. It is the recognition and application of technology to make fraud harder, trust in the social contract stronger. As the quality of evidence is improved things like collateral, insurance, equity, credit and non-violent conflict resolution are the bi-products.

For our purposes, this one cultural inheritance (the systemic impairment of dishonesty) is the central aspect of what we mean when we use the words "formal," "formality" or "formalize." Beyond the first requirement of writing, formal systems require validated signatures and other controls. The goal is a system in which the general standard of evidence is raised. Eventually, we approach the condition of *res ipsa loquitur* (the thing speaks for itself). It is a point at which the local sheriff can look at the plat map and the signature on the title or deed, determine without further requirement that the fence line is in the right or wrong place and slap an immediate restraining order on the trespasser.

The importance of stable evidence cannot be overstated when speaking of the "rule of law." If the *de facto* system of law enforcement regarding interests in land is one in which enforcement authorities act on logical determinations drawn from formalized evidence, then objective enforcement of the rule of law is the norm. If the public force regularly imposes decisions based on the oral arguments of one claimant versus another (or on corrupted or fraudulent documents), the authorities tend to become partisans in possession by force. To avoid partisanship, perhaps the appropriate authorities simply avoid the question, abrogating the duty of the State within the social contract, and leaving resolution of conflicts directly to

21

the parties. In Leavenworth, the police do not listen to the neighbors scream and yell about who should live in one or another trailer (well, OK, maybe sometimes they do). Preferably they detain those perpetrating violence and let the court enforce the right of quiet enjoyment, usually on the basis of the written evidence.

Conflicts over territory abound, and those not resolvable in civil law can quickly escalate to require application of the criminal statutes. To the extent solid evidence is made generally and easily available, peaceful resolution of conflicts and respect for the system of justice are greatly improved. To the extent evidence regarding the ownership of land is informal, that which might have been resolved as a civil matter inexorably devolves toward criminal. No matter what programs are implemented to better train police forces in underdeveloped countries, and no matter what efforts are expended to protect the independence, physical integrity and legal education of judges; if the system of ownership evidence is not formalized, the long-term prospects for peaceful resolution of conflict about land is slight. It is one of the great unremembered pieces of corporate wisdom that oral evidence is undependable, and that its broad acceptance is an encouragement to social disorder. Cementing this wisdom in the statutes of fraud is a victory of jurisprudential history. For Western countries to "professionalize" police and judicial systems in underdeveloped countries, but simultaneously fail to implement this piece of civilization regarding evidence, is a root cause of repetitive failure. It is a central reason why efforts to improve a government's human rights conduct are off-center when focused on criminal law and not on civil law, particularly as the latter applies to real estate. The construction of systems of reliable evidence is tantamount to preparation of the environment for effective adjudication of conflicting claims. This is parallel if not equal to what the military intelligence official, faced by internal disorder where the conflict over control of land has become violent and widespread, would correctly call the intelligence preparation of the battlefield. Unfortunately, most American intelligence officials, so used to a home where the practical engine of conflict information is taken for granted, do not think to address the laws, bureaucracies and technologies that serve to prepare authorities for success in identifying and locating the contestants for power.

Infinite divisibility of ownership

Under the system of property concepts generally shared among the states of the United States and rooted in English common law, the practical ownership of a piece of real estate can be infinitely subdivided.[17] A "life estate" can be granted that gives certain elements of ownership to a person only for the life of that person. A "remainder" might be bought or sold that gives rights in the property only after the death of the holder of the life estate. Possible subdivisions of the total ownership of real estate include the right of current use and enjoyment (such as an apartment rental) subsurface mineral rights or an easement for running a community sewer line. A "usufruct," or usufructuary right, gives use, enjoyment, and profits from land belonging to someone else. All these rights are associated with correlatives and opposites. While an apartment renter holds the right to use the apartment, the landlord and others have no right to enter without consent (or perhaps a search warrant). The law enforcement system should be assigned a duty to protect the renters' rights as well as those of the landlord. Potential horrors of landlord-tenant relationships are familiar in most jurisdictions, as is the rocky history of landlord-tenant laws.

To illustrate this point, consider a piece of ground on which a corporation owns a condominium built in a zoned part of suburban land

---

[17] Almost any law school casebook might do to express this concept to the point of pain. The text to which the author was subjected was an earlier edition of the 800-page text by John Cribbet, Corwin Johnson, Roger Findley, and Ernest Smith, The Law of Property: Cases and Materials 8th edition, (Foundation Press: April, 2002); For the economist, many of the same dimensions are laid out in that jargon using 11 pages in Armen A. Alchian and Harold Demsetz, "The Property Right Paradigm," The Journal of Economic History, Vol. 33, No. 1, The Tasks of Economic History, pp. 16-27.

controlled by a municipal corporation.[18] Assume there are various easements on the property (telephone cable, sewer, water and various other access easements), there are several taxes being paid and one of the condominiums has been turned into a public gym. The title to the underground mineral rights is in doubt because the majority shareholder in the corporation owning surface rights had sold a deed restriction limiting access to the subsurface value, and has since has died and bequeathed his shares in the property via a life estate to his nephew. Children walk to school over one corner of the property, an ancient burial site and some dinosaur fossils can be found under another corner, and the lots overlap four state and gerrymandered federal voting districts.

The division of ownership in many American real estate markets is no less complicated than in this Kansas hypothetical. So who is the real owner? Who owns the title? ...And so what, if pieces of ownership are evidenced in various deeds, contracts for sale, municipal codes, wills and court orders? There may be no "real" owner even while everyone mentioned is the real owner of some part. Additionally, every element of ownership in this complicated web involves more than just rights. Each element involves "non-rights" and duties, some of which are even less apparent than the ownership rights. The owners of the land where the school children walk to school have a duty to ensure the children's' safety while there. Identifying the owners with that specific duty becomes a very important money question for a tort lawyer if one of the children were to fall and get hurt. The lawyer will identify the appropriate owner based on the injury, and he or she will probably start looking for rich owners first. The plaintiffs' lawyer will attempt to convince a judge or a jury to establish an unmet duty. Others, with tenuous ownership interests the neighborhood, will have non-rights associated with the land as well. For example, a burglar has no right to enter the apartments. The State, probably manifested in police and prosecutors, will perhaps meet their duty to the apartment

---

[18] The examples offered on this page are adopted from Demarest, Geoffrey. Geoproperty: Foreign Affairs, National Security and Property Rights. London: Frank Cass, 1998, p.13.

dweller's right to deny access and will try to punish the trespasser. More complicated still is the non-right of persons living hundreds of miles away to pollute the air with acid rain, which diminishes the value of the right to unfettered enjoyment. It is very possible that someone would make legal demands respecting this type of non-right. Additionally, our example of suburban land is placed in a North American common-law jurisdiction. That is to say the tradition of decisions and case precedents weighs on the manner in which each right might be brought to and considered by the courts. Still, so many codes, covenants and local statutes apply that the division of ownership or its analysis would not be very different if the location had been set in some other Western country with a code-based property law tradition.

If someone were to own all the various rights in a piece of land, it would be said, under English common law, that the land was owned in "fee simple absolute" or that the owner "held the fee". Of course, no piece of land is really held in fee these days. The government always finds the right to tax, over fly, zone or condemn. The closest a would-be total owner can come is to hold a clear title to a remote piece of dirt outside any school district or municipality, insured by a reputable and solvent title guarantee company. Not many of us want or can afford to live on such a plot. If we did, we would find that complete ownership of the land still entails some public and private duties. A restraining order could be slapped on us at the request of even distant owners if we waste the land or despoil it in some way that endangers their lands, enjoyment of public lands, or even that endangers some species of animal. An owner, unless he is the nuke-armed tyrant king, cannot do just anything he wants.

The community is going to hold some common rights in private property no matter how dear a price is paid for the dirt. In addition, the worth of land and the measure of its worth in the marketplace are intimately related to personal priorities consciously or subconsciously assigned to various kinds of rights in land. As we gain a greater control of some rights, we find that the value of the property (probably reflected in its market price) is very limited in relation to other rights.

In other words, if we escape city water easements, we must dig our own well. If we invest in a place as a source of income, we will have a different sense of the attractiveness of the market price depending on its exposure to shared rights. The hermit and the restaurateur relate to a piece of land differently because of the relative importance of distinct, definable rights and duties associated with the land. While in possession, the hermit will place greatest emphasis on the right to exclude access. The potential for expressing and enjoying one type of right as opposed to another rests greatly on geographical location as it compares to the envisioned use. In deciding if we might buy a specific piece of land, the location, price and allowed uses guide our decision -- the price and allowed uses in turn having been determined in great part by the location.

The point will be made that property is not a recognized concept in many non-Western cultures. I don't believe this to be the case, although property may be poorly recorded, and the possible distribution of rights associated with land more restricted. Moreover, we can apply a property-based analytical approach to conflict regardless of the varying nature of legal or belief systems. At the root of the definition of property is the idea of claims about relationships between persons and things – relationships that involve preferences and advantages. If a people, whatever the nature of its belief system, makes a competitive claim against a rival group or culture, or attends to any competitive claims among its members, these are, logically, claims of ownership. One may say, for instance, that the belief systems of North American Indian tribes were completely distinct from that of the arriving White man, and that most Native American belief systems contemplated no private ownership of land. However, the Native American belief systems obviously included an understanding of land ownership at some level. Otherwise, what logical complaint could a Cheyenne have made that Sioux were hunting in Cheyenne hunting grounds. What argument could the Arapahoe make that land was taken from him by the White man? What could be taken away if not rights, at least shared rights, to access, use and enjoyment, or to preservation? If it were not for a perceived loss, there could be no complaint. For the practical

26

purpose of examining conflicts--if there is no complaint, there is no conflict. Apt consideration of ownership conflict incorporates and reconciles potential incompatibilities among diverse systems, but that wisdom hardly disables the applicability of property theory.[19] The notion of property as an infinitely divisible basket of rights and duties encompasses any cultural variation. Some perhaps purely Western legal jargon appears in the explanation of the model, and as Mr. De Soto allows,

> "This is not to say that culture doesn't count. All people in the world have specific preferences, skills, and patterns of behavior that can be regarded as cultural. The challenge is fathoming which of these traits are really ingrained, unchangeable identity of a people and which are determined by economic and legal constraints....Legal property empowers individuals in any culture, and I doubt that property per se directly contradicts any major culture."[20]

I would go further than Mr. De Soto to say that property *per se* offends no cultural schema, major or otherwise, and that even the less venerable cultural traits are not offended by the prospect of identifying and formalizing rights. Property statutes, registry systems and real estate markets reflect the development of ownership rules with a Western cultural stamp, marked by the application of fraud-control technologies. While these characteristics may be absent elsewhere, why would this suggest that accuracy, precision and transparency in the allocation of rights and duties be a disrespectful cultural imposition? The scope of personal or private property, forms of tenancy and degree of communal ownership will all have their relationship to and influence on cultural norms. Unintended consequences of changes in the forms

---

[19] The most vigorous theories of international human rights, as well as most geopolitical theories, are Western inventions. It would be picayune to accuse a property interpretation of human rights or of geopolitics as being ethnocentric. The terms of reference are no more or less universal than the term being questioned.
[20] Hernando De Soto, *supra*, p. 226.

of ownerships are, needless to say, a real possibility. Still, the most likely cultural characteristics to fall prey to the formalization of property, with its demand for precise and visible evidence, will almost everywhere be those cultural characteristics serving paternalism, concentration of power, impunity, and tendencies toward enslavement. While this logic may not be perfect, it is compelling. If interests in church lands, royal palaces, matrimonial holdings, or the extensions of communal lots such as Mexican *ejidos* or Israeli *kibbutz* are mapped, registered and published, it rarely works against equity or egalitarianism, provided that the descriptions of preferential, shared and overlapping rights are precise and comprehensive. "Culture," at any rate, is a soft and absorbent concept, like toilet paper. Much can be stuck to it. If as an inherent aspect of a culture we admit and admire the absence of writing, and therefore the absence of stable evidence regarding agreements within the society, we must accept that the reach of justice will be limited by the strength of personal honesty, obedience to unwritten social norms, and to quirk. That we might admire such a society, if successful in fulfilling human needs and aspirations, goes without saying. We would have to prepare ourselves, in such a rare circumstance, to face the violence sure to ensue as that little society bumps up against anything better armed.

Although property regimes pertain to interests other than just those associated with real property, we are first aware of struggles relating to land. Differences in land ownership practices (culture-to-culture and age-to-age) are well documented, but none of that documentation supports a conclusion that any of those ownership practices are particularly difficult to describe using English jurisprudential language. In this age there is little weight in arguments claiming that a culture has no room for specificity regarding rights and duties, or no capacity to have those rights recorded and preserved. Making the division of rights in land explicit and stable through the application of available technologies has been the hallmark of peaceful and free societies.

28

The enthusiastic assertions I've made above about formalized property are not new, and they indeed carry a potential for ethnocentric mistakes in application. As Toby Dodge puts it,

> For British colonial administrators across the Empire, property rights were seen as universal and applicable to all territories they controlled no matter what the superficial differences between them appeared to be. ... Although the imposition of European notions of land tenure was interpreted by administrators as merely codifying what was already in existence, it had profoundly transformative effects. By its very nature, this system of solidification and homogenization could not countenance or even recognize local differences in approach to social organization.[21]

Owners and the reach of identity

It is good to have rights precisely expressed and the evidence stabilized, but to whom might the carefully divided and recorded rights and duties pertain? "Bourgeois means an owner of property. The bourgeoisie are all the owners of property taken together. A big bourgeois is the owner of big property. A petty bourgeois is the owner of small property."[22] If we adopt this definition from Vladimir Lenin at face value, then we might say that what we are proposing as an aid to peace is the "bourgeoification" of society -- making everyone an owner. Indeed, the idea of property supplied here supposes that every member of society is already an owner of property, since each person holds at least some basic rights regardless of his or her identity, the formality of ownership records, or the latitude & longitude where the person stands. As noted, just listing all the owners associated with a single piece of land can be a task, but beyond the simple identification

---

[21] Toby Dodge, Inventing Iraq: The Failure of Nation Building and a History of Denial, (New York: Columbia University Press, 20030 p.105.
[22] Simon James, *supra* p. 18.

of owners is a problem involving the cohesion their identities. In the example of the condominium, rights are enjoyed by families that vary in their sense of identity, unity of purpose and feelings toward the rights and duties they claim and admit. One group may be closed, jealously protective of their privacy, and proud of their home, while the temporary residents next door might be a tad more gregarious and not as proud of their residence. Ownership documents only hint at the descriptors and determinants of ownership identity, even while they state who the owners supposedly are. The otherwise unrelated parents of the children in the suburban real estate example could form a powerful class-action argument to protect that single right of access. Their appeal might only have to influence a few city council members or ward healers who are responsive to a vague sense of equity within their electorates. The appeal of the parents could ultimately be manifested by a city ordinance, a lawsuit or other court action, or the outright purchase of a property right. Owner cohesiveness can be strong in relation to even a single specific right, even while no cohesiveness exists otherwise. Where there is a solid sense of shared ownership, where the "we-ness" is strongly related to a palpable property right, it follows that such owners are more likely to express and defend the rights they have as a group.

The ownership status of individuals can be credited to multiple owner identities. One of the parents of the children mentioned in the suburban example might fit all of the following groups: mother of children who cross that piece of land on their way to school, citizen of Lansing, Kansan, Black, immigrant from the Dominican Republic, Hispanic, owner of ten shares of Texaco, property tax payer, Republican, speedboater, female, Baptist, wife, Irish, short person, twin, lefty, kids hockey team representative, mother against drunk drivers, and alcoholic. Each descriptor can be matched to a right related to land that the mother is variably willing to defend or attempt to obtain. As a member of a racial minority she may be fiercely opposed to badges of racism. As a mother of school children and payer of property taxes, she may be opposed to allowing undocumented immigrant Mexicans from attending school in the district, but favorable

30

toward Hispanic immigration to the state. Other identities may be at odds with one another as far as property rights are concerned. For instance, she may find it difficult to vote for a proposed ordinance against serving alcohol in the county. She is both an alcoholic and a member of Mothers Against Drunk Driving.

Which of her identities is momentarily operant? Many of her listed identities may be individually less stable or substantive than one might think. Almost all of our Kansan's identities are artificial to some degree. Our Kansan, for instance, could look forward to having one of her kids play on the hockey team of a nearby Indian tribe. "Because of low populations, some tribes accept members with only one qualifying grandparent."[23] The need to maintain tribal membership is directly linked to legal recognition, which is in turn connected to preferential property rights. Our Kansan (until she moves across the river to Missouri) can choose which identities apply, and to what intensity she decides to pursue a given issue at a given moment.

The foregoing paragraphs make it apparent why the emotional intensity of ownership claims can be so situation-specific. An individual may feel intense group solidarity in relation to competition over one right associated with a piece of land, but may feel little sense of common identity in respect to another right associated with the same land. This is one reason why many analyses of international conflict can mislead. They often treat blocks of people and pieces of land in a way that does not allow for variable weighting of identities based on the specific rights in question. In domestic property adjudications, courts focus on specific rights, and plaintiffs' and defendants' lawyers are attentive to the cohesiveness of identity of all would-be owners. In addition, most ownership conflicts involve human characteristics such as capriciousness, ambivalence, error and ignorance. Analyses of international behavior, especially those that focus on state decisions, tend to underplay these human vagaries.

---

[23] Carl Waldman, Atlas of the North American Indian, (New York: Facts on File, Inc., 1985), p. 199.

The above examples tell us that simple cadastral maps would hardly be enough to impart an understanding of ownership in any sizeable piece of geography, and indeed that is the case. There are many other maps, however, that show parts of ownership, such as the boundaries of a spoken dialect, a soccer league schedule, telephone exchange, or the geographic distribution of an exiled minority or diasporas. All bear on ownership identity. Nevertheless, land registries and cadastres are the base maps of rights. They reveal (by presence or exclusion) the best capitalized, most invested, most accountable, and sometimes worst harmed. Where good records do not exist, their creation is an opportunity to give visible expression to ownership claims and contentions.

How finely rights are distinguished, along with how specifically the identities of claimants are defined, combine with the precision and durability of recording technologies in order to establish clarity of allocation (exactness as to who has what). This clarity, which we also call the quality of evidence, constitutes one of the three streams of inquiry by which we can judge the quality of a property regime.

Making use of the Evidence

> *"There are many things that free trade does passably. There are none which it does absolutely well: for competition is as rife in the career of fraudulent practice as in that of real excellence."*[24]
> John Stuart Mill

The Court

Conjoined with the quality of the evidence of ownership is a quality less tangible: the internalized presumption on the part of the

---

[24] Simon James, *supra* p. 81.

government of duties pertaining to it under the social contract. Although Leavenworth County extracts a property tax, most of which flows to local education and road maintenance, it goes unquestioned that the sheriff and court meet a primary responsibility to affirm and protect Horace against trespass. This may seem too obvious to mention, except that today, in many countries where aid organizations attempt to create property, they begin with an argument about improving the tax base. By neglecting to emphasize the duty of the government rather than the duty of the possessor, these efforts implicitly paint the "rule of law" as the power of government, rather than as a civilizing agreement the government is obliged to service. They fail to establish and underline the government's duty of conflict resolution as the first reason for surveying and registering land. At any rate, the example of Leavenworth County, Kansas is offered as a springboard -- to place land ownership first in a US context before launching toward foreign lands. It recently came to the author's attention that as late as mid-2005 no accurate accounting of people had been made in Iraq, that no comprehensive system of individual identification had been instituted and that property records were formalized in a very small percentage of the country. There is no mistaking the direction in which this argument leads: no hope should be wasted on the idea that Iraq will become a democratic and peaceful land, proofed against the excesses of radical charismatic elements, if the time-proven institutions of conflict resolution and control of wealth are not established. Unless the society can know who owns what, history and logic tell us that there is no hope, despite whatever immediate electoral exercise succeeds or whatever piece of physical infrastructure gets built. Lawfulness is based on good evidence as much as on good rules.

The Market

The process of buying or selling residential property in the United States can be exciting, tedious or both, but it is never without paperwork. Many of us have experience in the matter, but few have attached the lessons of that experience to anything remotely concerning international peace or counterinsurgency or the like. The administrative details of selling a home can seem oppressively picayune and legalistic. An agreement to provide a termite inspection, a professional appraisal, or title insurance, or that there is no lead paint, etc. -- all perhaps toiled before a buyer is even whiffed. But in the whole these annoyances reduce and spread risk, and, although the balance may be tipped at some point, create a more fluid market by reducing the friction of doubt and mistrust. The documents displace some of the need to see the thing itself. They become evidence of conditions, protecting rights to be gained and lost in the sale. Fraud is the constant enemy against which the documents are a hedge. The behavior of the sales professional is itself the subject of legal scrutiny and inspection, and the representations of an eager salesperson are always the subject of potential disagreement. The buyer has a right not to be tricked into buying a pig in a poke, and the bank a duty to its investors not to be a participant in, or successfully accused of, a fraud.

In addition to the reassurances of product quality, however, there is a world of expectation regarding the effort to market a residence (or business, etc.) and it is upon this effort that the sales professional earns or doesn't what can be a sizeable commission. Today, a property owner will likely sign an agreement that his home be placed on an electronic multiple-listing service. Finding the exact location of an offered property is increasingly a snap, and more-and-more information about taxes, schools and the like is available immediately on the Internet to prospective buyers. All this open information does not necessarily increase the price that a given house will fetch, but in the aggregate the vastly increased speed and distance of information about property means that certain rights of ownership are given greater effect, greater meaning. After all, if in the meaning of 'owner' we infuse the right to sell, then that right is made whole only if a desire to sell can be effectuated. The right to sell is made better if a proposal of sale can be made clearly and quickly to a huge audience of potential buyers, all with reasonable expectations regarding what they might buy. So it is not just access to a quiet-title court that gives meaning to the owners' rights. Some rights can only be given meaning through access to a functioning market, and what makes that market functional are the same qualities of accuracy, comprehensiveness and transparency of information that give the property regime strength as a conflict resolution mechanism.

The relationship of an efficient market in real property to general economic and social progress is not the direct subject of this book. That relationship has perhaps been best treated by Nobel Prize laureate Douglass North.[25] To economists like professor North, the institution of formalized property owes to an advantage over violence in transaction costs, described as follows:

> Transaction costs are the costs of specifying what is being exchanged and of enforcing the consequent agreements. In economic markets what is being specified (measured) is the valuable attributes - the physical and property rights dimensions - of goods and services or the performance of agents. While measurement can frequently be costly, there are some standard criteria: the physical dimensions have objective characteristics (size, weight, color, etc.) and the property rights dimensions are defined in legal terms. Competition also plays a critical role in reducing enforcement costs. The judicial system provides coercive enforcement. Still, economic markets in the past and present are typically imperfect and beset by high transaction costs.[26]

---

[25] See generally, Douglass C. North & Robert Paul Thomas, The Rise of the Western World, A New Economic History, (Cambridge: Cambridge University Press, 1973).

[26] Douglass C. North. "Lecture to the memory of Alfred Nobel, December 9, 1993," nobelprize.org at http://nobelprize.org/nobel_prizes/economics/laureates/1993/north-lecture.html; see also, as it relates to interstate boundaries, Beth A. Simmons, "Trade and Territorial Conflict: International Borders as Institutions," Paper presented at the annual meeting of the International Studies Association, Le Centre Sheraton Hotel, Montreal, Quebec, Canada, Mar 17, 2004 Online <.PDF>. 2006-10-05 http://www.allacademic.com/meta/p73352_index.html.

When transaction costs to secure the benefits of rights related to land appear too much higher than the private use of force, violence seems is a fairly common human economical option. North and Thomas expanded their historical observation of this phenomenon, suggestion that innovations in property arrangements stem from the need for common protection.[27] Reinold Noyes' research on the origin of formalized property indicates it was not one of response by a group to threats from outsiders, but rather a response within clans to resolve internal conflicts.[28] The two are reconcilable. North and Thomas were observing developments in the Middle Ages, not early Rome, and, in any case, much of the difference in perspective lends to imagination regarding who is 'inside' and who falls 'outside' an ownership identity. In either case, the construction of formalized property terminology and institutions is related to the management of violence and to the growing complexity and success of a society.

Political Action

Persons who consider themselves dispossessed, or are otherwise disaffected, often seek empowerment in numbers. That is to say, they may empower leaders able to define, engage, or exploit a unifying claimant identity. Innumerable possibilities for claimant solidarity -- race, religion, class, or any of the interests noted in relation to our Kansas mom—can attract or grow leaders. Those are successful who represent an identity that serves to affect a material change, even if only for the leader and only for a moment. Disaffected claimants, a unifying identity and effective leadership are standard variables in formulas of internal conflict. Since the late eighteenth century, but much accelerated since WWII, organizational innovations have strengthened this set of variables, especially in relation to claims for possessory rights in land. For the sake of efficiency, we can call these innovations

---

[27] See North & Thomas, The Rise of the Western World, note 24, page 19.
[28] See note 8. above.

36

'socialist activism' or 'participatory democracy.' Attendant movements have championed programs labeled land reform, agrarian reform or something more radical such as nationalization or communization.

The relationship that political democracy has to property ownership is no mystery, and is an eternal friction. To be property at all there must exist a social contract that recognizes preferential rights; but how stable is the contract if at any moment a new majority can change the government's end of the bargain? It is the question of modern times, of the American and Communist revolutions, of the taking laws, and of almost all fights. The answers are essential, too. If we hold firm to what we know of the experiences of market economics, we see that some folk become richer than others, and that sometimes the material winners create dangerous levels of resentment and envy among their neighbors. The rich then confront the reality of property... that property is an agreement with social authority to recognize preferential rights so that the preferential rights don't have to be defended tooth and nail. Those with a larger slice of the ownership pie may act indifferently or arrogantly to the perception of unjust differentials. The rich may be oblivious to underlying social formulae of mass action (steered by creative leaders as well as by the vagaries of human emotion) that can cause renegotiation of the social contract. Protection of property rights and the status quo is almost synonymous with conflict resolution, but only up to some point of tension that is marked by ostentatious advantages, at which time the balance of equities sometimes passes to those leaders who can mobilize and manage political action, maybe in the context of electoral democracy, maybe not. We need not be surprised at the tension between democracy and property, but we might seek the details of the matter, facts we rarely have in any appreciable measure.

Basic Ownership rules

"It should be remembered that the foundation of the social contract is property; and its first condition, that everyone should be maintained in the peaceful possession of what belongs to him."

Jean Jacques Rousseau

Liberality

Besides fixing the division of rights associated with things (especially land) and then identifying owners of the various rights, we must gain understanding of the regimes of rules that allow, disallow, protect or delimit those rights. The systems of ownership rules may be manifested in formal, written laws or may be expressed in other dimensions of belief systems that are more difficult to specify. In the examples of United States domestic real estate, rules exist as statutes, regulations, ordinances, covenants, deed restrictions, court decisions, etc. The rules often influence rights indirectly. Laws requiring registration, documentation, signatures and witnesses go to improving the quality of evidence, thereby allowing a court or police a greater possibility of being decisive, precise, even-handed and efficient. Laws that require real estate agents and salespersons to be licensed, trained and formally contracted also ease the burden of conflict resolution by lessening the possibilities of fraud and negligence in the marketplace of rights in land. Electoral laws such as those specifying what size of majority is needed on a city council to establish a zoning ordinance, or the rules for changing the basic rules of ownership, all weigh heavily on the nature of the property regime.

The rules that delimit the universe of possible owners, however, are generally among the basic distinguishing features of cultural variation. While minor cultural traits are rarely offended by the prospect of identifying and formalizing rights, questioning the rules regarding who may and may not become full owners is nonetheless a risky enterprise if conflict resolution is the goal. Challenging characteristics of a real property regime at its base may constitute the most direct cultural confrontation, even while simple formalization of property may not. Issues about who can own what indeed challenge the essential makeup of many societies. That said, formalizing such property regimes bears witness to cultural aspects that, for all the tolerance one might have toward another culture, expose what twenty-first century Western measurement could only classify as unjust.

Even within the highly formalized regime of real estate rules in advanced economies, broader social influences play in the ownership environment for land. If a would-be landlord, even with little documented evidence of ownership, gives an eviction order to an occupier, and that occupier does leave, the event shows an exercise of mutually acknowledged power, if not formal ownership. "Possession," as they say, may still be "ninety percent of the law." If the power and arrogance of the taker are sufficient that others do not care to somehow challenge the seizure, or cannot, the new possessor (even having taken possession illegally) can eventually become the legal owner. This possibility serves as a reminder that legal ownership is related to the force necessary to support a claim. It is a fact of acquisition that may seem to condemn the entire edifice of records and procedures that we are advocating as a civilizing tool. Indeed, the assertion is emphatic that without formalized property the less-developed countries have little chance of internal peace, but the opposite was not claimed. Just because property records are created and courts established does not mean that peace or freedom is necessarily secured. A government bent on tyranny and control can replace any records with its own, and can buy or threaten courts. These events are occurring today in some countries that were on their way toward more formalized property regimes.

This is not a cynical declaration that 'might makes right,' but an observation that the enjoyment of rights associated with domestic property is not perfected without some basis of enforcement. Legal ownership, whether by title, contract, deed, government regulation or court order, can be lost in even the most formalized and maintained system of laws if the supposed owners do not assert their ownership in some way. In a country where the legal system is less respectable, formal legal ownership is more easily lost, often to a tyrannical government mechanism, to private interests enjoying the conspiracy of the government, or to preventable fraud or negligence. Landlord-tenant relations were already mentioned as an example of competing ownership problems. In geography with matured legal jurisdiction, if the owner of an apartment complex wants a tenant to vacate, the owner must follow certain laws, usually statutory. At times it annoys the owner that the tenant does not treat him like the possessor, and it annoys the tenant that he is not being treated like a full owner. To ease the potential for violence in these situations, legislatures try to enact precise, comprehensive landlord-tenant laws. In some jurisdictions, the laws favor the tenants, while in others the laws help the landlord repossess. Always these laws have an effect on market value, the pace of market activity and on legal regime itself. Rent ceilings, for instance, typically cause black market transactions in selected possessory rights, which decreases the level of confidence in the quality of sale and purchase, simultaneously lessens respect for the legal regime, and consequently diminishes the durability and strength of the rights themselves.

Homelessness

A city park serves the common good by providing open space, psychological relief from the urban landscape, a place to play outdoors, to meet, to bird watch, to breathe. The community of park owners has an understood set of rights distinct from the rights they have over their apartments or offices (even while the value of these places is greatly affected by the value of the common property). These park rights amount to easy access to and limited use and enjoyment of a few very expensive commodities. With few exceptions, the homeless are kept or booted out of city parks because their claims are incongruous with the concert of rights normally associated with commonly owned urban real estate. Lawyers for the homeless may claim on their behalf that they must be provided the kinds of rights owned by apartment dwellers, but parks are not apartments. To give apartment-like rights to the homeless in a park requires that the common property value associated with the park's original intent be greatly diminished, and that all the rules and regulations bearing on an apartment be contorted. Do building codes matter? And why have rules regarding the number of portapoties at Oktoberfest if none are provided for the park-bound homeless? Every time the question of homeless care is revisited it confronts a thousand pieces of evidence of established and codified rights, the vast majority of which came into being as the result of some conflict resolution event, or some reasonable resistance against negligence and fraud. Regardless of anyone's theory about the justice or efficacy of private property as a concept, the set of palpable, individually identifiable rights associated with land continually reproves itself as being subject to market forces and generally resistant to insult. When, in the short term, political decisions are able to trump the market of property rights in order to favor immediately attractive claimants, the regime of rules may be disrespected, and possessory violence invited back into the society.

In Bogotá, Colombia one of the central issues of the latest mayoral race was that of public space in the city. Would the incoming socialist administration revert to allowing mobile street vendors to choke key sidewalks and parks? The answer included political and geographic compromise, informal business being allowed to fill certain public ways, but not others. This compromise, deft and perhaps necessary, may further weaken conformance to and observation of rules guiding urban land use and planning. Activists were encouraged to work by means of political organization and demand, and not through the morass of rules it currently takes to formalize ownership of businesses. Efforts to respond to Hernando de Soto's call to reduce the number of steps required to legalize the street vendors' businesses are hampered in the process. Vendors who buck the political organizers' decisions regarding location preferences are rebuffed and disciplined. The problem in Bogotá is not to be cured by greatly improving the cadastre. Bogotá has an excellent cadastral office, but suffers the general informality of the property regime in the country of which it is the capital. People gravitate to areas where property is better formalized. So, if there is no comprehensive national effort at formalizing property, even a relatively efficient city will still suffer an influx of claimants whose first option in a democracy will be political organization for the purpose of forcing improvement in their possessory rights. In this manner, the rules of political action, which favor fluid claimant identities and redistribution based on democratic force, are often at odds with the more bureaucratic rules generally associated with formalized property.

We noted the economists' observation that the use of violence may have apparent transaction costs below that of engaging formalized property institutions. Democratic action can also at times present lower transaction costs than the legalities of formalized property. In either case, if accession to the system of property is too expensive, even a liberal and formal regime may not present an economic decision preferable over the use of violence.

Imagine a situation in which the numbers of homeless in the city park gets out-of-hand due to a natural disaster or because the villages in a rural area outside the city are being threatened or even pillaged. The homeless population can change character. It may be peopled by capable, but desperate individuals whose talents and aspirations can be led to challenge the distribution of material benefits. A peaceful challenge might be mounted if an electoral democratic formula exists and makes economic sense, that is, the cost and speed of transaction appears favorable to the homeless' leaders. Often it does not, and the option of extortion and theft present a relative advantage sufficient to overcome moral constraints on the use of violence. For the well-healed owners in Boulder, Colorado, homelessness means balancing moral sensitivity and aesthetic luxury. To owners in many cities of the world, homelessness presents a more dangerous set of choices. Knowledge of who has homes (and workplaces for that matter) is intimately related to who does not.

From the urban conflict in Medellín, Colombia in the 1990s comes an observation about the formation and consolidation of small illegal armed groups, such as militias that can grow into larger groups of brigands and rebels. In Medellín, where broad geographic factors caused a near perfect storm of flash urbanization, numerous infrahuman conditions arose as squatters established their flimsy residences. Life for many included the travail of sewage disposal. Laziness and arrogance on many and increasing occasion led to the flinging of bags of human waste onto the shanty roofs of downhill neighbors, and this needless to say, angered. Garden hoses were stretched to pirate water from more distant public pipes, and then more petty piracies occurred as people taped from those lines. The same occurred with the piracy of electricity, phone and TV lines. With each tap, the new node of piracy required enforcement, organization of greater force and more elaborate expressions of territory and extortion. Finally, the costs of violence were recognizably higher than formalization of property by the constituted government. At that point of cost understanding the government had psychological space to act decisively. When it did so, it also formalized property rights in the wake of its actions. If it had not done so, nothing would have been solved.[29]

Communism

It is at this point then that we mention the ponderous psychological weight communist theory has lain against practical understanding of land ownership. No body of literature or political philosophy has been as influential as Marxism-Leninism in confounding the logic of property. Campaigns to concentrate and direct the power of loose identities (workers, women, the downtrodden, the proletariat) have for a century-and-a-half popularized a false distancing of common and private property, excused the sub-rosa

---

[29] For a competent journalistic rendition of this history see generally, Ricardo Aricapa, Comuna 13: crónica de una guerra urbana (Borough 13: Cronicle of an Urban War), Medellín: Editorial Universidad de Antioquia, 2005.

private ownership inherent in socialist governance schemes, and dismissed the variable and usually positive impact that the market sharing of rights in land has on its total worth.

The demise of the Soviet Union discredited but did not dispose of the manifesto's influence on economic-developmental logic. Marx and Engles attacked "bourgeois property" emphatically, treating the notion as a palpable thing of which the proletariat did not have enough, and that had to take from the higher classes. Development writers continue to treat property as a problem of land distribution between classes, the distribution almost always measured in hectares rather than market worth.

Much of the supposed scientific basis of communist theorizing derived from assertions regarding the nature of ownership in primitive societies and the natural evolutions of the same. Even before the end of the nineteenth century, there was sufficient academic exposure of the dubious anthropological foundation of Marxist historical scholarship.

> Modern communism finds no precedent in the institutions of early society, its conceptions and aims are of purely modern origin; and it can neither justify them on the ground of conformity with original sentiments of justice, nor, on the other hand, can be charged with going back to barbarism for its theory of rights. The original ownership of moveables by communities shews [sic] that the early usages of mankind are not models for our imitation. If separate property in land is contrary to primitive ideas and institutions, so is the separate ownership of chattels and personality of every description. If indeed we ought to revert to common property in land because it is primitive, why not also to communism in women, if that too can be shewn

[sic] to have been the primitive system?[30]

It was already too late. The notion that private property was ethically and naturally inferior to common property had been offered to a world ready to confirm intellectually a revulsion against the human greed manifested by flamboyant excesses of private wealth. But the nature of man was not evolving away from the sense of security inherent in private rights, or from territorial motivation. One of this author's favorite statements on man's nature as it might apply to real property is from Robert Ardrey's Territorial Imperative:

> "What has been good—or so I believe—about an opening inquiry into the role of territory in animal and human affairs in that it gives us in the future some place to stand. The night may be no less dark, the stars no less distant, the human outcome no les uncertain, the voices that advise us in forgotten tongues no less incomprehensible. But we have made a little place in the forest that we may regard as our own. We have sniffed about, recognized a few of its potential resources, found a hiding place or two that seem secure. We have marked out as well as we could the boundaries of our new domain and deposited scent on this tree trunk, that bush, to inform intruders that someone is home. We are predators, of course, and from time to time we shall go out looting and raping and raising general havoc in the surrounding countryside. There will be reprisals, naturally. And that is another reason why it will be so good to have some place to stand to regard as ours."[31]

---

[30] Emile de Laveleye (translated from the French by G.R.L. Marriott), Primitive Property, (London: Macmillan and Co., 1878).

[31] Robert Ardrey, The Territorial Imperative: A Personal Inquiry into the Animal Origins of Property and Nations, New York: Antheneum, 1966, p. 352.

In the arguments laid out herein, however, the history or anthropology of ownership, or the relative validity of competing visions (private versus communal) are considered moot points.[32] As a practical matter, rights are infinitely sub-dividable, some more suitably individual and private while others best understood and enjoyed in common. As it does with objects such as clothing, cars and food, the marketplace can serve as an efficient decision-maker for the distribution of rights in land. Central planning regarding real property rights, like central plans that tinker with markets for goods and services, suffer unwanted and unforeseen consequences.

The distinction between private and common property is generally not as clear as might be argued by those opposed to or favoring one form over the other. For the restaurateur, the system of ownership rules now in place in the US holds that the proprietor has no right to exclude patrons on the basis of their race. That is to say, everyone in the general public has the property right to enter the restaurant, whatever his or her race. The decision to use property as a restaurant means, as a result of acceptance of or acquiescence to the legal regime, that the private right to deny access is delimited. An implied invitation to the public creates a public expectation of fairness, and that expectation creates a new duty on the part of the restaurateur. With the invitation, everyone in the public "owns" a slice of the restaurant. Since the cohesive identity of the US public (at least in the context of the formal regime of ownership rules) now includes no distinction based on race, the correlative duty requires that everyone, regardless of race, be served. Note also that this and many other interpretations of ownership have not been historically constant, but have changed over time.

In examples used earlier, mention was made of Indian reservation lands. These common properties, belonging as they do to collective identities within a larger polity, carry their own set of private

---

[32] On the subject of competing visions, see, Gregory S. Alexander, Commodity & Property: Competing Visions of Property in American Legal Thought 1776-1970, (Chicago: The University of Chicago Press, 1997).

ownership problems. Internally, limited private ownership can keep a possessor or occupier of a residence from enjoying important elements in the set of possible owner rights, such as the right of alienation -- to control the disposal of one's rights in land through sale, gift, testament or some other means. In Colombia, for instance, it appears that ethnically or tribally-based ownership has been a factor in both hindered prosperity and vulnerability to violence. Ownership rights and their defense end up being represented through whole-identity politics, with small leadership groups becoming targets for genocidal threats, extortion, and bribery.

Chapter Two: The Globalization of Trespass

Chapter Two: The Globalization of Trespass

"In the absence of justice, what is sovereignty but organized brigandage? For, what are the bands of brigands but petty kingdoms? They also are groups of men, under the rule of a leader, bound together by a common agreement, dividing their booty according to a settled principle. If this band of criminals, by recruiting more criminals, acquires enough power to occupy regions, to capture cities, and to subdue whole populations, then it can with fuller right assume the title of kingdom, which in the public estimation is conferred upon it, not by the renunciation of greed, but by the increase of impunity. The answer which a captured pirate gave to Alexander the Great was perfectly

accurate and correct. When that king asked the man
what he meant by infesting the sea, he boldly replied:
'What you mean by warring on the whole world. I do
my fighting on a tiny ship, and they call me a pirate; you
do yours with a large fleet, and they call you a
Commander."[33]

St. Augustine, 5th Century Cleric

Omission and the structure of life

"The life of nations merely repeats, on a larger scale,
the lives of their component cells; and he who is
incapable of understanding the mystery, the reactions,
the laws that determine the movements of the individual,
can never hope to say anything worth listening to about
the struggles of nations."

Attributed to Marcel Proust, French Novelist

To the extent it is a term for something dangerous,
'globalization' refers to an amorphous set of phenomena, spurred by
technological change, that causes or allows ambitions, aspirations,
illnesses, foibles, frivolousness and even hate and psychoses to be felt
at distant, multiple, and often unpredicted points on the globe.
Globalization and trespass are natural partners, and together replace, in
21st-century style, the awful but slow four horsemen of the apocalypse,
or at least their horses. Globalization brings closer to us the dangerous
behaviors spawned in distant places. Globalization seems to make the
new threats to security harder to comprehend, and so makes their
reduction or defeat seem a daunting task. As this chapter extends to a
global scale the cause that property be made a central concept in the

---

[33] Saint Augustine, The City of God (edited by Vernon J. Bourke and translated by
Gerald G. Walsh, Demetrius B. Zema, Grace Monahan, and Daniel J. Honan) (Garden
City, New York: Doubleday and Company, Inc., 1958), p. 88.

search for peace and security, it necessarily contemplates the correlation between the quality of property regimes and social peace. The text proceeds by listing a number of dangers, discussing them in property terms. Admittedly, it looks at the world from a United States security perspective. This is not to equate absolutely the security of the United States with that of every other land, but rather to highlight the role of property and property theory in such a way that by extrapolation it might be understood as a central component in the security outlook of all countries.

'Globalization of trespass' encapsulates for us three broad trends that shape the national and global security challenges. These three are the particularization of power, the extension of legal regimes worldwide, and a resulting increase in moral asymmetry. That is to say: The number of identities that can wield power at a distance is ever increasing; an array of legal controls on the use of law-abiding power also continues to expand; but behaviors guided by this growing body of law are over-matched by behaviors that wholly reject the constraints of that same law and civility. The three phenomena -- particularization of power, growth of national and international legal regimes, and immane rejection of the norms prescribed by those regimes -- together create a moral gap, a moral asymmetry, between the actions countries such as the United States are constrained to take, and those its enemies are likely to take.[34]

The world of globalizing trespass presented here is one of hostile intent and exercised animosity, but globalization of ownership is simultaneously one of increasing civilization and opportunity. How can we observe the shrinking of the world – the acceleration of discovery, ease of individual travel, potential to create complex associations and to exchange and publish ideas, or to transmute

---

[34] This is not the same use of 'asymmetry' that is sometimes made by military people in reference to improvisational or capital-poor tactics, techniques and procedures employed by an enemy against a more materially girded foe. A smart fighter will of course seek affordable ways to overcome his enemy's strengths. When has this not been the case?

fungible capital from one enterprise into another -- and conclude that these are the predicates of an unpredictable and unsafe world? How can that be when so many places where these phenomena are most operant are predictably peaceable, even boring? Our Kansas property owner does not live in a world where violence is the norm. And the violence that she does suffer is rarely to be associated with political or organized violence beyond the level of local criminal conspiracy.

It is something else, something missing in the world, which we can change. Perhaps the absence of basic conditions of human prosperity and fulfillment (human flourishing in the new developmental parlance) positively correlates with the geographies were the perpetrators of international and transnational crime are grown. Yet we really don't know this to be certain, given that so many terrorists and insurgent leaders come from comfortable economic backgrounds. That those leaders represent the downtrodden out of some sense of responsibility, guilt or moral inspiration is itself a huge leap of faith. Nevertheless, to some degree, the failure of societies to meet what the National Security Strategy of the United States refers to as the 'non-negotiable demands of human dignity' probably correlates geographically and organizationally with behaviors that threaten America and its allies.[35] Places where basic rights are not observed are often places where dangers behaviors are encouraged or overlooked, and where the non-rules of moral asymmetry take hold. Governmental tyranny and corruption, even while perhaps motivated in isolation from any attitude toward America, the West or Western culture, we believe contribute to the danger.

The globalization of trespass is more than the increase of enmity or new evil forms. Much of the formula for a dangerous world relates to missing elements in the civilizing process -- omissions rather

---

[35] Bush George W., The National Security Strategy of the United States of America, (Washington, D.C.: The White House, 2002) p. 3. The listed non-negotiable demands are the rule of law; limits on the absolute power of the state; free speech; freedom of worship; equal justice; respect for women; religious and ethnic tolerance; and respect for private property.

than commissions -- on what has not spread globally rather than on what has. Law is spreading around the world, but it is a light veneer, and it binds only the already civilized who have a stake in the social contract that the law reflects. The rule of law as we know it in the successful societies of the First World -- the operant, civilizing social contract -- is set on formal property, but in most of the world evidence of property does not exist or is effectively incomplete. The leaders of the Colombian FARC or of Al Qaeda manage considerable wealth and defend territory by secrecy and force. If secrecy of ownership were unavailable to them, their wealth and sanctuaries exposed, then their ability to use violent force would be insufficient to keep them from losing power. Such leaders are well aware of that fact. They control wealth that has been grown and protected by the social contracts their ruthlessness insults, but even while they work and rail against the system, they are careful to protect the records and confidentiality of the wealth that the system legally assigns to them. Not only can we take their wealth away, it will lead us to them. It is their Achilles heel.

The sub-sections that follow describe the three aforementioned trends that change the nature of our common security challenge: the particularization of power, the spread of law, and moral asymmetry. These three phenomena do not paint the whole world or the complete formula of violent conflict, but they are central to the challenge. Presumably the first two will continue to increase, but it is not necessary that the third increase as a result. What threatens us is described in greater detail by the situation in our Chapter Three case study, about Colombia. As new inventions generate new demands they give rise to new, commercializable resources -- new objects, ideas and places worth fighting over. Basic geography shapes the human territorial tendency to prefer local impositions and decision-making to those from a distance. As technology shrinks the world and loosens the confines of that geography, more and more would-be owners enter the bidding over preferential rights everywhere.

Particularization of power

Property and power are closely associated, but their distinct connotations matter here. Diffusion of property refers to the constant re-division and redistribution of rights and duties, while particularization of power refers to the greater and greater number of individuals and entities that can assert and enforce rights and duties (or violate them). Particularization of power refers to the multiple concentrations of cohesiveness and the appearance of leadership initiative sufficient to translate cohesiveness into resolve. We could say with an acceptable degree of imprecision that the particularization of power gives practical effect to both resistance against and support to the diffusion of ownership claims.

In Chapter One, we outlined the property ownership and owner-identity of a single Kansan woman. That person can effect her own foreign policy, visit countries pretty much as she chooses, write a congressman to ask that aid be restricted to a foreign country, send money to a special interest group supporting a variety of causes overseas, use her Blackberry to send political propaganda around the world, invest or withdraw money from a company doing business in a given country, publish opinions and recommendations about foreign governments, sue in international courts, even become the defense minister of a foreign country, all with passing regard for the opinions or preferences of her own or any government. If she carries an emotionally powerful owner identity, perhaps as an Armenian refugee or a Chilean leftist, or especially if she has attained some degree of material wealth or artistic renown, she can exert a great deal of international influence. If she is a sociopath she may become the enemy of a whole nation state and if she has exceptional computing skills, even more so. She is the emblem of particularized power. This power, good or bad, is one product, evolved alongside physical technologies, of political innovations that radically changed the possibilities of dividing the ownership pie. America reinvented property, allowing a single person to exercise rights as substantial and far-reaching as those of government. That change has brought its unintended consequences, but they can be tamed.

Aside from the individual there are uncountable kinds of owner identities that manifest global policies, some in close coordination with nation-state governments, some oblivious to governments, and some in diametric opposition. Organizations that deal with finances or information have especially powerful foreign policies and these in turn attract the participation of individuals and other organizations. In each case some person is benefiting from a right to access, use and enjoyment, expectation of safety, or profit. The government of the United States is not unified within itself in its foreign policy, thus the individual company or citizen picks and chooses which government foreign policy to support--that of a congressional committee staff member, that of the National Security Council, or maybe the foreign policy of a federal court. Not only is there no hope of a unified voice or a *summa potestas* in American foreign dealings, there is more and more a marketplace for foreign policy in which the government of the United States is but a major player. If an item of foreign policy interest enjoys a central position on the current administration's foreign policy agenda, the government will be a very important player. There is, however, a finite amount of attention that can be given by varsity leaders, and when this attention space is occupied, matters fall to the second and then third string. With each lowering of the bureaucratic level of attention that the executive system can lend to a problem, other parts of the government, and influences outside the government, gain a greater share of power.

What is true about the particularization of power and its expression in the United States is becoming the truth throughout the world, the particularization of power not limited to non-violent or legal expression. Within a country, property claims may be mounted via labor sectarianism, brigandage, religious cultism or extremism, armed insurgency, or any combination thereof. Some of these are what E. J. Hobsbawm called primitive or "archaic" forms of organized political action.[36] Writing in the late 1950s, Hobsbawm looked at the political motivations and aspirations in what today might be referred to as gray area phenomena or "ungovernability." In 1959, the kinds of movement about which Hobsbawm wrote were to remain a secondary academic concern while three more decades of Cold War unfolded. If written in 2004, Hobsbawm's examples might have included environmental, species protection, anti-abortion or anti-cloning activists. Technological advancement has lent the possibility of sophistication and renown to an ever-increasing number of the types of archaic movements that drew Hobsbawm's attention 30 years ago. The intermingling of the legal and non-legal, violent and non-violent becomes more and more complex as technology empowers a greater number and variety of participants. The mob, for instance, is an ownership identity often generated by seemingly limited events, but determined by emotions that lend cohesiveness, and by the incapacity of other identities to satisfy expectations of ownership. The mob, while seemingly *ad hoc* and immediate, is a phenomenon with political longevity and utility that many individuals depend on and draw upon as a source of political power. Understanding the long-term political power of the mob is necessary to the understanding of the complete political calculus of many areas. Hobsbawm makes a convincing description of the evolutionary nature of the mob phenomenon, showing historical examples of changes from relatively spontaneous expression of shared frustrations and opportunism to a more sophisticated manipulation of the threat of mob violence for political leverage.

Challenges to a nation-state's government come increasingly from property claimants that are tenuously related or not related at all. Most of these operate within the bounds of existing national and international laws and ethics. Many, in fact, are dedicated to the improvement of legal and moral regimes. Some organizations, such as the International Red Cross or Amnesty International, deal with other

---

[36] E. J. Hobsbawm, Primitive Rebels: Studies in Archaic Forms of Social Movement in the 19th and 20th Centuries. New York: W.W. Norton & Company, Inc., 1959.

non-governmental organizations and with the highest levels of many state governments. These are among thousands of organizations of every description that can claim international membership and exert partial or wholly independent supranational or transnational influence. Banks, because they hold the convertible wealth of many other owner identities, are also among the most powerful and least understood non-governmental actors internationally. Banks can translate the cohesiveness of one owner group into support for the project of another owner group. They not only can launder money--eliminating the connection between cash or commercial paper and the manner of its accretion--they can also launder group resolve, using the funds of one organization to support the aims of others.

In property terms, a transnational criminal organization can have great power because it can maintain cohesiveness of identity that can be translated by effective leadership into resolve for the purpose of gaining wealth. It can apply organizational and physical technologies to its enterprise and quickly reapply any wealth gained into the business of gaining more. The transnational criminal organization depends on little population or territory, but is always in the business of gaining wealth and can gain wealth at the expense of legally constituted ownership systems.[37] This fact of 21st century life is alone enough to expose the inadequacy of State-oriented defense strategies. At the same time, there are no perfectly landless entities. Everything must touch ground someplace, even if only in a small computer in a small building on a small island. This raises the importance of geographic precision in matters of forensics and security strategy. Every transnational criminal organization, however agile, is led by humans who must sleep someplace and who move money that must be saved someplace. These 'someplaces' can be found.

Dangerous individuals and entities thrive within the new universe of diffuse ownership and particularized power, and

---

[37] Graham H. Turbiville, Jr., "International Organized Crime and Its Impact on U.S. Interests." Prepared for the National Strategy Information Center Conference, International Organized Crime, June 1993.

neutralizing them requires an analytical approach unbounded by either an obsession with national borders or the taxonomy of ideologies found in the encyclopedia. Property theory and property knowledge offers such an approach. After all, the scale of danger presented by an individual or organization is somehow commensurate with their material wealth. Evidence of that material wealth, and of all the places that it touches ground, will almost always be available to the diligent investigator, and can be used in one way or another to counter dangerous behavior. Furthermore, to the extent such evidence does not exist, it can be created.

The spread of law

The rule of law; limits on the absolute power of the state; free speech; freedom of worship; equal justice; respect for women; religious and ethnic tolerance; and respect for private property – in other words, the non-negotiable demands of human dignity -- are not concepts that will be easily acknowledged and digested everywhere. In the long run, however, resolve in meeting these demands will build a world that is less physically dangerous than it is today. Faith in that assertion is required. Like it or not, America at the beginning of the twenty-first century is striving to contribute optimistically, if aggressively, to the structure of life.[38] St. Augustine, quoted at the outset of the chapter, outlined for us fifteen hundred years ago the strategic dilemma faced by the West today: It must not let the world's criminals acquire power enough to subdue populations, but at the same time it must not act in

---

[38] The reference to the structure of life is to a 1943 speech of Franklin Delano Roosevelt in which he defended his concept of "Four Freedoms" saying, "We concede that these great teachings are not perfectly lived up to today, but I would rather be a builder than a wrecker, hoping always that the structure of life is growing-not dying." Found in Philip Zelikow, "The Transformation of National Security," The National Interest, Spring, 2003, online at <http://www.findarticles.com/cf_0/m2751/2003_Spring/99377572/p1/article.jhtml?term=%2BNational+%2Bsecurity+%2Bmanagement, taken from an address by President Roosevelt delivered in Ottawa in 1943. Zelikow in turn cites Samuel I. Rosenman, Working with Roosevelt (London: Rupert Hart-Davis, 1952), p.356.

such a way that it appears no better morally than did Alexander to St. Augustine. If the West promotes international law, it cannot unwittingly let that law be used as a strategic tool to stop the broad promotion of human rights principles. Perhaps the need exists for an international body that can prosecute heinous crimes, but emphasis might be better placed on civil law institutions, where the underbrush of conflicts can be cleared. When everyday rights and duties are transparent, and when more courts exist to resolve initial property disputes, then we may escape the dilemma.

Development of formal property regimes in service of long-term social peace implies development of administrative and civil law. In some cases also implies the development of international law. That said, there is a notable difference between public international law (focused on conflict or human rights) and international law related to commerce and what we commonly conceive of as property rights. The latter -- development of the international legal regime dealing with commerce and property – may be more likely to ease and prevent violence than the public international legal efforts that have been directly aimed at violence.

From unfriendly and unscrupulous pens, international criminal law can be a powerful tool in competitive diplomacy, and even favoring tyranny and the maintenance of illiberal property systems. The most aggressive use of international law threatens not only US interests, but also any civilizing development of international law itself. International law has a quality and power beyond the written aggregate of public and private international statutes, regulations, treaties, conventions, and customs we search to *find* the law. While there is sufficient inconsistency within that written body to cause a world of conflict, it is the law beyond the writing that disquiets. A defendant's fate in an international court is likely disconnected from written law.[39]

---

[39] In a recent explanation of domestic American law, Alan Korwin states, "Once you cross the line from law-abiding (or unnoticed) to law breaking (or at least charged as such), the meaning of the law is a whole new game. Injected into the court system, the written law plays only a small role in your fate. Rules of evidence, procedural

International law quickly becomes propaganda, and legal procedure gamesmanship. Mention of a few recent trends in public international law suffices to outline the danger. The growth of extraterritoriality, or erosion of the principle of territorial jurisdiction, is a direct product of high profile human rights outrage cases.[40] China's Li Peng, Zimbabwe's Robert Mugabe, Guatemala's Rios Montt, Chile's Augusto Pinochet, Israel's Ariel Sharon, and the United State's Henry Kissinger are among the better-recognized names that have been the subject of efforts to extradite and prosecute under the new tolerance for assertions of global jurisdiction by local courts.

Unfortunately, it is practically impossible to challenge or punish the misuse of international criminal procedure, and it is correspondingly likely that further acceptance of extraterritoriality will lead to its use against US and other Western officials, most of whom will have less stature and defensive resource than a Mr. Kissinger. In order to give prosecutorial reach and administrative agility to the concept of global jurisdiction, however, many internationally minded jurists promote the development of the International Criminal Court.[41] While the ICC might one day emerge as an important civilizing tool, it

---

rules, get-tough policies which may be in effect just then – or not, how crowded the courts are and with what, deals you can make in the hallways and back rooms (called plea bargains), the personalities of the players – from the arresting officer to the clerks, to your defense team, if any... the law, what it says, what it means, and how it is enforced and interpreted in light of every court precedent currently set, these all affect you in concert to comprise "the law." Alan Korwin, Gun Laws of America (Phoenix: Bloomfield Press, 1999) p. 6. The truth in this description applies to international courts, but multiplied.

[40] See Pat M. Holt, "The push for human rights could hurt Americans," Christian Science Monitor, August 2, 2001 online at <http://csmweb2.emcweb.com/durable/2001/08/02/p9s2.htm ; Henry Kissinger, "The Pitfalls of Universal Jurisdiction" Foreign Affairs, July/August 2001. This article can be found in its entirety online at <http://www.thirdworldtraveler.com/Kissinger/Pitfalls_Univ_Juris_Kis.html.

[41] See, for instance, Coalition for the International Criminal Court <http://www.iccnow.org/. "The Coalition for the International Criminal Court is a network of well over 1,000 non-governmental organizations (NGOs) advocating for a fair, effective and independent International Criminal Court (ICC)."

is difficult to see how such a court could meet basic standards of equal protection and due process in the face of competitive strategic pressures, especially those aimed primarily to counterbalance or challenge the United States.

The hallmark document of public international law, the United Nations Charter, has from the moment of its birth been excepted or disregarded on hundreds of occasions while respected and enforced on only a few. Within the last half decade, the United States government has taken decisions in regard to Iraq and other places that admitted a distance between the security perspectives of the United States and the probability of gaining effective UN support for those perspectives. The development of international security law within the UN system is presently stagnant, but this is not necessarily a bad thing, at least to the extent that "law" is applied aggressively as a strategic tool or as a manifestation of generalized anti-Americanism. The disheartening violence of Iraq's climb away from totalitarianism after the takedown of the Hussein regime, along with the discrediting intelligence failure in regard to weapons of mass destruction, have raised both the underlying sentiment of anti-Americanism as well as the energy of international jurists who would apply international law specifically to check the alleged excesses of the United States. Had the proscriptive suasion of international law been empowered by an independent UN budget, the UN might have been dangerous rather than just exasperating in its opposition to US takedown of the Hussein regime. Whatever one's opinion about the decision of the US to enter Iraq, it is apparent in the aftermath that pecuniary interests from within the United Nations could have caused it to physically oppose the invasion if it had better controlled both the expression and enforcement of international law. It is also apparent that nothing about the Saddam Hussein regime merited its defense.

While public international law related to global security has been a relative failure, the march of private or commercial international law, as well as the body of international technical regulations, continues with positive effect. It is in this realm, as much as in the

61

context of public international law, that the expansion of formalized property systems will find growth. Even as public international law and international criminal trials become more politicized and less effective as tools of conflict resolution or dissuasion, a universe of international commercial rules and regulations interconnects rights and obligations globally. Taken as a whole this can be rightly described as the development of the international property regime. Surprisingly, while executive attention, and that of national intelligence services, is keen in regard to the application of international public law and its diplomatic and strategic consequences, the complexity and detail of private or commercial international law is relegated to unheard technical experts. Nevertheless, it is in the realm of private and commercial international law that much of the battle over globalization will be waged.

Moral asymmetry

America's enemies naturally resort to methods that avoid or obviate America's capital and technological advantages. These methods of attack might be called *asymmetric* in reference to the relative absence of physical capital invested in weaponry or operational scale. This recognition of capital imbalance is not particularly useful, however, once it is realized that underdogs have always everywhere depended on cunning and economy to overcome material disadvantage. The most dangerous asymmetry is the moral abandon that allows the ruthless to act in ways that America and its allies cannot. The West's civilizing standards, its cultural progress in law and behavioral norms are what today provide an asymmetric edge to its enemies, but only in the short term of violent enterprises. In the longer term, it is the fact of civilizing standards and discipline that separates and justifies a culture. It would be a shame if, in response to moral asymmetry the West and especially the United States were to fall prey to unintended consequences. That is, if America's reaction makes it still more vulnerable to the threats it had hoped to avoid.

Terrorism is not as physically dangerous as the classic threats posed by other nation-states, or as constant and likely as organized crime. As the name implies, terrorist attacks are intended to inspire fear, are a surprise even when expected, and undermine our sense of civilization in a way other violence does not. Terror may be the action of the weak who decide they must, if they are to be of any consequence, seek advantage in ruthlessness. When intermixed in terms of sentiment, timing, and logistics with other outlaw conduct, terrorist-style action becomes supremely dangerous. When ruthlessness combines with advanced technologies and organization (and even more so when sponsored or encouraged by formal state governments) acts of terror rise to the stature of a principal threat.

If Al Qaeda is the model terrorist organization then terrorism as a conceptual category is further complicated. Arab governments may have played an abiding role in the establishment of fundamentalist Moslem schools around the world, perhaps as a Faustian bargain to keep radical violence at a distance, perhaps out of some measure of sympathy. It is in these schools that the majority of active Moslem terrorist leadership is nurtured and prepared for jihad. Private and perhaps public financial support contributed to the elements necessary to produce educated, trained, committed radical Imams prepared to empower Islam through violence. To the extent that sponsorship of Al Qaeda was intended to further state interests (if indeed this is the case) then American conceptions of terrorism's causes, terrorist objectives, and the required responses might have to be adjusted accordingly. At a pre-Iraq war address to an audience at the National War College, James Woolsey seconded an assertion of Johns Hopkins professor Eliot Cohen that the US was in the beginnings of World War IV (He considers the Cold War to have been WWIII.).[42] According to Woolsey, the WWIV enemy is a three-headed beast of Islamist Shias,

---

[42] James Woolsey, "World War IV" speech given 16 November 2002, National War College, Washington, D.C. See also speech to students at UCLA in 2003, < http://www.derechos.org/nizkor/iraq/doc/wwiv.html.

middle-eastern fascists, and Islamist Sunni.[43] Woolsey's construct did not damn the Moslem world, but instead specified a targetable selection of indocile actors and described why they were worthy of classification as enemies.

The connection of terrorism to legitimate states, either as a tool of state foreign policy or as a side effect of indifference or appeasement, presents a mottled area for determinations of friend or foe. The United States cannot simply cite Switzerland or Saudi Arabia, for instance, as enemies; the US and these countries share wealth and find common ground on myriad matters including security. Besides, some American citizens have themselves supported Al Qaeda, and more the FARC. Public and private worlds are so intermixed, and the situations of many of the world's governments so variegated and confused that perfect policy or diplomatic consistency at the national level is not possible. Property (sometimes pertaining to individuals, sometimes to larger entities) presents a more logical scale of approach to the problem of support activities to insurgent, gangster and terror organizations. At the property level of analysis, entities can be targeted surgically, proportionately and State-to-State diplomacy can be brought to bear within the confines of lesser offending identities. Such an approach, however, requires precise property knowledge.

In northern South America, the nexus between established government and terror deserves our worry. Hugo Chavez prized Saddam Hussein and prizes Fidel Castro among his friends, presents

---

[43] Woolsey, and by reference, Cohen, may be mistakenly focused on the Middle-East as the preeminent danger zone. The threat to Israel is palpable, but the complex threats posed from northern South America and the Caribbean are potentially more costly to the United States. As in the Middle East, terror groups benefit from accessorial behavior on the part of established states. The FARC is a terrorist entity under any reasonable definition, and accessorial behavior on the part of the Venezuelan government in favor of the FARC is hardly to be doubted.[43] The Caribbean is also home to a population of radical Islamic Jihadists. Mix these facts with the potential political consequences of the Castros' deterioration, and the near-abroad looks ever-uglier as a source of security challenges.

himself as the ordained leader of socialist revolution and is excitedly anti-US.[44] His regime will favor and nourish the FARC and FARC similars. Assured of sanctuary in Venezuela and Cuba, the FARC could become more dangerous to the United States than Al Qaeda.

Enthrall, Extort, Pique

> *[K]idnapping, extortion, bank robbery, and drug trafficking—four favorite insurgent activities—are very lucrative.*[45]
>
> US Army Counterinsurgency Manual

Brigandage

Brigandage is evil with social organization and a plan. Brigands (or gangsters, organized criminals, thugs, etc) are often the master employers of terror and terrorists, and, because they combine organizational expertise, aggregated disposable wealth and amorality, they are to be feared in direct relation to the destructive capacity of the weapons that may come into their hands. Bridging what is a police problem and what is military, brigandage straddles the cut-line between civilized-but-unlawful and uncivilized behavior.[46] As corporate

---

[44] See, Washington Post, "Venezuela's Conscience," washingtonpost.com, October 30, 2005; Page B06, <http://www.washingtonpost.com/wp-dyn/content/article/2005/10/29/AR2005102901043.html;Juan Forero, "Chávez Restyles Venezuela With '21st-Century Socialism'," New York Times on line, October 30, 2005, <http://www.nytimes.com/2005/10/30/international/americas/30venezuela.html.

[45] Department of the Army. Field Manual 3-24, Counterinsurgency. Washington, D.C.: Department of the Army, 2006, p. 1-11.

[46] Sir Michael Howard recommends the medieval term *latrunculi*, used to distinguish the fight against these common enemies of mankind from wars against *legitimus hostis* or legitimate enemies. Fighting the former required less in terms of

outlaws such as Colombia's FARC thrive, observers begin to speak of ungovernability and failed states, but those characterizations might misdirect. It may be that the States in question, Colombia's, for instance, are simply under siege. Physical coercion for profit is wedded by the brigand to the timeless political aspiration of avoiding government regulation and taxation, and of acquiring impunity for criminal acts by any means – best of all by assuming government power itself. Governments can become confused or divided by what may be seen as a question of "public safety" vice what is "national security" and so respond inappropriately. When states fail initially to confront organized crime, they risk grave errors of omission -- first simple irresponsibility or appeasement, then corruption perhaps, then on to criminal negligence -- until the state no longer has the power to contain the criminal enterprise. America normally falls victim to brigandage when its citizens stray into trouble abroad or because its commerce is subject to parasitism (although the history of the strategic power of the Sicilian mafia in America is not to be dismissed). Today, criminal enterprises have greater and greater global reach, and their day-to-day activities, while perhaps not rising to the dramatic level of a terrorist event, are of the same character and lead to the same result. Far more people have fallen in Colombia (or Nigeria, Thailand and other countries) to the piecemeal terrorism of illegal armed groups than died in the World Trade Center attack. As for the Colombian FARC, the United States government recognized its terrorist character years ago, but declined until recently to explicitly help the Colombian government defeat it. Over the last decade the FARC has murdered, kidnapped and bombed on thousands of occasions, and became too powerful to destroy without concerted military effort. It has cloaked itself successfully as a revolutionary force engendered and motivated by Colombian social injustice. The argument, long since void, continues sufficient as a justification for (especially European) accommodations to that organization, accommodations sweetened by FARC money and anti-American sport.

---

international law, often more in terms of patience and fortune. "It's not so much war it's more like a hunt," London Times, October 2, 2001.

When successful, criminal organizations metastasize, internationalize, and politicize. They call at first for routine compromises of the law, using minor coercion, perhaps justifying themselves under a cloak of social rebellion. Their initial presence and activity rarely rises to the level of strategy and military response. When it does, it is often too late for peaceful cure. Many of these organizations plague the world, and as a convenient part of their efforts to establish or feign legitimacy they often disparage, or even target, the United States. Most of the world's countries acquiesce or collaborate with these outlaw organizations to one degree or another, so US efforts to curtail outlaw finances are at times impeded by a lack of political will within local governments – either because they fear domestic political repercussions, or because they gain directly from the illegal enterprise. Others simply disagree with the US view of the nature, progress, or virulence of the problem.[47]

Today's greatest outlaws may include outwardly licit corporations. What St. Augustine's pirate captain said to Alexander is repeated today by self-assured thugs who ask what other recourse besides violence they have if they are to compete with that caliber of robber baron exemplified by Enron or WorldCom and legitimized by western governments. Therein lays the heart of the argument of the anti-globalization movement, and why stridently criminal entities such as the FARC have any support at all from the morally attuned. Curiously, America is one of the world's least globalized countries, economically speaking.[48]

---

[47] P.7 Terrorist Financing Council on Foreign Relations Maurice Greenberg, chair 2002; p. 26 "...the Task Force finds that currently existing U.S. and international policies, programs, structures, and organizations will be inadequate to assure sustained results commensurate with the ongoing threat posed to the national security of the United States. Combating terrorist financing must remain a central and integrated element of the broader war on terrorism."

[48] 2003 A.T. Kearney/FOREIGN POLICY Magazine Globalization Index, online at <http://www.foreignpolicy.com The index measures a country's global links, including foreign direct investment, international travel and Internet servers. Out of a total of 62 rated countries, the United States was rated 50th in overall economic

We might call crimes of strategic magnitude, but that do not involve direct use of violence, grand felony. Non-violent crimes such as embezzling, distribution and sale of illegal drugs, counterfeiting, smuggling, and related business ventures induce ruthless efforts of self-protection, and are often concurrent with more violent criminality. Enron's collapse would have to be considered a grand felony the scale of which has an impact on national security. The explanation of Argentina's early 21st century bankruptcy is varied and complicated, but it is no stretch to assert that the Argentine nation fell victim to an Enron-type of felonious assault on the value of major Argentine firms.[49] The felons that produced the Argentine debacle were not international terrorists or armed pirates. However, financial felons and violent gangsters slouch toward uncomfortable partnerships with each other as one set of criminals begins to depend on or extort the other for security, financing, and money laundering. Perhaps a harbinger, Argentina, as a result of initially non-violent but massively felonious behavior, is now more subject to violent criminality than it was only a decade years ago. Protection against grand felony requires transparency of records, aggressive professional auditing of large firms, as well as regulation of trading and accounting practices.

Uppermost in America's response to the growth of grand felony is the effort toward business discipline and the promotion of valid corporate standards. In the end, the best leadership is leadership by example. There may be no other enduring method to mitigate St. Augustine's charges, or to lessen the irony that the synthesis of American economic/cultural success (manifested in the multinational corporation) creates the antithesis of empowered anti-Americanism (manifested in armed, organized criminal mega-business). In the shorter term, America cannot act indifferently to the growth of thug

---

integration, 60th in international trade. Ireland soars in the index as the most globalized country in the world.
[49] See generally, Andrew Marlatt, Economy of Errors (New York: Random House, 2002). While a satire, the humor in the section titled "Enron Admits It's Really Argentina." is valuably disturbing.

organizations. Especially in the Western Hemisphere, where proximity to the homeland makes the danger more immediate, the US will vigorously assist its allies, militarily and otherwise, to defeat organized outlaws.

The quotation at the beginning of the chapter warns that arrogance of a dominant sovereignty can cause it to be considered no better than a brigand, at least according to the assertion of Alexander's pirate foe. But the modern twist is of second or third-tier sovereign states trading on that accusation while they themselves perpetrate complicities with criminal organizations, or even act directly as brigands. Add to this the explosion in the number of non-governmental and international organizations. Many, often those with the gentlest names, are guilty of the same complicity with or enablement of criminal organizations and regimes. St. Augustine's observation is flipped on its head and back again. Formalized sovereignties, NGOs or international organizations, or any conspiratorial combination can be brigand. It is behavior, not organizational genera, that matters in calculating the moral necessity of defensive reaction. Analysis of threats must not be distracted by the arguments of clever pirates, whether they wear an eye patch, a revolutionary armband or a presidential sash.

States are still the most powerful political entities that can organize resources for violence. Most states enjoy unity of command and considerable unity of purpose, can implement policies across borders, keep secrets to fund the ineffable, marshal manpower, expropriate land for military construction, provide sanctuary to others' outlaws, and ally with friend or foe for unworthy purposes. As in the case of North Korea, for instance, the factor of conventional force is wrapped into conditions of geographic control and influence. North Korean infantry divisions threaten the South Korean capital. That North Korea might strike at Japanese sovereign territory with nuclear weapons is plausible, but that threat underwrites the intimidation that North Korea's conventional divisions generate against South Korea, giving North Korea additional military leverage. Conversely, it is

North Korea's conventional military power that protects its ability to pose a nuclear threat.

If the Venezuelan national military were to further split in response to a growing challenge to the regime of President Hugo Chavez; and if some part were to devolve into a force disciplined to protect an exclusive Chavez dictatorship; it would likely also harbor and encourage the FARC (a charge the Colombian government has already made), which would in turn continue to attack the free development of regional energy resources, kidnap travelers, expropriate land, traffic in illicit drugs, and associate with other international terrorist organizations. The US military could be obliged to prepare to fight a national army of Venezuela, a contingency that the US, its military, and its allies in the region do not and cannot want. Venezuela's formal military power may not seem to present a grave challenge to US forces, but there are some who feel the United States still has not prepared itself to fight in the full variety of terrains and geographies, or the full range of conflict types.[50] The US military is notoriously reluctant to fight in urban or mountainous areas. Northern South America is either heavily populated, mountainous or both.

Insurgency & counterinsurgency

"You may buy land now as cheap as stinking mackerel."
Shakespeare's Falstaff on a consequence of civil war

It might have been better to use a more inclusive term, "internal warfare' as the title to this section.[51] An appreciable literature on the

---

[50] On this point, see for instance, John A. Gentry, "Doomed to Fail: America's Blind Faith in Military Technology," Parameters, Winter 2002-03, pp. 88-103.
[51] By the 1980s, "Low Intensity Conflict" (LIC) became the doctrinal container for most of whatever was not heavy unit maneuver warfare. LIC was the subject of military doctrine writing for more than two decades, but was always an un-favored title. "Low intensity" was an appropriate modifier to the extent that the ratio of metal

related subjects exists within which can be traced a body of accepted, if dubious, theories as to why there are insurgencies, how they grow and how to defeat them. *Insurgency* is a currently popular term due to its use to describe the forces opposing the government of Iraq. It is also used to describe the armed leftist guerrilla movement in Colombia. In both places the term may be an overstatement. Insurgency suggests that to some appreciable degree the population is surging in revolt, but in Iraq it seems that much of the violent opposition is a mix of remnant Hussein regime supporters and foreign jihadists. In Colombia the term insurgent might at one time have been appropriate, but it has been years since the principle guerrilla organizations could reasonably claim anything more than marginal support from within the Colombian civilian population. In Colombia, both the supposedly leftist guerrillas and the supposedly rightist paramilitaries are brigands far more than they are insurgents.

---

to men (that is, the relative capital investment in materiel) was lower than in a mechanized conventional war (in this sense the idea of LIC and 'asymmetrical warfare' are almost identical). The overpowering connotation of LIC, however, was always one of relative unimportance. But what was low intensity for the United States was a question of survival for some directly involved ally--this was the common complaint from abroad. Thus the term "LIC" fell on hard times, and was ineffectively replaced by Operations Other Than War (OOTW), the latter more explicitly encompassing multinational peace operations and disaster relief. The newer title proved as debilitating as the old in that it replaced a connotation of unimportance to the country with one of irrelevance to the soldier. The term left the daily lexicon of the US military when GWAT, or Global War on Terror, took up acronymic space after the World Trade Center attacks in 2001.
See Department of the Army, Field Manual 100-20, Military Operations in Low Intensity Conflict (Washington, D.C.: Department of the Army, 1990) which superseded Field Manual 100-20, Low Intensity Conflict (1981) which superseded Field Manual 100-20, Internal Defense and Development (1974); See also Field Manual 7-98, Operations in a Low Intensity Conflict (Washington, D.C.: Department of the Army, 1992). None of these texts mention property as an issue or focus. They address urban environments cursorily and they mention organized crime briefly in the context of narcotics trafficking. A 1994 draft of the updated Field Manual 100-20 is titled Operations Other Than War, and while it incorporates Peace Operations, it maintains much of the Vietnam counter-revolutionary war flavor of its predecessor manuals.

A suitable term for the course of action favored by gangsters and insurgents or terrorists is might extortionary warfare. Extortion supposes an illegitimate demand backed by the credible threat of force. The extortion may be strategic or very individual, and is often both. The method may be a letter to a local government, a kidnapping or bombing, but the term defines violence applied in the absence of war, perhaps in the absence of revolutionary strategy, with or without a political goal, and regardless of advantageous correlation of forces, save that advantage gained by amorality. Extortion is an available option for a whole array of identities, and is aided by every advance in communications and information technology. It is supremely flexible in that some form of violence can be leveraged against almost any vulnerability. Successful extortion, as well as resistance to extortion, requires detailed knowledge of the wealth to be extorted and where the extortionists can most efficiently and safely endanger that wealth.

Throughout this book there is discussion of three defining aspects of internal warfare and two specific technologies which the United States has yet to dominate. The three defining aspects are: 1. the ability of an insurgent military force to disuniform and 'disappear' into the civilian population; 2. the essential requirement of the insurgent commander to concern him or herself with lines of communication; and 3. the need of government armed forces to operate within the confines of domestic law. The two pieces of modus operandi are the use of the landmine and kidnapping.

The great military advantages of the West and of the United States in particular seem to be the projection of kinetic energy and massive logistics. If there is a need that can be met by great physical destructive force delivered at great distance, the United States military is without doubt in its own league. Because this is so obvious it makes the likelihood that enemies will avoid kinetic competition all that much greater. Interestingly, the West and in particular the United States has another comparative advantage and strength that is appropriate to the new universe of threats. That advantage is its organization of rights and duties related to wealth. It is an advantage that has previously not been considered a military one, or for that matter considered at all, but nevertheless presents an important advantage in counterinsurgency.

The fact that an enemy does not maintain outward appearances and emblems of combatant or military status requires an approach to intelligence more akin to the investigatory methods of domestic police detectives. The detective method is greatly enabled by the presence of public records, ID cards, finger prints, property records, school attendance sheets, and all manner off public preparation of the environment to include such ubiquitous phenomena as school bus routes, phone books and street signs.

The essence of strategy for an insurgent leader revolves around maintaining safe passage to sanctuary. This is discussed at greater length in Chapter Four in the section titled '*A general whose road homeward is cut is ruined.*' The secret for his opponent to finding his routes homeward lies in detailed intelligence of geographic behavior, and that geographic behavior is often revealed by public documents, especially property documents. Any environment where public documents reveal relationships between people and places is a going to present a less survivable battlefield to the insurgent leader.

The need of the government armed forces to operate within the confines of the law creates a corresponding need for precision in finding and fixing individual leaders. The standard of conduct for a plaintiff's lawyer in the United States, if he wants to bring financial pain to a prospective defendant, is to have a piece of paper handed to that potential defendant appraising him of the action. That high standard of locating is possible because of the existence of extensive public records. The records make it possible for an average private investigator (with some requisite knowledge of local culture) to find all but the most clever and secretive individuals. Service of process cannot be accomplished with a canon, or can criminal arrests. If a military unit regularly goes out on patrol without a precise idea of where to find a suspected insurgent, it is safe to say that the level of intelligence is still inadequate to meet the conditions of civil law. The intelligence that the private eye or a policeman has at his or her disposal almost never includes data from a remote sensor or overhead system. The intelligence that serves process on defendants and arrests criminals is almost entirely a combination of local cultural knowledge and public records that are analyzed to determine likely whereabouts within the confines of law. Property intelligence is exactly suited to insurgent situations to the extent that the government continually tries to move its behavior in the direction of legal constraint.

Property information and property-based analyses are more naturally suitable to three defining aspects of internal war: legal constraint on government forces, the ability of the insurgent to shed outward signs of insurgent status, and the need of the insurgent commander to avoid a decisive engagement with a physically superior government force (also expressed as his need to preserve the security of his line of communication for withdrawal). The two modus operandi mentioned above as being unsolved challenges for the United States military are the employment of IED (Innovative Explosive Devices) and kidnapping. Both of these technologies, one mostly physical and the other mostly organizational, are being constantly advanced by insurgent enemies of the United States and its allies. As to both activities, the location and defeat of the insurgent leadership will likely be the fastest rout to stopping them. Once again, going back to the three defining aspects of insurgent warfare, property intelligence is probably the most effective and suitable.

So What?

"Mine is better than ours."

Benjamin Franklin
from Poor Richards Almanac

Land worth

The worth of real estate is determined, according to the old saw, by three things – location, location, location. If there *are* three determinants of worth, physical location is actually the least of the three – sort of. The first determinant of worth (and market price) is the content of the mix of rights purchased and duties shouldered. The price of a place is higher if the subsurface rights are included, if there are no easements, no lingering leasehold, and so on. So, while the distance to a school and the quality of the water certainly influence price, it is a mix of rights that we purchase, not just the environment. The other remaining determinant of value is the nature and quality of the regime of ownership rules. If the rules do not allow the ostensible owner to sell or bequeath, then the market value of what is bought and sold is likely to be less, all else remaining equal. This idea of buying rights goes unstated by the Kansan of our earlier example because property rights and rules are taken for granted in Kansas, and so seem to beg the question of value entirely. These non-physical ingredients of what gives real estate a good price have often been ignored in land reform measures, and their neglect has been a cause of failure.[52] At the beginning of the paragraph an assertion that physical location was the least of three determinants of value carried the disclaimer "sort of." That escape was included because the regime of ownership rules guides what rights can or cannot be purchased, and so, since the regime of rules is usually delimited by a geography with a political name (such as Kansas or Leavenworth County or Bogotá or Colombia), it can as well be argued that indeed it all boils down to *location, location, location.*

---

[52] They are likewise ignored in developmental engineering projects. See, for instance, George Mason University, Rethinking Institutional Analysis: Interviews with Vincent and Elinor Ostrom, (Vienna, Virginia, 2003). Renowned developmental economist Elinor Ostrom gives a prime example: "The initial plans for many of the major irrigation projects in developing countries focused almost exclusively on engineering designs for physical systems and ignored organizational questions. This engineering bias leads to neglect of proper incentives. Project engineers, for example, face strong pressures to focus on the design of physical works while ignoring social infrastructure, and to focus on larger rather than smaller projects. Few engineering schools offer any courses on property rights or institutional arrangements. Ibid, p.10.

The market of property rights is not a zero-sum world. The value of rights in land often increases as other rights are relinquished. For instance, if visitors enter a restaurant freely, the possibility of making a profit from the property increases. By giving up an exclusive right to entry, and not enforcing the right to deny access, the value of the right to rents increases. We also incur a duty to protect our visitors while on the property. A change in the mix of rights and duties associated with real estate can increase its value, but only if owners wield enough control over the changes to insure that the new mix of rights fits their priorities, the market demand for rights and the willingness to shoulder duties. In addition, property adjoining the restaurant may increase in commercial value, but may decrease in value as residential property. In the aggregate, property values can be measured by sale prices, taxes assessed, average local insurance appraisals, municipal bond ratings, commercial loan rates, stock quotations or even the number of tourist visits. Still, value remains a personalized concept, and as in any market, a higher price is available as a greater number of potential buyers are exposed to a reasonable potential for satisfying their preferred use. The recluse might not be well compensated by the added income generated by a restaurant. As zoning or land use plans reduce the potential uses of a piece of land, the potential can, but is not necessarily, reduced. It may be, for instance, that in a given area no parcels of less than ten acres may be sold, but the area becomes especially attractive to buyers seeking to live on gentrified hobby-farms. Or perhaps a warehouse zoning decision improves the marketability of an area otherwise unwanted. On the other hand, an area that cannot be reached because the road is not safe, or where there is simply no information about the value and potential price of land will suffer chronically lowered land values. The presence of landmine fields near a mountain community is not a positive element in most personalized senses of value. On an international scale, a country that cannot easily be entered, or from which one cannot freely travel, may become similarly hamstrung in terms of the aggregate value of its real property.

In order to understand all the influences that might bear on the worth of real estate, and therefore the price of a piece of land, we need to do more than list the identities of potential owners and the rights that might attract them. We also require a grasp of the cohesiveness of identity. It may be more costly to induce a group of existing owners who have a strongly cohesive identity to sell or share their ownership portions. It may also be harder to get them to meet duties implied by their ownership and associated with whatever rights they enjoy. Thus an analysis of the value and price of a set of property rights must go beyond two-dimensional identification of rights and related "owners." The analysis must also consider the nature of the identity of those owners. Finally, no strategic understanding of the value of land is possible without consideration of relevant aspects of the overall system of ownership rules--the market value of a Kansas restaurant will be greatly influenced by a pending change in zoning laws, as will the value of rural land in Colombia if the legal political authority is willing to cede land whole-fee to an armed outlaw group.

Almost every law influences the market value of real estate. Where the legal emphasis is on protection of tenant rights (and ignoring all other market factors) the prices of apartments would logically tend to be higher. After all, the value of possession is made greater by the greater security provided by the legal regime. It might be supposed, then, that the market value of rental property as an income producing investment would go down since there would be more risk involved in owning the complex. Curiously, given additional protection of the tenant by the legal system, the value of the apartment complex as an income producer may go up, since the rents may be higher and the clientele may, in turn, be more solvent. Of course this depends on other market factors. It is possible that the owner of the apartment building would see the profitability of his rights increase even after what seems an erosion of his rights in favor of the tenants'. The landowner has a right to gain income from the rental of other rights. That is to say, he receives payment for renting the right to possess space in his building. Although he wants to retain the right to eject renters because he feels this ensures the collection of his rental income, the government might limit his right of repossession once the landlord-tenant relationship has begun. Government may have bolstered the tenant's claim to exclusive possession, but the value of the landowner's right to rents may have actually gone up with the value of the tenant's possession. This is because prospective tenants may see greater security in the apartments as potential homes. The value of ownership is often increased for all parties when rights in the property are dispersed and shared. Likewise, sharing sovereignty, like dispersing rights in domestic real estate, can increase the value of a nation's aggregated property. But this is not necessarily so. Value can be decreased when ownership is dispersed too much.

Gottfried Dietz, in a compelling statement on the subject, argued that eroding respect for private property in favor of common property (a result, he claims, of the assaults of socialist philosophy and decadent living) is a principal threat to the cause of freedom.[53] Decadence aside, it is good to recount the fuzziness of the boundary between what is clearly a private right and what is held in common. A private club is an example of shared rights owned in common. The club gains value in the counting of its members as much because of the sharing of rights as because of the exclusion. It is nevertheless important to the value of the whole that within the club the status of membership and payment be precise, complete and transparent.

So, how does this discussion about the perceived and market worth of real estate touch directly on the link between the formality of property and social peace or global security? The answer is four-fold: First, and least, a side effect of formalizing property is an increased likelihood of material prosperity. In the long run, material prosperity may indirectly promote peace. Secondly, experience and logic tell us that people fight over land, often focusing on supposedly advantageous geophysical attributes while oblivious to the nature of property institutions and how they conduce greater or lesser real estate worth.

---

[53] See generally, Gottfried Dietze, In Defense of Property, (Chicago: Henry Regnery Company, 1963).

78

Also, every violent insult to human rights (a bomb, for instance) influences the market value of a place. Human security can be measured to some degree in the market for land. this is especially true in select industries -- like tourism. Finally and mostly, the issue of real estate worth touches directly on the link between property and peace because the institution of property is in essence and has been from the beginning a means of conflict resolution. Institutionalized conflict resolution based on clear evidence of ownership, along with effective mechanisms for giving meaning that evidence, greatly increases the worth of real property because the cost of peace is made to be less than the cost of violence.

Since the end of the Cold War, a number of popular books on the general subject of property have been published, most dealing with the importance of property for attaining general prosperity, or as an integral element of a free society.[54] The appearance of these titles is in some measure attributable to the manner in which the Cold War ended, with communism and its criticism of private property discredited. Hernando De Soto is perhaps most widely read among those writers who identified property development as a key to economic prosperity in poorer countries. Mr. De Soto, a Peruvian, has dedicated himself to marketing a powerful idea: a country's institutional and legal framework must recognize and protect the value behind ownership if there is to be any widespread creation of wealth. Mr. De Soto

---

[54] See, for instance, Gregory S. Alexander, Commodity & Property: Competing Visions of Property in American Legal Thought 1776-1970, (Chicago: The University of Chicago Press, 1997); Tom Bethel, The Noblest Triumph: Property and Prosperity through the Ages, (New York: St. Martin's Press, 1998); Geoffrey Demarest, Geoproperty: Foreign Affairs, National Security and Property Rights, (London: Frank Cass, 1998); J. W. Harris, Property and Justice, (Oxford: Clarendon Press, 1996); Andro Linklater, Measuring America, (New York: Walker Publishing Company, 2002); J.E. Penner, The Idea of Property in Law, (Oxford: Clarendon Press, 1997); Richard Pipes, Property and Freedom, (New York: Vintage Books, 2000); Svetozar Pejovich, The Economic Foundations of Property Rights: Selected Readings, (Northhampton, MA: Edward Elgar, 1997); John P. Powelson, The Story of Land: A World History of Land Tenure and Agrarian Reform, (Cambridge, Massachusetts: Lincoln Institute of Land Policy, 1988).

convincingly establishes a causal link between formal property and material success of the population at large.

> "[M]ost people [in the third world] ...do not have access to a legal property rights system that represents their assets in a manner that makes them widely transferable and fungible, that allows them to be encumbered and permits their owners to be held accountable. So long as the assets of the majority are not properly documented and tracked by a property bureaucracy, they are invisible and sterile in the marketplace."[55]

There appears to be, however, an obstruction in the intellectual path taken by the property writers of the last decade: the link between property and security has been greeted as an afterthought. Peace is anticipated as a secondary benefit when poverty's cruel choices become less and less a cause of criminal and subversive behavior. It may be presumed that widespread economic desperation presents a common seedbed for willingness to commit violence; this has long been a staple of counterinsurgency theory, although some phenomena argue against it. Regardless, the important nexus between the existence of formal property and the condition of security is not indirect via prosperity. The link between property and security is direct and substantial -- greater than the link between property and prosperity. Prosperity, a worthy goal in its own right, can be promoted in many countries via the development of formal property regimes. This prosperity should have a positive effect on the general prospects for peace. Nevertheless, such an effect is speculative, while the linkage between property formalization and social peace are concrete and often immediate. Mr. De Soto, principally concerned with the benefit of formalizing property as a measure to defeat poverty, almost recognizes as much. He states,

> Widespread legal property will even help solve one of their loudest and most persistent complaints about

---

[55] Hernando De Soto, *supra* p. 211

expanding urban poor – the need for more "law and order." Civil society in market economies is not simply due to greater prosperity. The right to property also engenders respect for law.[56]

The essential purpose, the historical purpose inherent in the process of formalizing property is one of conflict avoidance and resolution, as much as it is the creation of capital or of an efficient and equitable tax-base -- although the latter has been an attractive motivator for a number of governments to partially formalize property. The original reason for a definite, public, court-assured demarcation between the lands of two would-be owners was to keep them off each other's throats.

Human rights

Pre-WWII scholar Reinold Noyes contributed an elaborate observation regarding property as a psychological and linguistic concept. Purists have long held property to be merely a concert of rights, and Noyes furthered this view with an interpretation of the early evolution of Roman legal terminology. According to Noyes, words leading to the very ability to consider property as a substantive thing were, in the days of the early Republic, descriptors of legal or pre-legal court actions. Noyes found that the word property had referred to a complaint that an early Roman court would normally be willing to hear. In other words, an early Roman might have pleaded, "He hunted where only I may hunt, or "he took grain from land where only I may harvest." These claims of violated rights were called property, which led to the idea of property as a separate class of complaint and *then* as a special class of thing. According to Noyes, prior to the recognition of preferential rights in courts, the noun *property* could not exist to encompass legally owned things. Since the vocabulary leading to the notion of property *as a location or object* was legalistic, Noyes

---

[56] de Soto, supra p. 196.

discovered, in effect, that the invention of property law came before widespread usage of the noun. Furthermore, much of the early semantic debate about the property concept revolved around fundamental, abstract and prehistoric distinctions between law and power, power and right, right and claims. In other words, at some point in the Western jurisprudential past, distinctions between human and property rights, and the act of asserting them in court, did not exist, or at least could not be formally expressed to the court. This understanding of the commonality between human rights and property is today shared by leading developmental economists. The words of Svetozar Pejovich, for instance, could hardly be more to the point.

> "About the right of ownership, I. Fisher said: "A property right is the liberty or permit to enjoy benefits of wealth while assuming the costs which those benefits entail....property rights are not physical things or events, but are abstract social relations. A property right is not a thing." (I. Fisher, Elementary Principles of Economics, New York: Macmillan, 1923, p. 27) Instead, property rights are relations among men that arise from the existence of scarce goods and pertain to their use. This definition of property rights is consistent with Roman law, Karl Marx's writings, and the new institutional (property rights) economics.
>
> This definition of property rights makes two important points. The first is that it is wrong to separate human rights from property rights. My right to vote and my right to speak on issues are my property rights because they define the relationship between myself and other people. In other words, the property-rights definition applies to all rights of an individual vis-à-vis

82

other people. The second point derives from the first, in that property rights are relations between individuals."[57]

From his perspective on the less-than-essential quality of the term *property*, Noyes had concluded that modern legal protections afforded to real property could be expanded to include every right associated with things in general. In the half-century since Noyes' treatise was published, US courts indeed took the same direction and accepted an ever-growing list of theories of protectable rights litigated as property. It was a later trend to litigate the violation of human rights as a separate category of public action. Developmental economics passed through no such period, however, *property-as-rights* having been all but overlooked as a conceptual focus of developmental programs.

Under examination, grave violations of human rights, such as mass murder, will often be tied to competition over land that has not been civilized into a formal property regime. In this sense, human rights violations are a final result of a failure to detail, announce and enforce property rights. It would be counterproductive to routinize horrific crimes and diminish the urgency in confronting them by approaching them as property questions. Nevertheless, clashes over property are often the object if not the cause of the most serious human rights abuses. Many abuses are rooted in competitions for the rights of enjoyment and profit associated with land. In many geographies still, the human rights challenge is one of measuring not just the extent to which property rights are being protected, but the extent to which humans are being treated as property. A venerable American geopolitician, Theodore Roosevelt, stated,

---

[57] Svetozar Pejovich, The Economics of Property Rights, (Boston: Kluwer Academic Publishers, 1990), p. 27; also see generally, Svetozar Pejovich, The Economic Foundations of Property Rights: Selected Readings, (Northhampton, MA: Edward Elgar, 1997). For a more general primer on the economics of property, see Harold Demsetz, "Toward a Theory of Property Rights," The American Economic Review, Vol. 57, No. 2 Papers and Proceedings of the Seventy-ninth Annual Meeting of the American Economic Association (May, 1967), pp. 347-359.

"In every civilized society property rights must be
carefully safeguarded; ordinarily and in the great
majority of cases, human rights and property rights are
fundamentally and in the long run, identical; but when it
clearly appears that there is a real conflict between them,
human rights must have the upper hand; for property
belongs to man and not man to property."[58]

Significant historical examples exit of impairments to the property
rights of collective victim groups.[59] These impairments, which have
included restrictions on professional licensing, divestment and purchase
of real estate, clothing markings, special naming conventions, marriage
and intercourse restrictions, off-limits locations or concentrations,
marking of transactions, special taxes and others. These have been
specifically established as formal impairments in the social contract as
to a vulnerable collective identity. Such impairments have preceded
horrific mass violations of basic human rights and constitute an
important intelligence indictor of future collective violence.

Detractors of *property* as an ordering concept of society may
determine their opposition on the basis of self-imposed straw man
argumentation. Such obstinacy ala Proudhon (that property is theft)
makes its application as an instrument of reconciliation of rights and
duties difficult.[60] When Proudhon stamped his imprimatur on the

---

[58] Theodoreroosevelt.org, "The Man in the Arena: Citizenship in a Republic"
(Address delivered at the Sorbonne, Paris, April 23, 1910), Theodore Roosevelt
Association Speeches, online at
http://www.theodoreroosevelt.org/research/speech%20arena.htm.
[59] On this point, see, Raul Hilberg, The Destruction of the European Jews, (New
York: Holmes & Meier, 1985) pp. 10-11; also, Benjamin Leiberman,. "'How Much
Worse It Is Than Massacre!': Turkey, Russia, Serbia, and Macedonia, 1914-1918"
(Chapter 3) in Terrible Fate: Ethnic Cleansing in the Making of Modern Europe,
(Chicago: Ivan R. Dee, 2006), pp. 80-117.
[60] P.J. Proudhon. What is Property? (1840). An Inquiry Into the Principle of Right and
Government. Translated by B.R. Tucker, 1876, (New York: Humbold, 1890; New
York: Dover, 1970; Cambridge, Cambridge University Press, 1994).

thinking of generations of anti-capitalists, his own thinking was channeled by existing formal definitions of property -- the codes of mid-19th century France that gave the concept rigidity and tied it to the interests of a small minority of owners.[61] Proudhon was not informed or not impressed by the revolutionary nature of land surveying and marketing that was well under way in the United States.[62] Rights in land nearing the complete "fee simple absolute" were being sold at auction at low prices to whoever had the gumption to homestead or speculate. Also, just as Marx had not envisioned the spread ownership of common stock, or of trade union bargaining power, Proudhon was obviously not engaged by the history of free stock companies that first settled New England, and did not foresee the complex and flexible interpretations of rights delineated in relation to every kind of thing. Much less could he have envisioned the breadth of claims and causes that have been successfully championed under property theories, or the reach and detail of markets for property rights. Proudhon, however, wrote at a time before universal acceptance of the idea that humans should be owners, but not themselves property.

---

[61] In Proudhon's writing, for instance, "The Roman law defined property as the right to use and abuse one's own within the limits of the law -- *jus utendi et abutendi re suâ, guatenus juris ratio patitur*. A justification of the word *abuse* has been attempted, on the ground that it signifies, not senseless and immoral abuse, but only absolute domain. Vain distinction! invented as an excuse for property, and powerless against the frenzy of possession, which it neither prevents nor represses. The proprietor may, if he chooses, allow his crops to rot under foot; sow his field with salt; milk his cows on the sand; change his vineyard into a desert, and use his vegetable-garden as a park: do these things constitute abuse, or not? In the matter of property, use and abuse are necessarily indistinguishable. According to the Declaration of Rights, published as a preface to the Constitution of '93, property is "the right to enjoy and dispose at will of one's goods, one's income, and the fruit of one's labor and industry. Code Napoléon, article 544: "Property is the right to enjoy and dispose of things in the most absolute manner, provided we do not overstep the limits prescribed by the laws and regulations Ibid. at p. 43 (electronic text version from the Electronic Text Center, University of Virginia Library, <http://wyllie.lib.virginia.edu ." Proudhon, a master of circular argument, defines property in such a way as to find it unacceptable.

[62] See generally, Andro Linklater, *supra* note 28.

Nicolas sums up the slave's position in this way: Being endowed with reason...he was inevitably a peculiar thing and could, for example, acquire rights for his master. But he himself had no rights: he was merely an object of rights, like an animal. It was not until the first and second centuries AD that any attempt was made to regulate the master's treatment of his slave, and such regulation as there was took the same form as our regulation for the protection of animals.[63]

Property's Roman roots and its principle advocates suffered or apologized for the "peculiar" institution of slavery, and so the word itself carried subliminally an unspoken and irreconcilable association.

When, in recent decades, international defense of human rights was targeted at Soviet treatment of its citizens, the elemental philosophical differences between the American and Russian revolutions were newly bared. A Soviet treatise on international law written by Soviet jurist and Marxist ideologue G. I. Tunkin in the early 1970s is exemplary.[64] It was presented as the official Soviet academic statement on the principles of international law. Many sections of Tunkin's tome expose ownership as a fundamental sin, and are ironically betray the seeds of the Soviet demise. For instance, Tunkin's explanations of the right to self-determination seem tailor-made as arguments for the various republics to separate themselves from the Soviet Union. More to the point are references to the Soviet theoretic understanding of the relationship of the Soviet, as a central government, to the rights of its citizens. "Conventions on human rights do not grant rights directly to individuals, but establish mutual obligations of states to grant such rights to individuals."[65] The drift of

---

[63] Peter Birks, New Perspectives on the Roman Law of Property, (Oxford: Clarendon Press, 1989), p. 61, citing Barry Nicolas, Introduction to Roman Law, 3rd. edn., Cambridge, 1972, p. 133.
[64] G. I. Tunkin, Theory of International Law translated by William E. Butler, (Cambridge, Massachusetts: Harvard University Press, 1974).
[65] Ibid., p. 83.

Tunkin's description, with its rejection of natural rights, exposes the Soviet citizen as part of national sovereignty in the same way that cattle belong to ranch land. The US Constitution, on the other hand, does not grant the citizens of the United States rights. That document is intended to protect the citizens of the United States from denial and violation of natural rights, including and especially denials and violations by the government. To be sure, the Soviet citizen exercised rights, even rights recognizable as use and possessory rights in real estate, but the Soviet citizen was simultaneously considered an object of property rights to be exercised by the State.[66]

There is nothing new to the observation that systems of ownership can incrementally approach the state of slavery. If we are the full owners of our land, we can do what we please on it, including speak as we please, worship as we please, or leave. The importance of the right to leave property is so obvious when referring to domestic property rights that it is disregarded unless forced under pedantic analysis. Even a prisoner holds some property rights in "his cell," but it would clearly be more valuable to him as property if he could come and go as he wished. Internationally, we have seen the value of this right reflected in the desperation of peoples whose poverty in the ownership of their native lands has led them to dare dangerous escapes.

Tunkin's expression of the Soviet relationship of the individual to the state suggests how we can treat human rights in property terms, but the link between individual liberties and property rights is already scarred into the American cultural experience. Nothing more clearly proves the point than the agonizing debate of man as chattel that led to

---

[66] The Chinese are today struggling with similar issues, and seem to be seeking an un-communist path. See generally, Congressional-Executive Commission on China, One Hundred Eighth Congress, First Session, Ownership With Chinese Characteristics: Private Property Rights and Land Reform in the People's Republic of China, (Washington, D.C., U.S. Government Printing Office, 2003); Li Li, "China entering era of enlightenment for property rights," Beijing Portal, online at <http://www.beijingportal.com.cn/7838/2005/07/25/210; Cao Desheng, "Court Rules on Property rights," China Daily, online at <http://www.chinadaily.com.cn/english/doc/2004-11/25/c.

the American Civil War. Few understood better than Abraham Lincoln the continuous weave of property and human rights. Lincoln himself equivocated over interpretation of the constitution's respect for private property and the "peculiar institution" that allowed treatment as property of beings supposedly endowed by the creator with the right to liberty.[67] It is useful to remember that black slaves were held often enough by other Blacks or by Indians.[68] More than a historical curiosity, ownership of Blacks by other Blacks shows that the acceptance of property rights as defined by the regime of property laws had consumed recognition of human rights as argued by the nature of humanity. The point is that civil or human rights have often been organized and understood intuitively as property. Basic human rights concepts can be placed on the same plane of analysis as other rights associated with ownership. The historical references are not comfortable ones, but it is instructive in some situations to highlight human status in property terms. The 14th Amendment to the United States Constitution, ratified in 1868, not only prohibits that any State "deprive any person of life, liberty, or property, without due process of

---

[67] See Noah Brooks, Abraham Lincoln and the Downfall of American Slavery (New York: G.P. Putnam's Sons, 1898). "Not at once did he throw in his fortunes with those who were to be the leaders of the new Free Soil party. He always moved slowly and with deliberation that deceived many and annoyed not a few. They thought him too slow, over-cautious, even waiting to see which was to be the winning side.. . . But the time came when he took his final stand and declared that he must thenceforth be the champion of freedom against slavery..." Ibid., 152; See also Robert W. Johannsen, Lincoln, the South, and Slavery: The Political Dimension (Baton Rouge, Louisiana: Louisiana State University Press, 1991).

[68] See Annie Heloise Abel, The American Indian as American Slaveholder and Secessionist, (Cleveland: The Arthur H. Clarke Company, 1914). "With them (Indians who had been transplanted to lands south of the Mason-Dixon line) it had been a familiar institution long before the time of their exile. In their native haunts they had had negro slaves as had had the whites and removal had made no difference to them in that particular. Since the beginning of the century refuge to fugitives and confusion of ownership had been occasions for frequent quarrel between them and the citizens of the Southern states." Ibid, p.22.

law; nor deny any person within its jurisdiction the equal protection of the laws," the writers of the amendment felt it necessary to specify that financial claims for the loss or emancipation of any slave were illegal and void.

The subject of human rights is omnipresent in US foreign policy. It invites constant accusation of hypocrisy and challenges the comfort of consistency. In one form or another, United States foreign policy has always been conducted in light of or in spite of a hefty measure of human rights content. Winston Churchill, anticipating the entry of the United States into WWII and appreciating Roosevelt's efforts to support Britain logistically, states the case:

> ...[I]n the long run—believe me , for I know—the action of the United States will be dictated, not by methodical calculations of profit and loss, but by moral sentiment, and by that gleaming flash of resolve which lifts the hearts of men and nations, and springs from the spiritual foundations of human life itself.[69]

Specific use of the term "human rights," and integration of the term into policy has been more recent phenomena. Property rights have not seen such a fashion. The moral complaints of communist theorists precluded and sullied discussion of rights in property terms.

It is safe to say that human rights performance has always figured as an element of the United States' relationships with other lands. Violations of human rights most decried by our government, or by private citizens working through non-governmental organizations, include lack of habeas corpus, torture, organized rape, extrajudicial execution, forced exile, disenfranchisement, and genocide. Less heinous, but more typically practiced abuses abound, and these can be usefully described in property terms. An exclusionary government

---

[69] Winston Churchill, The Great Republic: A History of America, (New York: Random House, 2000) p. 599.

might exercise property ownership in disregard of what should be the ownership rights of populations within its geographic reach. A government can represent the ownership arrogance of the majority of citizens against a minority population or against another nation. In other cases the government is unable or unwilling to enforce the property rights of citizens that do identify with it. The combinations of dysfunction are many, and each can be detailed in terms of three elements: 1, lack of acceptable evidence delineating rights, duties and the identity of owners; 2, incapacity of owners (or claimants) and the government to act on conclusions drawn from the evidence; and 3, exclusionary conditions in the basic rules delimiting the social contract. Any situation involving the violation of human rights could be expressed in ownership terms, but with reference to the most serious violations, the use of property terminology might sterilize descriptions. At that point, the utility of a property-based description of events, conflicts and institutional shortcomings might be exceeded. What is perhaps most important in defending broad attention to property rights in the analysis of national and international security affairs is observation of the close linkage between denied property rights and evolution of basic human rights abuses. That said, and if an easy distinction between human rights and property rights is comforting, it seems that in general people accept the proposition that the protection of a property right be made to depend on expression of the right in a document. A human right should not require expression in a document.

Concern about human rights inspires or modifies United States foreign policy almost daily. The human rights performance of a small country's government may come to decide the likelihood of United States financial, diplomatic or military assistance. Violations of rights, duly publicized, can become the most important reason for involvement of American forces in areas otherwise lacking strategic interest for the United States. Within this context of moral luxury, the failure to acknowledge powerful relationships between human rights and property ownership forces human rights abuse into a category of interest apart from standard policy. Not all violations of human rights are as morally gripping as governmentally-sponsored mass rape or the organized disappearance of dissidents. The right to do business on equal terms, or to expect that the natural environment will not be abused, or a patent respected are all ownership rights. They do not have the same psychological urgency as rights associated with the physical integrity of a person. Like all rights, they are associated for policy purposes with geographies, group identities, and systems of ownership rules. The United States government created policy positions on the treatment of dissidents "in the Soviet Union," or the alleged abuse of Palestinians "in Israel," or the cause of majority rule "in South Africa." Policy, and any military force imputed to back it, will have a geographic reference, and usually an explicit or implicit reference to owner groups. They will also be made in the context of some kind of system of ownership rules (also at times explicit, at times not). Observers can find what appear as inconsistencies, partiality, or even hypocrisy in the application of human rights standards in many countries' foreign policies. But when we define basic human rights together with rights more commonly interpreted as property rights, we can more easily identify and reconcile strategic priorities. Perhaps more importantly, human rights abuses, like international wars, can all be traced back to property conflicts. If we establish the system for settling property conflicts we will go a long way toward obviating the course taken toward violence.

Agreeing with Teddy Roosevelt that human rights and property rights are fundamentally and in the long run, identical, and that property belongs to man and not man to property, I believe a practical, operational difference will become clearer and clearer. In successful societies, there is no valuable tangible property without a written instrument. That is the result of the statutes of fraud and their rejection of oral evidence. If the evidence is not perfected to the satisfaction of whatever type of court exists, the right barely exists in practical terms. That is the logical consequence of the right being a product of the social contract. Meanwhile, there are some rights, at least according to those streams of philosophy arguing natural or God-given rights, that don't stem from human agreement, or that at least do not depend on the existence of any written evidence (a fact that would require a human agreement). The difference can be sorely tested at the edges of semantic logic, but as a practical matter, and for the assertion of this book, preferential rights in land require formal evidence. The individual right to physical integrity does not.

Violence and Peace

So why is the legalistic organization of real estate ever a military concern? Answering this question is tricky, given that the connection is at once *un*intuitive and obvious. Taking and holding terrain is an essential vocation of the military commander about which no convincing is needed. At the same time, the existence of cadastral records presupposes the rule of law, while military operations are, in the ideal, conducted beyond the confines of domestic law. Therein lays the nub of the matter. When the soldier is called upon to confront something less than the raw taking of terrain from a uniformed foreign enemy, there is always a bit of an identity problem. He is being asked to delve into matters of a police nature, or within that band of incomplete governance where society is not quite policed, and where the enemy is hard to define, and so is the law. The soldier will be torn between a desire to define his environment in such a way that his supra-legal mission and training are more applicable (to close with and destroy an enemy, and to take and hold terrain for that purpose) or to create the conditions of governability that would make his services no longer necessary. Enroute to the condition of the rule of law, which would allow the soldier to retire from the field, is development of a set of civilizing institutions. The property regime is so fundamental an institution that not creating it means never to supersede the condition that makes the presence of the soldier necessary. Bluntly, in a place such as Iraq or Haiti, if the occupying forces do not establish Western-style property regimes, those forces will not be able to leave without the polity devolving back toward warlordism and tyranny. The military commander easily handles the notion that he build roads and run hospitals during his occupation, but this owes as much as anything to the presence of engineers and doctors within his command. A savvier leader sees the central importance of establishing property courts and the evidence they must have in order to function well. Providentially, the evidence that the property court needs in order to function as a conflict resolution mechanism can also provide some of the best intelligence for defeating the kind of armed foe that bedevils the military in insurgency-type environments.

At the time these paragraphs were being written, the international news media reported the arrest of Dorothy Stang, a catholic nun and naturalized Brazilian of American birth working for years in support of indigenous rights in the Amazon region.[70] As the news media put it, she had complained that the Brazilian government was not doing enough to stop land-related violence. Sister Stang was apparently murdered for having been a partisan activist in an on-going land dispute. According to the reports, Brazilian troops were being sent to the region to help track down the missionary's killers. Meanwhile, in Plateau State, Nigeria, in a clash between Muslims and Christians (in which tens of thousands have been killed and hundreds of thousands displaced) the visible and inciting questions of ethnicity and religion are secondary. The central object of this violence, grown well beyond the possibilities of police control, has been real estate.[71] A look at the Muslim-Christian conflict in Mindanao shows similar land disputes at the source of the conflict, although in Mindanao land acquisition and denial may be more of a strategy in service to ethnic conflict.[72] From the US Department of State Background Note on Lebanon we find the following:

> "Palestinian refugees, predominantly Sunni Muslims, whose numbers are estimated at between

---

[70] BBC News World Edition, "Brazil charges nun murder suspect," Monday, 21 February, 2005 at <http://news.bbc.co.uk/2/hi/americas/4280919.stm.
[71] Mark Doyle, "Poverty behind Nigeria's violence," BBC News World Edition, May 19, 2004 online at <http://news.bbc.co.uk/2/hi/africa/3730109.stm.
[72] See, for instance, Keith Bacongco, "Mindanao Land Dispute: Lumad selling CLOSAs to recruit more allies," Cyberdyaryo, online at <http://www.cyberdyaryo.com/features/f2001_0801_02.htm.

200,000-400,000, are not active on the domestic political scene. Nonetheless, they constitute an important minority whose naturalization/settlement in Lebanon is vigorously opposed by most Lebanese, who see them as a threat to Lebanon's delicate confessional balance. During 2002, parliament enacted legislation banning Palestinians from owning property in Lebanon."[73]

It doesn't take five minutes research to find real property at the center of conflict almost anywhere, from the scale of a single murdered woman to the scope of national constitutions. It is usually easy to understand the *why* of violence, once details regarding the distribution of property rights are known. So it should be a wonder why any leader assigned the task of dealing in any way with almost any human conflict would not want to be appraised of the details of land disputes. Those details are best understood where the evidence of property ownership has been carefully compiled and exposed.

Violence can be usefully studied through a property lens, divided into parts that match the three streams of inquiry regarding the quality of the property system, or regime (evidence, capacity to act on the evidence, and basic rules of participation). One stream attempts to match claimant identities as closely as possible with the specific rights and duties over which violence occurs, another considers the practical exercise of ownership rights and the reasons why violence was deemed by someone necessary or preferable; and the third considers the basic rules of ownership bearing on the violence and its outcome.[74]

---

[73] US Department of State, Background Note: Lebanon, online at
<http://www.state.gov/r/pa/ei/bgn/35833.htm.
[74] To an extent, this formula is inspired by a standard law school class material dating back at least to the writings of Yale Property Professor Wesley Hohfeld. See, in this regard, Wesley Newcomb Hohfeld, Fundamental Legal Conceptions as Applied to Judicial Reasoning, (New Haven: Yale University Press, 1919) reissued 1964. Also reprinted in Edward Allen Kent, ed. Law and Philosophy: Readings in Legal Philosophy (New York: Meridith Corporation, 1970). See, however, J. W. Harris,

Comments in the literature about the relationship between ownership regimes and conflict run the cultural gamut.[75] Of special note is University of Colorado Economist John Powelson's The Story of Land.[76] Powelson surveyed the history of land tenure and reform, and proffers the hypothesis that,

> "customary land tenure, non-literate society, trend migrations, slavery, and continuous warfare (conflicts not expected to be resolved) all go together; they contrast with fixed tenure (land registration), literacy (written contract) settled existence, free wage labor, periodic peace, and the expectation that contracts will end."[77]

Powelson has been under-recognized, considering the originality of his research, its careful exposition, and, coming as it did in 1988, the intellectual self-confidence of championing *property* as an ally of civilization and peace. His observation, modestly presented by a scholar not familiar with military strategy or the practice of property law, need not have been so timid except perhaps for the ideological norms of the day. His exposition of historical correlation between formal property regimes and periods of peace matches the original purposes of property creation, and the obvious logic of possession by force vs. occupation by rule of law. Admittedly, there is somewhat of a leap from Powelson's carefully disclaimed "bold hypothesis" that peace correlates with fixed tenure, to the assertion that without formal property peace cannot last. But the implications of the assertion

---

Property and Justice, Oxford: Clarendon Press, 1996, p. 120 for a critique of Hohfeldian analysis.
[75] On this point see, Rose, Carol M. Property and Persuasion: Essays on the History, Theory, and Rhetoric of Ownership. Boulder: Westview Press, 1994.
[76] John P. Powelson, The Story of Land: A World History of Land Tenure and Agrarian Reform, (Cambridge, Massachusetts: Lincoln Institute of Land Policy, 1988).
[77] Ibid, p. 308.

demand further investigation into the correlation that Powelson announced. As well, the experience of domestic property law as a conflict resolution enterprise, and the constant outbreaks of land struggles in countries suffering internal violence and war suggest that the correlation be presumed – that the burden of proof be shifted to those who might name any large group of people having lived in democratic peace without formal property.

Powelson further hypothesizes that, "negotiation and compromise are a last resort, to be employed only when war and conquest have failed over centuries and only when land shortage prevents enemies from escaping each other any more...."[78] To this observation something must be added: The amount of land in the world may be all but fixed, but the amount of property worldwide, brought about mainly by innovation, is constantly increasing. Real property, understood as the set of rights and duties associated with places, is constantly rearranged and re-divided. Moreover, as new discoveries are made, the monetary value of different parts of the natural environment changes. Until molybdenum was a useful mineral, it was not a contested natural resource, and the places of its extraction not the object of conflict. Inventions, and the increase in property they entail, are as much a cause of conflict as are shortages of foodstuffs or farmland. Powelson's hypothesis about land shortage is made in the context of an historical survey, mostly of rural land questions. But technological change has a marked effect on the relative value of one piece of land vs. another, such changes invariably bringing new conflict that must be resolved. A small community of developmental economists has begun to identify the powerful nexus between underdeveloped property and failing prospects for peace.[79]

---

[78] Ibid, p. 310.
[79] Leading this group is Karol Boudreaux, "What's Missing in the Darfur Debate: Addressing Property Rights Could Help Bring Peace," IREN Newsletter, Nairobi, Kenya, September, 2004, online at
< http://www.mercatus.org/article.php/877.html; "Property rights: a key to development," Moneyweb, June 15, 2005, online at
<http://www.mercatus.org/article.php/1407.html;"Property holds Africa's answer,"

In Colombia, tension has existed for centuries between small-extension agriculturalists and great landowners.[80] Meanwhile, more violent competitions over comercializable natural resources erupted in relation to inventions and fashions taking place outside Colombia, unrelated to population pressures inside it. This point in no way opposes Powelson's broader hypothesis. A formalized property system offers a better chance of resolving conflicts brought on by land shortages, as well as those brought on by technological change.

Powelson makes another hypothesis that is relevant here:

> …that economic development requires a culture in which individuals and corporate bodies are clearly bounded and identified; in which rights, duties, and obligations with respect to property, also well defined, are clearly assigned to those individuals and corporate bodies, including the state; and where the distribution of rights and resources is not unduly concentrated in any of these bodies, including the state.[81]

Avoiding the excessive concentration of power (supposing that power and property have an especially rigid correlation) was a purpose of the authors of the US constitution, and a column of America's democratic heritage.[82] Excessive concentration of power is also a constant critique made against developing societies where political violence is commonplace. It is out of fashion to rate cultures as more

---

Moneyweb, September 23, 2005, online at <http://www.mercatus.org/article.php/1408.html; Karol Boudreaux is a Senior Fellow at the Mercatus Center at George Mason University.
[80] On this point see generally Catherine LeGrand, Frontier expansion and peasant protest in Colombia, 1850-1936, (Albuquerque: The University of New Mexico Press, 1986).

[81] Ibid, p. 312.
[82] The term democracy is found in three of the eighty-five essays making up the famed Federalist Papers; property is mentioned and discussed in twenty-four.

or less primitive or advanced, but the cultural progress to which Powelson refers is a degree of civilization. Civilizations are advanced that order and protect property rights, and that devise against concentrations of power. To remain civilized, and to remain in being, the regime of property ownership must be able to cope with changes brought about by three simultaneous and interrelated trends. The first two are environmental change and population growth, and the third is technological advancement. The importance of all three lies in the stress put on the ability of regimes of property ownership to peacefully reconcile competing claims. The linkages between property and peace, furthermore, are not macro only, but have thousands of specific, palpable and realizable tactical expressions known intimately by the county judge, local police officer, residential developer, town mayor or property attorney. Clearing the underbrush of social conflict is the aggregate accomplishment of all these players. It is a routine in successful societies, lubricated by the stable evidence of millions of property records allowing liberal democracies to function peacefully. It is a routine grown from necessity, aided by jurisprudential heritage. The heritage, however, is often drawn upon only after economic necessity tests the quality of law in the realm of raw property competition. Few economic studies deal directly with the relationship of real estate and violence. One relevant exception is a study of the California Gold Rush. From his study of that history economist John Umbeck concluded that...

> "Whenever a group of individuals agrees to some system by which exclusive rights to scarce resources will be rationed, they are implicitly agreeing not to use violence. Yet this contract must provide for the use of violence to punish any member who does not follow the rules and maintain the rights of members against attacks from nonmembers. If the group is not willing or able to use violence in either of these two situations, their property rights over resources will be lost to those who are. *Ultimately, all exclusive rights are based on the threat or the use of violence.* [italicized original] Even

the individual who has the exclusive rights to coconuts because he is the only one who can climb the tree may lose these rights if he cannot keep others from chopping down the tree for firewood.

This unique characteristic of violence places an important constraint upon individuals who enter into a contract that specifies the initial distribution of property rights. No individual would be willing to accept a contract in which he was assigned property rights of less value than he could obtain by personal violence."[83]

In this book's appendix we offer a design for measuring the relative quality of real property regimes in places around the world. This is not the same as comparing the market value of real estate, although we might suppose that the quality of the property system would correlate positively with market value. Nevertheless, so as to not put the cart before the horse, we don't look to the value (or the prices) of land as a measure of the quality of the property regime. Instead, we disregard briefly the factor of physical location and look more carefully at the rules and mechanisms, the institutions that serve to distribute rights and duties associated with land and permanent fixtures we know as real estate. In a sense, we are looking to compare institutions to the extent they serve to optimize the value of property, given whatever geophysical advantages or disadvantages a place might boast or lament. Umbeck's conclusion that "no individual would be willing to accept a contract in which he was assigned property rights of less value than he could obtain by personal violence" may be an exaggeration of human willingness to resort to the use of force. Still, it is possible to measure the overall social contract regarding real estate, the real property regime, to see whether or not a given polity is continuously traipsing along that line of values that flirts with violence.

---

[83] Umbeck, John R. A Theory of Property Rights: With Application to the California Gold Rush, (Ames, Iowa: The Iowa State University Press, 1981).

Within our domestic experience, we know that the price of a Kansan's home is influenced by the physical characteristics of location (how many square feet, how far from the school); the rights and duties sold and purchased; and the regime of rules guiding what can be bought and sold, and in what manner. Since the rules channel and shape the market of rights, and since the regimes of ownership rules are delimited geographically, we are back to location. Countries with advanced regimes of property rules will have more valuable locations. Simultaneously, to the extent a country establishes precise, transparent, comprehensive evidence of shared and private rights; and goes about applying that evidence to resolve quotidian claims, that country is more likely to prosper in a democratic and peaceful context. Eventually we may be able to assess and compare systems of property rights and duties country-by-country. With such an index we may be able to better prescribe improvements.[84] After all, property systems can be improved more easily than the geophysical environment or human nature, even while these latter two may tell us a great deal about a given conflict. Although improving social contracts by formalizing property (and thereby increasing prospects of social peace) is an attractive notion, remember how the operant assertion is framed: Places that do not have formal property do not enjoy peace. Attractive as a course of action or not, improving the property regime may be a necessity if there is to be any long-term success in building social peace in a given country. Sadly, we do not know enough about the property regimes of foreign lands.

Are there dangers close by?

---

[84] Since the writing of this text, the Property Rights Alliance http://www.proertyrightsalliance.org published its International Property Rights Index (IPRI), <http://www.internationalpropertyrightsindex.org>, rating seventy countries according to a study methodology prepared by Alexandra Horst in 2006. This is a tremendous step forward, and while it is not aimed directly at an understanding of the relationship of property regimes to the likelihood and control of internal violence, it is sure to accelerate the kind of research proposed herein.

*"I should warn, however, that the philosophy that
sovereignty is not so important is in fashion, that what
they call democracy and human rights is more
important, as if there could be democracy and human
rights without independence and without sovereignty."*
Fidel Castro

Cuban upheaval

Is Cuba a threat to the United States? No, it is not, but
respecting Yogi Berra's wisdom that it is difficult to make predictions,
especially when talking about the future, we are on safe ground to
predict that change is coming to Cuba, and that the change could upend
the American political applecart.[85] Cuba is not a threat, at least not in a
military sense. Almost any period of violent instability the island
would attract thousands of US citizens and residents intensely
interested in steering the outcome, and any official United States
intervention would be conducted in a muddled citizenship environment.
It should not be lost on anyone who doubts the importance of this
problem that actions of the US government in detaining Cubans have
already invited legal challenge.[86] Courthouses will have a direct effect
on any missions and orders. Because parties to any Cuban conflict will
have access to mainline US news media and to US courts, the link
between legality and legitimacy of government actions will be
constantly and quickly tested and changed.

Castro's Cuba hangs a well-recognized weight over US
electioneering. Lobbying exercises by the intensely Cuba-focused can
warp and radicalize politics in Florida and elsewhere in the United

---

[85] Calling wolf about Cuba is perennial stuff, however. See Edward Gonzalez and
David Ronfeld, Storm Warnings for Cuba (Santa Monica, California: Rand, 1994).

[86] Andres Viglucci, "Repatriation of Rafters Is Blocked," Miami Herald (26 October
1994): 1A, 5A.

States -- increasingly as the Castro brothers' control finally begins to come undone. US politicians and their handlers will perceive a need to play every episode in that unraveling to their electoral advantage. Little in that play, however, will facilitate reasoned policy promoting a peaceful, free and prosperous Cuba. Office winners will be left without control over Cuba-related issues once elections are decided. Massive human migration throughout the Caribbean will be more than a bothersome phenomenon. Worse, a Cuban transition could devolve into violence on the Cuban islands and beyond.[87]

Any impending upheaval in Cuba also poses a threat to US foreign policy construction and implementation. A Cuba crisis would absorb a disproportionate amount of executive attention, and would be the object of much gratuitous international criticism regardless of what policies or actions the US government might take. If only in view of these two likelihoods (the deleterious and unpredictable effect Cuban upheaval could have on domestic electioneering and the anti-American opportunism sure to transpire in the international ambit) any option of outsourcing the Cuba question might be carefully considered.

Cuba's future presents an array of palpable, dominant property issues. Latent real estate claims overshadow the return of exiled anti-Castroites, and competition for pieces of post-Castro Cuba will be awash with partial, overlapping identities and outlaw agendas. Transnational organized crime, the criminalization of ex-soldiers, black market commercialization of excess military hardware, racial and religious superimpositions, talent draining, and every form of fraud and demagoguery will blossom. Troubles there will be covered vigorously, if superficially, by both US and foreign news media. For the interrelation of destabilizing and threatening phenomena to be understood, however, they can be viewed as ownership struggles, even

---

[87] For analysis tying together news of Fidel Castro's health, Cuba's transition and the prospect of violence see for instance, William M. LeoGrande, "Fidel's Swoon and Other News From Havana" Los Angeles Times, July 15, 2001 Part M, p. 1, online at Lexis-Nexis Academic, < http://american.edu/faculty/leogrande/Cuba-swoon-LAT7-15-01.htm.

where the property involved is more subtle or intangible than possession of real estate. Without question, Cuban property competitions will transmute into future human rights violations if no legitimate system of reconciliation is available during Cuba's coming change.

Former President Jimmy Carter's 2002 trip to the island reawakened an interest for many of us who perennially announced an impending collapse of the Castro regime and the beginning of the long-awaited 'transition.'[88] Mr. Carter was adamant on the human rights

---

[88] For a compendium of reports on the visit see, <http://www.latinamericanstudies.org/carter-cuba.htm; In 1994 Edward Gonzalez and David Ronfeldt outlined some of what seemed then to be alternative possibilities for the unfolding of possible endgames for the Castro regime. More than ten years later their assessment seems to have made sense, but are we still waiting for the endgame to start, or did option I already occur?
> * Endgame I. The Castro regime survives over the
> short to medium term by means of the current
> transitional model. [retaining totalitarian control,
> but creating a dual model economy with an
> external foreign exchange producing sector.]
> * Endgame II. Over the short to medium term, the
> regime adopts major economic reforms and
> muddles through with an authoritarian market-
> oriented model--most likely a Cuban-Chinese
> hybrid based on "market-Leninism."
> * Endgame III. In the short or medium term, the
> regime begins to lose control and Castro halts all
> reform (regardless of the model); stasis and heavy
> repression follow.
> * Endgame IV. In the short or medium term,
> popular resistance increases, Castro leaves the
> picture, pro-reform factions in the regime
> regroup, and nonviolent change takes place from
> above and below. This sequence leads to a new
> coalition-type government with elements of the
> internal opposition, possibly ushered in with
> elections and including some former exiles.
> * Endgame V. In the short or medium term,
> violent change from below occurs as widespread

---

issue, and serving President Bush followed up with a mild surprise, hardening rather than softening US policy toward the Cuban regime. Nevertheless, Fidel Castro's public appearances, as well as Internet audio of the Cuban leader talking on the phone with Mexican President Vicente Fox, revealed a still wily but aging king.[89] Since then, Fidel Castro has shown further signs of physical weakening, but the Castro brothers have hardened their dictatorship (along with anti-US identity) and have shored-up alliances with populist demagogues, especially Hugo Chavez of Venezuela. Due to the support and compatible aspirations of the latter, it may very well be that the principle features of the transition are already visible, with the revolution surviving in the persons of second-tier managers engaged in international capitalism alongside repressive domestic socialism.[90] In 2005, the question of human rights continued to reign as various countries posture and waffle in the unsightly diplomatic dance that is the annual process of human rights certifications and condemnations.[91]

---

popular unrest erupts, leading to civil war, the downfall of the Castro regime, and a seizure of power by a new set of (dictatorial? democratic?) leaders."

Edward Gonzalez and David Ronfeldt, Storm Warnings Over Cuba (Santa Monica, California: RAND, 1994), p. xi.

[89] Valley Multimedia Corp, "Conversación telefónica Castro-Fox revela mentiras y contradicciones," (Castro-Fox telephone conversation reveals lies and contradictions) audio and transcript in Spanish online at http://www.elclamor.com/contradicciones.htm

[90] On the issue of a transition that already happened, see, for instance, Blanche Petrich "Ricardo Alarcon: 'Ya ocurrió en Cuba la esperada transición post Fidel Castro'" (Ricardo Alarcon: 'The awaited post-Fidel Castro transition in Cuba already happened') La Jornada (Mexican in Spanish) Viernes 6 de julio 2001 p. 1 & 6; Ricardo Santa Maria, "Los sucesores de Fidel"(Fidel's Successors) Semana (Colombian in Spanish) Julio 9 - Julio 16 2001 edition 1001, p. 58

[91] Richard Waddington, "UN Body Keeps Pressure on Cuba," Reuters online at Yahoo! News < http://news.yahoo.com/news?tmpl=story&u=/nm/20050414/wl_nm/rights_cuba_dc; U.S. Department of State, "United States Hails U.N. Resolution on Human Rights in Cuba" USINFO.STATE.GOV online at <http://usinfo.state.gov/dhr/Archive/2005/Apr/15-666219.html.

Whoever manages Cuba's political change will either place the question of property at the center of transition planning, or the question will go there on its own. "Property" will immediately displace almost all other considerations as far as United States-based interests are concerned. The Castro revolution, after all (more even than socialist revolutions of Europe), changed the property regime, giving to the central government whole-fee ownership of almost all real estate, urban and rural. In no other transition from socialism (if transition from socialism is in fact the future) will there have been involved such a prominent, vocal, emotionally invested and financially capable community of dispossessed.

Mention of dispossession leads us to a bifurcation. In one sense when we speak of the Cuban property problem we speak of actual claims to existing pieces of real estate and other tangible quantities of wealth.[92] In other words, the property question is one of clarifying claims created as a result of expropriations by the revolutionary government. There are 5,911 claims by US citizens and business entities with a total value of about 1.8 billion dollars as registered in the U.S Foreign Claims Settlement Commission (FCSC).[93] Add to this an unknown number (but many times greater) of claims by exiled Cubans and their heirs and assigns. Finally there is in addition an unknown quantity of claims likely to be levied against the state by Cubans still resident on the Island whose property was expropriated by the government.[94] But having recited the nature of anticipatable property

---

[92] The issue of the resolution of property claims is expertly summarized in a chapter titled 'Property" in Mark Falkoff, Cuba: The Morning After: Confronting Castro's Legacy (Washington, D.C.: The AEI Press, 2003), pp. 72-96.

[93] Foreign Claims Settlement Commission of the United States report online at <http://www.usdoj.gov/fcsc/annrep03.htm#3a5b.

[94] For an outline of possible privatization steps that would deliver restitution to many claimants see Matias Travieso-Díaz and Alejandro Ferraré, "Legal Foundations for a successful privatization program in Cuba," Cuba Transition Workshop Internal and External Factors in Cuba{s Economic Transition (Washington, D.C.: Shaw Pittman, Potts & Trowbridge and the Association for the Study of the Cuban Economy, March 25, 1999)

claims, the more important question in terms of creating the conditions for peace is what form the property system will take during and after the transition period. The first question, about claims, bears on the second, especially as it relates to credibility in re-creating the rule of law. If, however, the property regime is not radically and quickly changed, there is little hope for a satisfactory settlement of extant claims -- or for the Cuban future.

Transition toward a property regime conducive to peace and prosperity in Cuba is a more important question than is the settlement of existing claims to real estate. Nevertheless, it is difficult to envision how such a transition might occur without resolution of the real estate claims present in the conflict calculus, so some discussion of the possibilities for resolution is obligatory. Two excellent points are made by Gary Maybarduk, that action will be best taken quickly, and that the quieting of titles be a main objective, an objective to which acts of compensation should be subordinated. He states,

> Sorting out property cases has been a problem in most ex-socialist countries, but in Cuba—perhaps more than any other economy in transition—the need to move quickly will be imperative. Justice to the owners will be hard to achieve, but the danger of the case-by-case approach is that it will do serious injustice to Cubans in Cuba who will be looking for and deserve rapid economic growth. Separating the decision as to who gains title from the question of compensation may provide a solution. At a minimum any solution must give high priority to establishing property titles.[95]

---

[95] Gary H. Maybarduk, "The Post Fidel Transition: Mitigating the Inevitable Disaster" in Cuba in Transition: Volume XI, Papers and Proceedings of the Eleventh Annual Meeting of the Association for the Study of the Cuban Economy (ASCE) Miami, Florida
August 2-4, 2001, 164-171 at 167 online at
http://lanic.utexas.edu/project/asce/pdfs/volume11/maybarduk2.pdf

The specific property disputes in Cuba can be easily resolvable. We must suppose that the central government (now and through whatever period of transition might be envisioned) is in effective possession of a great deal of real estate not under former claim, or easily compensable without restitution. That nationally-owned real estate is the necessary startup capital for Cuba's future. While the world, and especially the world of Cubans, needs to know the exact dimensions and relative market values of Cuba's real estate holdings, it may be more than enough to satisfy claims, distribute wealth to the dispossessed, leverage the development of infrastructure and impel a vigorous marketplace.

A great deal is made in the Cuban-American literature of Cuba's rural agricultural lands and industries, either because the agricultural patrimony has been mismanaged by socialism, because it is somehow essential to root Cuban identity, or because of personal emotional ties to lost estates. Whatever the case, the marketplace, with some restraints, is the best mechanism for determining the future demographic balance rural-to-urban, as well as the mix of land uses. It could be mostly through the creative alienation of rural lands that a transition government would discover the capacity to pay debts, resolve conflicts and attract investments. Currently, however, it appears that preferential rights in many tracts have already been assigned as a way of maintaining revolutionary loyalty, or as a method of creating golden parachutes to carry leading revolutionaries into the next phase.

> "On the other hand, this control of a great part of the agricultural production may follow under-handed plans to constitute the high commands as business entities, thus, directly by way of government concessions, arriving at the kind of "Great Piñata" that occurred in Nicaragua.[96]

---

[96] Arturo Pino Navarro, "La Propiedad en Cuba... Medidas Urgentes' (Property in Cuba...Urgent Measures) Municipio de Camagüey en el Exilio, undated, online at <http://www.municipio-de-camaguey.com/page32.html article in Spanish, extract translated by author.

The property concerns of exiled Cubans may be dwarfed by complaints of Cubans who stayed in Cuba and were nevertheless victims of uncompensated expropriations. Worse still might be a phenomenon that is rarely mentioned. When urban development, especially in the Havana area, begins to accelerate, apartment dwellers (let's say those whose rights could be appreciated and solidified by ownership documents such as condominium deeds) could find that their buildings are nearly worthless. As such, any transition to a market economy would probably have to be softened for many apartment dwellers. Those in less favorable building locations might be offered subsidized exchanges. Meanwhile the greater problem may involve buildings in especially favorable locations. These will beg for demolition and replacement under the pressure of profitability, forcing apartment dwellers to move. If building deeds are given by the regime under a "piñata" plan to create landlords out of favored revolutionary leaders, then the dwellers in these buildings will have been greatly cheated. These are but examples of transition problems, and if a Cuban transition is to go well, the evidence of all claims to real estate must be made precise, comprehensive, and transparent – and quickly, or every intention toward reconciliation will be dashed and new injustices impossible to follow or rectify.

Some claimants will be non-Cubans attempting to take recourse in the system of international business law to capture equity from previously owned properties. For many commentators this question of pre-revolutionary business holdings is at the forefront of the Cuba problem, but attempts at a pre-collapse property grab by the communist insiders will be a far more exacerbating aspect. The Nicaraguan experience after the election of President Violeta Chamorro provides a hint regarding the potential for violence between pre-revolutionary claims against confiscated property and communist party seizures.[97]

---

[97]. Oppenheimer, Castro's Final Hour, p. 324. In Nicaragua, the Sandinista Army was able to maintain its political identity and physical integrity in spite of the Violeta Chamorro election. This fact provided a coercive backstop allowing the Nicaraguan communists to resist claims of pre-revolution owners. A similar environment could exist in a post-Castro Cuba; Tim Johnson, "Property disputes cloud Nicaragua's

As in Nicaragua and some of the East European countries, the impending ruin of the communist ownership system caused the dictators to redistribute and formalize lucrative real estate interests. The Castros will have vested key security force leaders with ownership slices that, if they can be translated or leveraged into equivalent rights within a capitalist framework, constitute the golden parachute. First, the give away shores up support for the regime within armed institutions. Second, the move offers a means to resist the political consequences of having key real estate, and the power that accompanies it, fall under control of a zealous opposition. Third, whatever the nature of the transition, a transformation of property ownership protocols can preserve political power and wealth for the communist party elite. With important properties (transportation, water works, power generation, beach fronts) under possession of an armed organization, any demand for reconciliation of old claims might invite a violent defense.[98] Yet another property strategy seems to be the sale of partner shares to foreign companies, thus vesting future foreign allies in claims that, even if not secured completely, promise to establish a base for court arguments in whatever system ultimately arrives. The piñata problem (a give-away to friends) is hardly intractable, however, requiring the same analysis regarding what rights carry what prices that any quiet-title action might demand. Title can always escheat or revert to the State.

---

economic future," The Miami Herald (12 March 1993) . "Many people are upset at offer of substitute property being offered for property taken by Sandinistas after the Sandinistas lost the 1990 elections. They quickly gave away 11000 houses farms and lots--to Sandinistas."

[98]. See Kenneth Freed, "National Agenda; Cuba's Army Becoming More Important Than Party; The Military Commands the Economy as Communists Lose Credibility. But Fidel Castro Seems Safe for Now." Los Angeles Times, December 6, 1994. (from The Xinhua News Agency). Freed, aside from reporting that the Cuban Army was running department stores, travel agencies, construction companies and farms, suggested that this was because the army had more professional capability and public credibility than the Cuban Communist Party.

Some crisis predictions foresee violence.[99] If violence becomes widespread or acute, the United States government, alone or with international partners, might be obligated to intervene to stabilize, ease or fashion Cuba's change. Other organizations based in the United States, or with significant American membership, might intervene as well. The Cuba problem could simultaneously become a growth industry for all manner of opportunist from baseball scout to cocaine distributor to religious missionary to foreign spy.

Cuba is not and will not be a military threat, but a poor US response to societal change in Cuba will be diplomatically and fiscally costly, and will be politically costly to some contenders in US domestic politics. More importantly, the transition of Cuba, hopefully to the First World, represents an opportunity of the highest caliber, one that can easily be missed.

The future of Cuba is mentioned here in the discussion of globalized trespass for several reasons. A simple announcement of threats would be an incomplete presentation of the foreign challenges facing the United States. There exists another kind of cost -- lost opportunity, which is grave to our national purpose if not our safety. This is so because the test of a better Cuba is a test of the relative worth of our own country; because the conditions of the 'third world' are not inevitable; because the United States will be stronger for having a

---

[99]. See generally Transition in Cuba: New Challenges for U.S. Policy. Miami: Florida International University, 1993. This is a good place to enter the writings on Cuban Transition that have been produced since the end of the Cold War. The product of a research project sponsored by the Office of Research, U.S. Department of State's Bureau for Latin America and the Caribbean and the U.S. Agency for International Development, it was undertaken by the Cuban Research Institute of the Latin America and Caribbean Center at Florida International University. It has had a significant impact on U.S. government planning regarding Cuba's future. The study posed nine possible scenarios for Cuban change. The first set a baseline, characterizing the responses of Cuba's government and people. It needs to be noted that several of the possible scenarios posited mid- to long-term survival of a communist government without a violent crisis.

110

stronger, healthier neighbor; because to have a healthy polity on our southern border means a more secure border; and finally because Cuban-Americans exiled from the Island of Cuba cannot be disregarded as strident or emotionally disqualified for having maintained fervent opposition to a dictator. They are citizens of the United States and deserve particular attention regarding the recovery and healing of their homeland. In every aspect of this reasoning, analysis of the conditions in Cuba, and design of a way ahead involve careful consideration of property rights, both in their palpable form as existing rights to real estate, and in the design of the social contract.

So far from God

Is immigration from Mexican a threat to the United States? The answer is as easy and emphatic as that related to Cuba. No, Mexican emigration is not a threat to the United States. Still, the calculus of migration, and we might highlight the legal component of that calculus, provides a favorable context for the contraband of illegal goods, movement of violent organized criminals and terrorists, etc. Again obeying the obvious geographic fact of distance, the ownership environments of Mexico and the United States are distinct but intertwined. The practical effect on United States territory of any Mexican instability is a matter of record. Instability in Mexico and illegal migration to the United States are related almost as the readout on a car's tachometer is related to that of its speedometer. As RPM on the tachometer go up, speed increases, albeit after a short time lag. When instability in Mexico worsens, migration to the U.S. increases. Every breakdown in Mexican law and order invigorates cross-border activity. The most disruptive and damaging effect of Mexican political violence, if it were prolonged, could be guerrilla warfare within the borders of the United States. That being a worst-case view, the approach the United States has taken toward the migration of Mexicans into the United States has two lesser strategic ill-effects. One is a lost opportunity to engage the migrant population in security-favorable behaviors, and the second is to create cover for a range of illicit activities that in turn provide cover for the dangers we fear most. These things can be changed, and a property-oriented vision of the challenge will reveal the specific methods.

There is much about the Mexican national indoctrination and self-concept that has not been favorable to anyone's security. Alan Riding's translation of a harangue by nineteenth century revolutionary Miguel Hidalgo still has active emotional content:

> "My children...a new dispensation comes to us this day. Are you ready to receive it? Will you be free? Will you make the effort to recover from the hated Spaniards the lands stolen from your forefathers three hundred years ago?...Mexicans, Long Live Mexico! Death to the Gachupines!"[100]

Therein lies a good deal of what scares some Americans, especially in the southwest of the United States, regarding the psychological substrata of Mexican migratory intention. Hidalgo was addressing a mostly indigenous crowd, riling them against the Spaniards. Gringos have replaced Gachupines quite nicely in the Mexican psyche. This popular and (at least until recently) officially approved anti-American Mexican catechism allows greater intellectual and psychological freedom to commit illegal activities, the negative effects of which are felt mostly in the United States. Gangs such as Mara Salvatrucha will continue to appear, with US, Mexican and other foreign authorities continuing to suppress them, but along the way there will be instances of at lease low-level government officials in Mexico helping the gangs.[101]

---

[100] Alan Riding, Distant Neighbors: A Portrait of the Mexicans (New York: Vintage Books, 1986) p. 46.
[101] On Mexican criminal gangs including Mara Salvatrucha see *Kevin Freese,* "The Death Cult of the Drug Lords Mexico's Patron Saint of Crime," Criminals, and the Dispossessed, Foreign Military Studies Office online at
<http://fmso.leavenworth.army.mil/documents/Santa-Muerte/santa-muerte.htm.

One of the most important cultural distinctions formerly separating Mexico from the United States, language, almost no longer exists. Mexicans find it possible to remain indefinitely in United States territory without the necessity of learning English. Widespread use of the Spanish language combines in some locales with public deference to Mexican national symbols to a degree that it is offensive to some English speakers who have a strong emotional connection to US symbols. Trouble is to be predicted. In various towns and counties in the Southwest, native Spanish speakers represent a formidable political block, and it can be expected that, unless current trends change, native Spanish speakers (of predominantly Mexican origin) will outnumber English speakers in an increasing number of jurisdictions. The language shift will carry along with it a shift in symbolism and cultural identities that can change the balance of group cohesiveness. Changes in musical selections at official functions, the raising or displaying of Mexican flags, progressive changes in the content of school texts, and widened promotion of bi-lingual education in public schools are other common occurrences. Not only do none of these things constitute illegalities, no one of them might ever cause a spark capable of igniting armed conflict. However, at some point the identity of common ownership will have shifted to the point of threatening existing ownership rules and relationships. Incremental reactions against the culture shift will earn rebuke in the opinion media as being intolerant or as offenses against the rights of free speech and expression.

If the ignition of internal conflict is Anglo-American or Black-American reaction against Mexicanness (perhaps even from multiple-generation Mexican-Americans) the United States government may at some point be obliged to take the next steps leading toward armed violence. The federal government will more than likely intervene to protect the rights of immigrants. Many organized armed groups of disaffected citizens could take federal intervention on behalf of immigrants as evidence that the government is not the legitimate protector of citizens' rights, particularly property rights. Their reaction will not be spontaneous, irrational or novel. It will be a critical milestone in what is already a budding grass-roots movement of

113

rebellious expression. In the American west and Southwest, groups are already organized, and while their strategy of action is yet undefined, their dissatisfaction with the role of the federal government (focusing on property rights in most cases) provides a latent purpose.[102] The symbolism favored by these groups is evocative of both patriotism and territorial ferocity. The federal government can unwittingly unify these armed organizations, which might easily redouble violence against Mexicans, which in turn could provide both provocation and justification for guerrilla activity within the United States.

The Southwest of the United States has always displayed a Mexican cultural flavor that is perceived in much of the rest of the country as benign and enjoyable, exotic, even resplendent. The idea that a dangerous threat to national security is brewing as a result of Mexican nationalism might not impress Americans from other parts of the United States whose direct property interests are not affected. Oddly, those Mexicans most likely to promote an aggressive expression of national identity at the cost of Uncle Sam will be able to count on spiritual solidarity, if not material support, from throughout the Western Hemisphere, including from within the United States. In fact, an opportunity to promote the kind of internal disorder in the United States (that the U.S. has for so long derided in Latin American countries) may be irresistible. News of such a predicament would be agreeable *shadenfraude[[* in many corners of the world.

Slumping real estate values, exodus of labor able to seek options elsewhere, increasing insurance rates, disruptions in public services, collapse of municipal bond ratings, depression in tourist revenues--the list of symptoms is well known. What may not be understood is that a guerrilla movement capable of causing a property

---

[102] See, for instance, Brock N. Meeks, "Crackdown on southwest border begins," MSNBC March 30, 2005 online at <http://www.msnbc.msn.com/id/7340214/;Jon Dougherty, "'Border militia' critic gets cold feet: Pro-immigrant activist fails to follow through on promise of confrontation," WorldNetDaily.com, May 28, 2003 online at <ttp://www.worldnetdaily.com/news/article.asp?ARTICLE_ID=32782.

disaster can be haphazard, poorly led, without concrete or consistent ideological foundation, in want of an achievable strategic goal, and with support from only a small fraction of the total population. It does not have to move in accordance with any military concept of strategy, even though the movement may enjoy international supporters with great-power strategy in mind. It can be improvised, rag-tag, intermittent, multiply led, irrational and still be effective. All the more so if it enjoys an engaging set of symbols, like the recovery of ancestral lands, retribution for violence committed, anti-racism, obvious economic disparities, and a cohesive owner identity associated with a place that promises to provide sanctuary. With these attributes, an effective insurgent movement can survive for decades--to give sport if nothing else.

Meanwhile, back in Mexico, a number of factors could worsen conditions in the United States still further. Many Mexicans would take pleasure in the internal difficulties unfolding in the United States, even if this enjoyment competes for mental space with the logical desire for economic success. The fact that the majority of Mexicans do not think in such an Anti-American competitive way will be of not particular comfort. Some will be enthusiastic supporters of American trouble and will find ways to fund or otherwise encourage guerrilla activity inside United States territory. In addition, one of the consequences of a transition of political power in Cuba may be another mass migration into Mexico similar to the exodus of the Spanish Republicans after the Spanish Civil War. Like the wave of Cuban migrants that arrived in Miami decades ago, the new wave to Mexico may include a slice of leftist rancor combined with mafia style loyalties. Some will occupy themselves with political party activities flavored by a robust anti-Americanism. Resentment toward the United States will be a strong enough emotional quantity that direct action to punish the U.S. could be a staple release.

The answer to all these admittedly alarmist possibilities is not rejection of things Mexican, but a much greater development of contractual and ownership formality between US entities and those

115

sectors of Mexican society wanting and needing a healthy and productive relationship. This includes respecting immigrant rights, and creating formal stakeholders of Mexican nationals seeking greater stability for their families and assets within the United States.

Venezuela's Hugo Chavez

Is Hugo Chavez' regime in Venezuela a threat to the United States? Looking at the question within the confines of the theme of this book, that is to say, the relationship of property to peace and how systems of property bear on the prospects that places might foster dangerous behaviors, the answer is emphatically yes. We noted about Cuba that the shape of anticipated change there hinges in some measure on a realization that the current basic law of Cuba, what is called the 'Cuban Constitution,' is an accurate reflection of the social contract there. That document reposes rights to make decisions regarding occupation, use, preservation, profit, and alienation of land almost entirely in the hands of the centralized State, and those hands are very few. The future of Cuba's social contract (Will Cuba is proceed apace to the ranks of the first world or rise only to the half-failing condition typical of Latin America?) depends on revision of how 'property' is treated in the basic legal documents that guide and restrict. Cuba is an opportunity, a chance for change in the right direction, toward a formal, liberal property regime. Hugo Chavez, meanwhile, is leading Venezuela in the opposite direction, centralizing real estate ownership in the State.103 The nature of property is a central theme in Chávez'

---

[103] This is patent in even a cursory review of the Venezuelan media. See for instance, Ministry of Communication and Information, "JUSTICIA: Guerra al Latifundio (JUSTICE: War on the *Latifundio* [Great Landholding]), Bolivarian Republic of Venezuela June 5, 2005,
http://www.mci.gob.ve/noticiasnuev.asp?numn=6719;
English.el Universal.com, "Government Continues to Confiscate Estates" English.el Universal.com, September 17, 2005,
http://english.eluniversal.com/2005/09/17/en_pol_art_17A611731.shtml;

ideology. Since taking power (democratically), Hugo Chavez has changed the basic law, the denominated 'Constitution,' to do for his regime what the Cuban constitution does for the Castro brothers.

So the question will be put: What difference does it make how the Venezuelan government, the leader of which was elected openly, decides to divvy up Venezuelan land, or what powers over land its constitution reposes in the executive? If the reader needs the answer at this point, you fail the quiz! If the social contract in Venezuela devolves away from formal, liberal property (and the speed of change appears greater than what 'devolve' connotes) the geography we call Venezuela will be the locus of economic failure, tyranny, corruption and violence. It will be a threat to its neighbors whose land and economic intercourse are cheek-by-jowl with Venezuela. The Chavez regime will be forced to seek aggressive external options for survival. It will collude with, harbor and encourage outlaw groups whose amoral pragmatism can be influenced by disposable income and a psychological justification for disrespecting the property of others. So consideration of the obvious is made unnecessary -- never mind that President Chavez self-proclaims as an enemy of the United States, that he is acridly critical of Colombia or that the FARC finds sanctuary with the borders of Venezuela. Just looking from the perspective of a property-based analysis, prospects are that Hugo Chavez' Venezuela will be an increasing security challenge for the United States. The flexible power that oil-revenue disposable income gives the Chavez regime, and ties it has or has been trying to make with other autocratic regimes bring the challenge closer in time.

---

dfrente.com. "Sentenció el Presidente Chávez Guerra contra el latifundio" (President Chávez declares war on the *latifundio* [large land-holding]), dfrente.com, September 20, 2005, http://www.dfrente.com/noticia.php?IDN=24908;
Gustavo Azocar Alcala, "(INTI) Burning Plains," English.el Universal.com, September 24, 2005,
http://english.eluniversal.com/2005/09/24/en_eco_art_24A613879.shtml;
El Universal.com, "400 properties in Maracaibo may pass into State hands," El Universal.com, September 27, 2005,
http://www.eluniversal.com/2005/09/27/pol_art_27109C.shtml

Of all the deleterious effects that Hugo Chavez' personal success might have on America's future, however, his interest in preserving the Castro revolution in Cuba may be transcendent. Hugo Chavez may bankroll survival of a property regime that provides safety, prosperity and liberty for a small nomenclatura, blocking Cuba's passage to the First World for decades.

Venezuelans are the newest wave of political immigrant to Miami, and like Cubans and others before them are grateful that there is a place to go. At the same time they are similarly exasperated at the relative indifference of the US nation to events transpiring so close by the United States. Their country is undergoing a transformation of property such as that undergone by Cuba after the Castroite take-over. The government of Hugo Chavez is dismantling the property regime in Venezuela, doing exactly the opposite of what this book describes as the steps necessary for long-term conflict resolution and material prosperity.[104] This is not to say that the property regime in Venezuela was correctly formed or that all the actions taken by the Chavez government will prove harmful. To some degree the property regime may have had to be scourged in order that it be rebuilt on a proper foundation. But that is going to be hard to measure or describe as Venezuela closes to any investigation regarding the distribution of rights, duties and power. If we follow the property ball in Venezuela we can see the route toward dictatorship. It is a route that extends a covetous eye on its Caribbean neighbors as well. It is not an amorphous threat of influences, propositions and common ideological agendas. It is the purchase and bullying of specific rights and duties related to critical industries and terrain, in most cases associated with energy sources. It is painted as anti-hegemonic or pan-indigenous or Bolivarian, but it is worthy of concern. It welcomes anything and everything that confounds the web of civilizing laws on which defense against dangerous transnational behavior depends. Harboring fugitives, proliferating the component elements of dangerous weapons, protecting

---

[104] Typical of news coming out of Venezuela is Jose de Cordoba [["Farms Are Latest Target In Venezuelan Upheaval: Co-ops of City Dwellers On Seized Acreage Are Mostly a Bust So Far," The Wall Street Journal, Thursday, May , 1u, p. 1.

illegal accounts or the contraband and counterfeiting of national monies. They are hard to see on a map of geophysical features and national boundaries, but they are trespasses--globalized.

Chapter Three: The Colombia Case

Chapter Three: The Colombia Case

*"Lo que en este momento tiene lugar en Colombia es
una lucha por la dominación territorial."[105]*
(What is taking place right now in Colombia is a
struggle for territorial domination)
Alvaro Valencia Tovar, retired army officer, author, journalist

---

[105] Alvaro Valencia Tovar. "Conflicto armado y territorio." El País de Cali. 21 July, 2003. online at <http://elpais-cali.terra.com.co/HOY/OPN/op5.html.

The calculus of violence

"Colombia necesita la fuerza brava de todos sus hijos
para defenderla contra la avalancha del imperialismo.
No hay otra solución para el problema de la tierra que
la expropiación sin indemnización de todas aquellas que
no se cultiven para entregarlas gratuitamente a quienes
sí las cultiven. No ha de importarnos nada que nos
llamen socialistas, porque nuestro credo consciente,
meditado, pensado y estudiado es ése."[106]

(Colombia needs the angry force of all its sons to defend
it against the avalanche of imperialism. There is no
other solution to the land problem than to expropriate
without indemnity all those lands that are not being
cultivated and give them for free to those who *will*
cultivate them. It should be of no importance to us
whatever that they call us Socialists, because that is
exactly our conscious belief – meditated, considered,
studied.)

Jorge Eliézer Gaitan,
Colombian populist assassinated in 1948

Colombia is strategically located at the center of a part of the
world in danger of regressing toward tyranny, and where breaches of
basic human rights are more than occasional. It is one of the world's
leaders in murder rates, kidnappings and landmines, and its abundant
agriculture supports production of most of the cocaine used in the US.
It also exports a wide variety of desired and legal products and is a net
energy exporter, although not in quantities like that of its oil-rich
neighbor, Venezuela. Colombia is a country in which the United States
has invested billions of dollars, and where US citizens are being held

---

[106] Jorge Eliézer Gaitán, Speech given in Bogotá, September 25, 1945 found in Luis
H. Aristizábal, editor. "Diccionario Aristizábal de citas o frases colombianas". <u>Banco
de la República</u> online at <http://www.lablaa.org/blaavirtual/diccio/dicg.htm#g04.

hostage. It is also a country that experienced more years of valid electoral democracy in the twentieth century than did most of the countries of Europe, and with which the United States has a growing and indelible cultural and familial bond. It is, in short, an important place for U.S. foreign policy to succeed, but where success hangs in the balance.[107]

In Colombia an imperfect property regime has enabled internal conflict. Property creation and formalization will contribute to long-term social peace; and property intelligence can speed an outcome favorable to the people of both Colombia and the United States. Understanding property is key to understanding the Colombian conflict, and improving the property system key to solving it. For these reasons, the Colombian case is offered here to place the theoretical in the context of stark reality.

Colombia has a partially and unevenly developed property regime, but violence and internal warfare are not *caused* because the property regime is informal or because the rules of ownership illiberal. The complex calculus of Colombian violence involves the rapacity of human nature, Colombia's compartmentalized physical geography, spectacular geophysical wealth in items for which there is commercial demand, competing ideological currents that bear on how wealth is distributed, and an insufficient of civilizing constraints in the practical organization of Colombia's social contract. Of the derivatives in the formula just cited, the last is the most available for improvement. Informality of land ownership is not the cause of violence, but rights in land *are* the object of violence, and failure to civilize the manner of land ownership is the relevant omission of Colombian social

---

[107] Beginning in late 2001, the author led an investigation into the feasibility of creating a database of real property ownership in Colombia. In the course of the study, a picture was gained not only of the central position of real property in the calculus of Colombian violence, and of the overlooked (and still available) opportunity to change the direction of Colombia's political history through property formalization.

organization. It is an omission that Colombians can and are attempting to fix.

Noble Revolution

Some aspects of Colombia's internal conflict are not so hard to understand, or not as hard to understand as they once might have been. There is no longer much room for ambivalence regarding the noble strivings of good revolutionaries whose aspirations to social justice provide them moral space in which to justify organized violence. The major surviving illegal armed insurgent groups, the *Fuerzas Armadas Revolucionarias de Colombia* (FARC), *Ejército de Liberación Nacional* (ELN), both at one time impelled by ideological arguments about the defects and indignities of the reigning social contract, have devolved away from all but the most callous pretension of worthy motive. A third major illegal challenger, the come-lately and currently disbanding *Autodefensas Unidas de Colombia* (AUC) barely defined an ideology beyond opposition to the aforementioned ELN and FARC. All three finance themselves through illicit drug trade, kidnapping, smuggling, counterfeiting, extortion and other predation.[108]

---

[108] See Jeremy McDermott "Colombian report shows FARC is world's richest insurgent group" Jan Jane's Intelligence Review - September 01, 2005 posted 19 Aug, 2005. Part of a balance sheet of FARC finances prepared ostensibly by the Colombian government includes the following detail on FARC income.

INCOME	USD	%	
Trafficking of cocaine	617 million	45.49	
Extortion	560 million	41.30	
Kidnapping	91.6 million	6.75	
Earnings from investments	41.2 million	3.04	
Cattle rustling	18.8 million	1.39	
Theft of hydrocarbons	15 million	1.11	
Tax on coca base	7.2 million	0.53	
Taxes on illegal airstrips	2.55 million	0.19	
Bank robbery	992,000	0.07	
Protection of crystallizing drug labs		936,000	0.07
Security for coca leaf	340,000	0.01	
Protection of coca base laboratories		316,000	- 0.1

It is has been standard to disregard an exasperating fuzziness of
sets and divide Colombia's malefactors according to four broad
categories – drug traffickers, guerrillas, paramilitaries, or corrupted
officials.[109] The resulting analyses, however game, bog down without
inspiring recommendations beyond "improve human rights practices,"
"relieve socio-economic conditions of the poor," or "increase
government presence in contested areas." The analyses often lapse into
polarized debate about the psycho-political motivations of the
contenders, whether or not a military victory is possible, if the elite is
committed, or if political settlement is the only solution. When, after
digesting these analyses, one remembers the suspension of disbelief
that was required in order to cleanly separate the offending identities,
which in reality are terribly intermixed, it becomes apparent how
difficult it is to know exactly against whom to fight, when success
might be honestly claimed, if the causes have been sufficiently
relieved, or the motivations for homicidal behavior negated.

If, on the other hand, we take Colombia's history as a dynamic,
continuing fight over property, especially real property, and we demote
the particular labels of contestant categories to secondary importance,
then the nation's geography itself tells us something about the soul of
the violence. Colombians have forever fought over key terrain, the
value of the most contested lands being tied to the profitability and
taxability of an export product.[110] Coal, coca, coffee, emeralds,

Security of coca fields	193,000	- 0.1
Material captured	54,000	- 0.1
Extortion of territorial entities: no figures available		
Smuggling: no figures available		

TOTAL … [$]1.36 billion

[109] See, for instance, Marcella, Gabriel and Schulz, Donald. Colombia's Three Wars:
U.S. Strategy at the Crossroads. Carlisle, PA: Strategic Studies Institute,
1999;González, Manuel et. al. Una Mirada Argentina sobre Colombia. Buenos Aires:
Instituto de Investigación sobre Seguridad y Crimen Oranizado (ISCO), 1999.
[110] On the history of agricultural and extractive products as a factor in Colombian
conflict see, for instance, Frank Safford and Marco Palacios, Colombia: Fragmented

quinine, ink, feathers, fur, flowers, gold, oil, poppy, sugar, cattle – all these saleable items and many others have specific geographic references.[111] Their profitability is influenced by exigencies of transport, vulnerability to taxation (both legal and illegal) and control of the labor required for resource exploitation, said costs in turn correlating back to geographic conditions.[112] Obviously, resources can be extracted and marketed without being a catalyst of armed violence. In Colombia, however, compartmented terrain makes centralized governance difficult, and highly marketable resources focus materialist genious. Natural rapacity is all the more tempted by the promise of easy profit and difficult governance. Possession by force has been the natural consequence of human territoriality unchecked by civilizing structure.

Land, Divided Society (New York: Oxford University Press, 2002); and Indalecio Lievano Aguirre, Los grandes conflictos sociales y económicos de nuestra historia [The great social and economic conflicts of our history] (Bogotá: Círculo de Lectores, 2002).

[111] The list of Colombian items susceptible to smuggling is seemingly endless. It easily includes ink, leather, edible rodents, hardwoods, African palm oil, cigarettes, quinine, counterfeit monies, music CDs, bananas, etc. The smuggling of tobacco cigarettes is a major industry. On this point, see Center for Public Integrity, "El lado oscuro," Semana, 5 March 2001, pp. 40-48.

[112] The theme of conflict over cash products and their geography is not at odds with another common thread in the literature of Colombian conflict -- the struggle for control of labor. Historically, Colombian labor, whether of indigenous populations, imported slaves or otherwise, has been variously courted and abused for the purposes of exploiting a natural resource, or controlling terrain for the same ultimate purpose. Thus the two themes (resources and labor) are interwoven and complementary. Political assumptions and preferences of Colombian authors toward this phenomenon show a marked ideological tendency, those focusing on abuse of labor generally favoring socialist solutions. See, for instance, María Clemencia Ramírez, Entre el estado y la guerrilla: identidad y ciudadanía en el movimiento de los campesinos del Putumayo [Between the state and the guerrilla: identity and citizenship in the campesino movement in Putumayo] (Bogotá: Instituto Colombiano de Antropología e Historia, 2002); Orlando Fals Borda, Historia de la cuestión agraria en Colombia [History of the agrarian question in Colombia] (Bogotá: Carlos Valencia Editores, 1982); Margarita González, El resguardo en el nuevo reino de Granada [Defense in the new kingdom of Granada] (Bogotá: El Áncora Editores, 1992).

126

Colombia's most powerful outlaw organizations directly and indirectly sap the value of Colombia's bounty using a variety of tactics and strategies. Some are specific to certain products and locations, while other aspects of their modus operandi, such as bribery, are perfectly generalized. (See Figure 3, Colombian Resource Predation) In almost every Colombian locale that deals in some way with the extraction, cultivation, processing or transport of a natural resource (and by no means just coca and oil), armed criminality has a direct effect on the value of real estate, the quantity of human confidence, of positive aspiration, and of positive social ethic. To be sure, these values, save positive social ethic, are increased, often dramatically, for some enterprises and persons favored by the illicit exploitation. However, generalized insecurity and violence reduce market value for most landowners, and good times are short-lived in areas where organized armed criminals fight for advantage. Organized criminality weighs constantly on the quality and enjoyment of citizens' rights. The effect is especially visible in rural land, and is double-edged: Illegal behavior, especially as it concerns real property, undermines market value. Conversely and concurrently, failure of the society to clarify and stabilize property rights in rural areas encourages that illegal behavior.[113] If one is looking for a single essential political shortcoming tying natural bounty to violent conflict, in Colombia that shortcoming is the absence or under-development of formalized property. Rights and duties related to land have not been expressed in detail so that the essential social contract might be readily fulfilled. We can anticipate that Colombia's abrupt terrain will ameliorate only in

---

[113] Semana, "Necesitamos una respuesta inmediata del Estado" (We need an immediate response from the State) Semana (weekly news journal)interview with José Félix Lafourie, 26 Sep, 2005, <http://semana2.terra.com.co/opencms/opencms/Semana/articulo.html?id=89992 Lafouri is President of a Colombian national cattlemen's association and former director of the ministry that stewards the properties registry. Mr. Lafourie argues forcefully in this interview that the absence of State presence to protect small and medium size ranchers leaves them vulnerable to predation by outlaw organizations, particularly the guerrilla. One clear suggestion from the interviewee -- that in the absence of assistance from the State, formation of paramilitary groups for self-defense is a natural consequence.

geologic time, that marketable resources will continue to abound, and that human base instincts will change little. Colombia can, however, improve the practical supports to the social contract that check and discipline territorial instinct. In the short term, the same ordering of rights and duties in land provides the Colombian government with a powerful forensic tool with which to find and deny wealth and power of Colombia's illegal armed groups.

Four Ownership Plans

Creating a better social contract in order to limit violence is no new idea in Colombia, or that the social contract and the regime of real property ownership were intimately joined. Violent competition in Colombia did not begin last month or forty years ago either. Since the arrival of the Spanish Conquistadors in the early 16th century, four dominant and intermingling intellectual-ideological currents have changed and fed the Colombian land fight. Each has had its particular imprint on the manner in which ownership rights have been evidenced and conflicts resolved. The first of these currents was conquest and evangelization -- a straightforward expression of imperial arrogance and dominating spirit, easily understood by both conquered and conqueror: Subdue by force, take the land, self-justify and domesticate. Spanish conquest and evangelizing created the immediate, obvious and urgent need for the crown to delineate boundaries, to the extent practical at the time, among conquistadors -- and by conquistadores among their lieutenants.[114] Likewise the Catholic Church demanded and received great tracts of land for various purposes of the church mission.

The second current, beginning around the turn of the 18th and 19th centuries, was that of federalism/anti-federalism. This is perhaps

---

[114] Principal among these was Gonzalo Jiménez de Quesada, who some say was the model for Cervantes' don Quixote. The first major conquistador intramural in northern South America involved Jiménez de Quesada, Sebastián Belacázar and Nicolas Federmann meeting in Bogotá.

the most "Colombian" of the violence-propelling intellectual streams in that it seems to fit both the terrain and national disposition. Even though it depended for its destructive energy on a polarized interpretation of the North American revolutionary experiment, it matched Colombia's exotic geography, giving accidents of terrain political meaning. How far from the capital can or should the central government hold sway? What is the proper balance of individual freedom and power with that of the State? The civil wars of the 19th century were guided by this question (or by cynical reference to the question in order to clothe simple arrogation) up through at least the disastrous War of a Thousand Days at the turn of the 19th and 20th centuries.[115] No serious student of Colombian history, of any ideological bent, can separate land from violence or from ever-conflicting schemes to stabilize ownership rights, or to realign them or redistribute them. Most of these schemes I place in the category of federalism-anti-federalism because the associated arguments expend most of their energy on the play between geographic distance and varying authority to tax.

In the middle of Colombia's nineteenth century melee to decide the matter of civilizing arrogation came the news of European socialism. This third current might be described as imported class struggle. One can make the argument that the *Comuneros* uprising in the late 18th century was a forbearer of later class revolt, and perhaps socialist revolution can further trace its roots to conflicts of squatters against speculators in the late 19th century, or to dissidence on haciendas, or indigenous rebelliousness and land invasions of the 1920s and 1930s.[116] Many in Colombia today will point back to the assassination in 1948 of Jorge Eliécer Gaitan, quoted at the start of this section, as the birth of the current socialist revolutionary movement. Regardless, the federalist/anti-federalist debate remained the powerful

---

[115] On the War of the Thousand Days, see Geoffrey Demarest. "War of the Thousand Days" Small Wars and Insurgencies, Spring 2001, pp. 1-30.
[116] Regarding land conflict during the second half of the 19th century and beginning of the 20th, see generally, Catherine LeGrand, Frontier expansion and peasant protest in Colombia, 1850-1936, (Albuquerque: The University of New Mexico Press, 1986).

undercurrent, manifested and dominated from the mid-19th century until recently through the two principal political parties, Liberal and Conservative, and now through illegal armed groups.

There has always been a demand for greater social justice in Colombia, but class, race and religion have not provided popular representative identities to pursue it -- through violence or otherwise. On the other hand, there is little question that social and economic inequities have contributed to recruitment potential for rebellion. Traditionally, however, the rural agriculturalists were conservative Catholics tied to paternalist dependency and party loyalty. The Marxist-Leninist argument more often did not inspire them, and succeeded most when overlaying better-rooted determinants of competition, almost always territorial and familial. While revolutionary writers may claim that the *Violencia* of the 1950s was class-revolutionary in nature and the seedbed of the current crop of Colombia's leftist guerrillas, it is also argued that the *Violencia* owed much more to the old federalist/anti-federalist polemic, and to the two-party loyalties engendered by it.[117] After the *Violencia*, the radicalizing effect of revolutionary thinking and its opposites increased--spurred by organized efforts at concientization, foreign intervention, and by growing ideological dissipation and ambivalence within the Liberal and Conservative parties. Explicit collaboration between those parties in the late 1950s and 1960s, in what is known as the National Front, served to calm the federalist/anti-federalist polemic on which the *Violencia* had thrived. It also presented a common target (a single oligarchic concept) against which the new stream of communist revolutionary organizations could argue their moral purpose and justify violence. Paradoxically, compromise inside and between the most effective competitive identities (Liberal and Conservative parties) in the federalist/anti-federalist contract battle gave the socialist-revolutionary idea an opportunity to sustain itself.

---

[117] Among the more intriguing histories of the Violencia is Ramsey, Russell W. Guerrilleros y Soldados. Bogotá: Ediciones Tercer Mundo, 1981.

The fourth intellectual (or perhaps counter-intellectual) stream, particularly noxious and currently reigning, is unrepentant gangsterism. The notion is still one of taxation and its avoidance, and of changing the balance of individual rights with those of the government and society. There has always been an admixture of purely mercenary criminality in Colombian organized violence. Smuggling has been a science in Colombia for almost five centuries, but the violence today is not the same as in the past. Some insidious methods, such as widespread kidnapping, are new, as is the indifferent sowing of inexpensive, easily deployed explosives. Abandonment of moral motivation in favor of material expediency became commonplace rather than exceptional – the moral asymmetry described in Chapter Two. This or that gangster might make a convenient argument about local territorial identity or representing workers, but the volume of their insincerities owes to illicit disposable income. Maintaining that income encourages further justifications for opposing established standards of morality. In this vicious syndrome of challenged norms, ruthless criminal organizations set about to establish their own taxing authority and tax territories. Thus the Colombian fight slouches back both to justification of pure conquest and to its polarized federalist/anti-federalist self -- all of it territorial and homicidal.[118]

Four historic catalytic currents favoring violence were just listed: conquest and evangelization, federalism and anti-federalism, revolutionary socialism, and gangsterism. Regardless of the measure or mix, the object of conflict and the frontline geography of violence in Colombia has been real estate and its product. All of the four currents

---

[118] As to the causes of violence in Colombia, quite a literature exists, especially by Colombian authors. To summarize in a few paragraphs what remains unexplained in hundreds of titles is not a conceit the author will risk here. Outstanding among the explanations favored by the author is that of retired Colombian General Alvaro Valencia Tovar, one of the most widely respected and most prolific writers on the nature of Colombian violence. General Valencia stresses individual human faults as root causes of Colombian violence (ambition, caudillo-ism and power hunger). See, for instance, Alvaro Valencia Tovar, Inseguridad y Violencia en Colombia. Bogotá: Universidad Sergio Arboleda, 1997. Regardless, the object of these spiritual failings, is almost always territorial or has powerful territorial correlations.

are strategic ownership plans. None have been conducive to long-term peace because they do not contemplate property as a social contract with just peace as its purpose, or that itself required maintenance.

Figure 2. Special Colombian land-use challenges

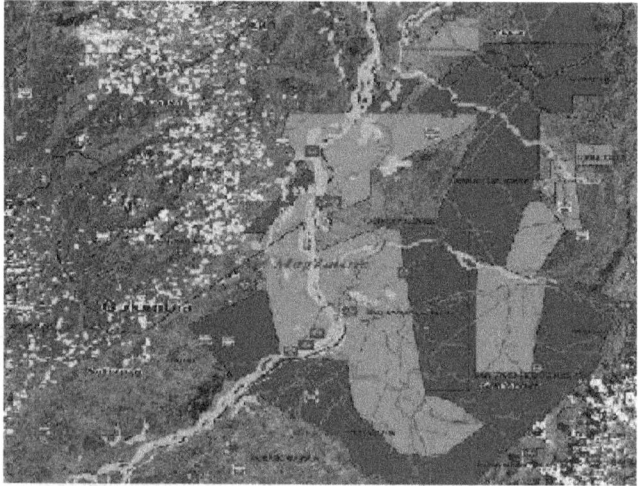

This image of the 'Middle Magdalena' region of Colombia was prepared from various open sources by the GIS Team of the Foreign Military Studies Office. It was part of an attempt to test correlations between coca crops (yellow dots) hydrocarbon exploration and exploitation concessions, transportation infrastructure and land mine fields.

The object of organized conflict

¡Vamos a buscar este indio dorado!

(We're going to go look for this golden Indian!)
Sebastian de Belalcázar, Conquistador

ELN, AUC, FARC[119]

The following examination of the ELN, FARC and AUC is from a prominent Colombian commercial lawyer. It is based on number of local sources and is included here as a summary not only of the evolution of the three principal illegal armed groups, but as an apt

[119] FARC-EP is the acroynm for the Fuerzas Armadas Revolucionarias de Colombia - Ejército del Pueblo (Revolutionary Armed Forces of Colombia - People's Army), ELN is the acroymn for the Ejército Nacional de Liberación (National Liberation Army). Roots of these two communist guerrilla groups reach back to at least the early 1960's. See, on the history of the Colombian guerrillas, Michael Radu, <u>Violence and the Latin American Revolutionaries</u> (New Brunswick, 1988); Russell W. Ramsey, <u>Guerrilleros y Soldados,</u> Segunda Edición (Bogotá: Tercer Mundo Editores, 2000); Cordillera Editores, <u>Historia de las Fuerzas Militares de Colombia: Ejército, Tomo III</u> (Bogotá: Planeta Colombiana, 1993) pp.124-141; Eduardo Pizarro Leongómez, <u>Las FARC: 1949-1966</u> (Bogotá: Tercer Mundo, 1992); Carlos Medina Gallego, ELN: Una historia de los orígenes (Bogotá: Rodriguez Quito, 2001); AUC is the acronym for the Autodefensas Unidas de Colombia (United Self Defense Forces of Colombia), another illegal, armed irregular force popularly described as 'paramilitary' and as 'right wing,' although it has made few ideological statements beyond opposition to the communist guerrillas. For more on this organization, see David Spencer, <u>Colombia's Paramilitaries: Criminals or Political Force?</u> (Carlisle, PA: Strategic Studies Institute, U.S. Army War College, 2001); Maurico Aranguren Molina, <u>Mi Confesión: Carlos Castaño revela sus secretos</u> (Bogotá: Editorial Oveja Negra, 2001); 'Place' as used here alludes to a body of theory in the study of geography, a centerpiece of which is called 'central place theory,' that considers competitive weeding-out and survival of businesses. Associated normally with urban economics and geography, place theory has obvious application in Colombia. See in this regard, <http://geography.about.com/cs/centralplace/

description of their equivalent, territorial, strategic and mercenary nature.

"Although [the FARC] arose by the middle of the 60's, its growth is verified mainly starting from the 80's, coinciding with the expansion of the coca cultivations and the escalation of kidnapping. In 1982, when president Betancour's administration began, there were 16 fronts with nearly 1,300 men. Two years later, in 1984, the figure increased to 27 fronts and around 1,700 men. In 1987, when during the Barco administration the peace agreements broke, there were already 39 fronts and 4,300 men. In the decade of the 90's the growth didn't stop. In 1991, year of the Army's offensive into the FARC headquarters at Uribe, Meta, to evict the FARC from Casa Verde, there were already 49 fronts and 8,500 men. In 1995 at the beginning of the Samper administration, it increased to 58 fronts and 10,000 men. And in 2000 there were already 66 fronts and 16,000 men. In 2001 and 2002 the fronts and the men didn't increase notably, but it is necessary to note that multiple columns and mobile companies were created that modified FARC's military activity, passing from the war of guerrillas to the war of movement, with significant attacks on military bases. ...

In the 60's and 70's ELN located its combat fronts in the Middle Magdalena River valley. A very mineral and cattle rich environment; likewise they had presence in urban areas like Bogotá, Cali, Medellín, Bucaramanga and Barrancabermeja. They were strengthened starting from 1983 through extortions of the foreign companies, as in the case of the manufacturer of the pipeline of Occidental Petroleum and through Kidnapping. The numbers of men and fronts corroborate this situation. While in 1987 there

134

were only three fronts and sixty men, in 1983 it passed to five fronts and 150 men and in 1987 went to 14 fronts and 1200 men. In 1994/5 there were already 26 fronts and 2,454 men in arms. Their growth slowed down in the second half of the decade. Today, most ELN fronts have been overrun by either FARC, or AUC. ...

AUC was born in the Middle Magdalena Valley in the early 70′s as a response to FARC and ELN penetration of the rich cattle and oil producing areas. In general, they can be described as groups formed or supported by land owners, that sought by means of armed confrontation to maintain the status quo and to weaken the insurgency, assuming the double task of not allowing the expansion of the guerrillas and on the other hand penetrating the areas where these organizations had their most stable sources of financing. Although they have the support of varied groups affected by the guerrillas, among them farmers, merchants, peasants and other, their expansion in the 80′s has been associated to the drug traffic. ...

The current self-defense forces were established in the 1980's, when drug barons bought a millions of hectares of land in rural areas, according to Defense Ministry estimates. Drug dealers acquired cheap cattle farms in the Middle Magdalena valley, in the plains of Meta and mainly in Córdoba, Antioquia and Sucre, in the northwest of the country. These areas had been under guerrilla siege and influence. Routinely FARC demanded money in exchange for protection. The drug dealers counteracted these demands, organizing militias that evolved as the self-defenses. According to author Alberto Valencia, between 1986 and 1988 armed groups at the service of drug dealers that had acquired enormous extensions in the Ariari (Center south of the country) undertook a regional war against the FARC, and were able to expel them from some municipalities like San Martin, Granada and Vista Hermosa, in Meta. In Caquetá, the presence of these groups was smaller, due to the dominant power of the FARC. By the end of the 80's, for a short time, between two and three hundred men of Gonzalo Rodríguez (also known as The Mexican) tried to take control from the FARC in areas like El Recreo, Yaguara II, Las Sombras, Los Pozos, Las Delicias, with the purpose of depriving them of the strategic corridor between the Region of the Cagúan, the Lozada and the Macarena.[120]

The trend toward pure profit motivation is a latest phase in the long history of Colombian territorial competitions. It is no surprise that violence occurs in positive geographic correlation with the sources of profit and their movement routes.

---

[120] From Ernesto Villamizar Cajiao, "Terrorism in Colombia," presented in Williamsburg VA, 26 May, 2004, at a conference hosted by the US Army Training & Doctrine Command. Mr. Villamizar, Fulbright scholar and managing partner of Villamizar Abogados Asociados, has also served as a criminal attorney in high profile human rights cases.

Figure 3. Colombian Resource Predation

Unlawful/ unethical Behavior	Implicated Actors	Major Resources Affected	Consequences	Principle Geographic Locations	Counter-Measures
Extortion, including support violence	FARC, ELN, AUC, DTOs (DTO=Drug Trafficking Orgs)	Oil, natural, natural gas, coal, electric power, water, coffee, other transport, other	Strengthened outlaws; government programs, business profitability, resource exploration all diminished; murders, bombs and general mayhem	Norte de Santander, Boyacá, Arauca, Sucre, Nariño, Cauca, Huila, other	Destroy outlaw leadership, improve personal security, audits, transparency, legal system, other
Illicit crop cultivation, processing and transport	FARC, AUC, DTOs, ELN, others	Natural habitat, protected species, licit agriculture, licit extractive industries	Strengthened outlaws; Production of illicit drugs for export, loss of habitat/species, population displacement, loss of tourism, increased energy exploitation costs	Putumayo, Caquetá, Guaviare, Bolívar, Nariño, Cauca	Eradicate crops, interdict transport, pursue and eliminate outlaw leaders, formalize property, strengthen forfeiture laws
Theft	AUC, FARC, ELN, others	Gasoline, various agricultural products	Strengthened outlaws; higher domestic energy costs/ weakened economy; lower government revenues	Middle Magdalena between Baracabermeja and Salgar Port	Regain territorial control, anti-fencing measures, technology, destroy outlaw forces
Bribery	FARC, ELN, AUC, others	All	Environmental protection and enforcement regimes weakened, energy exploitation regimes	Select, resource rich municipalities	Sting ops, amnesties, confidential comms, audits, etc.
Territorial control	FARC, AUC, ELN, factions within	Lines of communication, gas pipelines, illicit drug cultivation areas	Government programs stopped, legal regime for environmental protection compromised, resource allocation shifted	AUC: Uraba ELN: Parts of Cesar, Antioquia FARC: Venezuela border, part of Ecuador border	Destroy outlaw forces, terrain and property intelligence, owner strategies, property formalization

Landmine emplacement	FARC, AUC, ELN	Oil, natural, natural gas, coal, electric power, water, coffee, other transport, other	Civilian maiming, depressed land values, generalized fear, resource exploitation cost increase	Approx 50% of counties affected, about 5% severely	Destroy outlaw forces, increase funding to protect infrastructure, mining deactivation
Highway robbery	FARC, ELN AUC, lesser known criminals	All	Strengthened outlaws, resource exploitation cost increases, depressed tourism, generalized fear	Road network	Destroy outlaw forces, increase checkpoints, detachments, convoy, escorts,
Kidnapping	FARC, ELN, AUC, others	All	Strengthened outlaws, Resource cost increases, facilitated extortions	Select urban areas and roads	Destroy outlaw leadership, personal protective measures
Population displacement	AUC, FARC, ELN, government	Farmland, forests and woodlands	Exploitation cost increases, depressed land values, social care costs	Areas of conflict among illegal armed groups	Destroy outlaw leadership, formalization of property
Embezzlement	Government functionaries	All	All	All	Corruption regulations and practices
Poaching and smuggling	Cross-border actors; unknown	Flora and fauna	Loss of species/ loss of viable sustainable development options	NA	Patrolling, checkpoints, international agreements
Abuse of legal process	Unknown	All industries, specifically power companies, mining operations	Increased costs, bankruptcy, encourages violent action	NA, but recent efforts against gold industry	Facilitated procedures against abuse of process
International strategy	Foreign government officials	All	Strengthened outlaws, increase in contraband, border tensions	Venezuela	International pressure, other

138

Figure 4. 16th century gold coin of Charles I at the Prado Museum, Madrid.

A legend heard by the author in Spain (maybe one of those 'urban' legends, e.g. spurious, but nevertheless entertaining) holds that this pristine gold coin, recently obtained by the Prado Museum in Madrid, was illegally possessed for almost all of the first four hundred and fifty years of its existence.

Doubloon at rest

Compartmentalized geography, geophysical wealth, predatory human nature, and the mix of contentious philosophies have together furthered Colombian violence. To state that this or that has been the single cause of violence would be to foist questionable logic. The determinants are scarcely subject to independent treatment. The weakness of the social contract that civilizes the interaction of these other variables, however, is a condition that *can* be improved. The most directly relevant of the civilizing institutions of a successful social contract is a transparent, precise and stable property regime. This last variable in the equation of violence, inadequacy of civilizing institutions, can be dramatically and favorably improved by improving the property regime.

Violent territoriality and illegal arrogation of real estate in Colombia today correlates generally to business factors involving the processing, warehousing, delivery and sale of an illicit commodity; fenceablity of a legal but stolen commodity; or risk-benefit calculations regarding human targets potentially paying extortions or ransom. Each parasitic activity-type has a specific geographic reference. Because a parasitic behavior matches a portion of the logistical web of the illegal armed group, and marks an important line of communication, the best military understanding of key terrain in Colombia is informed by the commercial value of given set of places, as much as by their classic military characteristics.

Colombia's internal conflict centers geographically on resource extraction areas, processing points or movement routes, in accordance with their importance to profitability.[121] The favorite natural resources

---

[121] During the early stages of the on-going leftist insurgency, the greatest violence was centered geographically on newly colonized lands and marginalized populations, rather than on a specific natural resource. See, for instance, Eduardo Pizarro Leongómez, Las FARC: 1949-1966 (Bogotá: Tercer Mundo, 1992). Looking at Pizarro's map figures, such as those on pages 129 and 190, both the limited geographic extent of guerrilla territorial influence, as well as the non-correlation with

targets for illegal armed groups are hydrocarbons (oil, natural gas, coal and refined products), illicit drugs (the products of coca and poppy plants, cocaine and heroin respectively), electric energy, water and minerals (especially gold). There are many lesser resources spurring armed violence, not the least of which are bananas, coffee and African palm.[122] Admitting many commonalities, each of these products is associated with a certain criminal modus operandi due to geographic concentration and peculiarities of the product. As expressed in Figure 3, the parasitic method of Colombia's illegal armed groups includes extortion and bribery; illicit drug trafficking; theft; guerrilla assaults; outlaw territorial control; landmine emplacement; highway robbery; kidnapping; population displacement; embezzling; poaching and smuggling; abuse of legal processes; and international strategy. Some towns and small cities have suffered generalized extortion, in which any enterprise irrespective of product, is subject to forced illegal taxation, a condition typical of locations where mafia-style presence becomes dominance.

Underground and placer mining activities, especially for gold and emeralds, but also for lesser gems and minerals, are the more traditional objects of internal discord.[123] Before the arrival of the Spanish conquistadors, pre-Colombian tribes living in mountainous northern South America prized these elements and fought over them.

---

natural resources are notable. While the geography of armed political conflict in Colombia was centered on remote areas with communist-influenced populations rather than on commercial resources, this is not to say conflicts were not property-based, even at the historical roots of revolutionary organization and violence. Pizarro points out early in the text how much revolutionary violence, and Colombian violence in general, are connected with tenancy and ownership.

[122] "Aumenta en Colombia la piratería de videos, libros, música y muchas mercancías más" [Piracy of videos, books, music and many other goods is increases in Colombia], El Tiempo (Bogotá) 28 January 2003, online at <http://eltiempo.terra.com.co/judi/2003-01-29/ARTICULO-WEB-NOTA_INTERIOR-262989.html. Colombia has become a world leader in the piracy of almost everything.

[123] For a review in Spanish of Colombian gold history see Juan José Hoyos, El oro y la sangre [Gold and blood] (Bogotá, Editorial Planeta 1994).

Not, however, with the dedication and organizational bent of the Spanish. Beginning in the 16th century these items (along with lesser mentioned resources such as ink and animal pelts) became focal points for geographic dominance, then the motivation of taxation schemes and the smuggling routines and practices to avoid taxation. Colombia's social-revolutionary tradition is rooted directly in opposition to oppressive taxation, and the geographic flashpoints of revolution were often places associated with mining activities.[124] A culture of criminal extraction, clandestine transport and outright theft had been firmly established well before national independence in the 19th century. Today most gold extraction, transportation and exchange are still accomplished outside the legal mechanisms intended to regulate them. This failure begins at the base ownership rights of access and extraction. Subsurface resources belong initially to the federal State. Exploration licenses and extraction licenses are issued, and mining conducted with small regard for the holders of mere surface rights. The extent the government can monitor, inspect and enforce the legal balance of rights determines the level of conflict resolution, or of waste and trespass associated with mining claims. Historically, little has been done by the State to secure the rights of licensees, or surface owners, or to establish an efficient mechanism of conflict resolution based on clear evidence of the rights contested. This has forever opened the door to resolution by force.

As old as the history of gold conflict is in Colombia, its ups and downs have clear historic, often transnational, details, even recently. In 1971, the President of the United States announced the suspension of convertibility of dollars into gold, and in 1974 American citizens could

---

[124] See, for instance, accounts of the late 18th Century "Comuneros" uprising in Aguirre, Indalecio Liévano, "La Revolución de los comuneros" in Los Grandes Conflictos Sociales y Económicos de Nuestra Historia (Bogotá: Intermedio, 2002 pp. 381-404; Henao, Jesus María y Arrubla, Gerardo, Historia de Colombia: Tomo 1, (Bogotá: Plaza y Janes, 1984), p. 315; Gutierrez, Javier V. Historia de Colombia y educación cívica (Medellín: Editorial Bedout, 1975), p. 95.

once again legally hold gold coins and bullion.[125] In 1975 and 1976, the US Treasury and the International Monetary Fund began sales of gold reserves. Gold purchases, especially from the Middle East, caused the market price of gold to rise from what had been 35- 45 dollars a troy once in the early 1970s to over eight hundred dollars a troy once in 1980. This change coincides with social upheaval in the gold mining areas in Colombia, and in particular in southern Bolivar Department. In 1980, the ELN moved into the southern Bolivar mining counties to take advantage of an increasingly violent dispute between established residents and itinerant prospectors from neighboring Boyacá and Santander departments who were attracted by the rise in prices.[126] The town of Simití became the geographic focal point of an ELN effort to leverage its 'mediation' of the conflict into tax concessions on gold mining, concessions that soon amounted to effective control of the mines, since absence of government authority in the region created impunity for extortion. Gold was the natural resource object, and the gold region, with its unsettled population and stressed economy, became the geographic locus of violent conflict and organized outlaw exploitation of that conflict. It is not that property was not created in the gold region, but that the authority for dispute resolution was outlaw and non-transparent.

In obedience to the notion that one bad thing leads to another, the history of Southern Bolivar in the last two decades links natural bounty to violent competitions of all kinds. Besides the nearby gold, it is a concentration area for coca cultivation and for the suite of parasitic activities associated with hydrocarbons. Southern Bolivar, more broadly the 'Middle Magdalena' (middle reaches of the Magdalena

---

[125] Earle B. Amey, "Significant Events Affecting US Gold Prices since 1958," Gold in Commodity Statistics and Information, online at
<http://minerals.usgs.gov/minerals/pubs/commodity/gold/300798.pdf.
[126] Norbey Quevedo Hernández, "El tesoro de las autodefensas" [Treasure of the self-defense forces], El Espectador, 26 November 2000 online at
<http://www.elespectador.com/2002/20020728/periodismo_inv/2000/noviembre/nota2.htm; see also "Las aventuras de los paramilitares en San Lucas" [Adventures of the paramilitaries in San Lucas], eln-voces.com, 2001 online at <http://www.eln-voces.com/ultno/un_minavieja.htm.

River valley), is a natural hub for oil and gas transport infrastructure. Extortion targeted at the oil industry had become the preferred modus operandi of the ELN, doubtless in obedience to the quick submission of the industry and the propagandistic advantages of 'taking from the rich.' Geographic proximity to the Bolivar gold region made imposition in the gold fields a natural step, followed by exploitation of an ideal coca-growing zone, also contiguous.[127]

Gold mining, however, retained a central role in shaping the contest over natural resources, a role disproportionate in terms of the total value of disposable income generated for outlaw groups when compared to drug or hydrocarbon-related parasitism. Around 1997, the AUC began to invade Southern Bolivar and the middle Magdalena valley, taking over extortion contracts, physically occupying territory and denying the ELN the ability to collect in a wider area that eventually included the hub city of Barrancabermeja, just east of the Magdalena River. Local geographic differences in the gold fields also contributed to violence, as have Colombian government gold policies.

> *"En el sur de Bolívar según el Ejército hombres al mando de alias Montañez y de alias Julián han desplazado a los guerrilleros del ELN en el control de las minas de oro. Allí no solo controlan la minería illegal sino que exigen 'contribuciones' a quienes tienen títulos legales de explotación."*

> English translation: "According to the Army, in southern Bolívar (Department) men under the command of Montañez and Julián [aliases] have displaced the ELN guerrillas for control of the gold mines. They not only control the illegal mining there, but also require 'contributions' from those who have legal mining titles."

---

[127] On the clearance zones, see Geoffrey Demarest, "In Colombia: A Guerrilla Sanctuary?" Military Review, March-April 2002,. pp. 48-50; also online at <http://www.smallwars.quantico.usmc.mil/search/LessonsLearned/LatinAm/colombia.htm.

Globalization, and in particular the movement toward extraterritoriality of legal jurisdiction, especially in human rights cases, has, along with active participation of international NGOs, made the competition over gold all the more complex and difficult to decipher. *El Sindicato de Trabajadores de Mineria Colombiana* (Colombian Mine Workers' Union, SINTRAMINERCOL), a miners' union active in Southern Bolivar and, entered a case in the US Federal Court for Northern Alabama against multinational corporations for human rights abuses against its members, alleging, moreover, collusion with paramilitaries. Since the parties in this and related cases seem to align themselves perfectly with competing outlaw groups, one is led to speculate that the ELN feigned a role of innocent victim in part because it had control of organizational and legal/propagandistic assets that its competitors did not. In any case, the presentation of the conflict in Colombia as a war over natural resources is clear:

> "There are people ["The US and the great world powers... {and} multinational corporations in league with the Pentagon"] responsible for this War, with names and clear interests. It is our duty to remove their masks and the blanket of impunity that covers them. In Colombia the war against SINTRAEMCALI and the communities of the Atlantic Coast is called privatisation, handing over public and state resources such as Water, Electrical Energy and Telecommunications to the multinationals. The war against the Oil Workers Union Unión Sindical Obrera USO and against the U'WA indigenous people is because of OIL. The War against mineworkers union SINTRAMINERCOL is based on GOLD. The War on the workers of DRUMMOND is because of COAL." [128]

---

[128] Berenice Celeyta, "Humanity's Ethical Duty," Nadir.org, 15 February 2003, online at <http://www.nadir.org/

Emerald smuggling is another traditional illegal activity in Colombia, and one that has very specific geographic identity, most recently in the *municipios* of La Palma, Yacopí and other *municipios* of northern Cundinamarca Department and southern Boyacá Department.[129] La Palma is the unofficial capital of the headwaters area of the river Rionegro, which flows into the Magdalena. It is a central location, not too far north of the nation's capital, or south of the strategically essential middle Magdalena valley, yet its difficult terrain makes it remote in the sense of military pursuit. It is fought over by all major terrorist organizations. The area has become one of the country's most frequent battlefields, an area over-sown with improvised landmines, and a favorite hiding place for kidnapping victims.

The links between emeralds and the current conflict include coincidence of difficult terrain, experience in the growth of criminal organizations and their private armies, smuggling routes and fencing apparatus, and a broader agenda of aversion toward the government and application of violence to create impunity. Here again, it would be too much to say that a quick improvement in the condition of property records, the creation of property courts, professionalizing of the real estate profession or any improvement in the property regime in Boyacá department would have a noticeable short-term impact on the violence there. However, just as discipline in policing the misdemeanors of graffiti and window breaking has the effect of interrupting devolution toward felonious violence, so too will an expectation of enforcement of the rule of law regarding the details of property have an ameliorating

---

nadir/initiativ/agp/free/colombia/txt/2003/021415FEB_Colombia.htm. The FARC has had the greatest leverage over mining industries in Colombia; the quoted assertion is from an organization sympathetic to the FARC.

[129] See María Victoria Uribe Alarcón, Limpiar la tierra: guerra y poder entre esmeralderos (Clean the land: war and power among emerald men) (Bogotá: CINEP, 1992), p. 74; Jineth Bedoya Lima, "La Guerra del Rionegro," El Tiempo (Bogotá), 15 July 2003, pp. 1-4.

effect on the illegal organizational impulse toward territorial violence. That this is not mere speculation lies in the immediate uses to which property records can be put in order to identify ownership associations, anomalies of land-use, and questionable tax-paying events. Until property records are available that expose interests and associations, there is no comprehensive way of establishing the actual battle-lines of violence there. Entering into this geographic area with the intention of imposing the rule of law, or of bringing felons to justice, but without an understanding of who owns what and with whom, is shortsighted and inconsequential. Paraphrasing for our own purposes the quotation used above, "There are people ... responsible for this War, with names and clear interests. It is our duty to remove their masks and the blanket of impunity that covers them.

In Colombia, oil infrastructure depredation has also been extensive along Colombia's northern border area, especially in Arauca Department. Oil pipeline attacks have been especially costly to the local and national economy and are visibly detrimental to the environment. Extortion and bribery require less technical expertise and physical risk than outright theft, and do not require post-act logistic preparation for product movement and fencing.[130]

> ...[T]he department of Arauca receives 80,000 million pesos [approximately 28 million dollars] annually royalties. Of this amount authorities estimate that between 10 and 15 percent goes to the coffers of the guerrillas,

---

[130] Some of the most publicized environmental insults of the conflict have been attacks by the ELN or the FARC against the Caño Limon-Coveñas oil pipeline. "Presidente Álvaro Uribe gobernará por tres días desde Arauca" [President Álvaro Uribe will govern for three days from Arauca], El Tiempo (Bogotá), 14 July 2003, online at <http://eltiempo.terra.com.co/coar/noticias/ARTICULO-WEB-_NOTA_INTERIOR-1177394.html. Guerrilla bombings of oil infrastructure have spilled three million barrels of oil--more than ten times the amount of oil caused by the Exxon Valdez disaster. Semana, "El nuevo narcotráfico" [The new narcotraffic], Semana, 23-30 September 2002 No. 1,064 p. 27.

FARC and ELN, the product of direct extortion. In 16
years, Arauca has received 1.2 billion dollars in royalties.
It is estimated that of this amount, 180 million dollars has
ended up in the hands of the guerillas.[131]

Guerrilla violence in Colombia has evolved to the point that
every Colombian understands the seriousness of guerrilla threats and
the matter-of-fact ruthlessness with which the illegal organizations
prove their strength of will. The specific fund-raising activities of the
major illegal armed groups cover the entire range of parasitism, and
resemble as much as anything else the extortionist activities of the
American mafias of the 1930s, but aided by computer literacy and
heavier weapons. In areas where resource extraction industries
proceed, the illegal armed groups extort money "downstream" by
taking a cut of royalties from local government officials. They also
extort "upstream" by instructing exploration, extraction and support
contractors.

> The diversion of official budget monies toward the
> guerrillas is almost always accomplished by means of the
> protection insurance racket targeted at contractors.
> Occasionally it is city hall itself that acts as the middleman,
> keeping a percentage itself.... City Hall would kept a
> percentage of the contract: One of the most common forms
> that the guerrilla has in order to control county budgets in
> the various zones of the country, particularly in Arauca, is
> to infiltrate the mayor's offices and intervene directly in the
> adjudication of contracts, especially the public contracts.
> Only those contractors that have the authorization of the
> subversives, and that pay a percentage of the official
> contracts, are able to execute the works without
> difficulty.[132]

---

[131] Semana, "El Nuevo Narcotráfico" Ibid.; see also "El otro cartel" [The other cartel],
Semana, 17-24 June 2002, p. 52.
[132] "¿Cómo intervienen las Farc en los presupuestos municipales en Arauca?" [How is
the FARC intervening in the municipal budgets in Arauca?], El Tiempo (Bogotá), 30

Foreign investors almost always have a strict policy against paying these illegal armed groups, claiming that they would be propagating the problem. Instead, they devote money to social programs (schools, agricultural projects, etc.) and rely on defense by the community. Some companies also provide training to help community leaders identify funds within their own government structure to pay for programs and augment those funds with their own donations. However, the contractors and sub-contractors of these companies are often left with no choice but to pay outlaw taxes. All movement is subject to illegal fines or forced contributions, and nearly all transportation for foreign companies is contracted out to locals. Company executives know this well, and so transportation costs are understood to include necessary pay-off overhead. The coal industry, for instance, is effectively subdued by extortionist groups, which have occasionally blown up a coal train along the route southwest from the Guajira peninsula mining areas in northeast Colombia. Tolerable arrangements appear to have been reached after only a few such attacks. The major coal companies, as in other industries, profess to never negotiate with the illegal armed groups. Nevertheless, security managers and energy executives report that their subcontractors could not complete their contracts successfully without factoring in transportation costs that include arrangements for placating extortionists.

Theft of refined gas is prevalent especially in Cesar Department and in several counties in the middle reaches of the Magdalena River valley where long, vulnerable stretches of Colombia's gasoline pipeline infrastructure run. According to information from the *Empresa Colombiana de Petróleos*, (Colombian Government Petroleum Company, ECOPETROL), some 37.5 million gallons of gasoline were stolen in the first four months of 2003, and of 1,387 illegal valves found on the gasoline pipelines during 2002, 238 were found in the

---

January 2003 online at <http://eltiempo.terra.com.co/coar/noticias/ARTICULO-WEB-NOTA_INTERIOR-263747.html.

149

Barrancabermeja area alone.[133] Conversely, natural gas theft is unusual because it requires too much technical preparation and investment to avoid self-inflicted injury. The theft of refined gas, however, cost the government a reported four and a half million dollars a month in 2002.[134] Most of the value of illicit profit gained by illegal armed groups from this gas theft appears to be converted into combat and coercive power in order to protect the illicit activity, mostly from other outlaws. The relationship of this particular natural resource to internal conflict is clear and uncomplicated. The natural resource is vulnerable and attracts attention. A powerful criminal organization such as the FARC or AUC can easily make the initial technical investment and provide local security to steal the gas. The net income can be enormous, especially if the armed group can control territory inside which they can insist that citizens buy stolen gas, a common practice. An armed group will buy or exchange (if able to transport the gasoline with sufficient impunity) for armaments so that it can maintain its revenue source not just in the face of government law enforcement, but more immediately in the face of other, competing outlaw predators on their territory.

Direct theft of crude oil in large quantities is a newer phenomenon than the theft of natural gas.[135] Most parasitism targeted against crude oil infrastructure had been in the form of extortion of companies backed by bombing of capital inputs or kidnapping personnel. This newer form of theft is revealing and challenging due to the category of buyers on the black market and the concentration of the theft geography.

The above litany of parasitic behavior is intended to show the relationship in detail of violence to geography, and the extent to which much of Colombia has been driven away from the rule of law. An

---

[133] Ecopetrol, "Crece el robo de gasolina" [Robbery of gasoline increases], El Tiempo (Bogotá), 27 May 2003, p. 1.

[134] "El otro cartel" [The other cartel], Semana, 17-24 June 2002, p. 52.

[135] Arturo Peñalosa Pinzón, "Mercado negro de crudo" [Black market of crude oil], El Tiempo (Bogotá), May 22, 2003, pp. 1-3.

observation that such bold acts of parasitism are distant from nuances in the property records, or from civil actions in property courts, would be gratuitous -- the State has been unable to bring effective kinetic firepower against illegal armed predators in many areas, much less prosecute them for trespass. Nevertheless, formal ownership allows a record of extortion and loss to be established, creates the possibility of insurance coverage and the establishment of bond values. Formalized ownership spreads and specifies responsibilities for vigilance and protection, and helps seal neighboring properties from illegal arrogations and direct extortion. There comes a moment when it is too late for the details of the rule of law, and so violent measures are engaged to force a return to that rule. In Colombia, in many jurisdictions, but not all, the rule of law has been overcome. It cannot be returned to the areas of predation by the physical presence of the State alone, but by the reestablishment of respect for the invisible lines of preferential ownership.

Colombia's property legacy

> *El título de la propiedad en el Quindío lo dio el hacha del labriego que rompía la selva para establecer su casa rústica y su parcela.*[136]

(The hatchet of the laborer, who broke the jungle to establish his rustic home and land parcel, is what gave title to property in Quindío.)
Luis Eduardo Nieto Arteta, Colombian historian, diplomat

---

[136] Luis Eduardo Nieto Arteta. Extract from María del Carmen Tafur, "Mensajes bajo un mismo cielo. Cartas de amor de Nieto Arteta", 1995, online at Banco de la República, <http://www.lablaa.org/blaavirtual/diccio/dicn.htm#n02.

Law as legitimacy

The history of property rights in Colombia is typical of many Latin American countries.[137] The Spanish crown justified appropriation of "New World" lands within the context of Christian proselytizing affirmed by Roman ecclesiastical authority. Division of lands went to governors or captain-generals who swore allegiance to the crown and confessed their faith. The assignment of urban *solares* or rural *estancias* correlated to the importance of the individual participant in a particular conquest expedition. Originally, a system of *morada y labor* was applied in which the receiver of lands had to stay resident on them for five years and work the land in order to gain permanent title. Later, under Bourbon reforms, the system was changed to that of conditional sale of royal holdings. The crown reserved to itself mining and subsurface rights. At first, indigenous people, while not considered property outright, were virtually chattel under a system of territorial *encomiendas* that gave managerial control over indigenous labor sources, these *encomiendas* being territorially demarcated. Later, when treatment of indigenous people as property was outlawed, blacks were introduced in the equivalent condition.

Colonial titles were clouded, and in cases remain so even today, in two principal ways, first by imprecise boundaries and secondly because many of the *mercedes reales* (royal grants or favors) were often not authorized by competent officials.[138] Some property rights were claimed without the *morada y labor* having been fulfilled. The distinction between private and public property was often uncertain because the *merced* might be conceived of more as a royal tolerance and not as delivery of the fee simple. Also, there was often little

---

[137] Thanks and apologies to Professor Mauricio Rengifo Gardeazábal of the University of Los Andes. Much of the material on the history of the Colombian property regime is adopted and translated from his Los Derechos de Propiedad en Colombia: Una Interpretación Comprensiva (Property Rights in Colombia: A Comprehensive Interpretation). Bogotá: Ediciones Uniandes, 2003.

[138] For brief definitions of various historic real estate terms see, Jaime Sierra García, Diccionario Jurídico, (Bogotá: Librería Juridica Sanchez R. Ltda., 2001).

152

distinction between the local functionary and the landowner, since many favored subjects of the crown exercised public and private roles simultaneously. Urban properties were relatively well marked, given that the Spanish urban planning system required rectilinear forms and generally standard sizes, but rural lands were often huge, irregular, and the terrain unknown.

Real property with documented ownership did not change hands often in colonial Colombia, but tended to stay within the same family group. Obstacles to the development a freely functioning market for even documented real estate included obligations known as *décimos* and *censos*, the *décimo* being at first a ten percent ecclesiastical tax based on the value of land (generally undervalued by the possessors until the point of sale). In the first half of the 18th century these *décimos* were denied to the church, but continued in various forms in support of civil government until mid-century. The *censos* were a variety of mortgage types, often involving annual payments to an individual for life in exchange for basic possessory rights. Both these encumbrances made purchase and sale less attractive. Hording or setting aside of lands by the church, the doubtful character of many titles, slow processes of registration of encumbrances; unlawful expropriation of indigenous reservation lands; questionable paper transformation into real property of what had begun as indigenous labor control rights; state monopolies over the production of certain export commodities; and the abundance of royal patrimonial lands and their actual or fraudulent grants -- all had a dulling effect on market development.

Aside from market barriers related to direct encumbrances we can add debilitating aspects of Colombian jurisprudence. Many locally determined laws and regulations opposed norms unsuccessfully pronounced by the Spanish throne that were intended to protect the indigenous work force. The royal juridical system rarely even contemplated the growing condition of *mestizaje* (racial mixing), creating large gray areas and loopholes in the law. Most of the clergy also escaped regulation by the crown.

153

Colombia's immediate post-colonial political reordering, influenced by the extreme nature of its geography, prolonged some idiosyncrasies of royal land policy. It also left regional divergence and disarticulation as Colombia lived a violent process of deciding the federalist debate. Eventually the whole range of western ownership rights including alienation, compensation and free marketability found expression in the Colombian civil code. Bureaucratic evolution competed mightily with juridical evolution, however. The property regime pertaining to subsurface resources and government open lands was built on a theory of government prerogatives fundamentally at odds with the guiding principles of the civil code.

In recent decades, contemporaneous with the above-mentioned current of ill-fitting revolutionary ideology, Colombian legislation has seen the advance of the concept of 'social property.' Tangible effects of the movement to deduce social property include regulations determining unit minimums of real property ownership (such as the agricultural familial unit which is an attempt to set the minimum amount of land needed for an agricultural family to survive), redistribution plans, and the organization of collective ownership entities. Social redistribution of real estate has been a political and academic favorite, implemented sporadically in the following forms: Voluntary negotiation, rural condemnation and taking, forfeiture for disuse or misuse, freezing of rents, urban expropriations, environmental expropriations, distribution of unused lands by petition, etc. The three major initiators of these processes of redistribution have been: the government under the auspices of established programs, class action lawsuits by claimants or dispossessed, and on occasion the private sector. In Colombia, a perpetual re-servicing of the theory that inequitable distribution of land is a primary cause of conflict tells us four things: One, that real estate is indeed important to Colombians; two, that redistribution efforts generally have not worked; three, that a fixation on the object of property has reigned without the necessary accompaniment of understanding of property as a social contract involving distinguishable and divisible rights; and four, a failure to

154

perceive the determinants of land value as it is reflected in the market for rights.

The institutional history of land ownership in Colombia has unevenly and for the most part negatively affected the quality Colombia's property regime. The quality of evidence delineating rights and the identity of owners often has been purposefully debased; marketing rights in land has been awkward or impossible. Protection from trespass has been nonexistent or ineffective, and the basic rules delimiting the social contract – who can be owners and what rights they might claim – has been illiberal.

The resulting cadastres and registries

While the history of the development of the property regime is in many ways unfortunate, millions of Colombians nevertheless claim ownership of land parcels recognized in one of the five cadastres and the national land registry. Tenancy conditions are highly varied from one part of the country to another, even within a single department. Quality of land ownership in southwestern Nariño department, for instance, is typically varied, as a thematic map of tenancy there indicates.[139] The Colombian cadastres have existed more or less in their present form since 1940, and they include mostly rural and urban claims from the eastern mountains west. Aside from their central role in tax appraisal, the Colombian cadastres are today recognized as a fundamental source of information for growth and conservation planning.[140] The cadastres and the registry, however, are not

---

[139] See, Instituto Geográfico Agustín Codazzi, Análisis geográficos: Aspectos geográficos del sector Andino Nariñense (Bogotá: Instituto Geográfico Agustín Codazzi, 1982) p. 26.

[140] Yovanny Arturo Martinez & Nyrian Angelica Ubáque, El catastro del nuevo milenio (Bogotá: Instituto Geográfico Augustín Codazzi, 2001) p.1.; See also, Ernesto Parra Lleras,. Apuntes de Catastro (Notes about the Cadastre). Bogotá: Universidad Externado de Colombia, 2002.

reconciled. The cadastres are not up-to-date, sufficiently digitized, and are woefully incomplete in many of the *municipios* most effected by violence. Perhaps most important of all, they are not transparent. That is to say, the data that represents the social contract of rights and duties related to Colombia's precious geography are not readily available for public inspection and are therefore subject to every type of instability and corruption. Rural Colombians almost always can produce some kind of writing indicating ownership, even in the most remote and marginalized areas. But to the degree these documents are not validated by the government and made representable to the market, they are correspondingly vulnerable to the modus operandi of the armed gangs.

The cadastral offices are responsible for appraising land values as the basis for taxation.[141] They are charged to keep records of the size, location, use, potential use and tax currency of all properties. In order to fulfill all the requirements of Colombian administrative law, a seller must produce certification from the cadastral offices to show the boundaried description and location of land to be sold, as well as any tax debt. This process seems to be followed as an exception, however, in many rural areas, and often in the city. The cadastral offices are not the official record of ownership of a property. That function belongs to the registry offices of a separate ministry, the Superintendency of Notaries and Registries.[142] In the course of many land transactions,

---

[141] The tax rates vary as a percentage of market value and no general figure for the relationship between the appraised value and market value would be broadly accurate. According to many familiar with the system of appraisals and the market for real property, an appraisal of around fifty percent of market value would be typical.
[142] Real property registrars are named to all of the departmental capitals and to a number of other cities. Registrars to the departmental capitals are named directly by the President of the Republic. Registrars are subordinate administratively to the Superintendency of Notaries and Registries (*Superintendencia de Notarios y Registros*) and those registrars named to non-departmental capitals are generally named by the Superintendent, who is in turn appointed by the President. The Superintendency is subordinate to the Ministry of Law and Justice (*Ministerio de Justicia y Derecho*). The registrars direct the registry offices, known as Offices of the Registry of Public Instruments (*Oficinas de Registro de Instrumentos Públicos*),

new owners often consider it sufficient to register using a bill of sale in the registry without consulting the cadastral office or having received a certificate of description and assessment from the seller. Therefore, the cadastral records, while determinant of the location, shape, size and tax value of a piece of land, are not legally sufficient to establish definitive ownership. Historically, the cadastral office records have not been compatible with the registry files, or at least, no comprehensive comparison has been made to measure the match. Today there is at least a technical intention and a technical method for reconciling the cadastres and registries.

The Colombian national cadastral office is a directorate of the national geographic institute, The Instituto Geográfico Agustín Codazzi (IGAC), which is a dependency of the Ministry of Interior and Public Credit (*Ministerio de Hacienda y Crédito Público*). The office is pursuing a process, supported in part by international loans, to digitize the property lines found on the analog cadastral maps, and IGAC recently signed a contract with a Colombian GIS firm to modernize its file system.[143] A potential for greater transparency and, therefore, stability of ownership evidence does exist.

In addition to the national cadastral office there are four autonomous cadastral offices -- the Federal District of Bogotá, Antioquia, Medellín and Cali.[144] The existence of these independent

---

which are organized into what are called Registry Circles (*Círculos Registrales*) and into which may fall several to many counties (*municipios*). That is to say, only about one in ten counties has a registry office.

[143] The current process of vector-digitizing is labor intensive, requiring laborious tracing of the property lines using a mouse. The process, often termed "live digitizing," produces vector images as opposed to raster images, the vector images being subject to a different type of value assignments and mathematic manipulation. The importance of this technical point is only that full use of cadastral files in the context of current information science requires some investment.
[144] Cadastral information for the Federal District of Bogotá is almost entirely digital, aggregated in an ArcInfo® database. The district is divided for cadastral purposes into just over 1,100 cadastral sectors and 41 separate layers of information. These layers

offices is directly related to historic anti-federalism. While the offices are politically, administratively and fiscally autonomous, they take technical guidance from the national cadastral office and theoretically follow the same technical protocols

The Federal District of Bogotá has one of the four independent cadastral offices, with over 250 employees. The office is well-funded and well-led.[145] Bogota is one of the safest areas of the country, and while there are many other factors to which credit is due, the existence of a functional and increasingly formal property regime is not to be dismissed.

Medellín also has a modern cadastral and registry process. The Medellín office coordinates some appraisal activities with the other counties that make up the Valle de Aburrá, or the greater metropolitan area.[146] In 2003, Medellín suffered a severe outbreak of organized armed violence as units of the FARC, AUC and ELN vied over select neighborhoods considered essential to maintain control of smuggling and re-supply routes through the city. Medellín lies across a vital line of communication between the western lowlands and the interior of Colombia. It would be a stretch to suggest that better developed urban property and records would have prevented this violence. While Medellín has made strides to formalize property, it is in areas of the

---

are available for sale to the public and are priced by virtual map sheet (most at 1:2,000 scale) and by layer. The cost of the layers per map sheet area ranges from about six to fifty dollars. Almost the entire digital map, in the form of ArcInfo® files with all 1,100 sectors and all correlative data layers can be purchased retail.

[145] Cadastral information for the Federal District of Bogotá is almost entirely digital, aggregated in an ArcInfo® database. The district is divided for cadastral purposes into over 1,100 sectors and 41 separate layers of information. These layers are available for sale to the public and reasonable prices.

[146] The Antioquia departmental cadastral office is not as complete as that of the city of Medellín, but enjoys some technical cooperation and guidance from the Medellín office. Antioquia department has 127 *municipios* (counties), about 40% of which now have digitized cadastral information on 1:10,000 and 1:25,000 scale base maps. Antioquia used AutoCad® software, which is compatible with the Intergaph® and ArcGIS® products.

least formal property ownership that much of the fighting broke out.[147] More than Bogotá, Medellín also pays a cost for the weaknesses of the region as a whole, and southeastern Antioquia Department is one of the most violence stricken rural areas in the country. (The condition of property records for this area is not known to the author.) As an interesting side note, Colombian drug kingpin, Pablo Escobar, was captured in Medellín, in part through the use of property files.

Cali Colombia is a center of lawlessness in southwestern Colombia. Approximately the same size as Medellín, Cali has been less successful economically. It has a much less formal property regime, and according to various informed Colombians this condition reflects an outright decision on the part of the Cali municipal government to not have a current, accurate and transparent cadastral record.[148] The most likely reasons for maiming the cadastral office are to disable their obvious forensic utility; appease special interests that do not want the tax assessments to reflect true values or identify their properties for taxation. In service of these first two reasons, the office had been purposefully overstaffed with unqualified political pawns

---

[147] Recognizing the economic, social and fiscal advantages of formalized property ownership, Medellín's city government has in the past several years legalized more than 8,000 lots in economically disadvantaged areas. City officers believe the process of cadastral formation has contributed to positive evolution of several neighborhoods. Some zones that are considered high-risk for environmental reasons have a low priority for formalization. As many as 150,000 of the 650,000 lots mapped by the office remained un-legalized in 2003.

[148] Organized similarly to that in Bogotá, the cadastral office in Cali has four divisions -- Cadastral Formation, Conservation, Cartography and Systems. At the time of the field study in 2002 the office had records on 505,000 urban plots and about 16,000 rural plots. It was in possession of a digital plan based on 1993 aerial photography and completed in 1995. The plan includes 35 urban data layers and 25 rural layers in ArcView® format, and it covers 37,000 urban hectares and 30,000 rural hectares. However, the Cali cadastral office had no employees who knew how to work the digital plan software, and while the city planning office apparently had a current ESRI license, the Cadastral Office did not. The 1995 plan has not been updated. From Jan 1, 1982 until December 31, 1995, the office had 235 employees, from Jan 1, 1996 to Jun 30, 2001 it had 90 employees, and from July 1, 2001 until mid 2002 it had 25 persons.

(reportedly including dozens of wholly illiterate persons) so that a subsequent radical reduction in personnel became broadly accepted as a reasonable efficiency measure.

The effect of the reduction was perfectly understood by technicians in the cadastral office who remained. Millions of dollars in tax revenue are forgone in Cali by the failure to update appraisals. Meanwhile, tax rates have been rising to make up needed income. Forensic uses for both criminal and civilian courts are stymied. Land-use planning is made unreliable and many opportunity costs are incurred by city services. Cali, more than Bogotá or Medellín, is a metropolitan area not guided by the rule of law, where the negative *isms* of a failing society are more prevalent. In the confusion and violence of cronyism, paternalism, and bullying populism, drug mafias are more likely to thrive and guerrillas to find safe harbor. Thug leaders, who have arrogated power and gained impunity in Cali's slums for bomb-making or storage of kidnap victim, are able to reach out into other neighborhoods of the city. As it stands now, Cali is unlikely to find a successful outcome to a major outbreak of urban violence such as that which occurred in Medellín. Cali's property values are on the decline and its general prospects for economic health are declining commensurately. Those seeking an answer to what appears to be a vicious economic down-spiral might claim a failure of social services, but they would be mistaken. They need look no further than the city's cadastral office. The government in that city decided emphatically to not be equitable in observing the rights of Cali's citizens in their residences and businesses. In the most favorable light, they pressed for greater redistribution of "social property." The result has been support to political elements most able to win a game of possession by force, aiding those elements by allowing anonymity and impunity. It is a perfect formula for strategic reduction of the value of property, the value of rights.[149]

---

[149] Not everything is going badly in Cali in terms of property, and it is by no means beyond hope of peaceful return to a path of broad economic prosperity. The real property registry (as opposed to the cadastral office) is in pretty good shape. The Cali registry maintains more than 700,000 files iincluding those for surrounding counties.

The above description of property records in Colombia paints a mixed condition of the general property regime across the country. Records are excellent in some offices, a disaster in others. We will not find a perfect correlation between local conditions of property regimes and the incidence of violence with any degree of accuracy, but the anecdotal evidence of such a correlation is intriguing, the logic compelling, and it is hard to imagine that violent competition over urban or rural territory would have unfolded as it has if ownership rights had been more clearly recorded, transparent, and protected earlier during the evolution of predatory behavior on the part of the illegal armed groups.

Un-property strategy

> *As a matter of Administration policy, we will not support*
> *Colombian counterinsurgency efforts. ...This*
> *Administration remains convinced that the ultimate*
> *solution to Colombia's long-standing civil conflict is*
> *through a successful peace process, not a decisive*
> *military victory, and believes that counterdrug progress*
> *will contribute to progress towards peace.*[150]
>
> President William Clinton, 2000

We look below at three specific phenomena of the Colombian conflict: aerial eradication of coca plants, Colombian negotiations with the FARC (on which the former Colombian government under President Andres Pastrana rested its security strategy), and landmines. These three do not paint the entire canvas of the Colombian conflict,

---

Eighty percent of the information managed by the registry is digitally systematized, but it is not transparent to the public, and without a reconciled, matching cadastral system, it is very difficult to use for forensic purposes.

[150] Presidential Decision Directive/NSC 73, August 3, 2000.

but they each serve in a different way to connect conflict strategy with the issue of property development.

Putumayo and Ploesti

Plan Colombia's Putumayo aerial eradication is a bit like the WWII raid on Ploesti.[151] Few spray planes are shot down, but the

---

[151]In 1943, WWII allied war planners felt a decisive raid on the Romanian oil fields around Ploesti could be a knock-out blow to German war-making capacity and so shorten the course of WWII in Europe. Churchill called the Ploesti fields, producing more than half the crude oil imported into Germany, the taproot of the Nazi war machine. An ensuing operation on August 1, 1943 was costly -- 54 of 177 of the B-24 Liberators sent on the raid did not return, giving the raid its nickname, Black Sunday. There was no knockout blow at Ploesti; the immediate results were insubstantial, and, in terms of the overall outcome of WWII, the effectiveness of the raids is still debated. A resilient, determined enemy took countermeasures and found alternatives. Eventually, Nazi use of Romanian oil had been reduced by as much as 85% by the time the Russians occupied the fields in 1945. Hurting the Nazi resource base was a good idea, and the oil bombing campaigns did speed the end of the war. The Battle of the Bulge, in which the final German offense stalled for lack of fuel, is an oft-cited proof. However, starving the Nazi war machine of Romanian oil was as effectively accomplished by railhead interdiction and destroying rolling stock as it was by bombing production facilities in the oil fields themselves. (Except perhaps later in the war, when a comprehensive, near simultaneous campaign against production facilities within Germany had a devastating effect on supply. Therein, too, may lie an important lesson. Eradication will be more successful in hurting guerrilla finances to the extent it can be done massively and simultaneously throughout the county. This may be practically impossible until the expanse of crop areas and the complexity of the outlaw logistics routes is reduced.) The overall air effort in Europe can be said to have been most effective when it supported major allied ground operations by interdicting Wehrmacht operational reserves. The air campaigns had to be part of a broad effort that correctly identified various critical vulnerabilities and attacked as many as possible. For Nazi Germany to be defeated, the Allies had to close with and destroy the Wehrmacht on the ground. See Michael Hill, <u>Black Sunday: Ploesti</u> (London: Schiffer Publishing, 2001); See also Hart, B. H. Liddell, <u>History of the Second World War</u>, (New York: G.P. Putnam's Sons, 1970) pp. 607-608.; United States Air Force Museum, <u>WWII Combat Europe, Ploesti, Rumania Mission Details</u> online at http://www.wpafb.af.mil/museum/history/wwii/ce10.htm.

162

strategies are analogous in that massive aerial attack against the dense and extensive Putumayo coca crop was supposed to cause grave harm to the FARC's cocaine-based financial health -- just as the raid on Ploesti was to deprive the Nazi war machine of its supposed lifeblood. The strategy identified Putumayo, hardly the geographic center of gravity of the war in the traditional military sense, as the locus of a significant amount of the FARC's overall war-making strength. The long-term value of eradication spraying will, like the Ploesti raid, be ambiguous. Spraying achieves the immediately visible result of knocking out a lot of commercially valuable vegetation. The extent to which the outlaws shifted to other income sources, protected other crop areas, dispersed cultivation, replanted, improved the species genetically, shipped from storage, increased kidnapping and oil extortion, exerted political pressure to end the spray, or took other countermeasures is yet to be precisely calculated.[152] Aerial eradication makes it a little more difficult for the FARC, the ELN and the AUC to fund their respective wars, but they will do so.

Neither the raid on Ploesti nor Putumayo eradication were abject failures, even if they were not decisive blows. The costly experience at Ploesti led to better planned and executed follow-on operations that evolved with the broader counter-oil strategy. Like Ploesti, the coca field targeting may have been the result of the obvious. That is to say, oil field infrastructure in the WWII case, and coca plants in the Colombia case, stuck out in aerial photos, prompting a planning momentum too impatient for the painstaking identification

---

[152] These responses also show that eradication is having an effect, and more than mere annoyance. Still, the effect could be worse than the cure. See, for example Juan Londoño M., "Violencia, peor que la broca," (Violence, worse than the blight) El Tiempo, December 5, 2001. Describing the effect of the war on the traditional coffee growing region, the *eje cafetero*, Londoño reports on an increase in violence, including the robbery of whole shipments of coffee beans by the guerrillas. Such acts may be compensatory means of reacting to diminished coca revenues. They raise a question about fencing. In order to convert coffee beans to cash, the guerrilla organization must have in place the correct set of owned or extorted businesses, and/or the right array of government bribes.

of less dramatic and more disperse transportation nodes and infrastructure. Had there been a methodology in place able to precisely scale the relative economic-military value of European terrain, then perhaps the Ploesti fields themselves might never have been rated as an optimal target as compared, say, to railheads. In Colombia, while drug traffickers will use all means at their disposal for product shipment, cost constraints have them employ roads and rivers, probably in a measure consistent with the carrying capacity of the route.

The Putumayo eradication strategy recognized a place in Colombia as particularly valuable economically to the outlaw enemy, and therefore a valuable military target. Fortunately, the eradication plan also assisted the government in compromising a major enemy LOC. Unfortunately, the Putumayo spray plan, like the Ploesti bombing raid, was not based on a sufficient understanding of the relative economic value of terrain as a targeting guide. Nothing had been done, upon looking at the crop extension blobs, to find out in detail *who* owned the land on which those blobs appeared. When shown the crop extension plotting on government maps, we asked who owned the land where the coca was being grown. The question was met with incredulity. In fairness, it was also met with sufficient funding to determine the feasibility of answering the question. But US planners had incorrectly assumed that all the land was no-man's land, or that knowledge of personal ownership was unavailable or would be inherently unreliable. Furthermore, the Putumayo plan neglected to identify terrain that might have been more important in the overall value of the product than the fields themselves. It was not based on geographic visualization of natural resources to include transportation routes as of equal or greater importance as source locations. The importance of the coca plant itself was perhaps over-rated as a factor in the commercial value of cocaine. Consider another widely available product on which there can be some physical dependency -- water. Bottled water is an extremely lucrative offering in the United States, and, as some note with chagrin, bottled water can sell for more money than the soft drink on the shelf next to it, even though the water was drawn untreated right from a municipal water service. This might make one question the value of sugar, but neither should we be fooled into thinking the price is associated with the quality of the H$_2$O. The plastic in the bottle is not worth much either. If we wish to choke off water-profits from some ill-doing water-trafficker, we might try drying up the sources of water, perhaps because we can identify an offending lake or water main. Still, that strategy seems unlikely to succeed. It would be more efficient to knock off the truck on the way to the store. Where is the most valuable geography in the bottled-water industry? It is not the lake, but the bottling plant or some point on the road to the convenience store, or maybe the shelf in that store. The value of bottled water is the fact that it is found in a portable form *in the convenience store*, not that it is water. While this analogy is soon overdrawn, the question it highlights regarding relative geographic value -- route vs. ingredient source -- is valid. The coca fields are not as important as they appear in an aerial photo. They are more replaceable than other parts of the product-market geography. This question of relative geographic value is much more easily understood when land is considered as property.

Counter-terror has now displaced counternarcotics at center stage of official US policy toward Colombia.[153] Not long after 9/11/2001, the Pastrana government's negotiations with the FARC collapsed, and a new government, with a different approach to the conflict, was voted into power. Current Colombian President Alvaro Uribe Velez set Colombia on a more martial course toward defeating the FARC, ELN and the AUC. The Uribe government, generally compatible ideologically with the US Republican administration of President George W. Bush, and sensing a mandate from Colombian citizens to act aggressively toward Colombia's illegal armed groups, sought a change in US policy. The fictitious pre-9/11 dichotomy of counter-narcotics and counter-terror ended. Accordingly, one would

---

[153]For a more recent US government statement regarding the Colombian situation, except in counter-terrorism terms, see United States Department of State, Patterns of Global Terrorism, Department of State Publication 10940 (Washington: Office of the Secretary of State, 2002) pp. 45-47.

suppose that the principal US military objective in Colombia was no longer reduction of the amount of illicit drugs leaving the country. It would be to establish the security conditions for development of a regional ally where liberty and property are protected, material progress is a reasonable expectation for the majority, and, most of all (but hand in hand with these other goals), that Colombia not become a haven for growth and empowerment of terrorist organizations. If this does not misrepresent US policy, it means the US is assisting a Latin American ally to improve internal security that is threatened by organized armed foes. Whether or not these foes deserve the label *insurgents* is a question apart. The US and Europe have settled on defining them as terrorists. Countering illicit drugs became a subordinate mission, but remained a key objective. The illogic that caused Putumayo to be the geographic locus of US military assistance and aerial eradication to be the principal method had all but disappeared, but bureaucratic inertia retained their positions at the center of US efforts. According to some observers, operations and priorities at the US embassy were changing very slowly. If a shift had been ordered toward greater US support of Uribe's effort to destroy the terrorist organizations and away from counternarcotics, the change would be implemented slowly.

It was not an irrational approach to make aerial coca eradication the centerpiece of US counternarcotics assistance, given the constraint of the counternarcotics-counterinsurgency dichotomy. However, the impact of aerial eradication efforts will diminish over time in accordance with outlaw reaction. Eradication programs can, however, increase in effectiveness within the right strategic context and supported by the right kinds of knowledge. The selection of what and when to eradicate can be better informed, and the logic made more transparent. Aerial eradication, especially to the extent it is identified with the United States, should be armored against criticism of targeting decisions by incorporating absolute detail regarding land ownership, along with public transparency regarding the targeting decisions. It is now practicable to establish a matrix of use, ownership quality and applicable law that can indicate the most appropriate method and timing for eradication of illicit crops, even in areas where *minifundios* (very small land holdings) dominate. Such data can also be used to reveal anomalies in market prices, ownership interests by outlaw organizations and hidden political or familial associations, the ignorance of which might warp eradication decisions. It also provides legal and technical justification for taxation policy. Much of the information can be obtained now, although basic cartography, surveying and registry will have to be accomplished in many areas where illicit cultivation is pronounced. Such an approach is more compatible with heroin poppy cultivation because poppy is grown in the midst of other, licit crops; is grown on sloped terrain at higher altitude where spraying is more difficult; and is prevalent in areas of small land plots.

Giving Property Away

In 1999, to find a way out of what the Colombian government claimed was an impasse, Colombian President Andrés Pastrana agreed to concede to the FARC a piece of Colombian territory the size of Switzerland. The government withdrew forces from the area as an assurance of security in order to resume another round of peace negotiations. The results were dubious: in three years the FARC gave up nothing, and in the meantime exploited the natural military advantages of safely occupying a huge zone situated in the heart of the country.[154]

---

[154] The natural military advantages the FARC gained by occupying the *despeje* included interior lines, rear area security, protected lines of communication, protected financial resource bases, marshaling areas, training areas, and faster access to strategic corridors (including into the federal district of Bogotá). The propagandistic value cannot be understated, either, propaganda and operational strategy being at some point linked. The FARC had long made explicit arguments in favor of belligerent status under international law. See, for instance, "Beligerancia," FARC-EP Documentos at http://www.farc-ep.org/. As the FARC pointed out, application of the conventions (and with it a strengthened argument for separate and legitimate international identity) includes a requirement that the dissident armed force 'exercise such control over a part of its territory as to enable them to carry out sustained and concerted military operations ....' More important still is the very fact of participating in a peace process while carrying on its violent activities. Sitting at a peace

Protected interior lines allowed the FARC to increase its effective presence in areas around the zone, expanding the territory under its control. The *despeje* and the Pastrana peace process were so linked, that elimination of the *despeje* meant the end of the process and the political benefits to the FARC that went with it. It especially helped secure the FARC's southern line of communication out of Colombia into Ecuador and Peru. Within the *despeje* (clearing) as the area was called, the FARC was able to hide and manage its inventory of hostages, accelerate terrorist training and manufacture bombs and mines. Three Irish Republican Army (IRA) members were captured in Colombia after having been accused of providing training to FARC members there.[155]

By 2001, as it became obvious that the land concession to the FARC was a perfect failure, President Pastrana prepared to give an even more valuable zone to the smaller ELN.[156] Aside from dominating the most important transportation route in the country, the proposed zone, commonly known as the *Magdalena Medio* (Middle Magdalena), included a major coca crop concentration, as well as oil-industry infrastructure. Asked by a newsperson about his decision, Pastrana answered "The country needs to understand that the ELN is prepared to make peace, but if it doesn't happen, it is prepared to make

---

negotiation lent the FARC both legitimacy and media profile, especially overseas. Without the peace process, the FARC image diminished. See Armando Borrero Mansilla, "La importancia militar de la zona del despeje," El Tiempo, 19 October 2001, online at http://eltiempo.terra.com.co/19-10-2001/prip118531.html
[155] "Colombia details fresh IRA link to guerrillas," Financial Times, September 17, 2001, online at <http://ft.com. See also "IRA denies sending trio to Colombia," Agence France Presse, Wednesday, 19 September 2001, online at <http://www.prairienet.org/clm/clmnews_files/010919AFP01.html. The long-standing issue of Cuban government sponsorship of Colombian subversive groups should regain currency. See, for instance, Ninoska Pérez Castellón, "The Cuban Connection," Latin American Special Report Vol.12, No.11, 30 Sep 01, p. 1.
[156] "Mi única prioridad no es la paz." Interview with President Andrés Pastrana, Semana, February 26, 2001, p 30.

war. And it has a great terrorist capacity."[157]   In a nutshell, a national president stated that his countrymen must simply resign themselves to the fact that if he did not offer up the most important corner of land in the country to a group of outlaws, that group would hurt them.

The Magdalena River runs generally south to north between Colombia's central and eastern mountain ranges to the Atlantic coast. It is the single most important transportation corridor in Colombia and an essential artery to Bogotá. The middle reaches of the Magdalena have always been of particular strategic value, and are more so today because of a concentration of oil industry infrastructure. The southern bulb of Bolivar Department is home to a huge coca crop concentration. In recent years, the area became a battleground between the AUC and the ELN, with the AUC having gained the upper hand. Government-ceded control of the area would have been doubly advantageous. The area lies across vital lines of communication for Colombian economy. Impunity in the zone would have allowed uncontested access to the favorite object of extortion for that group: petroleum infrastructure. Proximity to taxable coca harvests, as well as major transportation routes make it a near-perfect staging area for taxation and kidnapping sorties. Physical dominion in the zone would also have given the ELN a spatial advantage in terms of attacking into the heartland area of the AUC to the west. Incredibly, and in light of no appreciable benefit to the nation from the experiment with the FARC's *despeje*, President Pastrana pushed to concede three counties to the ELN, two in the southernmost tip of Bolivar department and one in Antioquia just to the south of the others.[158]   A militarily more valuable piece of ground

---

[157] Ibid.

[158] These counties are Yondó, Antioquia, Cantagallo, Bolivar and San Pablo, Bolivar. The Magdalena River itself was not to be included and, according to President Pastrana, the time would be limited to nine months. For a detailed description of outlaw competition for the area, including a series of maps describing *Magdalena Medio*, see Vicepresidencia de la República, Programa actual del Magdalena Medio (Current Program on the Middle Magdalena) online at http://www.derechoshumanos.gov.co/observatorio/04_publicaciones/04_03_regiones/ magdalenamedio/index.htm; For a chronology of the Pastrana government's policy regarding the ELN, see also, Departamento de Comunicaciones, Oficina del Alto Comisionado de paz, Santa fé de Bogotá, Colombia, Hechos de Paz (Peace Facts)

could hardly have been chosen. The Colombian government plan to concede the area was blocked by protests from local residents, and the government could not deliver possession to the ELN, in good measure because of the AUC, which began to exert physical dominance in the zone. A public perception shift against the guerrillas created by the World Trade Center attacks later in the year contributed to killing the idea.[159] Perhaps because many Colombians saw the AUC as the only force effectively defending key Colombian territory, that illegal group gained significantly in political confidence and recruiting ability. The Pastrana government, meanwhile, verged on demoralization.

The 'Middle Magdalena' has been prized territory for hundreds of years.[160] Assuring that the reaches of the Middle Magdalena are strategically denied to the enemy is one of the basic elements of Colombian military history, whoever the contestants. Trying to give it away is a bizarre exception. The Colombian government's move to engage the ELN in peace talks by way of ceding such a militarily critical place is hard to fathom. One is led to suppose that President Pastrana and his advisors assigned more power and terrorist capacity to the ELN than it actually had, were overly committed to the concept of negotiation, were under some unspoken duress, sympathized with the guerrillas or simply did not understand. Accepting that the AUC is a drug trafficking, terrorist organization that the government is obliged to defeat and not help, it may have been strategically fortuitous for the government that the AUC rejected ELN occupation of the Middle Magdalena.

---

online at
http://www.hechosdepaz.gov.co/es/load.php/uid=0/leng=es/5/cronologia_eln00.htm
[159] Vicepresidencia de la República, Ibid.
[160] Thrusts to seize control of the big river mark most of Colombia's civil wars. Typical was an early incursion by Liberal (rebel) forces at the outset of the War of the Thousand Days. On October 24, 1899 at a mid-river turn called Los Obispos, a group of rebels led by Barranquilla doctor Julio Vengoechea sank one of their own paddleboats and watched the government gunboat Hercules sink the rest. The rebel plan to wrest the Middle Magdalena was well-conceived, but botched. See Geoffrey Demarest "War of the Thousand Days," Small Wars and Insurgencies, Vol. 12, No. 1 (Spring 2001), p. 7.

Comprehending the value and ownership of land as a function of divisible rights, rather than simple location, could offer a unique perspective on President Pastrana's policy. If the world had a map detailing particularized ownership interests in the Middle Magdalena, a whole new realm of understanding might attend the Pastrana position. If it were possible to view the whole picture of preferential rights in land that would have been transferred or jeopardized by a concession to the ELN, a better understanding might emerge of what was at stake. Most of the land in the region is privately owned and has been appraised.[161] Why there is an isolated blob of coca cultivation and how that cultivation relates geographically to oil industry licenses and concessions should be of particular interest. These questions are not posed out of historical curiosity. The land remains under coca, and is still under outlaw dominance.

A president giving land away to outlaws in huge chunks is a rare occurrence. More common is programmatic give-away. Land reform, and especially agrarian reform, has been a staple of developmental and redistributive campaigns in Colombia for decades. Since 1962 more than 1,700,000 hectares of land ceded to, bought or expropriated by the national government has been turned over to campesinos and tribal peoples.[162] More than 18,000,000 acres of

---

[161] Knowledge of ownership by plat in southern Bolivar Department would not likely point directly to those responsible for drug cultivation (although it might indeed). It is more likely that ownership information such as residency of absentee owners, or hometowns of mortgage banks might tend to prove or disprove territorial theories concerning the lack of material progress in the area. One popular hypothesis holds that the departmental capital is simple too distant from the southern cone of Bolivar. It would be interesting to see, by way of the property ownership records, what the relative connection of the agriculturalists in the area is to the departmental capital of Cartagena on the Atlantic coast. See Orlando Fals Borda, Región e Historia: Elementos sobre ordenamiento y equilibrio regional en Colombia (Bogota: Tercer Mundo, 1996) p. 9.

[162] Instituto Colombiano de la Reforma Agraria – Incora, Colombia Tierra y Paz: Experiencias y caminos para la reforma agraria, alternativas para el siglo XXI, 1961-2001, (Bogotá: Incora, 2002) p.174, 175. This work contains several essays relating the agrarian reform efforts of Incora to social problems, including violence, facing

government open land has also been redistributed.[163] Curiously, while this seems to be a great deal of land, officials from the national agrarian reform institute (Incora), stated that the distribution of land ownership in Colombia remains radically inequitable.[164] The validity of the observation may be the subject of considerable economic and social debate, but it is a debate conducted in the absence of needed data regarding what happened to all the redistributed land. Incora [now Incoder (Colombian Rural Development Institute)], claimed to be able to show every acre of land distributed to whom and when. What it apparently cannot show, at least for redistributions done until the last several years, is *where*. The Incora mandate was to redistribute, but not to keep track of redistributed land. For that reason, most Incora records indicate a precision of location only down to the county (*municipio*). Apparently there has also not been any systematic effort done to determine the consequences of ownership or divestment during more than forty years of redistributive activity.

Without asserting that Colombian government land redistribution has been a total failure or has contributed to violence, it is at least fair to say that all analyses of the effect of programmed redistributions in Colombia are anecdotal or speculative. Today, it is technically possible, using commercially available software, to match the Incora database with cadastral and registry information to determine the ownership results of the Incora programs and, more interestingly, to expose any geographic correlation of redistribution programs with the incidence of violence. It appears that some of the Incora land has to have been redistributed more than once, especially in lawless areas.

Colombia. The essays should be compared to those in an earlier Incora publication, Marta Rojas, editor, Tierra, Economía, y Sociedad (Bogota: Incora ,1993).
[163] Ibid p. 187.
[164] Author interview of Colombian government officials who requested anonymity. Incora is the acronym of the *Instituto Colombiano de la Reforma Agraria* (Colombian Institute for Agrarian Reform). Incora was liquidated and replaced by Incoder, *Instituto Colombiano de Desarrollo Rural* (Colombian Rural Development Institute). The name change reflects economic theory and ideology held by national leadership, but not one necessarily shared by the rank-and-file of that bureaucracy.

When the Colombian army reentered San Vicente Caguán in the former clearance zone in February 2002, it found that fleeing FARC units destroyed government offices, with the exception of the land registry office.[165] The records of land ownership did not show a rash of takings by the guerrillas and, apparently, land values had not changed appreciably (although they were extremely low to begin with). In Puerto Leguísamo, the local FARC commander demanded and accepted letters of introduction from the office of the Presidency to permit workers of the cartographic institute to complete cadastral formation for hundreds of agricultural properties in the area under its immediate control. One has to ask why the FARC would be willing to have the government formalize property ownership. The answer is troubling, considering the implication of accessorial behavior by the Colombian government. If the FARC has control of the occupiers, it can enforce a sharecropping relationship, force sale or mortgage, tax, etc., all while using government-provided records to facilitate and legitimatize its actions. It also acquires options if the area is overtaken by government troops or by another outlaw entity. In case of some interim or final negotiated settlement, the outlaw leadership has put in place the basis of legally controlling population and territory, the population controlled by feudal connections to the land, and the land controlled by a client population. The guerrilla leader thereby succeeds in becoming a great landowner, or *terrateniente*.[166] This circumstance was made more frustrating by a parallel legalistic movement to make land ownership databases unavailable to the public, to decrease transparency under a theory of privacy. Brigands gained government-approved access to the evidence of the social contract, while lawful users were denied it. It is not a civilizing formula. Brigands were, and to an extent still are, succeeding in a strategy to preserve their own anonymity and impunity while gaining the power of control that

---

[165] On the clearance zone or 'despeje' see Geoffrey Demarest, "In Colombia: A Guerrilla Sanctuary?," Military Review March-April, 2002, pp. 48-50.

property records convey. In essence, they gain control of the social contract and become the de-facto government. It is with the brigand that the occupier then settles his corner of a debased social contract.

Land appeasement has been discarded as a strategy in Colombia, probably for good. So has blind obedience to the simple categorization of malfactors as drugtrafficker, terrorist, subversive or insurgent. Both errors, appeasement and semantic diffidence, offer powerful arguments for the formalization of property as a long-term foundation for Colombian peace. Any government so detached from the social contract, so indifferent to its responsibility under the agreement regarding agreements, that it could simply forfeit huge tracts of land to a criminal organization, without even a nominative intervention on the part of the courts, is simply not a democratic government in the Western sense. Imagine the Leavenworth County commissioners attempting to cut a deal with a gang of criminals by giving them a section or two of the county, oblivious of the rights of the affected landowners. As for defining the enemy, the government's strategic design does not have to depend on any particular taxonomy beyond that which helps locate lawbreakers on the ground. Except as it helps to order forensic and military predictions, it does not matter whether they are drug traffickers, kidnappers, murderers or thieves. They have surnames and addresses, and their relatives have addresses. And they all covet places. Transparency in knowing what persons are connected to what places is a strategic fact that can be created in order to protect the civilized from the predators.

Harvest of amputees

It would be an unresponsive oversight to touch on the military situation in Colombia in a book about property without addressing the poignant ecological disaster of land mines. In Colombia, the presence

---

[166] The translated denotation of the word *terrateniente* is landowner, but the connotation for some, especially in Colombia, is of an arrogant holder of more land than justice should permit.

of landmines (or improvised explosive devises, IED, to use the more generalized term) may actually be expanding as a result of government success against its guerrilla enemies in the past few years, and decisions of the latter to resort to the use of these inexpensive weapons.[167] According to local authorities, it costs the guerillas, who plant the vast majority of explosive artifacts, about 2 to 4 dollars per mine, while it costs the government between $4,500 and $8,000 to remove one and repair the damage caused. As the Colombian army advances out into more remote areas in attempts to pursue the guerrilla, the relative advantage of costs favors the guerrilla even more. One in three of the deaths that the FARC inflicts on government soldiers is by way of landmine detonations. Meanwhile, landmine injuries are most often suffered exactly in those parts of the country where the rule of law and the presence of the state is weakest. Conversely, it is more costly to implement formal property regimes in some corners of Colombia where it is most needed, due to the presence of landmines.

While landmines have been strewn at one time or another in 30 of the 32 Colombian departments, they are present today in about half of the 1098 *municipios* (counties), and between 40 and 50 of these *municipios* suffer an alarming density related to tactical or strategic value in the context of the internal war. (See figure5) These 40-50 *municipios* can be seen as the geographic center of armed conflict in Colombia, and there is hardly a need to argue the negative effect that the presence of antipersonnel mines have on the market value of a piece of farmland. Still, in the context of reoccurring combat and the impositions of competing armed forces, the fact of landmines descends to being just another dimension of the violence. The numbers for victims of landmines are not as immediately alarming as those for kidnapping and murder. "Only" about 2,600 victims (about a third civilians) have fallen in Colombia to landmines in the last decade, but the direct effect on land and security is enormous. It is by no means clear that the economic and social assistance programs directed at

---

[167] See, for instance Jineth Bedoya Lima, "Minas: se creció la amenaza" (Mines: the threat increased) El Tiempo 7 Mar 2004, p. 1,2.

Figure 5 Colombian minefields

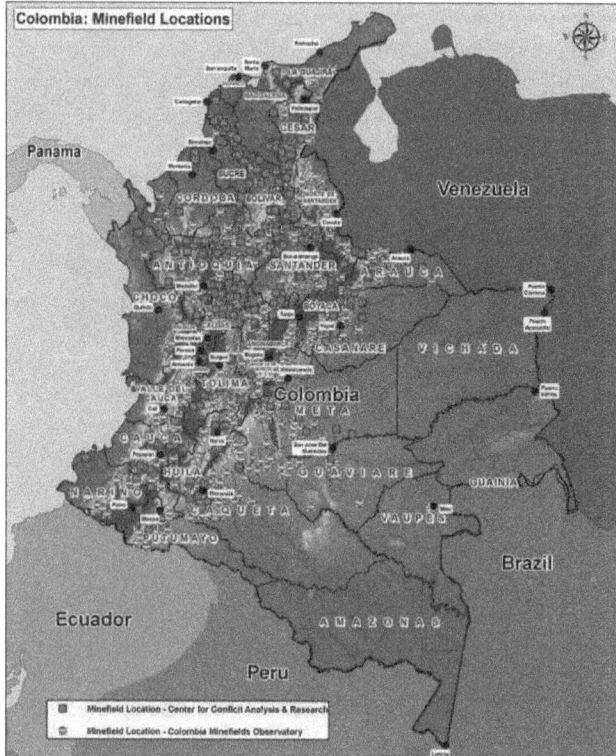

Composed from two data sources: The private Resource Center for the Study of
Conflict (CERAC) and the Colombian Government Minefields Observatory.

Colombia as a country in conflict have had the geographic precision that the landmines have. In other words, it seems, from comparative georeferencing of land mines and aid programs, that the *municipios* most affected by the war are not those in which the programs have been attempted. The reasons may be entirely valid; it is difficult to send a Peace Corp volunteer out to build a fishpond if it would be irresponsible risk to his or her life. But a more geographically rational application of aid and government presence is undoubtedly possible and would include an initial respect for the need to maximize the quality of property in and around (or perhaps first around and then in) the most affected conflict locales.

Landmines are arguably the worst ecological blight currently faced by Colombia, and are inseparably connected to the conflict. They are to an extent correlated to high-concentration natural resource locations, processing zones and movement corridors, but such correlation can be misleading because the mines are also planted on terrain that has specific value in the context of competitive military maneuvering and tactics (especially escape routes). As a result, the presence of landmines affects the value of Colombian land generally as well as specifically.

Landmines have been used to a limited extent by the government of Colombia to protect military bases and fixed pieces of strategically valuable infrastructure. However, the use of landmines by criminal groups has been far more extensive, undisciplined, cruel and environmentally destructive, especially as it affects less concentrated natural resources such as agriculture. Illegal armed groups plant mines in the context of three principle tactics: to hamper access to fixed locations of value such as a cocaine base laboratory, a gas siphoning point, a logistics cache or a base camp; to slow government pursuit during a withdrawal; and for offensive ambushes against enemy forces. These uses almost never entail recovery of the mines by the illegal groups. They make records of the locations of emplaced mines only when they plan to return quickly to the same locale. The result is an insidious danger civilian populations.

The Colombian landmine environmental challenge appears to be solvable, but at the present time, given the ongoing conflict and the continued sowing of landmines by outlaw groups, there does not appear to be much near-term prospect of solving the frightening imposition of these artifacts.[168]

> Out of a total of 1,097 Colombian municipalities, 140, in 22 of the 31 departments, were the scene of accidents or incidents involving landmines during the ten first months of 2001. In other words, there are anti-personnel mines scattered in 12.8 per cent of Colombia's municipalities. The department worst hit is undoubtedly Arauca. Not only has the highest number of victims been recorded there, but five out of its seven municipalities (71.4 percent) have seen accidents or incidents associated with anti-personnel mines. In Antioquia the number of municipalities affected is 34, most of them in the east and south of the department, on a geographical zone stretching into the departments of Santander and Norte de Santander, where accidents or incidents have taken place in 13 and 11 municipalities respectively.[169]

In Colombia the terrain calculus is immensely intricate and local, each hectare presenting its own mix of military and economic value. Reconciling the two (what we might call the maneuver view of terrain and the economic view) for the purpose of shaping strategy is

---

[168] See, for instance, "Objectivo: mutilar" (Objective: mutilate), El Tiempo. May 31, 2004, p. 234.

[169] "Geography of Anti-personnel Mines in Colombia," in Anti-Personnel Mines in Colombia (Bogotá: Presidential Program for Human Rights and International Humanitarian Law, 2001), p. 7., online at <http://www.derechoshumanos.gov.co/observatorio/04_publicaciones/04_02_temas/minas/minasingles.pdf.

crucial. The government of Colombia, with US assistance, could produce a comprehensive, detailed database of Colombian land use, relative value and ownership. As Chapter One argued, the most important determinant of the market value of real property may be the mix of theoretical rights associated with the land, along with the practical effect government enforcement gives to those rights. This is not an abstract comment on political philosophy. The market price of a piece of land in Colombia is closely correlated to the basket of rights attendant to it. The farm's longitude and latitude are important, but not as important as the mix of rights associated with it. Just listing and formalizing the understanding of those rights, however, is not enough to give them their entire value. If the police cannot or will not prevent the use of an empty lot as a place where drug dealers convene, the market value of the houses nearby may plummet. Likewise, if potential buyers of Juan Valdez' farm cannot travel the road to his farm without being assaulted or kidnapped, the farm's market value will be almost nil. And if it is seeded with landmines, the value might be less than nil.

Can the war be won militarily?

"The meek shall inherit the earth, but not its mineral rights."[170]
J. Paul Getty

Whether or not an insurgency can be won military is one of those recurring, vapid debate questions. Can Colombia's internal war be concluded by military means? The military part can, although there are many *ifs* that qualify a yes answer from the government point of view. It is a bizarre world in which an illegal armed organization can march thousands of uniformed soldiers around in a country, mount artillery attacks against government installations and resistant towns, move millions of dollars of materiel along thousands of miles of logistics routes, maneuver battalions, assert that it will take power by

---

[170] Attributed, see
http://quotes.telemanage.ca/quotes.nsf/quotes/1e76651eda7247098525697f008307b4

force--and still successfully finesse an argument to an international audience that there is no way for anyone to win the war militarily. "Resistance is futile." The vast majority of Colombians is fed up with the leftist guerrillas and their 'paramilitary' opponents, and lately became willing to make sacrifices to physically eliminate these groups. At the time of this writing, the Colombian government was attempting to translate this willingness into action. Upon coming to office in 2002, President Alvaro Uribe, rejecting defeatist analyses, set out to make peace negotiations something desperately needed by the illegal armed groups, rather than something hopelessly sought after by the government. The results have been significant.

> Analysis of our new, 16-year dataset on the Colombian civil war finds under Uribe: guerrilla and paramilitary attacks dropping sharply to long-run averages since 1988, lower for April- December, 2003; government-guerrilla clashes at all-time highs, exceeding guerrilla attacks; civilian killings dropping sharply and continuously to all-time lows, mainly from decreased paramilitary attacks; combatant killings rising sharply to all-time highs; guerrilla tactics shifting toward indiscriminate attacking, forcing civilian injuries to long-run highs; government-to guerrilla casualty ratios in clashes falling; government-paramilitary clashes increasing but still uncommon; paramilitary performance in clashes poor and worsening; guerrilla-paramilitary clashes dropping sharply; the ELN seriously weakened, mounting few attacks.[171]

---

[171] Jorge Restrepo and Michael Spagat. The Colombian Conflict: Uribe's First 17 Months. London: Royal Holloway College, University of London, 2004; For a Latin American analysis of the Colombian government conduct of the war, see César Bartolomé, Mariano. La Evolución del Conflicto Colombiano durante la Presidencia de Álvaro Uribe. Buenos Aires: Centro de Estudios Estratégicos, 2004ñ For the Colombian government statistics on violence in Colombia visit Casa de Nariño, Presidencia de la Repúbica Colombiana, online at <http://www.presidencia.gov.co/documentos/documentos.htm.

Respecting the above-noted success, if the government of Colombia does not win militarily, efforts to formalize property in service of long-term peace are shortchanged. As long as organized elements wield sufficient power to disregard the law at all levels, reform of the law itself will matter little. Debate about the possibility or efficacy of military victory can be discarded out-of-hand. Promoting the rule of law through formal property means establishing a way to avoid the condition of possession by force. The existence of multiple, large, organized, competing armed claimants within the same geographic space defines a condition of forceful competition for possession. The only property agreement in which the illegal armed groups have shown interest is that they have more. The Colombian government is in the process of building and improving a liberal property regime, but as part of that very contract it must defang armed trespassers.

Crossing Lines of Communication

Colombia's extravagant geography guides decision-making more than in most other countries. As noted earlier, the history of Colombian conflict is a record of competition for control of lands and movement routes related to export products or their taxation.[172] Rebels, pirates and their hybrids, arrayed against the Colombian state and each other, have forever fought over control of product sources, transportation routes, taxation and fiscal policies bearing on Colombia's natural bounty.

The author does not cite illicit drug profits as the characteristic distinguishing the current struggle from those of Colombia's past,

---

[172] On the history of agricultural and extractive products as a factor in Colombian see, for instance, Frank Safford & Marco Palacios, Colombia: Fragmented Land, Divided Society (New York: Oxford University Press, 2002); See also, generally, Indalecio Lievano Aguirre, Los Grandes Conflictos Sociales y Economicos de Nuestra Historia (Bogotá: Círculo de Lectores, 2002).

although this is clearly important to the scale of the problem. Rather, the key difference between today's civil conflict and its predecessors is the imported nature of the ideological base of the rebel (FARC and ELN) projects. The ostensible argument of the guerrillas is not rooted in the traditional Colombian federalist – anti-federalist debate, but rather in class struggle. It may be that the un-Colombian nature of the argument is part of the reason that the guerrilla has seemed to loose ideological compass. Interestingly, there is a new and growing body of political literature in Colombia that emphasizes regional and territorial issues, advocating the reshuffling of administrative political units of the state. Even those writings inspired by socialism seem less taken by class-consciousness than by the traditional Colombian centrifugal quarrel.

While the current civil conflict differs in significant ways from those of the past, the correlation of outlaw strategies to agricultural and mineral geography is the same, often exactly the same.[173] Leaders of today's FARC, ELN and AUC are intimately aware of the effects that the control of 'place' has on profit and on prospects for their long-term organizational health. Like the classic combat commanders, the Alexanders and Napoleons, a successful outlaw strategist recognizes the critical advantage of choosing favorable fighting terrain, protecting his lines of communication (LOCs) and compromising those of his enemy. In Colombia, he must also be sensitive to the relative

---

[173] See, for instance, 'Conflicto, Autonomia Regional y Socialismo Ecológico,' (Conflict, Regional Autonomy and Ecological Socialism) or 'Descentralizar para Pacificar' (Decentralize to Pacify) in Agenda Ciudadana, Las claves territoriales de la guerra y la paz, desarrollo regional, participación ciudadana y agenda de paz (The territorial clues to the war and peace, regional development, citizen participation and the peace agenda) (Bogotá: Agenda Ciudadana y Cátedra para la Paz, 2000); Jaime Castro, La Question Territorial (Bogotá, Oveja Negra, 2002); and Orlando Fals Borda, Kaziyadu: Registro del Reciente Despertar Territorial en Colombia (Kaziyadu: Record of the recent territorial awakening in Colombia) (Bogotá: Ediciones desde abajo, 2001); Alejo Vargas, "La guerra por el control territorial," (The war for territorial control) El Espectadorain , 17 Nov, 1998, p. 4A; "Guerrilla exigirá derecho a gobernar territorios" (The guerrillas will demand right to govern territories) El Espectador, 16 Nov, 1998, p. 6A.

commercial and industrial value of property and movement routes. Likewise, any winning government strategy seeking to defeat the outlaw, or for that matter, to establish long-term social peace in Colombia, must discover and respect the essential worth of land. Colombia's terrain cannot be considered only in terms of physical defense and attack, but also according to its material value. This marks a difference between internal armed conflict and international war. Especially in Colombia, land is not only a space over which materiel moves, or where firefights occur, it is an engine of disposable wealth and wellspring of the war-making strength of all the contending forces.[174] Moreover, the performance grade given to Colombia's national armed forces always includes a human rights component, yet it is failure on the part of the State to give meaning to property rights that leads to human rights violations. If the Colombian State is ever to clarify the human rights issue touching their armed forces, it must better understand and improve the contract between citizens and government that is called 'property.'

The Colombian FARC opted decades ago for wide dispersion of its subordinate units.[175] This was done not only for reasons related to the autonomous, obstreperous nature of guerrilla commanders, but also as a method to deny the Colombian army the opportunity for battles of annihilation. For the sixty-odd FARC fronts, organized into seven

---

[174] For a brief description of Colombia's current 'contending forces,' their methods and goals, see generally Max G. Manwaring, Nonstate Actors in Colombia: Threat and Response (Carlisle, PA: Strategic Studies Institute, US Army War College, 2002).

[175] Numerous unclassified maps of FARC dispositions have been published in recent years. Among the best see Alvaro Valencia Tovar, "Ubicación Cuadrillas FARC," in Inseguridad y Violencia en Colombia (Bogotá: Universidad Sergio Arboleda, 1997) p. 126; "Localización de los frentes guerrilleros (1995)," in Jesus Antonio Bejarano Avila, Colombia: Inseguridad, violencia y desempeño económico en las areas rurales, ibid. p. 119; Angel Rabasa & Peter Chalk, "Figure 4.3, Areas of Expansion of FARC Activity1996-1997," in Colombian Labyrinth: The Synergy of Drugs and Insurgency and Its Implications for Regional Stability (Santa Monica, CA: RAND, 2001) p. 49.; a map image is also available only from "The Center for International Policy's Colombia Project," at <http://www.ciponline.org/colombia/farcmap.htm.

blocks, logistics has been a primary occupation. For some fronts the most lucrative activity may be taxation of coca farmers, but in others perhaps the control of kidnapping contractors, or movement of weapons is more important. The fronts are also encouraged toward the FARC's strategic objective of controlling urban centers. To achieve this, FARC fronts work toward systematically influencing and eventually controlling movement corridors (lines of communication) into assigned cities.[176] Some cities, such as Medellín in Antioquia Department, are susceptible to being choked and extorted because their mountainous environs so constrict access.[177] Much of the combat responsibility, as well as maintenance of discipline among the fronts, falls to mobile columns, which have a wider geographic range.

In order to maximize security and for economy of force, the FARC created networks of movement corridors within the blocks, and mobility corridors between the blocks. Some of these routes follow standard road and river transportation infrastructure and are used to move large quantities of illicit product. Secondary routes are more often used for the movement of units and materiel. In mountainous areas it is common that the routes follow ridgelines. The FARC has worked to control owners and ownership of properties all along the movement and mobility corridors (it is suspected that this is especially true along remote ridge line routes), thus helping to assure operational

---

[176] See Thomas Marks, Colombian Adaptation to FARC Insurgency, (Carlisle, Pennsylvania: Strategic Studies Institute, U.S. Army War College, 2002) p. 16.
[177] A 1961 US Army field manual on irregular war states, "Surface lines of communication which have proved particularly vulnerable to attack and sabotage should be abandoned, at least temporarily, if at all possible. Long surface lines of communication cannot be completely protected against a determined irregular force without committing an excessive number of troops." Department of the Army Field Manual, FM31-15, Operations Against Irregular Forces (Washington: Headquarters, Department of the Army: 1961) p. 23. However sound this advice might have been in the context of the conflicts contemplated by the authors at the time, this would be disastrous advice for the Colombian situation, and is rejected here. Colombia's urban centers are dependent on a limited number of long-haul road routes. Colombia has the material wherewithal to not abandon legal commerce to its fate on the nations major highways.

security. Lately, the FARC is known to have assisted in the formalization of property holdings by peasants under their direct control in active drug cultivation areas, one being the Puerto Leguísamo area in Putumayo.[178] Additionally, there have been repeated rumors that the guerrillas have effectively purchased mineral mines. Labor tactics, selective extortion and bribery can be supported by using cutouts to gain control of licenses or by surrounding publicly owned mineral extraction sites with peasant clients and then formalizing the ownership of those properties.[179]

The FARC does not enjoy widespread mass support in the Colombian population, even in rural areas. It has, however, carefully proselytized or terrorized in select locales related to its nation-wide, logistics-based strategy. Meanwhile, the AUC, a newer force, appears to have a varied popular support base greatly exceeding that of the FARC -- but less so along many of the movement corridors for which the AUC and guerrillas fight. Apposite with the property discussion is AUC heritage, that organization having been born of the frustration of ranchers at the failure of the government to protect their rural properties from the FARC. A difficult political issue was born once the illegal character of the AUC became evident and less tolerable to the government: how to confront that kind of outlaw force as compared to the traditional guerrilla groups. The spawning of the anti-guerrilla paramilitary was an outgrowth of the failure or inability of the state to meet an obligation to protect persons and property from predation. It can be cogently argued that a local paramilitary defense structures is, if not a requirement for winning an irregular war, at least an historically

---

[178] Personal interview of the author in February, 2002 with government officials who requested anonymity.

[179] Colombia's outlaws have property-awareness. They know what property is most valuable and they know that property is a relationship between land, people and government. They know further that accurate records help govern. Outlaw leaders, especially guerrilla, understand property as a contract between government and people -- but they want that contract to exist between Colombia's countrymen and themselves, not the democratically constituted government the US supports.

successful element.[180] From the American historical perspective, it is also something honored and protected constitutionally. The legitimacy, establishment, or discipline of community defense organizations, of militia, are beyond the purposes of this essay; nevertheless, the debate rarely proceeds except in total ignorance regarding on-the-ground land ownership facts. Until recently this ignorance permeated debate about what kind of strategy to apply in Colombia's war. The Colombian government has moved in the direction of strategic property knowledge.

The observation that guerrilla forces, at the sight of potential government victories, can slouch back into a latency of civilian garb and popular protection impels an argument for community organizations that can spot and will report guerrilla presence. Having said that, an apparently grassroots movement of resistance to guerrilla violence bloomed in a few areas, and this phenomenon may present a vehicle for local organized resistance to outlaws in select areas.[181] The question, therefore, of local militias has not disappeared, and US posture regarding their creation could be better informed by facts on the ground.

The appearance of the AUC is attributable in some measure to the failure of the Colombian government to establish effective discipline and to crisply delineate the authority and range of initiative accorded to civil defense groups. The juridical turn in Colombia against legal establishment of militias can be blamed on excesses in militia vigilantism, to put it mildly, as well as to the fact that the paramilitaries were effective in opposing the leftist guerrilla, this effectiveness not setting well with elements within the State apparatus

---

[180] See, for instance, Spencer, supra. note 4;

[181] See Susannah A. Nesmith, "Colombian Rebels Face New Adversary," Associated Press, Thursday, 3 January 2002, online at <http://www.prairienet.org/clm/clmnews_files/020103AP01.html; "Rebeldes con causa," Semana, Noviember19-26, 2001, No. 1,020, p. 32; "La Resistencia," Semana, Noviembere19-26, 2001, No. 1,020, p. 54.

sympathetic to the guerrilla.. Moreover, the virulence of the self-defense movement can be associated more broadly with two factors. One is the failure of the Colombian state to defeat and remove the guerrillas, which became the *raison d'etre* [[of the AUC. The second is the lack of commitment to destroy the illicit drug industry, which provides autonomous financial power to groups like the AUC and corrupts the enforcement regime. Had the government of Colombia reformed the controls and linkages over the several types of authorized militias, and maintained a participation in their existence and discipline, it is less likely they would have turned into the drug trafficking mafias that they have. Because many in and outside Colombia consider the establishment of a militia system to be an effective and legitimate part of counter-guerrilla strategy, it behooves US planners to be informed about the home communities and memberships of future militias and vigilante groups. Such information can be optimally gleaned from census, cadastral and land registry records. Naturally, when the Uribe government entered into peace negotiations with the AUC, that organization sought to stabilize and legalize possession of lands it had extorted. [182] All of a sudden knowing where the relevant properties were located and who were the rightful owners became a significant question.

Conceivably, the historical and geographic bases of the struggle between the FARC and the AUC could be painted using existing cadastral maps by tracing back to relevant ranch properties. Furthermore, the property-based origins and purposes of the AUC logically drive it to augment formal ownership of land in areas it considers strategically important. This is not true of rural areas only. Recent urban combat among the FARC, AUC, ELN and lesser groups in the city of Medellín seem to attest to the selective importance of commercial property and its relationship to rural terrain. Combat between outlaw groups in Medellín broke out over control of the major land route to the Urabá Gulf and Atrato River Valley lowlands to the

---

[182] See, for instance, "Los senores de la tierra," <u>Semana</u>. #1,152, May 31. This is one of the most significant articles published on the conflict in Colombia In recent years.

northwest.[183] The Urubá/Atrato area represents a major illicit logistics corridor. If the corridor were better controlled by the government, the fighting in Medellín would logically not have occurred. Contest of the route between outlaw groups would be mooted if control were already lost to the government in the rural region to the northwest. To attain control, the government will have to pursue a strategy that recognizes land ownership as a key element. Formal, visible and protected property rights be the foundation of long-term government presence in the area of Colombia facing Panama. Until that is achieved the area will be outlaw in all respects, and Medellín will continue to suffer periodic violent eruptions. People of the Urubá/Atrato lowlands are likely to continue suffering forced displacements and mass killings.[184]

Along the same general axis in Antioquia, a secondary network of rural transportation routes runs through the Dabeiba, Peque and Ituango municipalities to the west of the Cauca River. It is a major confrontation area between the AUC and the guerrillas. Warfare imposed and suffered in this mountainous sub-region encapsulates the nature of the conflict in Colombia. Almost all combat, human rights cases and criminal encounters relate to the dominance of passage routes used for illicit purposes. Putting a stop to intra-outlaw combat in the area will require a greater presence of government military force in order to physically deny use of the zone's passes for illicit product shipment. To pacify the region in the long-term, however, may require a change in the mix and quality of real property ownership. There are few proven treatments for the kind of social poisoning that years of ruthless competition for the control of land causes. One antidote is to redistribute populations and property ownership. The Colombian

---

[183] "Milicias se pelean a Medellín," El Tiempo, 23 May 2002, p.1, 2.
[184] The Atrato area has been an especially unfortunate victim of mass civilian suffering and death. One of the worst human rights offenses of the war occurred in late April, 2002 at Bojayá in Chocó Department. In the context of a battle with the AUC for control of the area (the same general confrontation as that in Medellín) the FARC launched a gas cylinder mortar/rocket that detonated in a packed church killing at least 110 persons outright. See "Crece la pesadilla en Bojaya," El Tiempo, Bogotá, May 8, 2002, p.1.

government may decide to embark on programs changing ownership of land in local areas most affected by the violence, perhaps by empowering ethnic communities and better securing communal land rights, or perhaps by encouraging private ownership by persons and organizations more likely and capable of resisting outlaw incursions. Regardless of the details, any land-oriented part of a solution will depend for integrity on precise, electronically available, complete records of ownership interests at key locations. Precision lends juridical strength to the documentation, as well as future market confidence. Electronic availability (transparency) helps proof the ownership documentation against fraud and corruption, and allows individuals and non-governmental organizations to monitor land policies.

The value of terrain for illicit uses is heightened in many locales, like the Peque-Ituango passes; nevertheless, many properties will be abandoned or subject to forfeiture. These need to be identified in detail, but visible at a strategic level so that the evolution of ownership serves a peace-intending initiative of the government rather than outlaw competitiveness. If the government does not mount a national property strategy that helps placate the cycle of violence, property strategies mounted by outlaw groups will continue to catalyze it.

The notion of moving the illegal armed groups off the local beat, that is, identifying individual *municipios* where outlaw presence has been the norm and then concentrating on the civilizing of those counties is not an obvious or necessarily effective strategy. A counter argument may be, extrapolating from arguments about illicit drug cultivation, that moving the illegal armed groups out of one *municipio* only causes the effect of moving it to another. Within some range of geographic possibilities this may contain some truth, but it is limited by the relative strategic importance and military advantages of the geographies themselves. The reasons that a particular *municipio* is hotly contested generally derive from an advantage of movement or protection due to isolation, routes of escape, logistical lines of

189

communication, etc. The *municipios* of Florida and Pantera in southern Valle de Cauca Department are being proposed by the FARC (summer 2007) as suitable areas for renewed exchange agreements with the government and that those counties be cleared of government military presence. No wonder, since, as many government military analysts will point out, the two counties are hubs of outlaw clandestine lines of communication. Much of the calculus of geographic importance is founded on economics and business principles related to both legal and illegal activities. As noted earlier, Colombians have forever fought over exportable or comercializable natural resources and the routes products and input materials must follow to market and from supplier. Labor often features as an input that causes difficult and complex competition but still has clear geographic referents. (As an aside, but one that bears on the understanding of the relation of property and strategy, it is a shame that outlaw leaders and their apologists have been able to convince the legitimate government that it is a good idea to provide government service infrastructure to populations of coca pickers in areas of the country where there had not previously been a population.)

Another set of variables influencing the strategic value of terrain in Colombia is that set imposed by the warfare itself. Maneuvering, supplying and discipline of forces displays a geographic imprint that, while intimately related to the other variables of terrain value, is not exactly the same. Some of the geographic consequences and their relation to the question of property are discussed a bit further on, but immediately relevant is the following, Yogi Berra-like point: The next best places for outlaw survival -- once they are moved out of the best places for them to survive -- are not as good! In predictable increments it takes them longer to supply, is harder for them to communicate, harder to escape a government pursuit, more difficult to collect rents and extortion payments, more difficult to fulfill delivery contracts, more difficult to pay debts, kidnap victims, etc. Eventually, failure to hold the best terrain is tantamount to defeat, and in Colombia, because of the exaggerated accidents of terrain, the next-best terrain, militarily speaking, is often much worse than the best. For this reason the Colombian government ultimately decided on a security strategy designed to cut of guerrilla supply lines.

"Por primera vez en la historia del país todos sus municipios tienen Policía. Se trata también de cortar el paso en 12 zonas que antes eran dominio de grupos armadas."[185]

(For the first time in the history of the country all of its counties have police. That also cuts movement in 12 zones that before had been the domain of armed groups.)

Compare the above headline to the following from an article in Semana magazine about forced land sales and extortions:

"La presión de los paramilitares también se ha dado en Antioquia. Por ejemplo, en las áreas aledañas al túnel de occidente y del Nuevo trazado de la vía al mar los lugareños aseguran que ha habido una active compraventa de tierras asociada, en varios casos, a situaciones de desalojo o negocios bajo presión de miembros de estos grupos que operan en esta parte occidente del departamento."[186]

The pressure of the paramilitaries has also been felt in Antioquia. For example, in areas surrounding the western tunnel of the new stretch of the road to the sea, the locals assure that buying and selling of land has been active, this associated in several cases to situations of eviction or negotiations under the pressure of these groups that operate in the western part of the department.

---

[185] "Bloqueo a corredores de Farc" (FARC Corridors Blocked) El Tiempo March 4, 2004, p. 1-2.
[186] "Los senores de la tierra," Semana, supra note 78 at p. 227.

For outlaw groups, dominating special areas is not simply a matter of mastering military aspects of terrain, although these factors still matter. More important in the context of internal war and territorial competition among illegal armed groups is the control of rights associated with particular pieces of land. Whether extorted purchase, planned squatting, or more legalistic methods, criminal groups gain much of their control using the social and legal mechanisms in existence. Likewise, organized violence can be traced even if the records and property standards are not perfectly formalized.

Taking property away

The whole array of Colombia's ills cannot all be explained as a failure to develop a civilizing property regime. The assertions made at the outset of Chapter One, however, are reinforced and amplified by reference to almost every facet of disorder and violence there. One of those assertions extolled the power of property information for its forensic value. Looking at the cocaine industry, one can see how real property records quickly become "actionable" intelligence.

> "Después de la extradición, si algo temen los grandes narcotraficantes es la confiscación de sus propiedades. Más que la fumigación de cultivos ilícitos, que se pueden resembrar; la destrucción de laboratorios, que se pueden reconstruir, o el decomiso de un cargamento mientras otros 'coronan', lo que golpea de modo más rotundo al narcotráfico es que el producto de sus fortunas mal habidas pase a manos del Estado."[187]

---

[187] El Tiempo, "Las incautaciones de propiedades son golpes que duelen a los narcotraficantes." El Tiempo online April 20, 2004 at <http://eltiempo.terra.com.co/opinion/reda/2004-04-20/ARTICULO-WEB-_NOTA_INTERIOR-1588716.html.

(Next to extradition, if there is something that the big
drug traffickers fear it is the confiscation of their
properties. More than fumigation of illicit crops, which
can be replanted; destruction of drug labs, which can be
rebuilt; or capture of shipments while others make up
the difference, what hits the drug trafficker hardest is
that the product of his ill gotten gains passes into the
hands of the state.)

The above paragraph began a recent editorial in El Tiempo, Bogotá's
leading newspaper regarding a sea change in progress that occurred in
just the past year or so. According to the article, between 1996 and
2000 only fourteen successful forfeitures of property against major
drug dealers occurred, while in 2002 and 2003 one hundred eighteen
were completed, moving almost 2,800 real estate locations into
government hands. Just two years ago the forfeiture law in Colombia
was all but toothless and in doubt, but suddenly the war against drug
dealing in Colombia seems to have improved on an immensely
effective weapon. Asset forfeitures, which obviously depend on
ownership data, quickly come to mind as a law enforcement advantage
of a modern property system, but there are other forensic applications.
In Colombia, the possibilities are mixed, and reflect the varied and
incomplete nature of the property regime in that country.

The immediacy and deadliness of violence make reflection on
the benefits of civilized records seem a luxurious impertinence in a
place like Colombia. But the actions made available by formal records
include the legal forfeiture of property belonging to guerrilla,
paramilitary and drug cartel leaders. Relationships and affinities can be
determined that expose the structure of illegal organizations, or even to
anticipate whereabouts, leading to arrest or destruction. How this can
be done -- where information is made available on a precise,
comprehensive basis -- is suggested by the results of the experiment
described by the series of images below. The same kind of linking
sequence, if played out at the regional or national scale, would be able
to expose criminal affinities, real property wealth of known criminal

organizations, geographic strategies of outlaw organizations, or aberrations in market prices that often indicate money laundering or extortions. It would also aid in prioritizing illicit crop eradication, or in identifying optimal targets for police questioning. These are not speculative uses. Cadastral data is already a staple source of forensic information in jurisdictions in the United States where property is already formalized and information is readily available.

Can the war be won politically?

> *Los señores de la tierra: Grupos paramilitares se están apoderando, a sangre y fuego, de las tierras más valiosas del país. Las víctimas están desesperadas y no tienen quien le devuelva su patrimonio.* [188]
>
> (The landlords: Paramilitary groups are grabbing, by gunfire and bloodletting, the most valuable landholdings in the country. The victims are desperate and can look to no to return their inheritance to them.)
>
> <u>Semana</u>

The shape of the problem

Above is the title of the cover story of <u>Semana</u> magazine for early June 2004. It is an old story in Colombia. Many landowners across a broad gamut of economic means fold or die under the extortion of armed groups. A wave of forced sales was the work of armed militias whose claimed ideological position was anti-communist. This is to say they can be identified as not the guerrilla groups traditionally identified with armed leftist social revolution. Not too much more can be stated regarding any ideological or political color they might take. They simply take. The political left in Colombia clamors to accuse and demand redress, but they do not claim it is something the leftist

---

[188] "Los señores de la tierra," <u>Semana</u>, supra note 78 at p. 224.

194

guerrillas have not also done, and would do more of if it weren't for the physical will of the paramilitaries to prevent them. Many Colombians look at the situation and bleat, or shrug fatalisms and cynicisms, not able to imagine a course in which the power of the civilized state will reach all parts of their compartmentalized and federalized country. This Semana article is a watershed piece, however. It suggests, between the lines, the possibility of new vision. It brings to the forefront the possibilities for civilizing Colombia that the historic juncture of modern science, law and developmental theory offer.

> SEMANA consulto archivos del Incoder (Instituto Colombiano de Desarrollo Rural), donde también se guarda la memoria del antiguo Incora; los de la Red de Solidaridad, los del Instituto Geográfico Agustín Codazzi (Igac), los de las oficinas de Notariado y Registro, y los de la Fiscalia. La información conjunta que hay en todos estos no permite elaborar un mapa nacional o una estadística general sobre la cantidad de hectáreas de tierra que han sido expropiadas a la fuerza en los últimos anos.[189]

> (SEMANA the files of Incoder (Colombian Rural Development Institute), where they also guard the memory of the former Incora; the Solidarity Network, Agustín Codazzi Geographic Institute (IGAC), offices of the Notary & Registry, and the Treasury. The combined information of all of these did not permit the elaboration of a national map or a general statistic on the number of hectares of land that has been expropriated by force in recent years.)

Colombian government records don't yet permit the creation of good enough maps to serve as evidence necessary to protect rights. We cannot see the evidence of the obligations in the social contract that a

---

[189] Ibid.

democratic government is to fulfill. It is not just a question of the physical condition of individual records. Reconciliation is needed of registration documents that show base ownership and cadastral records that show parcel boundaries and values. Regulations requiring speedy registration of sales and other alienation could be considered; or that qualified notaries witness lease signatures, or that contact information of owners be surrendered to the government. In other words, that all real estate related information be transparent and continuously updated. Were this already the standard, then special allowances could be made for conflictive areas or areas where it appeared that extortions were being conducted. These could include any number of measures including special reviews of sales, moratoria, payment escrows, etc. If the market for rural real property were vigorous and transparent, with multiple listing services and an active agency profession, the pace of rural markets and any anomalies would be readily apparent. Massive extortions and population displacements would become much more difficult. Instead, the debate about the privacy of cadastral and registry information continues to embed anonymity and impunity as columns of jurisprudence in Colombia. Consequences of the disingenuous privacy argument about land and land records include what the Colombian countryside is experiencing this go-around with the paramilitaries. It is especially unfortunate in light of the fact that new technologies, as well as the current wave of De Soto-esque developmental thinking, makes creation of a comprehensive, accurate, transparent, and therefore stable and protected, property regime practicable.

The land records in Colombia can be used to trace ownership to national identification numbers and then to passports, telephone bills, etc. This application of land information for cross-referencing databases is doubly attractive to law enforcement because land records have inherent stability and reliability. People do cheat the records, often to avoid taxes, but such cheating is self-limiting, and can actually be helpful to the detective. The special stability of land records resides in the ultimate need of an owner ultimately to prove his identity (perhaps in a quiet-title court action) or risk losing ownership. Since property is a contract with the state for the recognition and support of specific preferential rights, an ostensible owner cannot pretend he is someone else for very long, or indeed his ownership preference will disappear. At any rate, the use of cutouts or dummy-owners is a red flag for the smart cop. There is rarely a legitimate reason to pretend someone else is the owner of your land. Nevertheless, the proposed use of property records for forensic database cross-referencing and mining has become a sensitive political and social issue. Colombians involved in illicit activities logically are opposed to the loss of anonymity, and therefore, impunity. More worthy of our sympathy are the many law abiding Colombian landowners who see public revelation of their property data as an invitation to predation by the mafias. 'Big Brother' records-keeping is one of those concepts that in the aggregate seems to Colombians a good idea for application of the rule of law, but from many individual perspectives is a patently dangerous proposition in the context of a dangerous land.[190] In addition, it is obvious that the process of reconciling records, monumenting the borders of plots, and investigating titles would surface additional conflicts--that stirring up the dust of land records is not necessarily a peaceful tactic, even while a requirement of a peace strategy. How Colombians decide this jurisprudential dilemma is one of the most critical that bear upon the promise of peace in the long term.

So can the war be won politically? The political part can be. Electoral democracy is an important and valued tradition in Colombia. The thing is, both questions -- Can the war be won militarily? and Can the war be won politically? -- miss the mark. The powerful question is not about the celebrity headiness of politics and elections, or is it about the glory and risk of combat. Conflict resolution (and civilization) is found in the boring details of civil administration. The answer is found in the statutes of fraud that require written evidence of duties and rights

---

[190] See Yamid Amat Ruiz, "Reajustan los avalúos catastrales entre 35 y 50 por ciento" Interview with Iván Darío Gómez, director of the Augustin Codazzi Cartographic Institute (IGAC), repository and managing agency for the Colombian national cadastre. In this interview, IGAC Director Gómez provides outlines of a concerted governmental effort to improve and expand the cadastral system. Yamid Amat blog http://www.yamidamat.com.co/Contenido/contenido.asp?Entrevista=177

in order to ease administration of justice and services. Boring, perhaps, like the study of property, but there is the key. Can the war in Colombia be won administratively? Let's hope so.

The developmental importance of cadastral mapping is not lost on Colombians in a position to know. The chief of the cadastral office of the Colombian geographic institute wrote a 2001 essay outlining the long-range goals of his office and asserting the importance of his organization's mission.[191] The InterAmerican Development Bank, in turn, has supported the government of Colombia, although haltingly, with loans. Work on the modernization of the cadastre has proceeded, but at an inadequate rate. The Colombian government is attempting to formalize land ownership throughout the country and to digitize the related data.[192] A major titling program aimed to legalize some seven hundred thousand informally owned parcels is underway. As it stands, benefits of that effort will not be realized for several years at best. Moreover, there is a strong possibility that the resulting data will not be made transparent, or not made available in a timely and comprehensive manner. A multi-agency program of assistance can be implemented to accelerate the Colombian government property program, foster and monitor transparency and gain timely use of digitized and digitally mapped description, ownership, use and value data for property throughout Colombia. Most of this data would be necessarily unclassified, openly obtainable and could be made available to the full range of participating agencies and interested scholars.

---

[191] Yovanny Arturo Martinez, Ibid., note 10.

[192] Cadastral maps and data do not constitute all the government property data readily available in Colombia. Several ministries, government and non-government enterprises maintain geographically referenced data. For instance, ECOPETROL, the national petroleum company, keeps GIS data layers of pipeline easements, exploration licenses, areas of geologic promise, etc. INGEOMINAS, the national mining and mineralogical institute, has similar map data on valuable minerals. Other agencies maintain ecological and agricultural data, and the National Police keeps a massive geographically coded database of incidents that could be displayed on a common map with the property information using software such as ESRI ArcGIS.

Bigger troubles

Colombia has another property problem, however, one that is quickly surpassing and overshadowing all others. The current leadership of neighbor Venezuela has radicalized that county's constitution in a direction contrary not only to private property ownership, but away from the transparency of records. The philosophical and intellectual motivations of the Hugo Chavez regime are the inverse of what the liberal government of Colombia is attempting in terms of property. Socialist revolutionary initiatives in Venezuela present a danger to improving the property regime in Colombia. The border between the two countries is not definite any more than the distinction of families and businesses along that border. There is no way that a liberal property regime can maintain health alongside one in which ownership resides in a personalist dictator. For one thing, people will be leaving Venezuela, escaping to Colombia. We can expect to see the Hugo Chavez regime increasingly encourage the Colombian FARC to confound Colombia's progress toward formal and liberal property ownership. Colombia will suffer the poisonous formula of a brigand organization with huge amounts of disposable income allied to a anti-liberal State government, also with a great deal of disposable income. The FARC and the Venezuelan regime share with the FARC an attitude of automatic opposition toward Colombia's most important foreign ally, the United States. The strategic prospects for Colombia are challenging. To understand the challenge, however, the government of Colombia and its principle ally need to know all the details pertaining to the wealth of their opponents. This means understanding oil and gas revenues, coca production and distribution, foreign bank accounts, exploration licenses etc. It also means knowing in perfect detail what rights and duties are assigned and exercised pertaining to real estate. The lines of communication, and especially the routes to sanctuary of FARC elements will increasingly lead into and through Venezuela.

Deserving to win

> *No one can feel as the owner of the country and no one can feel excluded from the right of property. We must all suffer Colombia.*[193]
>
> Alvaro Uribe Velez, President of Colombia

The United Nation's 2003 human development report for Colombia deals extensively with the conflict there.[194] The report weakly addresses the critical issue of land and property, and does not orient on or encourage victory over the illegal armed groups. These are critical flaws of the UN document, and of similar suggested strategies. On one count, the United States policies and programs in Colombia have suffered a common flaw -- in not bringing the question of formal property creation to the forefront and doing something about it. On the second question of physical confrontation with illegal armed groups, the United States has been a more effective ally, helping the Colombian government reduce the influence of its internal armed enemies. Until after September 11, 2001, US assistance under plan Colombia was hamstrung and contorted by a policy that reflected a current of US foreign policy thinking still partially sympathetic to the armed opposition or at least not ready to embrace a Latin American government in counterinsurgency. The World Trade Center attack changed the balance of attitudes toward the guerrillas. At the same time the lack a property-based understanding of the problem, or of the

---

[193] Brainyquote.com, "Alvaro Uribe Velez Quotes," http://www.brainyquote.com/quotes/quotes/a/alvarourib178540.html.

[194] The United Nations Development Programme. El Conflicto, callejón con salida: Informe Nacional de Desarrollo Humano Colombia – 2003. Bogotá: Panamericana Formas e Impresas, 2003. The report contains one of the largest collections available of geographically oriented data and analyses. Much of that data relies in turn on Colombian government maps and statistics, especially from the human rights office of the vice-presidency or from the national cartographic institute. These two Colombian institutions have produced volumes of credible data (most of which is in some way coded and referenced geographically) as well as detailed analyses. Their presence, currency, dimension and relevance oblige some consideration of their findings.

importance of property as a conflict resolution institution, or of the forensic value of property information, continues to hamper appropriate foreign assistance to Colombia, even in the purely military sense of applying kinetic energy against a known enemy. There are three key aspects of the war with which the government of Colombia has had to contend – the ability of the enemy of the State to dissolve into the population and even into the government itself; an enemy strategy careful to avoid decisive combat with superior government forces; and an ever advancing requirement that the government conduct itself in accordance with the law. (A forth aspect might be the scale of disposable income available to the insurgent as a result of parasitic activity, particularly the cocaine trade.) Not constrained to law and in obedience to the essential dictates of guerrilla strategy, the guerrillas have two modus operandi that are especially confounding: use of the landmine and kidnapping.

Colombia's geography, while blessed with unique bounty, is compartmentalized and restrictive, always making Colombia difficult to govern. A political culture of local territorial independence and armed defiance against central authority, in part the result of difficult terrain, deepens the sense of territoriality. Meanwhile, the commercial attractiveness of marketable resources makes internal conflict that much more acute.[195] Colombia's diversity of saleable natural resources assures that no government strategy based solely on defending one or two of those resources will solve the problem of parasitism or order the country for peaceful and sustainable exploitation. For peace to be achieved, it is imperative in the near term to break the existing predator organizations, and simultaneously to formalize property ownership and

---

[195] For an especially penetrating analysis regarding the effect of coca on the morale and strategy of the guerrilla in Colombia, see Joaquín Villalobos "Por qué las FARC está perdiendo la guerra" [Why the FARC is losing the war], Semana, 7 July 2003, pp. 22-28; but see also Vicente Torrijos, "¿Por qué no conviene cantar victoria ante las Farc? Respuesta a Joaquín Villalobos" [Why isn't it suitable to sing victory before the FARC? Response to Joaquín Villalobos], Semana.terra.com online at <http://semana.terra.com.co/opencms/opencms/Semana/articulo.html?id=71555.

environmental protection. Today, the most notable exports that US policymakers associate with Colombian violence are oil and cocaine, and certainly these two play a foremost role in the calculus of organized violence as the US promotes exploitation of hydrocarbons and battles against cultivation of the coca leaf. Granted their relative importance, oil and coca must be placed in the context of other Colombian products, the focus of repressive attention going to predatory behavior, and to the environmental effects of illegal behavior as compared to normal, peaceful exploitation.

The evolution of rational property law designed to provide the State with adequate property information and to promote social peace is not something that can be purchased quickly with the creation of geo-referenced lines. A regulated real estate sales profession and the development of institutions such as title insurance are longer-term and dependent on developments over which foreign influence cannot easily or quickly be brought to bear. Nevertheless, while it is the whole strength of the property regime that lends importance and power to the property records, development of the records will be an important inducement toward development of the whole regime. Property records, even when incomplete due to unreported leaseholds and other tenancies and encumbrances, allow the development of specific questions regarding anomalies of use and ownership. Those questions can lead to formalization of records. The process is likely to generate wider observance of the law and wider appreciation for the effect that appropriate ownership laws can have.

The American revolutionary innovators knew property as power, and so to succeed, their experiment had to protect individual liberty and property. Somehow, caught by the polarizing effect of the federalist, anti-federalist argument, Colombians failed to seize on a central point of the American revolution -- avoidance of excessive concentration of power that could impose itself on property. In the popular mind, participatory elections, rather than being just a visible expression of freedom and tool for its protection, later supplanted protection of property in the popular imagination as the central purpose of the social contract. The moral governor of the federalist -- anti-federalist debate was a shared understanding of the need to balance individual liberties with social discipline. In Colombia, the debate became increasingly, and especially at times of violent spasms, only a question of how to divide the taxation pie. What is the relationship historically of the American political revolution to what has taken place in Colombia? The development of property could have been the backbone of the Western argument in opposition to communist revolutionary theory and its justification for violence, but it was not. Open elections and civilian control of the military became the dominating mantras. Admirable, neither of these went to the point. Neither flatten the debate about federalism/anti-federalism. Neither clarified the debate about common as opposed to private property that was contained within socialist revolutionary thinking, and, worst perhaps, neither provided the least amount of protection against organized criminality.

Among the uses of real property information touched-upon so far are asset forfeiture or denial; precision eradication of illicit crops; prediction and prevention of human rights violations; corruption limitation, long-term capital creation, alternative development contract monitoring; improved understanding and expression regarding the economic effects of aid projects; and support to territorial military strategies. Other uses include money-laundering tip-off, avoidance of collateral damage in military operations, improved disaster relief planning, support to ecological protection strategies and equitable tax assessment practices. Of all the uses of property data, however, perhaps the most profound and radical derives from the ability to map market values. The value of land speaks volumes about the degree to which rights are established, recorded and enforced. The market for property describes in detail what an internal war does to the essential contract between government and the population.[196] That contract is

---

[196] See, for instance, Jesus Antonio Bejarano Avila (Director of Research), Colombia: Inseguridad, violencia y desempeño económico en las areas rurales, (Bogotá: Universidad Externado de Colombia 1997) p. 225. This work includes extensive

supposed to be one in which the government creates the possibility of property. In other words, when the contract is in practical effect, people can obtain a set of preferential rights, enforceable by the government, and associated with a specific place. When the contract is not functioning, property is reduced by degree to the base state of possession by force. To understand if a society is winning or losing an internal war, one need only trace the value of property over time—not just in places such as Bogotá (or Baghdad or Manila) where the war might be hidden and ignored, but across the country. If there is a general increase in land values in the countryside, it is a good sign some sort of internal peace is extant. If there are anomalies, exaggerations, collapses in real estate values, it invariably reflects something more dangerous.

Tourism is another property indicia of success or failure in counterinsurgency. When people travel for other than business reasons, whether to a local park the other side of the country or the other side of the world, they are making an important judgment with their spare time and money regarding the comfort and safety of a place other than their own home, as well as the routes the routes to and from. Colombians understand this intuitively and directly, having had access to much of their country taken away from them by the internal violence. As more and more places return to the market of pleasurable travel, the geography of growing human security in Colombia can be clearly and distinctly mapped. That map of security is precisely measured in the increments of property values.

Colombia suffers acute political disorder in which real estate matters a great deal. Having precise, transparent, comprehensive property records -- along with a legal regime that gives those records their full import -- would help Colombia and the United States achieve both countries' goals of security and prosperity. Property creation and

---

presentation of the relationship between violence and rural land use and markets in Colombia (Spanish).

formalization should be raised as a principal column of US policy towards Colombia, and that policy should seek fundamental expression in plans and programs. In line with this book's principle assertion, however, improving the Colombian property regime will not secure peace. Rather, to not improve Colombia's property regime will consign to failure other efforts to secure peace and security there.

In Colombia, the development of property has helped in the short run with the most palpable goals of law enforcement – to kill or capture criminals, take their ill-gotten wealth, repress the growth of their power. The military part of the conflict can and must be won by the government, and formalized property has helped. It is becoming a regular occurrence to read of a FARC or AUC commander who has had the backbone of his line of communication broken through the confiscation of real properties. Moreover, in the long run, development of the property regime can redress and eliminate much of what is valid in the revolutionary argument, and it can close space to the unchecked action of would-be terrorists. With better property, Colombia will be a more prosperous trading partner, a more stable and stronger military ally, will suffer fewer violations of human rights, and will export lesser quantities of illicit drugs. Furthermore, if Colombia's property regime is not improved, the likelihood of achieving long-term internal peace is minimal. There is no other democratic option. Property, as an area of academic investigation, links law to physical geography and physical geography to economics. Without stretching a syllogism too far, it is safe to say that property is geography in legal detail; conflict and geography in Colombia are intimately connected, and further investigation into the condition of property in Colombia is likely to offer insights into details of the conflict. In any event, Colombia's conflict should be addressed in terms of law, land, and economics. Without detailed facts about who owns what land and how much each piece is worth, most analysis is speculation.

The Uribe administration has been, in fact, attempting to apply a property understanding, and to evolve the Colombian property regime through several programs. A recent Colombian study claiming that as much as four million hectares of land have been abandoned by persons displaced by violence (usually extortion, simple direct threat to life, or impossibility of commerce) has captured the attention of the executive and lawmakers.[197] An unrelated effort is underway to title and formalize some 700 thousand informal residences, this in line with the De Soto observation regarding capital creation.[198] These kinds of measures, in the author's view, are the right path. Colombia appears to be winning its internal war.[199] It is harder and harder for the insurgents to hide within the population and still be able to maintain any degree of wealth. The Colombian armed forces have been making it continually harder for the insurgents to avoid combat, and government forces have been increasingly disciplined in observance of the law. As a result, indices regarding the two most difficult modus operandi to solve, landmines and kidnappings, have shown a sharp decline. Colombia's elite and the engaged elements of Colombia's governing institutions appear to want to deserve to win.

---

[197] See, Ramiro Bejarano Guzmán, "Proyecto para-inmueble," colombia.indymedia.org, Oct. 1, 2005 online at <http://colombia.indymedia.org/news/2005/10/31525.php; El Tiempo, "Procurador alerta sobre tierras de desplazados que están hoy en manos de 'paras' y narcotraficantes," eltiempo.com, October 2, 2005 online at <http://eltiempo.terra.com.co/judi/2005-10-03/ARTICULO-WEB-NOTA_INTERIOR-2554156.html.

[198] El Tiempo, "700 mil familias colombianas que viven en predios que no son suyos podrán legalizarlos" (700 Thousand families that live on lots that are not theirs will be able to legalize them), eltiempo.com, October 15, 2005 online at < http://eltiempo.terra.com.co/economia/2005-10-13/ARTICULO-WEB-NOTA_INTERIOR-2567675.html.

[199] See, as an expression of this view, Guardian Unlimited, 'The Rebirth of a Nation' at http://business.guardian.co.uk/insidecolombia/story/0,,2095249,00.html

Chapter Four: Hohfeld versus Haushofer

Chapter Four: Hohfeld versus Haushofer

*"Do not be narrow-minded, but think in large terms of
great spaces, in continents and oceans, and thereby
direct your course with that of our Fuhrer."[200]*

Karl Haushofer, Nazi Geopolitician

---

[200] James Trapier Lowe, Geopolitics and War: Mackinder's Philosophy of Power (Washington, D.C.: University Press of America, 1981), p.5. citing Edmund A. Walsh, Total Power (New York: Doubleday and Company, 1948), 6 and 45.

National Security Strategy of the United States

"Our Nation's cause has always been larger than our Nation's defense. We fight, as we always fight, for a just peace—a peace that favors liberty. We will defend the peace against the threats from terrorists and tyrants. We will preserve the peace by building good relations among the great powers. And we will extend the peace by encouraging free and open societies on every continent."[201]

President George W. Bush

Chapter One outlined property theory; Chapter Two described the environment of dangers in property terms; and Chapter Three presented a case study of an important country where property issues are obviously at the heart of internal conflict. This chapter examines the change in national security strategy that the book's overall thesis hopes to provoke. How does 'property' fit into or against the dominant expressions of US national and military strategy? Why would incorporation of 'property' improve that body of understanding, and what would property-security doctrine and strategy look like? The rationale of this chapter is built from the principle assertion of the book that without formalized property a society's prospects of internal peace are dim. Lands where violent internal conflict lingers, or where tyranny takes hold -- where freedom, safety and prosperity do not reign -- are places correspondingly likely to spawn and propagate behaviors that threaten the rest of the world. Today, the question of other peoples' social condition is all the more critical given the phenomena encapsulated in Chapter Two as the Globalization of Trespass. It is no longer an option that we isolate ourselves from the insufficiencies that

---

[201] George W. Bush, <u>National Security Strategy of the United States</u>, Washington, D.C.: The White House, 2005, online at <http://www.whitehouse.gov/nsc/nss1.html.

208

hamper human flourishing in other societies, and so part of the upshot this book is a call to infuse property concepts into explicit national security and national intelligence strategies – and not just those aimed at economic development. Property-based knowledge, theory and praxis can also contribute to resolve current conflicts and to defeat violent enemies.

This book calls for specific improvements in national security, military and intelligence strategies. The thesis is simple: US national security strategy could more effectively respond to the changed nature of the global environment by more fully incorporating property rights knowledge, concepts and imperatives. As expressed in Chapter Two, the global changes in question are the particularization of power, the projection of legal regimes worldwide and moral asymmetry. Human political culture has evolved in such a way that the map of discrete sovereign entities is insufficient to represent the volatile interests in play. Adjusting our understanding of national security strategy toward divisible property and away from discrete state sovereignty invites some predictable consequences. The broad observations and country power-balancing of the geopolitician are forced to give ground to the incremental market consciousness of the real estate agent, litigious calculating of the plaintiff's attorney and scrupulous mapping of the county clerk. Such an approach does not lament or revel in the global particularization of power, but rather maps, measures and civilizes it. Explaining how the approach fits into or against existing national security, military and intelligence strategy is the chore of this chapter.

The cause of the book, as stated at the outset, is to convince, on both the theoretical and practical levels, why the advancement of property regimes in foreign lands should become a principal column of plans for a secure and peaceful world. To see how that column might fit, we take a brief look at how the current plans came about. In other words, at the determinants of the strategy writings, national documents that historically have paid deference to specific currents of strategic theory.

It is difficult to discuss *strategy* without falling prey to the same kind of academic jealousies and semantic quicksand that lurk in the word *property*. The word strategy carries a wide-ranging set of formally accepted denotations. I confine myself here to two broad areas of understanding: The first use of the term applies to the provision of security before, after or beyond the condition of warfare -- decisions made on a broad scope that are intended to protect and acquire rights without the necessity or consequence of organized violence. These decisions are often developmental, economic or diplomatic in nature, and are taken for the most part, in the American context, by civilian rather than military leaders.

The second understanding takes strategy to be a set of decisions generated by military leadership in order to fix and destroy or capture an enemy. 'Enemy' can be defined for convenience as an individual or organization the behavior of which cannot be peaceably changed soon enough to prevent it from doing our friends or us grave harm. This latter, military strategy -- strategy that manages violence against an enemy -- optimally comprises decisions taken to increase the probability of success of subordinate commanders in battle.

Purposefully absent in this discussion of the above two categories of strategy is any challenge to the hierarchies of terms that habitually appear in treatments of the subject. Within those hierarchies, the terms 'vision,' 'policy,' 'geo-strategy,' 'grand strategy,' 'operational art' and 'tactics' typically appear. Strategy, for the purposes of this chapter, however, is the trump term -- something greater and more important than whatever other label of purposeful competitive thought finds itself in the same sentence, and which guides whatever else it is that needs guidance.

I believe that strategy (when used as a synonym for planning) is best designed upon conscious reconciliation of objectives, methods, and resources, and that it has an imperative relationship to its inferiors. That is to say, an excellent tactical move can rarely save a poor strategy, but a correct strategy can suffer considerable tactical error. In

210

that regard we also nod to the generally accepted notion that an understanding of the basic sources of power is necessary if we are to succeed in strategizing -- supposing that, in any setting, accurate insight into the nature and source of power is helpful if we are to determine reasonable objectives and rational means of achieving them. As for the place of property theory and knowledge in the formulation of security and military strategy: an absence of detailed knowledge of property ownership is presumptive evidence of ignorance regarding the details of power. In the sections that follow, the text will criticize the established strategic power measurements and will propose a property-based approach to measuring power that matches a property approach to analysis of conflict.

Geopolitics

Among the currents of strategy theory that has most influenced US strategic writing is *geopolitics*. While geopolitics is yet another term at times used in place of strategy or as something bigger, here it represents a phenomenon in academic history, an academic sub-discipline that for many decades served as the mental bridge between geography and strategy; was, to some extent, synonymous with strategy. For some readers, geopolitics conjures up a worldview at odds with human rights -- one that still carries unpopular connotations as a vindicating pseudo-science for national arrogance. As a school of strategic thought it was, as its name implies, a cross of geography and politics, but its dominant scholastic parent is Geography rather than Political Science. It serves us here because it informed the writers of US national security documents well beyond its prime as a recognized approach to security thinking, and across the full ideological range of US administrations. It is also a useful referent in that the shortcomings of the geopolitical view of conflict and violence contrast most sharply with the advantages of a property-based view. One attraction of geopolitics seems to have been its confident explanation of security questions on the basis of visible geographic evidence and supposedly immutable physical laws. Property analysis of conflict (or 'Hohfeldian analysis' as the chapter title alludes, or what this author pretentiously calls Geoproperty) is more tedious. The necessary evidence is detailed and complicated, the laws myriad, mundane, and never immutable. With its shortcomings, however, property analysis can give a more precise and useable view of today's violent human competition.

The United States was born into a world of sovereignty, wherein the sovereignty-based construct for dividing the political and diplomatic earth was in the process of consolidation. Nevertheless, formed on the basis of revolutionary perspectives regarding the relationship between the individual and the state, the new American nation began successfully to export principles and create cultural norms that have since continually eroded sovereignty's dominion as the organizing principle of global power. Every step in the direction of free trade, constitutional social contracts, decentralized elections -- not to mention the spread of technologies giving voice and privacy to individuals and groups independent of central governments -- has worked against the relative power of those governments. With the basket of post-Soviet phenomena we call, the corrosive effect on the power-monopoly of central governments (with some glaring exceptions) has accelerated. Meanwhile, the international strategy of the United States government, evolved to fit the world of contrived nation-states drawn on the world map, and eventually as analyzed through a geopolitics lens, has not adjusted to fit the new power divisions. Just at the time in the late 1800s that the United States began to see itself as a global power, as it took its first competitive steps at the end of the age of classic imperialism, the notions of modern geopolitics were coming into fashion. At the turn of the 19th and 20th centuries, geopolitics, a child of Geography, imprinted itself on the minds of American strategists. Strategy, geography, history and politics were intertwined in geopolitics, as was, to a considerable degree, propaganda.

After WWII, Geography waned in the United States as a departmental academic discipline, replaced in time by Area Studies, International Studies, Anthropology or other bits and pieces of the

212

social sciences. It appears that Geography was made to pay a price for having spawned the geopolitics that inspired the sort of assertion that the Haushofer quote at the beginning of the chapter exemplifies. Irrespective of this shunning of Geography on campus, the makers of post WWII US national strategy gave inertial afterlife to the pre-war geopolitics. Superpower competition against the Soviet Union after WWII lengthened the historical relevance of the established, if questionable, geopolitical concepts against which American diplomacy and military might were shaped. This was so even while expressions of the vision of American national purpose were increasingly at odds with a geopolitical understanding of the world. Some understanding of where geopolitics came from, and why it survives, helps feed the argument for change.

Nineteenth-century German geographer Freidrich Ratzel is considered the father of modern human or political geography. [202] Ratzel presented his creative theories of political organization in terms of "laws" related to space and location. He stressed space as of extreme importance to national power, and concentrated much of his study on the United States, which he felt would become a 20th century world leader. Nevertheless, Swede Rudolf Kjellen is more often credited as inventor of geopolitics (*Geopolitik*) as is Karl Haushofer for warping geopolitics to the advantage of Nazi dogma. [203] Early in the

---

[202] See generally, Harriet Wanklyn, Friedrich Ratzel: A Biographical Memoir and Bibliography (Cambridge: Cambridge University Press,1961). It is at least entertaining to note that one of Ratzel's most influential works, *Anthropogeographie* (2 vols., 1882-1891; Human Geography) established his reputation as an anthropologist.

[203] Arild Holt-Jensen, Ibid., p. 32; Note the following from a post-WWII textbook on political geography: "Before and during WWII, German geopolitics (Geopolitic) was used to blueprint world conquest, and the Nazi creed incorporated those portions of political geography that served to justify German expansion. The natural result has been an attempt by some scholars to divorce the discipline of political geography from geopolitics. In the words of Karl Haushofer, 'Political Geography views the state from the standpoint of space, while Geopolitics views space from the standpoint of the state.' In the final analysis the difference is one of emphasis..." N. Marbury Efimenco, ed., World Political Geography: Second Edition (New York: Thomas Y. Crowell Company, 1957), p. 5.

20th Century, Britisher Halford Mackinder built on Ratzel's notion of continental power, and attributed preeminence to the Eurasian continent in what became his Heartland Theory. Mackinder is considered a determinist in that he stressed basic geography as the dominant influence over the fate of a country. Determinism, (*environmental determinism*, or *environmentalism*) caused a post-World War I reaction among geographers that was referred to as *possibilism*, a term apparently invented by French historian Lucien Febvre. The possibilists stressed the power of human choice rather than environmental limitations to it. Although Mackinder himself swung toward the possibilists in his later thinking, the German translation of his Heartland Theory had great impact on German territorial acquisitiveness and then on arguments that would bring the United States into the Second World War. The theory, published in 1919 in a study titled "Democratic Ideals and Reality," is summarized by MacKinder's famous phrase: "Who rules East Europe commands the Heartland: Who rules the Heartland commands the World Island: Who rules the World Island commands the World."[204] With this he intimated that if the Germans or the Russians were to control east Europe and Russia (the Eurasian heartland), they would be in a natural position to control the world. Given the orientation of his theory on the world-controlling importance of central Europe (i.e., Germany, Poland, Russia), speculation turned toward the effect physical control of these areas might have on possibilities for world domination. This became the intellectual baseline for drawing the United States into a European war.

Geopolitics is a twentieth century instruction, Geography itself being fairly young as institutionalized academic disciplines go. The first English and American university geography departments and

---

[204] Halford J. Mackinder, <u>Democratic Ideals and Reality</u> (New York: W.W. Norton & Company, 1962), 150. There is some debate about when exactly the term Heartland was coined. Mackinder had delivered an influential lecture in 1904 titled "The Geographical Pivot of History" in which the term appears and in which the essence of his theory is propounded. See James Trapier Lowe, <u>Geopolitics and War: Mackinder's Philosophy of Power</u> (Washington, D.C.: University Press of America, 1981), p.5.

textbooks date back only to the latter half of the 19th Century.[205] Geopolitics was one of geography's early progenies. Because it was born in an epoch of high imperialist pretensions, and given its undeniable Germanic ancestry, geopolitics was destined for dishonor by entanglement with Nazi racism, and perhaps by Hegelian and von Moltkean love of war as a crucible of human and national character. The term has survived because it finesses a determinant connection between physical geography, strategy and therefore international diplomacy. Its pre-WWII abusers are little remembered. Geopolitics, ugly still for some, is a valid term to describe the theoretical parameters within which much military thinking about strategy still resides. This was as true for United States strategists in the late 20th Century as it was at its beginning. While many military planners may be unaware of the intellectual and historical baggage that geopolitics lugs with it, they are generally content that the term represents a more worthy engine for national decision making than does, say, human rights theory. For others, human rights concepts are attractive for perhaps the same reasons that led the Post WWI possibilists to reject the suspicious environmental determinism of geopolitics. It is no wonder that post-WWII American academe might move away from study in service of strengthening the State, and toward the study of the State's role in improving the environmental space. Regardless, geopolitical theory has had a transcendent effect on the U.S. security outlook, beginning with the influences not of the Germans, but of Mackinder.

That geopolitics has been a dominant intellectual influence in contemporary United States foreign policy is a point that strategic historian Geoffrey Sloan expertly argued.[206] Sloan weaved together American geopolitical theorizing, geopolitical expressions in U.S. policy, and the geopolitical determinants of other policy traditions. He pointed out a remarkable intuition displayed by America's best known

---

[205] German geography was established as a separate academic discipline about a half century earlier. See Arild Holt-Jensen, Geography: History and Concepts (Totowa, New Jersey: Barnes and Noble Books, 1988), p. 3.

[206] Geoffrey R. Sloan, Geopolitics in United States Strategic Policy, 1890-1987 (New York: St. Martin's Press, 1988.

geopolitical theorist, Nicholas Spykman. As a geopolitician, Spykman claimed that the power of a state was strongly related to its location and its physical features. His geographic focus, and what distinguished his work from Mackinder's, was what he called the 'Rimland of Eurasia.' Playing on Mackinder's Heartland theory, Spykman asserted "who controls the Rimland rules Eurasia; who rules Eurasia controls the destinies of the world."[207] Spykman's observation may seem gratuitous coming as it did in 1941. Anyone might have stumbled across a threatening power or two on the outer edges of the Eurasian landmass. But what Spykman stated as the consequence of this geographic observation set in motion what is an example of the impact pure theory can have on strategy. Spykman stated that the rimland powers of Japan and Germany would, after the end of the war, become allies of the United States to counter Russian expansion.[208] He had maintained that Soviet foreign policy aims, as Russia's before, were to break out of the heartland to warm water ports, and ultimately to dominate the world. Understandably, his predictions were not universally well received in 1941. Spykman died in 1943, and as the coming end of the war exposed the need to reappraise strategic threats in a changed world order, Spykman's geopolitics quickly gained influential weight even as the labels of geography and geopolitics were swept out of view. His observations were stated in the context of power-balancing within the state system. In this calculus world domination was a viable end in a zero-sum game of dominators -- all of which had a natural appeal to the strategy-oriented.

Sloan points out that Spykman's reputation nevertheless suffered vilification as the "American Haushofer."[209] The conclusions Spykman asserted or implied in his interpretation of geography--that the United States should not seek to destroy Germany and Japan, but

---

[207] Nicholas J. Spykman, The Geography of the Peace, edited by Helen R. Nicholl (United States: Archon Books, 1969). See also David Wilkinson, "Spykman and Geopolitics" in On Geopolitics: Classical and Nuclear edited by Ciro Zoppo and Charles Zorgbibe (Boston: Martinus Nijhoff Publishers, 1985).
[208] Sloan, Geopolitics, p. 19.
[209] Ibid.

only to change regimes and preserve the countries intact as allies--appeared for some to be in amoral if not immoral consonance with disgraced enemies, and using their same discredited bag of theory. Consequently, neither Spykman nor geopolitics would enjoy the open recognition during the early years of containment strategy.[210] Along with them slumped the welcome and fortunes of geography as an academic discipline. Sloan notes that Henry Kissinger called for an explicit geopolitics, but that he did not mean a theory of spatial and historical causation. He meant power equilibrium. *Geopolitik* morphed into *Realpolitic*. Of course, treatment of states and regions as discreet geographic entities among which power could be balanced was always both precondition for and effect of geopolitical and well as realpolitical thinking.

Skipping over a few decades of Cold War to 1986, we note that the United States Congress passed The Department of Defense Reorganization Act (the Goldwater Nichols Act). It stipulates that the President of the United States annually send to Congress a comprehensive report on the country's national security strategy.[211] The act orders that the annual report include a description and discussion of the following:

---

[210] Actually, Spykman called Haushofer's writing "metaphysical nonsense." Spykman was also adamant about not assigning too much weight to simple geography as a guide to policy. "The formation of policy is not to be simplified into one all-inclusive generality like geography. They are many; they are permanent and temporary, obvious and hidden; they include, besides geography, population density, the economic structure of the country, the ethnic composition of the people, the form of government, the complexes and pet prejudices of foreign ministers, and the ideals and values held by the people." Spykman, The Geography of the Peace, p. 7. Spykman's conception of power is still rigidly framed by the official action of states in a state system and only casually tries to incorporate technological change.

[211] United States Congress, Goldwater-Nichols Department of Defense Reorganization Act of 1986, PL 99-433, 1 October 1986, Section 104.

(1) The worldwide interests, goals, and objectives of the United States that are vital to the national security of the United States.

(2) The foreign policy, worldwide commitments, and national defense capabilities of the United States necessary to deter aggression and to implement the strategy.

(3) The proposed short and long-term uses of the political, economic, military, and other elements of the national power to protect or promote national interests and achieve goals and objectives.

(4) The adequacy of the capabilities of the United States to carry out the national security strategy, including an evaluation of the balance among the capabilities of all elements of the national power to support implementation of the strategy.

(5) Such other information as may be necessary to help inform Congress on matters relating to the national security strategy of the United States.

Earliest versions of the official National Security Strategy of the United States, the document prepared annually by the president to comply with the aforementioned act, show the influence of geopolitical thinking in the explanation, if not the construction, of U.S. foreign policy. In 1988, the essential "objectives" of the United States were summed as peace, security, and freedom. The report stated that the...

> first historical dimension of our strategy is relatively
> simple, clear-cut, and immensely sensible. It is the
> conviction that the United States' most basic
> national security interests would be endangered if a
> hostile state or group of states were to dominate the
> Eurasian landmass--that area of the globe often
> referred to as the world's heartland. We fought two
> world wars to prevent this from occurring. And
> since 1945, we have sought to prevent the Soviet

Union from capitalizing on its geostrategic
advantage to dominate its neighbors in Western
Europe, Asia, and the Middle East, and thereby
fundamentally alter the global balance of power to
our disadvantage. ... The national strategy to achieve
this objective has been containment, in the broadest
sense of that term.[212]

The continuity apparent in the 1988 strategy with past national
goals and policies ratified the Mackinder geopolitical slice of foreign
affairs scholarship. Also in introductory paragraphs, national "values,"
(human dignity, personal freedom, individual rights, the pursuit of
happiness, peace and prosperity) were tied logically to "an international
order that encourages self-determination, democratic institutions,
economic development, and human rights. A good sense of US
national strategy emerges. Starting with the constitution as the guide,
the US government states that Americans should be safe, free and
prosperous and, looking at the rest of the world, concludes that it would
be advantageous if other peoples were prosperous, safe and free as
well. Though not always observed in the specifics, this has been a
durable element of national identity and the wellspring of considerable
power. These statements are nevertheless at odds logically with
theoretical determinants that view the value of geographies
independently of the conditions of ownership rights within them.

In addition to the required annual National Security Strategy,
another major strategy document was published in 1988, the report of
The Commission on Integrated Long Term Strategy.[213] The
commission was co-chaired by Fred Ikle and Albert Wohlstetter. First,
it recommended that the United States emphasize a wider range of
threats than the two that had dominated policy and force planning for

---

[212] Ronald Reagan, National Security Strategy of the United States (Washington,
D.C.: The White House, 1988), p. 1.
[213] The Commission on Integrated Long-Term Strategy, Discriminate Deterrence
(Washington, D.C.: U.S. Government Printing Office, 1988).

decades prior.[214] Instead of concentrating on the extreme cases of a massive Communist attack through Central Europe or all-out nuclear war, the commission called for the ability to make discriminate military responses to lesser, but still major confrontations in other areas. The primary defense strategy documents in 1988 followed through on a course that had been set near the beginning of the Reagan presidency. They announced a long-term policy of technological, all-level, all-places competition against the Soviet Union. The resulting particulars were clear. The United States was officially dedicated to fighting and winning the Cold War, and Mackinder's geopolitics still fit.

How is it that Mackinder's geopolitics enjoyed such longevity on the back of a theory that originally claimed that whoever held the heartland of Europe would control the world? Americans were unwittingly co-opted to internalize the protection of Western Europe as essential to United States national security. Therein lay one attraction to British statesmen, if not British geographers (Mackinder was a member of the British Parliament), of theories holding that nobody should be allowed to get hold of the biggest chunk of Europe. Halford Mackinder's Heartland Theory was less and more than it appeared. More than scientific observation, it was also an intellectual device managed in the service of great power politics. It was for Britain an exportable fear and a simultaneously popular hope for Germans. Mackinder's was a theory promoted in part, even if only intuitively, to aid in involving the United States in the event of European continental war. The British applied political geography to a specific end, as did the Nazis. The Heartland Theory presented a nexus between control of central Europe and the security of the United States, and it made a subliminal appeal to American identity. That identity included solidarity both with Europe as a whole and with the English-speaking

---

[214] The commission report gives an excellent summary of U.S. Cold War strategy-- "The strategy can be stated quite simply: forward deployment of American forces, assigned to oppose invading armies and backed by strong reserves and a capability to use nuclear weapons if necessary." The report notes that the strategy had had considerable success and asserted that the commission did not propose that the strategy be replaced, only that it be revised. Ibid., p. 5.

British in particular. The theory may have proposed that specific territorial space was the principal determinant of world domination, but the political message was that 'they' (Russians or Germans) were in an important property competition against 'us' (British and Americans).[215] In retrospect, it hardly mattered one iota what nation controlled the heartland of Europe as far as American security was concerned. After all, at the turn of the 19th and 20th centuries, U.S. wealth and security depended immeasurably more on how America controlled its own land than on what nation controlled the heartland of Europe. *How* a Europe-controlling regime would deal with people and with ownership *did* matter. But geopolitics is almost oblivious to how land is owned, or to any ownership below that of the collective nation-State, and at the time all ability to project organized destructive power was believed to reside in the State. The Heartland Theory continued to be cited past the Great War, past WWII and throughout the Cold War, but by that time it was the presence and range of nuclear missiles that made the Soviet Union a direct threat--not political control of the Eurasian heartland. If the Soviets were ever to have possessed all of Germany, they would have gained about 5 percent more land and about 15 percent more people. Without ICBMs, rule of the Eurasian heartland would have meant rule of the Eurasian heartland. Likewise, he who controls Kansas...controls Kansas. The Heartland optic can be taken as a self-centered European

---

[215] According to Mackinder's theory, control of the heartland, or central region, threatened the "sea powers" meaning first Britain, and then the United States. N. J. Spykman (American Strategy in World Politics, 1942) picked up on the idea, but with a different thrust. He visualized the "rimland" countries as being more important. These included Japan, Britain, India, and the Mideast countries. He speculated that United States security depended on preventing the formation of an enemy coalition of rimland powers, or domination of rimland areas by the heartland (Russia). Necessity is the mother of invention, and Mackinder was as much innovative politician as innovative theorist. He sensed the strategic moment of the Heartland argument. Spykman, much less the politician, nevertheless recognized the durability of Mackinder's Heartland theory and anticipated the American need for a post-war strategic vision. This, together with the intercontinental range of missiles, made the heartland theory a survivor. John E. Kieffer (Realities of World Power, 1952) picked up the geopolitical ball, explaining the East-West polarization using a power belt theory. Though equally as logical or illogical, Kieffer was nowhere as influential.

a priori, continental control and world domination billed as one-in-the-same.

President Ronald Reagan's 1988 report, written just before the close of the Cold War, presents an enlightening contrast to President George H. Bush's 1993 report. Writing the National Security Strategy in 1993 was a different challenge than in 1988, since Cold War containment of and competition with the communist empire could no longer serve as an azimuth. The 1993 document featured arms control and limiting the proliferation of nuclear weapons, control of illicit drug trafficking, halting environmental degradation, advancement of free market global economics, fostering democracy worldwide, responding to straightforward aggressions, and building coalitions with allies to achieve all of the other goals.[216] The Russians were not yet entirely off the scope. They still held the ability to destroy America, had not left Cuba completely, or had they withdrawn troops from much of the former Soviet empire. The US national strategy document reflected on the possibility of a resurgent Russia, but the direction was one of greater specificity in describing the actions to be included in the government's strategy to provide for the general welfare and secure the common defense. At the outset of the first term of President William Clinton, differences of vision between the Departments of Defense and the Department of State delayed internal administration acceptance of a unified strategy document.[217] The Department of State oriented on the use of diplomacy to address human rights and environmental concerns while the Department of Defense sought to retain a geopolitical construct. As in the first Bush administration, the geopolitical perspective tended to overly simplify classification of foreign lands

---

[216] George Bush, <u>National Security Strategy of the United States</u>, (Washington, D.C.: The White House, 1993). On the question of coalitions, however, a statement was included: "Foremost, the United States must ensure its security as a free and independent nation, and the protection of its fundamental values, institutions, and people. This is a sovereign responsibility which we will not abdicate to any other nation or collective organization." Ibid, p. 3.
[217]. The first Clinton administration national security strategy document was finally published in July 1994. William J. Clinton, <u>A National Security Strategy of Engagement and Enlargement</u> (Washington: The White House, 1994).

according to physical geographical aspects. Oil, distance in terms of missile ranges, jet engine minerals, or sea-lane choke points led analyses. Many of these geopolitical standards are related to a hypothetical condition of international war. Thus, places gained importance and priority because of their contribution in the exceptional case of a global conflagration. Within these analyses, especially geopolitical in nature, priorities for the prevention of global conflict can be overlooked.[218]

Although one might remark on the strategy differences taken by the Reagan and Bush administrations, or on the differences of vision between the Bush and Clinton administrations, the strategy documents indicate more continuity than change. A concluding paragraph from the report of the Commission on Integrated Long-Term Strategy in 1988 is enlightening. "We live in a world whose nations are increasingly connected by their economies, cultures, and politics--sometimes explosively connected as in the repeated vast migrations since WWII of refugees escaping political, religious, and racial persecution. It is a

---

[218] Not just with regard to the United Sates do we see the difficulty of distinguishing abstract concepts in the formulation of national strategy. The Brazilians, for instance, have formally defined their national objectives as "interests and aspirations, vital and optional, that in a given phase of its historic-cultural evolution, the nation seeks to satisfy." Vital national interests that are expected to endure throughout the period of Brazilian history are termed "Permanent National Objectives." Superior War School, Basic Manual (Brazil: Escola Superior de Guerra, 1992), p. 24. Of these Permanent National Objectives there are six--Democracy, National Integration, Integrity of the National Patrimony, Social Peace, Progress, and Sovereignty. Integrity of National Patrimony, for example, is defined as "Territorial integrity inherited from our forefathers and enlarged by those increments resulting from the evolution of technology or international law, examples being the territorial seas or airspace; integrity of the public lands, natural resources and the natural environment to be preserved against predation; integrity of the cultural-historical patrimony, represented in language customs and traditions, to wit, preserving the national identity." Ibid., p. 27. Sovereignty refers to "maintenance of national intangibles, assuring the capacity of self-determination and to live together with other nations in terms of equality of rights, not acceding to any form of intervention in internal affairs, nor participating in like processes in relation to other nations. In essence, it is the search for its own destiny; and as well sovereignty signifies supremacy of the juridical order of the State throughout its territory." Ibid., p.28.

world in which military as well as economic power will be more and more widely distributed and in which the United States must continue to expect some nations to be deeply hostile to its purposes." These words could have as easily been written by administration strategy writers in 1974, 1984, 1994 or in 2004.

The basic elements of national strategy found in the major United States strategy documents can be usefully considered in property terms. For instance, outlines in President Clinton's A National Security Strategy of Engagement and Enlargement about what the United States should do--about the need to enlarge the community of democratic nations, protect the environment and promote economic integration--are easy to express in property terms. We would simply say that the United States seeks to expand acceptance of its ideology regarding rules of ownership, ensure that other possessors meet ownership duties (according to the accepted rules), and increase the value of property through open trade. There is an evident efficiency in so stating the problem, even while the ideological challenge is blatant. In the examples used above, we note that simple categorization of items as of 'national interest' may often proves unconstructive in terms of conflict resolution. By addressing other elements of the ownership environment, such as attitudes about the collective identity of owners, we can more easily define the points of potential disagreement.

Mackinder's was a limited determinism in that he always left a hint that human initiative was available to change the basic geographical space. In a submission to the march of history, Mackinder adjusted the measure of his theory, saying toward the end his life in 1943 that the human influence was a more important element in the future of a nation than was territorial endowment. The property approach, which crosses law, economics and physical geography, seeks understanding of contractual agreements expressed according to place. It is the same, but the opposite of geopolitics. Both point to the map and say, "This place has a competitive advantage." Within property analyses, however, human capacity to order the details of competition over territory is a civilizing ingredient, and a key determinant of the relative economic value of land. These two characteristics of human input: the civilizing of human interaction and the establishment of relative value, are obviated by the bare geophysical assertions of geopolitics. Geopolitics ignores the importance of the social contract, the innovation of divisibility of rights and duties, or the market for rights, as well as innovations to reconcile conflicts over land. Geopolitics ignores the possibility of increasing the whole power of a people as a result of the way in which conflict is resolved and the value of land increased.

Geopolitics presumes a struggle for the fee simple, and gives little weight to the strength that might accrue to a person, family, NGO, gang, business, people or a nation due to the way in which rights in land and other are ordered and evidenced. For this reason, geopolitics has to be constantly re-thought to explain why this or that place is advantaged by physical geography. Geopolitics is a mental construct born of another, sovereignty. It is still the guiding mental construct for strategists, confines our understanding and is something we need to escape. It does not fit globalization, does not adjust quickly enough to technological change, is not precise enough to help us see the new enemies, and will not lead to victory over terrorism, over brigandage or over poverty.

Geopolitical perspectives start from characteristics of the land, not ownership rights. However, digging at the substrata of geopolitics, one can uncover fascinating evidence of the universality of man's attitudes toward land. Ratzel, presented his theories of political organization in terms of "laws" related to space and location. He conceived of the state as a type of biological organism with spiritual and moral character derived from the ties which men shared due to common presence on a definable piece of ground. The spiritual dimension of the relationship between man and land reflected the antecedent and ever-nationalist writings of philosophers such as Kant and Hegel. These expressions, while not shared universally, are not far removed from other peoples' conclusions regarding their political and spiritual relationship to land. Consider the following expression of the importance of land to the American Indians in face of the privations bestowed upon them by the White man in America:

> Land, moreover, has many meanings for the Indian. The relationship of a tribe to its land defines that tribe: its identity, its culture, its way of life, its fundamental rights, its methods of adaptation, its pattern of survival. Land also defines the Indians' enemies-those who covet the land and desire to expropriate it for their own use. Because Indian land is, or may be, of value, it has been, and remains, the source of almost every major conflict and every ongoing controversy between the Indian and the white man. Indian land is synonymous with Indian existence. A tribe's title to land often proves to be its death warrant.[219]

With changes only in the group identities, this assertion could have been safely attributed to German geopoliticians. At the level of rights associated with land, differences in belief systems are not so great as is often claimed. Geopolitics responds to atavistic ties between man and place. However, especially in its most abrasive forms, geopolitics does not deal well with multiple dimensions of ownership.[220] Emphasis on space and location is the Ratzelian heritage of geopolitics. Intuition about domestic real estate tells us that space and location are indeed principal determinants of land value in fiscal terms, but the body of rights obtained in the acquisition of land also has a close relationship to its price. Geopolitical analyses are poorly conformable to multiple,

---

[219] Edgar S. Cahn and David W. Hearne, eds., Our Brother's Keeper: The Indian in White America (New York: New American Library, 1970), p. 68.

[220] An indigenous, or 'Fourth World,' movement is afoot that seeks to build solidarity among indigenous peoples of the world in order to promote similar if not common interests. One might suppose that this movement would find common cause with environmental protectionists. Greenpeace, for instance, played a sympathetic observer role in the context of Mexico's Zapatista uprising, which purported a significant indigenous claims dimension. Still, activists for indigenous rights just as often find their agendas at odds with the goals of environmental protection activists, especially when the bottom line is land use and ownership.

226

occasionally shared, changeable rights in land held by overlapping owner groups that only sometimes can be delineated according to nationality. The more distant a problem gets from competition by nation-states over the fee simple of demarcated land, the less useful geopolitics becomes. As legal and economic innovation sneaks up on space to divide it over and over, and to create overlapping owner identities associated with every overlapping slice, geopolitics is further and further relegated.

Another significant weakness of geopolitics is its failure to receive technological change. Geopolitical interpretations of national interest can be seen as lagging reflections of technological history. Much in US national strategy, geopolitically-based, has been built around control of natural resources, such as oil.[221] This is an indirect response to technological change. Strategic minerals and oil are geologically noteworthy because of the technologies that lend them commercial value. Geopoliticians, observing the demand for these natural resources, imbue with a correlated value the places where the resources can be found. The weakness is obvious. Many technologies are not well defined geologically, but nevertheless create changes in the value of places. Widespread use of the automobile, or the development of the jet engine were ultimately reflected in geopolitical analysis. Use of the Internet, electronic banking, or DNA labeling, however, are less likely to be incorporated into geopolitical viewpoints because the varying changes that they make to the value of places is not geologically, or geophysically, visible. In this century the most hotly contested natural resource is not likely to be some hydrocarbon with a physical geographic manifestation. It is more likely to be the incidence, concentration and preparation of high-end math minds.[222] Geopolitics is hard pressed to comprehend a geographic advantage for such a resource.

---

[221] See generally Ronnie D. Lipschutz, When Nations Clash.

[222] On this point see Geoffrey Demarest, "Organized Brigandage and the Structure of Life: The Top Ten Threats to America" at Foreign Military Studies Office http://leav-www.army.mil/fmso/documents/topten.htm

Even less physically visible are the relative commercial values of places owing to the varying mix of rights and duties attendant there. It is difficult to imagine the geopolitician painting a place as more significant strategically because its people have long expected that their rights to peaceful use and enjoyment of land was secure. This again is because geopolitics does not begin from an integral theory about what makes a spot on the surface of the earth relatively valuable. We would suppose that any theory capable of explaining the value of places must incorporate technological change. Geoproperty does that, not looking simply at location or the geophysical qualities of a place, but seeking its relative value in relation to all potential claimant identities and in consideration of all the practicable divisions of rights and duties. To the extent a polity is market-guided, the value of rights and duties is automatically responsive to new technologies -- whether they be physical, such as an aircraft that might overfly (or land on) a given place, or an organizational technology, such as a digital system that makes the borders of that same land visible online.

Specifically, property analysis demands as its kindling all knowledge exposing rights to the use of a place or thing (which we can also call wealth), and especially all evidence that ties owners in some way to a time and place. The logic of a property-based security analysis is simple: wealth, power and the capacity to manifest ill intent are all closely related; 'property' is a universally encountered form of agreement regarding preferential wealth; records of that wealth can be found almost everywhere, or created. Once this information tying persons to places is amassed, the job of presenting the data in a digestible form is made practicable by the new technologies of geographic information systems (GIS). GIS is but an elegant, civilian extension of what military planners have called the Intelligence Preparation of the Battlefield, or IPB. This bigger, better IPB reveals the exact places where bad guys must be if they are human enough to eat or sleep or evacuate, or to visit their relatives, inspect their farms, or check their bank accounts. On a much larger scale the same analytical starting point leads to why a country has more strategic potential, not irrespective of the country's environmental bounty or geophysical placement, but rather explicitly cognizant of important determinants of power-- determinants that are more possibilist than determinist.

Plate Tectonics

"We have said that by power we mean the power of man over the minds and actions of other men, a phenomenon to be found whenever human beings live in social contact with one another."[223] We can reconcile this statement made by Hans Morgenthau with the John Adams quotation above, but it appears Adams understood power better than did Morgenthau, and Adams also understood the societal consequence of the American Revolution, even then. Defense policy specialist Colin Gray's optic can be placed closer to Morganthau's -- that the essence of power is simply influence over behavior. "From a strategic viewpoint, military, economic, or cultural power can all be reduced to the common currency of greater or lesser control over behavior."[224] Following a property-based analysis, power can mean the ability to gain or protect property rights. Strategic power for a country means the ability to protect or gain ownership rights inside and outside its borders.[225] If a nation can take possession of a piece of distant

---

[223] Hans J. Morgenthau, Kenneth W. Thompson, Politics Among Nations: the Struggle for Power and Peace, Sixth Edition (New York: Alfred Knopf, 1973), p. 117. "We have spoken of the "power of a nation" or of "national power' as though the concept were self-evident and sufficiently explained by what we have said about power in general. Yet, while it can be easily understood that individuals seek power, how are we to explain the aspirations for power in the collectivities called nations? What is a nation? What do we mean when we attribute to a nation aspirations and actions?... when we speak in empirical terms of the power or of the foreign policy of a certain nation, we can only mean the power or the foreign policy of certain individuals who belong to the same nation." Ibid.
[224] Colin S. Gray, "Strategic Sense, Strategic Nonsense," The National Interest, Fall 1992, p.11.
[225] The adjective "strategic" should not be given more credit than it is due. We often suppose "strategic" to have some logical relationship to the noun "strategy," and thus a national strategy is related to a nation's strategic power. There is a usage problem disjoining the two terms, however. Military strategists try to enforce some semantic discipline, but do so somewhat arbitrarily. An armored division may be designated as

229

territory and hold on to it indefinitely against opposition, it seems to have great strategic power in the classic sense. The British showed as much in 1982 when they acted to repossess the Falkland/Malvinas Islands from Argentina and hold on to them. That event offers us a concise example of relative strategic *military* power. Consider the distance, the amount of geography disputed, the time it takes to gain physical control of the geography, and the amount of time total ownership can be upheld after taking possession. Within six weeks of the Argentines having possessed, the British moved an attack force 8,000 miles, repossessed 12,170 square kilometers of territory within four more weeks and maintained possession indefinitely against a hostile claim. Britain demonstrated greater classic strategic power relative to Argentina. The British traveled farther, repossessed, and then retained possession indefinitely. Does this type of strategic power have to be measured in relative terms? Does the measure of strategic military power always require competition? According to Morgenthau, apparently so – at least during the Cold war.

---

a tactical unit and a tank army as strategic--but it all depends on the context. The military staffs of some smaller countries may refer to a given battalion as "strategic" because it can be committed throughout the national territory, is released at the national staff level, or is capable of making decisive changes in the course of combat actions. In U.S. Army parlance, a third term, "operational," is inserted between tactical and strategic. It is another difficult term because "operation" and all of its derivatives--like "operations," "operative," "operational" or "operating" all have a variety of military meanings depending on the context of their use. Since the Second World War, "operational" has gained honored space in the hierarchy of terms as it refers to a level of military art or knowledge. At the operational level, maneuvers are planned and executed that achieve or support strategic goals and that involve multiple units at the tactical level. Meanwhile, the U.S. Air Force has become disenchanted with the adjective "strategic." The Persian Gulf War saw the B-52 strategic bombers flying tactical support missions while tactical fighters were doing strategic bombing. At the heart of its universal usage, "strategic" carries the connotation of comprehensiveness-- of being more than just military or local or short-term. For the U.S. military, strategy does not lie atop the pyramid of decision-making. Above it is policy, a term reserved in professional subordination for the leadership expressions of the highest government officials. Outside military vernacular, strategy may still be found in the middle of the hierarchies used to describe decision-making. Vision/strategy/projects/tactics is a typical ordering.

When we refer to the power of a nation by saying that this nation is very powerful and that that nation is weak, we always imply a comparison. In other words, the concept of power is always a relative one. When we say that the United States is at the present one of the two most powerful nations on earth, what we are actually saying is that if we compare the power of the United States with the power of all other nations, as they exist at present, we find that the United States is more powerful than all others save one.[226]

The relativity of national power is evident in many situations, but insistence on the relativity of power can produce a false logic for at least two reasons. The first reason concerns the diminishing marginal utility of many kinds of power. While we can always measure one person or firm to be wealthier or poorer than another in financial terms, there comes a practical point where additional personal wealth cannot provide much greater comfort, safety or fulfillment. In other words, as people come to realize, stating wealth in relative terms can perpetuate false logic regarding the possible application of wealth. One can have a cat as good as the king's. Likewise, a nation can achieve liberty, security and economic progress without aggregating power for the purpose of controlling other lands. Nations often gain wealth without relative reference to the power of other nations and can claim great national power--great because it is sufficient to achieve security and prosperity. More than one people can maximize their power without the imperative that they have great or even relative ability to influence the behavior of others. In fact, accumulations of the instruments that seem able to change the relative balance of power often add little to the practical well-being of a nation. While the power to resist the aggressive behavior of other nations may indeed be necessary, it is generally far less power than needed to project physical control outside the nation. We needn't suspend our disbelief regarding the goodness of the species. The point is not a denial of the competitive and

---

[226] Hans J. Morgenthau, Kenneth W. Thompson, <u>Politics Among Nations</u>, p. 117.

dominance-seeking nature of man. It regards only the parameters of logic about military and diplomatic power used internationally. Unfortunately, when power is defined in terms of the relative ability to influence others, there follows (by intuition if not by logical imperative) a corollary that well-being depends on the ability to control other nations. False though this reasoning is in many international relationships, it has motivated much strategic thinking.

> "[W]e must know that the territorial imperative—just one, it is true, of the evolutionary forces playing on our lives—is the biological law on which we have founded our edifices of human morality. Our capacities for sacrifice, for altruism, for sympathy, for trust, for responsibilities to other than self-interest, for honesty, for charity, for friendship and love, for social amity and mutual interdependence have evolved just as surely as the flatness of our feet, the muscularity of our buttocks, and the enlargement of our brains, out of the encounter on ancient savannahs between the primate potential and the hominid circumstance. Whether morality without territory is possible in man must remain our final, unanswerable question."[227]

The second reason that insistence on the relativity of national power is a false logic has to do with the less tangible ingredients of power. Perceived power is often as important as real power, and national will-- the quantity we have portrayed earlier as national morale translated by leadership into resolve--is often as important as all other factors combined. It is no surprise that in many pure property contests, nations around the world are emboldened to challenge the United States. This is often because of the widespread knowledge that although the United States has tremendous potential national power, both real and perceived, it is power only equal to the measure of national will

---

[227] Ardrey, Robert. The Territorial Imperative: A Personal Inquiry into the Animal Origins of Property and Nations. New York: Antheneum, 1966, p. 351.

232

applicable to a given situation. In 1993, it at first made sense to the military leaders of Haiti to defy the military might of the United States.[228] The U.S.S. Harlan County, carrying 193 U.S. and 25 Canadian troops, had been ordered to dock in Port-au-Prince. As the ship drew near the landing, it was met by a chanting, armed crowd of about a hundred people. Several small craft blocked the dock so that the vessel could not unload. The crowd grew somewhat, threatening diplomats who had arrived by car. Armed thugs began firing into the air. The Harlan County was ordered to withdraw. Chances of success against the Harlan County were far greater than they would have been against smaller contingents any number of much less militarily capable countries. The example suggests that at times national power cannot be usefully compared away from the context of a specific situation. The clearest theoretic measures of power are presented within the confines of some artificial test situation-- often that of imagined all-out, winner-take-all war. In such a context, the United States generally wins. So what?

Adding things up in a different way, we can see that the United States is the most powerful country not because it might or might not prevail in an unconstrained war, or because it has relatively more power than any other individual country. What it has is more visible property claims in more places and against more claimants than any other country. The possibilities of getting mixed up in a property dispute are greater for the United States because its citizens claim more rights and more duties in more places than anybody else. These ownership claims don't exist because of unilateral presumptions on the part of US citizens, though this is hardly unheard of. Mostly they are the result of evolved mutual or common understandings of rights and duties, contracts of one kind or another. Some of these contracts are specific and formal. Others are unwritten, binding because some current of public understanding accepts them intuitively. In cases that may seem strange to some and simple to others--like feeding a starving

---

[228] Donald E. Schulz and Gabriel Marcella, Reconciling The Irreconcilable: The Troubled Outlook For U.S. Policy Toward Haiti, (Carlisle, PA: Strategic Studies Institute, 1994) p. 1.

population, many peoples expect the United States and a handful of Western allies to do something, as though the pitiable results of every failed system of ownership created a responsibility. Such expectations resonate because so many persons in the United States and other Western countries *do* admit a responsibility. How then are psychological components of national will such as this group conscience to be factored into national power? They can't be correlated with access to strategic minerals, or control of ocean choke points. They can, however, be understood in a property context, given, as we have asserted, that property is a recognition of agreements entailing shared identities, rights and duties.

At the beginning of this section allusions were made to two specific strategic competitions, one small and one large. They were the war over the Falkland/Malvinas Islands, and the global competition between the United States and the Soviet Union. It is worth noting that had the Argentines not attempted the use of military power to retake the Malvinas/Falkland Islands, and had instead pursued a strategy that protected property rights and values, grandfathering citizenship preferences, exempting military service and the like (in other words, had it addressed in detail the gamut of divisible rights and duties associated with the place and that might apply in the context of a change of sovereignty), it is likely in retrospect that the British would have conceded sovereignty of the islands to Argentina. As for the Cold War, it can hardly be said that the great military expenditures of the United States and the West did not play in the demise of the Soviet Union, but the observation is also valid that Soviet military power was inept to protect it from its own misunderstanding of the interplay of daily rights and duties. The balance between the corporate will to repress and the individual will to express finally favored the latter to an uncontrollable degree.

In 1975, intelligence and national security expert Ray Cline wrote an analysis in which he explained why the balance of world power seemed for many to be slipping toward the totalitarian countries.[229] The book was published at a moment when United States power was perceived to be unfocused and the nation confused after the debacle of Vietnam. Dr. Cline's analysis featured a United States in apparent strategic decline faced by a "clear and present danger" of totalitarian assertiveness. Sir Halford Mackinder is admired in the book's introduction for his prescience in portraying the Eurasian heartland as key to command of the world's resources and peoples. While Dr. Cline was careful to reject adoption of the term "geopolitics," he set a geographical foundation for his strategic analysis and used the then novel theory of the movement of tectonic plates to propose a substitute term, "politectonics." The tectonic plate idea was evocative of the continental scale of bipolar competition--intercontinental missiles and so forth--but the methodology was not an offspring of plate theory. Cline derived calculations of perceived power using a combination of mathematical formulae and subjective weightings of several power factors. His formula looked as follows:

$$PP = (C+E+M)x(S+W)$$

PP= Perceived Power
C= Critical Mass= Population + Territory
E= Economic Capability
M= Military Capability
S= Strategic Purpose
W= Will to Pursue National Strategy

Without accusing Dr. Cline of perpetrating a statistical fraud, his mathematic was in some measure a Trojan horse to make a larger point about the importance of national will and coherent national strategy. The weights of the various factors are such that national strategy and will are the notably weak components in the United States rating for perceived power. The math seems to deliver a preplanned conclusion. Nevertheless, the particulars of the methodology deserve separate consideration, the real problem being the lack of a most important variable. Cline's measurements of power did not incorporate consideration of the value of different pieces of geography as seen by

---

[229] Ray S. Cline, World Power Assessment (Boulder: Westview Press, 1975)

different potential owners. They did not incorporate the essential question of *how* land is owned. His assessment of power also does not satisfy the basic question about the use of power. For the geopolitician, or great power theorist, power is the power to exert will over others. This definition, accepting it as true, still begs a question. While there is some pure pleasure in having control over others, the next question has to be asked--power to get others to do what? What do people want others to do when they gain power? The answer is that they want preferential rights, almost always over the uses of land, and often over the people on it. Unlike geopolitics, property analysis considers human conflict in terms of the subjective value of distinguishable rights associated with land and assesses power according to the ability to gain or protect these rights as they are divisible, and not necessarily as they are gained whole. Geopolitical analysis encourages consideration of pieces of geography taken whole, that is, taken with all the bundle of rights together (what in legal verbiage we refer to as the whole fee or the fee simple).

In Games Nations Play, author John Spanier enters the same kind of analysis about national power as that suggested by Dr. Cline.[230] In a chapter entitled "The Ability to Play: Calculating Power," Spanier lists the components of national power as geography, population, natural resources, economic capacity, military strength, political systems and leadership, and national morale. Spanier also notes that power may exist only in the mind, and so the perception of power is measured as well. The type of reduction of national power exemplified by Spanier's list is an ever-recurring axiomatic foundation in American military writings on strategy. It is not exactly wrong, but it is not so right that it deserves such pervasive acceptance. To begin with, the components could be organized into a variety of different taxonomies. The term Geography could subsume population and natural resources, if not the other everything else. Economic power, which some theorists might say is of ultimate importance, depends on the other factors, so

---

[230] John Spanier, Games Nations Play Eighth Edition (Washington: Congressional Quarterly, Inc., 1993).

economic power could be the lead term and the others subordinate, etc. There is just nothing essential about the components of national power as they are often portrayed, and the proposed relationships are less essential still.[231]

Another, more important problem stalks the measurement of national power. The elements mislead when we take them as aggregate statistics whose influence is greater when their size is greater, instead of taking them as mere introductions to human dynamics. It is obvious that great population or extensive territory might lend potential power, so there is a tendency to presuppose that incremental increases in population or territory, or minor advantages in these factors, correlate to power advantages country-to-country. When we look at the countries of the world we see many with great populations, Bangladesh perhaps, with insignificant power. Adding a new increment to Bangladesh's population does not make it more powerful; it probably makes it less so. The fact that the United States is a superpower is based in part on large territorial size and large population, but an increase in population or territory (isolated from accompanying factors) will not make the United States more powerful. National will is important, but, being completely situation-dependent, is a different type of quantity than population and territory. While the national population can be counted and reported at any given time regardless of other things, national will has to be measured in relation to a competitive issue of some kind. Not only is national will an intangible, it can't exist apart from other situational elements. Economic power is important, but only if it can be corralled by national leadership and backed by national will. Formulae for comparing national power such

---

[231] Other mnemonic devices, or 'laundry lists' are fashionable as prompts for studying national power, and these same lists are sometimes offered up as analytical tools for conflict. Currently in fashion in American military schools is the acronym PMESII (Political Military Economic Social Information and Infrastructure). To this is sometimes added other letters, like L for Law, I for Information Warfare, and F for Financial actions. On this see, Small Wars Council "DImE, PMECII and now MIDLIFE" at <http://council.smallwarsjournal.com/showthread.php?t=67>. The authors seem to set the right tone.

as those presented by Cline or Spanier cause confusion because of the long gamut of patterns of interaction, and also because they do not clearly comprehend what goes into the value of land – that not only does it matter what is on land, but how land is owned matters as well.

Writings on strategy continually revisit the idea of elements of national power because strategists seek perspectives of relative strengths and weakness to predict outcomes in interstate competition. As author Geoffrey Blainey, in his study, The Causes of War, states, "...[I]t is the problem of accurately measuring the relative power of nations which goes far to explain why wars occur."[232] Blainey cites sociologist Georg Simmel, who, in 1904 argued that the most effective way of preventing war was to possess exact knowledge of the comparative strength of the two opponents. Such knowledge, however, was generally attainable only by fighting the war. Blainey takes aim at theorists who have debated the importance of national power within the axiom that an imbalance of power promoted war and that a balance of power was an explanation for peace. According to Blainey, the balance of power theory of peace is not born out by the history of conflicts. Whether there have been seven major powers, or two, or one, the number and intensity of wars would vary according to other factors. A balance of power among major nations, according to Blainey, may be a formula for maintaining independence, but not necessarily peace. On the other hand, when power is understood, the relations between nations are less likely to lead to war than if the potential parties are mistaken as to their relative strengths and weaknesses.[233] Generalizing

---

[232] Geoffrey Blainey, The Causes of War, (New York: Macmillan Publishing Co., Inc., 1973) p. 114.
[233] "Chapter 8, The Abacus of Power," Ibid., 108-124 passim. Blainey also writes, "In peace time the relations between two diplomats are like relations between two merchants. While the merchants trade in copper or transistors, the diplomats' transactions involve boundaries, spheres of influence, commercial concessions and a variety of other issues which they have in common. A foreign minister or diplomat is a merchant who bargains on behalf of his country. He is both buyer and seller, though he buys and sells privileges and obligations rather than commodities. The treaties he signs are simply more courteous versions of commercial contracts." Ibid., p. 115.

about war aims, Blainey states that "the aims are simply varieties of power. The vanity of nationalism, the will to spread an ideology, the protection of kinsmen in an adjacent land, the desire for more territory or commerce, the avenging of a defeat or insult, the craving for greater national strength or independence, the wish to cement or impress allies--all these represent power in different wrappings."[234] Blainey correctly confuses power with property. Again, when asking what power is for, the logical answer is to gain and enforce preferential rights. The measurement of power is greatly complicated by the changing distribution, or diffusion, of power.

United States Military Strategy

> *"Once the reader understands...that before entering into battle a general must be most careful to secure his line or lines of retreat; he understands the leading principles of strategy, whether he can define the phrase to his satisfaction or not. He sees that a general whose road homeward or to his base is threatened or cut by a superior force must, if he loses a decisive battle, be ruined as well as defeated; while a general who has secured his line of communication will not be ruined even if defeated, but can fall back, procure recruits, replenish his waggons, and begin to fight again with a fair prospect of success."[235]*

T. Miller Maguire,
British military historian, barrister and geographer

The above statement by T. Miller Maguire, extracted from a work titled Military Geography, should focus the mind of the military

---

[234] Blainey, p. 149.
[235] T. Miller Maguire, Military Geography, London: C.J. Clay & Sons, 1899, p. 21.

239

reader of the present work more than any of the other quotations used to adorn its sections. Maguire wrote these lines around 1898. He belonged to a school of doctrinal thinking he referred to as 'imperialist' as opposed to a 'continental,' but not imperialist in the sense of defending and admiring Britain's territorial pretensions (although we can assume he did). He was a styled himself imperialist within the context of his concern for the study of military strategy and tactics. He juxtaposed his 'imperial' focus against that of the continentalist thinkers, who he described as obsessed with the time it might take to move an army from Metz to Paris. That is to say, Maguire looked out to the dozens of small wars, military commitments and challenges that Britain faced around the world (some not so small as small wars go -- the Boer War was contemporary to his writing), while the majority of his contemporaries concerned themselves with the conventional military challenges looming on the continent of Europe just a few leagues away. Maguire felt that not enough attention was being paid to the myriad engagements and fates presented by guerrilla as opposed to maneuver warfare. A reservist and a barrister, Maguire was a prolific writer and one of the great military theoretical writers of the day. That his name all but disappeared from the English-language military lexicon can be attributed to the great war in Europe swallowed whole his ruminations about lesser wars, and consigned his writings to the shadows. What is especially significant for the purposes of the present work is the open nature of Maguire's use of terminology.

Maguire does not offer a definition of 'strategy'; he simply states its essence to a broader audience. It is a statement of essence that is as true for Napoleon and the battle of Austerlitz as it is for a guerrilla commander in Mindanao. Here it guides us to the essential military reason for studying property and for collecting and analyzing property information. It says between the lines that in order to defeat a guerrilla general we must block his line of retreat, deny him his sanctuary. If we do not succeed in this, the guerrilla general may live to fight again, no matter how many battle defeats he suffers. The paragraphs below recall some of the influences, currents and changes in American military strategic thinking, but the text will return to Maguire's statement, underlining that in order to block his route of withdrawal, and to deny him sanctuary, the guerrilla's lines of communication must be found. As simple as that sounds, it is a truth that is forever overlooked or diminished at the expense of efficient intelligence effort and rational military strategy. Recent official US army doctrine defines insurgency as a protracted affair.[236] What an unfortunate result of forgetting strategy. Insurgent wars are not protracted by their nature. The insurgent general, careful to protect his way home, protracts them.

Right war, right knowledge

American military theory has drawn from an eclectic mix of thinkers such as Antoine-Henri Jomini, Carl von Clausewitz, Alfred Thayer Mahan, Emory Upton, Guilio Douhet, William Mitchell, Basil Liddell Hart and others. Jomini, for example, was influential for his structured, geometric approach to organizing a battlefield. Clausewitz proffered psychological aspects of war and the concepts of war as an instrument of policy. Clausewitz, a nineteenth century strategist who died before his famous On War was first published, became especially influential in American military thought after the Vietnam War. Mahan, an Annapolis graduate of 1859, promoted sea power to assure open maritime commerce.[237] He applied Jomini's concepts of concentration, interior lines and logistics to naval deployments. Major General Emory Upton argued, at the turn of the century, that civilian government should not interfere with operations of the army in the field. His admiration of German staff organization and professional schooling also had a lasting impact. Giulio Douhet, an Italian General

---

[236] See, for instance, Department of the Army, FMI 3-07.22 Counterinsurgency Operations (Washington, D.C.: Department of the Army, 2004) p. 1-1.
[237] English naval strategist and historian Julian Corbett has been making a comeback in the minds of American strategic thinkers. See James Goldrick and John B. Hattendorf eds., Mahan is Not Enough: The Proceedings of a Conference on the Works of Sir Julian Corbett and Admiral Sir Herbert Richmond, (Newport, RI: Naval War College Press, 1993); Corbett, Julian S., Some Principles of Maritime Strategy, (New York: Longmans, Green and Co., 1911).

of the 1930s, advocated massed bombing against enemy centers of industry and population, and outlined the three-dimensional aspect of air war. He argued that air power alone could win wars--a view that has seen some recent adherents. U.S. General William Mitchell taught centralized control of air assets to take advantage of the fundamental nature of air warfare. British officer and historian Liddell Hart (critical of Clausewitz) suggested an indirect approach to victory on the battlefield. Of all these, Clausewitz has been the most touted and debated in recent years, at least among the military population.[238]

As the Vietnam War drew to a close, the 1973 Arab-Israeli conflict offered a war fought to what seemed to be Clausewitzian specifications. It provided a basis for recapturing traditional military doctrine that had been obscured during the Vietnam decade. It was a refreshing example of maneuver by mobile, armored columns unhampered by the confusion of part-time combatants, civilian populations, urban complexity, or for that matter, foliage. In 1976 a new English translation of Von Clausewitz' On War rekindled interest in the fundamentals of strategy. On War quickly became a bible for tank and cavalry commanders predisposed to weighing description of the military problem in terms that celebrated the predominance of their role.[239]

Reinvigorated was a strong interest in the design and conduct of campaigns and large operations (operational art) and a conviction among U.S. military planners about the efficacy of overwhelming force to achieve strategic objectives. As Clausewitz said, "..war is an act of force, and there is no logical limit to the application of that force."[240]

---

[238] See Peter Paret, ed. Makers of Modern Strategy: from Machiavelli to the Nuclear Age (Princeton, New Jersey: Princeton University Press, 1986); See also Arthur F. Lykke, Jr., ed., Military Strategy: Theory and Application (Carlisle Barracks, Pennsylvania, U.S. Army War College, 1989).

[239] Colonel Harry G. Summers, Jr. used Clausewitz' principles of war to frame a critical analysis of U.S. policy in Vietnam. Harry G. Summers, Jr., On Strategy: The Vietnam War in Context (Carlisle, PA: Strategic Studies Institute, 1981).

[240] Carl von Clausewitz, On War, p. 77.

Not only did the absence of the Vietnam distraction allow U.S. military professionals the freedom to refocus on a preferred calculus of open warfare, Vietnam itself offered important strategic lessons. Slow escalation in the application of force, failure to fix the enemy, failure to secure support at home, failure to achieve the strategic offensive--these became Vietnam lessons to be avoided in future contests. But the post-Vietnam rebirth of operational art must be identified together with its earlier European roots; it not only boasted a German guru in Clausewitz, but also a Germanic hubris that arrived hand-in-hand with geopolitics.

This hubris can be explained by reference to another, less well-known German strategic thinker named Hans Delbruck.[241] Delbruck was not a military professional, but a civilian historian. During his lifetime, Delbruck's scholarship and methodology were dismissed by most military officers in Germany. Strategic wisdom in the late nineteenth century was the property of the German General Staff and the Prussian General Staff College. There, strategy professors adulated Frederick the Great. An author and philosopher, Frederick had also been a military strategist whom the General Staff looked upon as a paragon.[242] Modern day historian Arden Bucholz also attributes to the mainstream German military thinking of the day a one-sided interpretation of Carl von Clausewitz. "To that generation Clausewitz seemed to have captured the essence of the wars of unification: war was an act of violence carried to the utmost bounds. The destruction of the enemy fighting force by battle was the only valid goal."[243] This supposedly Clausewitzian reading of Frederick's Military Testament was interpreted to support the Prussian School approach of annihilation battles, but Delbruck alone noted a completely different lesson in Frederick's writing. "Frederick had always regarded battle as an evil to be undertaken only in necessity, as Clausewitz himself had pointed

---

[241] See Arden Bucholz, Hans Delbruck and The German Military Establishment: War Images in Conflict (Iowa City: University of Iowa Press, 1985).

[242] Ibid, p. 4.

[243] Ibid., p. 6.

out."[244] Delbruck felt that Frederick's strategy had to be understood in terms of the social and technological conditions prevailing in Frederick's day. Delbruck suggested an attrition strategy that would wear Germany's enemies down and allow its leaders to leverage advantage in political negotiations. His inglorious advice was to not look for a decisive victory, thereby avoiding decisive defeat or the loss of resources.[245] German failure in World War I would be debated in reference to Delbruck's attrition option to the German General Staff's

---

[244] Ibid., p. 9.

[245] The history of Soviet military thinking includes a similar debate. Marshal Mikhail Tukhachevskii best represents the decisive battle school of Russian military thinking that reached its apex during the interwar period of this century. For Tukhachevskii and his followers, the future of war was mobility and firepower. Defense was deemed senseless as one could not defend against the new weapons of future war. The objective had to be destruction of the enemy forces by a series of strikes into enemy territory (Germany in mind). On the other side was General-Major Alexandr Svechin. For Svechin, attrition strategies were sensible and perhaps the only path to victory. A resolute attack could consume incalculable resources and, as a rule, would not be justified by operational gains. Attacking troops run the risk of having lines of communication interdicted or of suffering flank attacks. Therefore, in the opening phase of a war it is more expedient to keep on the strategic defensive. War can be waged at the same time on economic and political fronts while gradual, favorable change is sought in the relationship of military forces. Of course, Svechin was looking from a Russian perspective, Delbruck a German one. Svechin taught a flexible generality about attrition and annihilation strategies. For him they were debatable, adjustable, and blendable quantities whose relative measure depended on the situation at hand. The balancing of strategies became part of "operational art." See Jacob W. Kipp, "General Major A.A. Svechin and Modern Warfare" in Alexandr Andreevich Svechin. Strategy edited by Kent D. Lee, Minneapolis: East View Press, 1992). Dr. Kipp argues persuasively, *inter alia*, that the American military strategy in the 1990 Gulf War fit the strategic model that Svechin called attrition. But this is almost the opposite application of the term attrition that this author seeks. It can, after all, be argued that the Gulf War exemplified the decisive battle philosophy of a Tukhachevskii. Strategy has been delimited as a blending of ways, means and objectives. The objective from the outset of the Gulf War campaign, the resources mustered to accomplish the objective, and the methods chosen were all geared toward decisively destroying the Iraqi Army and physically removing it from Kuwait. Whatever the mixing of diplomacy and economic leverage, it is difficult to assign the English word attrition to such a military undertaking.

obsession with seeking the decisive battle. While many Germans agreed during the interwar period with Delbruck's "I told you so," the German penchant would prevail. And where in Delbruck's pallid criticism was there sufficient room for the dark Hegelian esteem of war for its own sake?

For the United States, the Delbruckian lesson is not so much that the United States should today seek attrition rather than decisive strategies in military confrontations. The lesson is that the United States will not be given many opportunities to apply the favored Clausewitzian strategies because most opponents will take Delbruck's advice. Smart foes will not seek victory in open, decisive battle against the Americans. They will apply violence to erode resolve, constantly leveraging ruthlessness against weariness, fear, and moral self-constraint. In this way attrition becomes synonymous with interminable extortion. A strategy of permanent violence appears in which no final uniformed, tanked, maneuver battle is offered to the Americans. It is terrorist guerrilla war generalized. If American impatience and anger draws U.S. military might out of its holster, it will not find a final objective, or least that is the theory. Supposedly either there will be no Baghdad to go to, or if a target seems to exist that promises a satisfying military closure, it will be too distant given the confines of the same American impatience and moral self-constraint. Wealth and value will be extracted violently and piecemeal from a United States that is hoping for that situation where American military-capital advantages are insuperable. Worst of all, at some point, the whittling away at US warring strength, and a smart enemy's ability to recognize its proper occasion, might make traditional defeat of an American force an attractive possibility.

U.S. military manuals soon incorporated much of the experience of the 1991 Persian Gulf War, especially the notion that to win efficiently the U.S. must apply decisive force in simultaneous attack throughout the entire battle space.[246] In other words, instead of just a synchronized set of events and maneuvers, attacks against the enemy will be mounted in priority, all over, as much as possible, in a furious overlapping rhythm. This improvement (made possible by new technology) on the tried-and-true Germanic basics is appropriate in view of the large force-on-force battles that might yet have to be fought. It has nevertheless been partially mocked by the transformation in the strategic environment. Peacekeeping, humanitarian assistance, nation assistance, counterinsurgency and the like have been harder for the US military to embrace within its doctrine.[247] These tasks are treated as extraordinary--even as they have become the everyday challenge and occupation.

---

[246] For example, see Department of the Air Force, Air Force Manual 1-1, Basic Aerospace Doctrine of the United States Air Force (Washington: Department of the Air Force, 1992, Volumes I and II). "One way a commander can exercise operational art is through a strategic air campaign that directly attacks an enemy's centers of gravity. Providing these centers are accurately identified and can be struck effectively at a tempo that maximizes psychological shock, the campaign may be decisive through air action alone." Ibid., Vol. II, p. 129; "The principal means for the application of military force is combat--violence in the form of armed conflict." Department of the Navy, Fleet Marine Force Field Manual (FMFM) 1, Warfighting (Washington, D.C.: Headquarters, U.S. Marine Corps, 1989), p. 20;"We must be ruthlessly opportunistic, actively seeking out signs of weakness, against which we will direct all available combat power. And when the *decisive* opportunity arrives, we must exploit it fully and aggressively, committing every ounce of combat power we can muster and pushing ourselves to the limits of exhaustion." Ibid., p. 61; "The objective [of a campaign] is the employment of overwhelming military force designed to wrest the initiative from opponents and defeat them in detail." Chairman, Joint Chiefs of Staff, Joint Publication 1, Joint Warfare of the U.S. Armed Forces (Washington, D.C.: Joint Chiefs of Staff, 1991), p. 47

[247] Only in the 1993 version of Operations were "operations other than war" given a chapter at the end of the manual--but with a different set of principles. Overwhelming force and decisiveness gave way to perseverance and restraint. The tendency in Joint and service doctrine is to treat low intensity conflict (more recently operations other than war) as a thing apart from "normal" or traditional warfare; but commanders would use force structure designed for conventional war to support unique tasks such as nation assistance, countering illicit drug trafficking, and peacekeeping.

Soon after the immensely successful application of U.S. military power in 1991, Chairman of the Joint Chiefs of Staff, General Colin Powell offered a proposal for a twenty-five percent defense spending downturn to a "Base Force" level as a hedge against Congressional demands for more dramatic expenditure reductions. One critic of the Base Force was Congressman Les Aspin, who considered the proposed reduction as too timid and out of touch with the changed world.[248] With the subsequent change from the Bush to the Clinton Administration in January 1992, newly appointed Secretary of Defense Les Aspin began a "Bottom-Up Review" to assess the threats to the nation and to determine military force structure. The review was designed in good part "to rationalize reductions in the $120 billion range over the Bush Administration's defense spending plans for 1995-99."[249] The result was a force structure design that would purportedly deter nuclear attack and meet the needs of prosecuting two major regional conflicts (MRC) nearly simultaneously. The same collection of general purpose forces needed for two MRCs would provide the military resources for smaller-scale conflicts or crises.

Other challenges to US national security were beginning to become more visible with the Soviet bogyman gone -- black market trading of nuclear material, weapons proliferation in all its dimensions (including weapons of mass destruction in the hands of rogue states, terrorists and organized criminals), conflict over scarce resources and environmental values, ethnic and religious conflict, spread of uncontrollable viruses and other diseases, the transnational linkages of crime, drug trafficking and its stormy marriages with terrorism and insurgency, illicit electronic capital movement, migration and illegal immigration, famine, mob violence and spontaneous ungovernability.

---

[248] Harry E. Rothmann, Forging a new National Military Strategy in a Post-Cold War World: A Perspective from the Joint Staff (Carlisle, Pennsylvania: Strategic Studies Institute, 1992); See also, Dennis M. Drew, "Recasting the Flawed Downsizing Debate," Parameters, Spring 1993, p. 39.

[249]. Colin S. Gray, "Off the Map: Defense Planning After the Soviet Threat," Strategic Review, Spring 1994, p. 33.

Unrestrained by borders and the traditional protocols of the international system, these dangers threaten a nation-state system poorly prepared to deal with non-governmental global dynamics. United States military doctrine and force structure was designed almost exclusively around traditional concepts of overwhelming conventional force to achieve decisive Clausewitzian victory--an unlikely formula for success against most of the emerging threats. Yet the changes proposed were related to the opportunity to reduce conventional forces, not a restructuring to face the emerging set of new threats.

The long list, just summarized, of "other" dangers invites another list. Typical military tasks in what the U.S. Army briefly took to calling Operations Other than War (OOTW) include surveillance and investigation; intelligence gathering, reporting, and analysis; negotiation and mediation; patrolling, traffic control, monitoring transportation of goods, local security, search and seizure of contraband; medical care, supervision of internees and prisoners of war, humanitarian aid, evacuation and relocation of refugees, warding of undocumented migrants; engineer construction, mine clearing or other ordnance disposal, route maintenance, force security; and, still, combat. If the list resonates of police more than military responsibilities, it should come as no surprise that most of the tasks present themselves in conflicts for which no decisive battle-annihilation strategy seems reasonable and attrition strategy illogical as well, since it is so often impossible to be sure what there might be to attrite.

Has there been inconsistency between the dangers presented and military strategy (the resources, methods and objectives) established for meeting the dangers? Les Aspin's bottom up review stated,

> ...our emphasis on engagement, prevention, and partnership means that, in this new era, U.S. military forces are more likely to be involved in operations short of declared or intense warfare. Events of the past few years have already borne this out, as our armed forces

have been involved in a wide range of so-called
"intervention" operations, from aiding typhoon victims
in Bangladesh during Operation Sea Angel, to delivering
humanitarian relief to the former Soviet Union under
Operation Provide Hope, to conducting the emergency
evacuation of U.S. citizens from Liberia during
Operation Sharp Edge, to restoring order and aiding the
victims of the civil war in Somalia during Operation
Restore Hope.[250]

It sounded as though the new military operational environment
was seen clearly. After the 1991 Gulf War, and the coincidental end of
the Cold War, the US defense establishment made sounds leading some
to doubt that it recognized the panorama of new threats or that it was
reorganizing to address it. Admiration of the "military technical
revolution" (which soon became interchangeable with "revolution in
military affairs") provided observations about the relationship of new
technologies to the future of U.S. security challenges. [251] We can
define technical revolution as a fundamental advance in technology,
doctrine, or organization rendering existing methods of conducting
warfare obsolete. The question is, has the technical revolution
addressed forms of warfare that the US had never mastered, and that
have not become obsolete. Some theorists seemed to be trying to take
the technical revolution in the direction of threats that were understood,
and away from those that were more likely. Treatment of irregular
warfare seemed to betray a stubborn institutional preference for large
military technical systems. Leading security theorists described a
revolution in information, sensing, and precision strike technologies,
but not everyone was impressed. In a potent critique, A.C. Bacevich
jabbed that "however handsomely packaged, institutional advocacy of

---

[250] Les Aspin, Report on the Bottom-Up Review (Washington: U.S. Department of
Defense, 1993), pp. 8-9
[251] For instance, in April, 1994, the US Army War College held a conference titled
The Revolution in Military Affairs: Defining an Army for the 21st Century.

change almost invariably conceals a defense of orthodoxy." Bacevich stated:

> In truth, as currently touted by soldiers, the very concept of a Military Revolution is profoundly reactionary. Its true aim is to roll back the two genuine revolutions that have shaped war in the modern age, revolutions for which military professionals never devised an adequate response. The first of those revolutions was the advent of total war, culminating in the creation of nuclear weapons. The second--in large measure stimulated by the first--was the proliferation of conflict at the opposite end of the spectrum: terror, subversion, insurgency, and "peoples war."[252]

Critics of the establishment revolution could also scoff at the military's once again wanting to re-fight the last war. The technologies of the insiders' revolution were those that would have been applied with even greater effect had they been available in the 1991 Gulf War, and eventually, in the 2003 Iraq war, they were. The conventional revolution also serviced another goal, support of a professionally technified, *ergo* smaller, military. The second Iraq war seems to have justified much of the conventional revolution's precepts. Nevertheless, if America's strategic habit did not serve with distinction in the two forms of twentieth-century war that Bacevich mentions, why expect this conventionalism to meet the challenge presented by unconventional forms of twenty-first-century struggle? More kinetic precision, more capital, and more information paid off in taking out the Iraqi regime, as did, to be fair, more psychological preparation of the battlefield.

---

[252] A.C. Bacevich ,"Preserving the Well-Bred Horse," National Interest , Fall 1994.

A general whose road homeward is cut, is ruined

The Maguire quotation that began this section compels attention. It says to us that however different an insurgency is from conventional style maneuver warfare, there is an essence to strategy that supersedes the differences. The enemy leader has to be concerned for his escape route, his route home, and it does not matter that he is the leader of a German Army encircled at Stalingrad or Saddam Hussein caught in a dirt hole. Once his route home is blocked, the leader will not just suffer defeat in battle at the hands of a superior force, he will be done, ruined. Even if a leader looses a half million men on the frozen march away from Moscow, however, he might have the chance to reconstitute a force and threaten Europe again -- if he can escape his confinement. If this lesson is indeed the essence of understanding military strategy, regardless of how we attempt to define the term (and I believe it is), then it leads us to what we can do to win an insurgent war, or at least what will keep us from winning it. It also throws a wrench into the debate between our Prussian general staff and the historian Delbruck. If we cannot identify the enemy general's route of escape, or at least reasonably anticipate it, or establish likely choices, then we cannot act on Maguire's observation. We cannot block his route of escape or deny him sanctuary if we can't find his line of communication home.

In an insurgency there is going to be a system of leaders and leadership. Some activities of a population may be nearly spontaneous, driven by an understood common agenda and an occasion to act to a generalized call to action. Such phenomena are rare or sidelights, or unmemorable (with some significant exceptions such as the Tiananmen Square defiance). What we know about the application and management of force is that it is dangerous and effective in relation to the quality of leadership. What we know of the history of insurgencies is that they are successful when led by effective leaders and when those effective leaders are killed or captured, the insurgency is correspondingly weakened or dead. Once Gonzalo is captured, Sendero Luminoso all but ceases to exist, and when captured leaders

251

sing to interrogators, even their most able subordinates are vulnerable and can be rendered impotent.

Knowing that, whatever the nature of the conflict, the opponent force has leaders who eat, sleep and defecate, we can apply our system of property logic and data to identify where. If we do not have such a system, then we cannot apply a military strategy cognizant of or obedient to the essence of military strategy. Our strategy will have to be reactive, or one of hope, but it will not close with and eliminate the enemy by planned initiative. But the question is still begged: how do we create, in economic time, a system of intelligence that can find the lines of communication, and particularly the lines of retreat of an intelligent enemy insurgent leader (who is well aware of the essence of strategy -- since it is stuck so intimately to his skin)? The answer is formalized property. It is what almost every sheriff uses to find a perpetrator, fugitive or witness, but depending on property requires that the environment be shaped administratively to provide detailed information about the connections between individual habits and precise locations. This means that the military attempt what for civilians is commonplace -- to create a carefully drawn census, impose a system of individual identification cards for everyone, and map exactly who owns what and with whom, who is resident where, what the tenancy and debt relations are, the marriages and business associations, the descriptions of the cars or mules. It means street signs and phone books. With the availability of GIS technologies, the locations and linkages are exposed almost instantaneously, once the data is input. Will there be gaps, will people try to hide their assets and identities? Yes, but that is far beside the point. More important is that such systems are used in so many places today that it is surprising that no similar ones were timely emplaced in Haiti. When ownership rights are specifically assigned, not only do the owners have a stake in protecting preferential rights, but also it becomes easier to identify outsiders, to find the right candidates for interrogation and to precisely orient surveillance assets of all kinds. If this smacks of Big Brother, let there be no doubt. Population control is created on the basis of records, not batons. If a person wants to create impunity for his actions he is generally obliged to maintain anonymity for himself and his wealth. Once the authorities know the particulars of his motorcycle, phone or apartment, it is harder to act outside the law without consequence. It is difficult even to stand distant from home without that fact being apparent.

As long as no system of institutional knowledge regarding individual identity and wealth is created, other social, cultural and geophysical data about an environment is rendered less valuable for the capture of enemy leaders. If the lines of communication, and especially the lines of retreat and sanctuary of enemy leadership are not identified, military success against that enemy is not likely. In order to identify the finely drawn placement geography of insurgents, as opposed to the LOC of an army corps, maps must be drawn on the basis of individual identities linked to places and wealth individually and jointly owned. That wealth exists everywhere in the form of preferential rights to the use of places and things. These preferential rights are what we have come to call property, and records of such rights either exist or can be created everyplace. Once a system of laws and administrative and technical capacity are married in such a way as to enable the mapping of property rights, then control of a population is, if not easy, practicable. So maybe Morganthau is right about power, that it is simply influence over behavior. Influence over the behavior of a population lies in the condition and use of mundane public records. What has or has not been done in Iraq is not the purview of this book, but if a census has not been done, the population not thoroughly ID-carded and comprehensive property registries not emplaced, then finding lines of communication of insurgents and strangers has got to be a difficult proposition. In addition, the same administrative actions, and especially the creation of formal systems of real property registration, are so essential to material prosperity (particularly among the poor) that to not implement such systems would seem doubly troublesome.

Pat of military strategy in counterinsurgency, then, is simplified and clarified. One goal is to capture the insurgent leaders; to do so we can block their routes of escape and close their sanctuaries; to do this we identify the routes and sanctuaries geographically with sufficient precision that we can act on the information. It is a short distance from simple to simplistic, so to defend against accusation of the latter, I throw in some disclaimers. None of this insistence on geographic lines of insurgent communication suggests that psychologically appropriate messages to sway behavior might not be helpful, or that all kinds of other cultural information don't add to the useful mix of knowledge or that other actions to protect the friendly force or diminish the capabilities of the enemy are not valid. Every piece of cultural knowledge becomes increasingly valuable, however, once we orient on the tasks of identifying the LOCs. If we know of an important local holiday, a specific dish of food eaten on a given date, the favorite colors of a local sports team, the psychological profile of persons likely to render useful information, it can almost all be mapped and add to the refinement of understanding of time and space regarding the likely whereabouts of an individual or group. Property theory challenges the military leader to determine what belongs to whom. It says that in our civilian contexts, in developed societies, lawyers and judges and policemen every day use detailed knowledge about preferential property (even if only from the phone book) and cultural habits to forecast the locations of individuals and groups. It is not always possible to serve a summons on an unwilling defendant, but it almost always happens. It happens because the system of laws and the natural habit of people to order their lives according to preferential use of land has prepared the terrain for identification of personal placement.

If it is not possible to replicate this condition of a developed society in a given geography, it is at least possible to move in the right direction. Closing a line of communication or an escape route does not necessarily mean a physical blockade. It may mean that movement and whereabouts is betrayed by citizens or members of the insurgent group, that the insurgent has too little time to prepare security or move furtively, or that other conditions of life require the presence of the leader in unsafe places. Maguire's 'essence' is not a geometric contemplation. The blockage of a route of escape is a matter of factors that make capture or elimination possible because all leaders have human needs, and all organizations must be maintained through some sort of supply, communication and discipline.

The paragraphs immediately above concern a narrow understanding of military strategy, aimed at a dangerous enemy, within a country suffering some form of internal conflict. As noted earlier in the text, the geopolitical or power-balancing school of strategic thought is naturally guided by the boundaries that make up the modern community of countries. Many of the most dangerous threats to the United States and globally, however, are transnational and paramilitary. The same arguments about the utility of property information and its construction apply to international and transnational organizations, lawful and unlawful. The geography of their wealth crosses political borders, but can be mapped. Sanctuaries and 'routes home' that cross and defy formal borders can also be mapped on the basis of property information.

Appropriate organization and weapons

Military strategy is more than action, comprehending also the organization and equipment with which action is to be achieved. Army strategist William Mendel wrote that the warfighting structure of the United States has been good for what it is good for--fighting and winning maneuver wars. Mendel pointed out, however, that the dominant doctrine of annihilation warfare left little tolerance among top military leaders for the idea of expanding the specialized force structure that deals with missions that are not maneuver war.[253] US military leaders insisted that "these capabilities [missions] could be provided by the same collection of general purpose forces needed for MRCs (major regional contingencies), so long as the forces had the appropriate training"[254]

---

[253] See generally William W. Mendel A Joint Command for Engagement Policy (Ft. Leavenworth Kansas: Foreign Military Studies Office, 1994).
[254] Les Aspin, Report on the Bottom-Up Review p. 29.

In 1994, the Rwanda humanitarian crisis operation, a Haiti intervention, and a Cuban refugee surge came nearly simultaneously. "The Americans came in full of plans and promises to put everything right, and as soon as they came in, they started talking about getting out," said a senior relief official about Rwanda.[255] One could not help but impact on the others. Joint Chiefs of Staff Chairman John Shalikashvili, expressed a common military attitude: "My fear is we're becoming mesmerized by operations other than war and we'll take our mind off what we're all about, to fight and win our nation's wars."[256] Civilian defense leadership was showing its frustration as well. Secretary of Defense William J. Perry said, "My job is managing an army, not a Salvation Army."[257] Irrespective of these complaints, the United States continued to apply military resources to resolve or at least influence violent struggles that did not reach the military leaders' idea of the status of one of the "nation's wars."

In spite of repeated and continuing use by US national leadership of conventional force structure (and doctrine) to accomplish police-type missions, results are mixed, but as the US defense establishment warms to the idea that special operating forces are becoming the key unit of employment, and that a full-time expeditionary-constabulary force may be inevitable, the kind of intelligence promoted by this book will gain in currency. Such forces are more likely to covet, seek and employ the kind of information that property formalization generates.

As asserted in Chapter One, every right that constitutes property is ultimately related to some form of enforcement or is subject to physical loss. The gap between protection of select rights in land and

---

[255] R. Jeffrey Smith, "Spooked by the Shadow of Somalia, the Pentagon is Ready to Pull Out of Rwanda After Delivering Much Less Than the U.S. Promised," The Washington Post National Weekly Edition, September 12-18, 1994, p. 16.
[256] Ibid.
[257] Ibid.

protection of the whole basket of rights (the fee) is one way of distinguishing police from military activities. Police forces are designed, equipped and trained for the purpose of defeating threats to rights that are less comprehensive than loss of the whole ownership, less than the entire sovereignty. This is reflected in the difference in weaponry and organization. There is a firepower gap, narrowing perhaps, between police and military weapons. Although there is no exact line between the two, it appears to fall somewhere around the use of the crew-served machine gun and certainly begins at the point of indirect fire weapons and bombs. This difference is a corollary to the difference in the reign of legality within most nation-states as opposed to among them. To the extent that the rule of law within a polity breaks down, the gap between the use of weapons appropriate for police purposes and those suited to military purposes often seems to close. When military forces occupy an area, but their mission is not to take and hold terrain, their weapon set may be inappropriate to a task that is more akin to police work. In other words, military weapons are more likely to be used even when inappropriate or excessive in relation to the rights and duties being enforced or challenged. The professional military forces are subject to committing actions that liken themselves to the acts of moral asymmetry about which the guerrilla or brigand forces are generally accused. This leads us back to the role of international law and jurist, and the question of proscribed weaponry. International conventions against the use of specified types of weapons have seen mixed obedience, but their influence on military practices should not be discounted.

The majority of explosive devices in many battle areas are of local manufacture, at least partially. Their use has a most direct relationship to rights in land. Landmines are regularly employed as a technological strategy for denying free use and access. In one typical use of the weapon, a guerrilla might cover a withdrawal route with explosives after having assaulted a town, a bridge, or a military outpost. The mines delay the pursuit by government forces, allowing the guerrilla to escape. Often the use of the mine supports a more strategic calculation. In order to leverage unspecific political concessions, or simply to lower government morale and tighten recruitment, guerrilla leaders may decide to inflict continuous casualties on government (or occupation) security forces. In order to do so, the guerrilla plots routes along which landmines can be best employed, then conducts an assault on a town or a bridge or a military outpost as an inducement for enemy regular forces to pursue the guerrilla and fall prey to the mines. In such cases the government casualty is the intermediate physical goal of the operation and the ultimate goal is attrition of government military morale or of the will of the public to support the government's counterinsurgency. So the landmine may be a weapon that supports an operation, or it may be the instrument whose employment is supported by the rest of the operation. Given the powerful relationship of this one weapon type to successful guerrilla strategies, both combat and psychological, the prospect of seeing an end to its use by guerrilla forces is dim. As noted earlier, the landmine is emblematic of moral asymmetry. Sadly, the number of geographies that are afflicted by the lingering presence of landmines is growing.

Guerrillas aside, the United States still needs big units with tanks and bombers and aircraft carriers that can go out and defeat uniformed, well-led and well-equipped military enemies. As Machiavelli opined,

> " those are able to maintain themselves who, from an abundance of men and money, can put a well appointed army into the field, and meet anyone in open battle that may attempt to attack them. And I esteem those as having need of the constant support of others who cannot meet their enemies in the field, but are under the necessity of taking refuge behind walls and keeping within them."[258]

---

[258] Nicolo Machiavelli, The Prince, Chapter X, translated by W. K. Marriott, online at http://www.the-prince-by-machiavelli.com/the-prince/the_prince_chapter_10.html The United States has one of about a dozen militaries in the world that maintain over 400 thousand men and women in uniform.

The US needs to root terrorist and subversive organizations out of their sanctuaries, but it cannot abandon all of its heavy force structure or mobile, combined arms method of warfare, since it may still be called on to close with and destroy modern military formations, and to take the fee simple. This book is about the importance of formal property as an indispensable condition for long-term peace, and as a tool that can help win at war against select enemies. Nevertheless, the age of warfare has not ended because we wish it has, and in some realms of endeavor property rights are still a luxurious detail. There will continue to exist a need to be able to take by force what we have referred to here as the whole fee. Meanwhile, we cannot continue to use the forces, methods and knowledge appropriate to whole-fee warfare in the contexts of internal conflict.

People and real estate: countering urban violence

The American military does not like fighting in the city. There are too many buildings and too many people.

> *"A major difficulty...is the deeply entrenched military*
> *opinion, that goes back many centuries, that cities are*
> *places where battles should not be fought.*
> *Consequently, when it occurred in urban areas, conflict*
> *tended to be regarded as an unfortunate aberration to*
> *be avoided in the future, rather than an example to be*
> *analyzed so that lessons for the future could be*
> *drawn."[259]*   G.J. Ashworth

---

[259] G.J. Ashworth, War and the City, (New York: Routledge, 1991), p. 92. Ashworth cites Yi-Fu Tuan, Landscapes of Fear (Oxford: Blackwell, 1979), p. 112. "It is difficult to draw a clear distinction between defense against external threats and that against internal insurgency. Such distinctions have rarely been drawn in history. City walls were intended as much to keep citizens in, and accounted for, as to keep enemies out. The wall had a practical, as well as symbolic, jurisdictional purpose, enabling the urban authorities to exercise a control over the movement of goods and people, and thus served police, customs, fiscal and immigration purposes (as such flows could be channeled through the limited number of gates which would be opened and guarded at specific times). Thus the distinction between police and

It should seem natural that information detailing the associations connecting real estate to its users would be key to population control, protection, and exposure of violent actors in urban areas. This, however, appears to be a more obvious conclusion within police intelligence culture, or even business culture, than for military intelligence. Existing military literature addresses the question of urban violence in terms of conventional combat, or of insurgency.[260] In conventional urban warfare doctrine the population is treated as either a physical obstacle or an annoyance, and stability or security of the population is considered a rear-area issue. Existing counter-insurgency literature also portrays urban environments as unique principally because of the nature of the terrain.[261] It fails to stress the world of records and signs that link the built environment to persons and persons to each other.

The direction of the best urban counterviolence can be expected to follow architecture as well as law. Architectural technology has proven successful in containing rioters and to limit the options of

---

military structures was generally blurred, with the same forces being called upon to perform both functions. Indeed, the only distinction between the modern situation--especially in countries with the Anglo-American aversion to paramilitary police forces--and that which prevailed in most countries until the last century, is that the military now operate "in support of the civil power', whereas previously they were frequently the only effective instrument of that power." Ibid.

[260] Jennifer Morrison Taw and Bruce Hoffman, The Urbanization of Insurgency (Santa Monica, California: RAND Arroyo Center, 1994).

[261] See, for instance, Bard E. O'Neill, Insurgency & Terrorism, (Washington, D.C.: Potomac Books, 2005), p.61; Anthony James Joes, Resisting Rebellion: The History and Politics of Counterinsurgency, (Lexington, KY, The University Press of Kentucky, 2004) p. 20; and Ian F. W. Beckett, "The Transition to Urban Insurgency" in Modern Insurgencies and Counter-Insurgencies: Guerrillas and their Opponents since 1750, (London: Routledge, 2001), pp. 151-217. In none of these books does the word property appear in the index. The analyses of the reasons why urban guerrillas fail do not hit on the essential facts tha anonymity works in favor of the would-be informant, that public records cause strangers to be highlighted, and that the need to create a support base cannot be reconciled against the need of that support base to register wealth somewhere with the government.

opposing groups intent on managing mob behavior. We can expect defense planners to survey urban landscapes using a methodology that keys on architectural phenomenon both to anticipate violence and to control it. In most of the world, architectural control strategies will not resemble the massive capital investment made by Los Angeles businesses to immunize their downtown area after the Watts riots, but they will reflect existing conditions of urbanization.[262] For instance, in many cities, the form and dynamics of the public transportation system guide the development of any impending mass demonstration. Security forces not only monitor and adjust aspects of the transportation system, they can create temporary architectures that restrict, canalize, diffuse or otherwise confound potentially violent congregating. Similar methods can be used to protect legally formed congregations against terrorist acts.

If we were to look at the evolution of organization and equipment of a standard US Army engineer battalion, we find that it changed little for a half century. Although this same half century saw incredible urbanization throughout the world, few urban-oriented changes occurred in how the Army organized its engineers. If we were to look at the standard requirements expected of a military police or military intelligence unit we would discover something parallel -- that they did not include conducting a census, building a cadastre, establishing an ID system that tagged everyone to a place of residence and work or building precise social labeling of places (such as the creation of street names and assignment of business addresses). In other words, the two aspects that make urban urban -- people and architecture -- were not until very recently reflected in military organization, equipment and doctrine. As far as the revealing linkages between people and place in the city, it goes without saying that it has been overlooked. The closeness of shantytowns to target crime areas, to high value real estate, or to vulnerable public service nodes can all be analyzed according to courses of action available to anti-state actors

---

[262] See generally Davis, Mike. Urban Control: The Ecology of Fear. Westfield, New Jersey: The Open Magazine Pamphlet Series, 1994.

and their containment. In addition, the specifics of property ownership, as detailed in land title registries and other ownership instruments, can be studied. This may suggest assignments of financial responsibility for strategic defense costs, provide information about the value and vulnerability of target areas, and reveal outlaw profit motivations. As urban violence evolves, so do the measures for countering it. Architects may become, in the urban context, the new military engineers--modern counterparts to the designers of the fortified cities of the early Seventeenth Century.[263]

Some will argue that broad social programs aimed at the socioeconomic causes of economic marginalization offer a more sane and humane approach to the problem of urban violence than does control architecture and Big Brother records-keeping.. Security forces should indeed address the sociological phenomenon of the excluded populations. Governments can seek new means of opening shantytowns to the presence of the state. These should pay particular attention to such things as the psychology of the abandoned child, and intimidations by criminal organizations that dry up publicly provided information. In a book titled New Visions for Metropolitan America, Anthony Downs outlined some government policy strategies for large cities in the United States. Downs presented a full matrix of options that included such things as expanding minority membership in local

---

[263] Two studies in Spanish, Manual de Métodos Geográficos Para el Análisis Urbano, Chile (Manual of Geographical Methods of Analysis, Chile) (México, D.F.: Instituto Panamericano de Geografía e Historia, Comisión de Geografía, Comité de Geografiía Urbana, 1988); and Nelly Amalia Gray de Cerdan, Territorio y Urbanismo: Bases de Geografía Prospectiva (Territory and Urbanism: Bases of a predictive geography) (Mendoza, Argentina: Consejo Nacional de Investigaciones Cientificas y Tecnicas, 1987) are examples. In Manual de Métodos, mapping was done of Santiago, Chile that includes the type and age of construction, value of homes, and many other aspects of the urban terrain and properties. The style of analysis not only promises to show potentially conflictive areas and urban targets in broad graphic terms, but perhaps can predict the most probable unfolding of events in the case of violent crises. Territorio y Urbanismo also delves into the application of geography-based modeling for the description of urban social problems and the rational determination of social programs.

police forces, decriminalizing the use of drugs, and expanding suburban school access to inner city children.[264] Elements on the strategy matrix reflect the full range of government program-based thinking about how to tackle the problem of what may be a growing urban underclass. Taken together, the strategy suggested by Downs as a preventive to urban violence is reminiscent of some broad-based socioeconomic program approaches to rural counterinsurgency. As Downs points out, such program approaches require a substantial redistribution of wealth, a requirement often unsupported by political realities. Moreover, many argue that such social programs generally do not work, that they create an addiction to programs that entrench dependency on government, rob human dignity and instill resentments that fuel the culture of violence even further. Major 'Third World' cities can expect to muster less public program funding than cities in the United States, and so the supposedly enlightened control of violence by way of social engineering will remain an unrealized dream.

As evidenced in the above discussion of urban conflict, one of the most useable aspects of a property vision of urban conflict is clarification of the overlapping frontier between what are military and non-military applications of power.[265] It is the evolution of legal strictures that formally define the details of legitimacy of military efforts. Property is not just a question of records that tie places to people, although this forensic aspect is immensely important to effective military and police operations. The greater advantage to a property approach comes with the understanding that property is rights and duties, and that the legal constraints on law enforcement and military maneuver are embedded or part-and parcel of the terrain. The need to gain a wire tap warrant might be an extreme example only for a geography where property is better developed, but legal systems relate

---

[264] Anthony Downs, New Visions for Metropolitan America (Washington, D.C.: The Brookings Institute, 1994), p. 176.
[265] The intangible but profound distance between military and police mentality, and the organizational preparations that attend the difference, are perhaps best described by persons who are neither police nor military. One such description is Bob Shacochis' "The Immaculate Invasion," Harper's February 1995.

the specific rights that people have wherever they stand sit or lay, and for a counterinsurgency force to be successful in the long run it must know these rights. Early in this decade the Colombian police found it impossible to serve a legal warrant in the slums of Medell[[in. The streets and shacks were so irregular that violent actors could confuse addresses and identities. Part of the solution was to apply best-practice street naming and numbering conventions, installation of durable street signs, and the assignment of fixed addresses to residents.

Developmental Strategy

> *"Many years of observation in the developing nations...have convinced me that in these vital areas the most important economic and political question is: who owns the land?"*[266]
>
> Chester Bowles, US diplomat and economist

Land reform

Attention to property matters has not been wholly absent from U.S. strategic thinking. With regard to contexts that are describable as "low intensity" or "other than war," the most recurring property theme is land reform. As an adjunct to U.S. military land reform (or often "agrarian reform") strategy has come and gone during the twentieth century. One distasteful factor is that many land reform schemes have been promoted by the ideological left during a century in which so much geopolitical advantage has been associated with polarized ideologies. That is to say, land reform ideas have often been discredited as benefiting an ideological and strategic enemy. Land reform is a label given to a wide array of property-focused strategies for resolution of political struggles. The results have been mixed and

---

[266] Thomas Melville, Guatemala: The Politics of Land Ownership (New York: Free Press, 1971) p. xi. Chester Bowles was a former U.S. Ambassador to India.

264

depend ultimately on subjective measures. Their history is obviously relevant to the current theme. However, land or agrarian reform as it has been historically stylized is not prescribed here as the key to strategy of any kind. Too many land reform notions have been bad ideas. Dissecting a typical land reform program according to all the affected rights and duties in land usually bares inefficient statist hubris and numerous unintended consequences.[267]

All strategies, and especially those aimed at attaining objectives beyond immediate physical possession, are land reform strategies in a sense. Their essential flaw has been a presumption that the land itself is the dominant source of wealth and therefore political power. Lost has been a full understanding of the nature of property. Property, even real property, is not the thing. Property is the concert of rights, associated with the thing, that regulates relationships between people. Strategies that begin with a complete understanding of the preferential rights and duties of all owner interests are more likely to succeed than any strategy that only envisages preferential occupancy of a delimited slice of land. It is safe to claim that every land reform project so far attempted in Latin America at least has suffered from unexpected and unintended affects of tinkering with forces and relationships that were incompletely understood.

That political strategies can be based on property is difficult to question. A review of the history of Israel is enough to dispel doubt. The initial strategy of the Zionists was one of simple land purchase combined with efforts to make that land productive enough to support further settlement.

---

[267] This assertion depends, of course, on one's point of view. For leadership interested in centralizing and securing state power, land reform has had a record of successes. Economic advantage, individual liberty and upward mobility have not fared as well. As Professor Powelson expressed, "The most disheartening conclusion...may be that whenever a reformer (such as a king, a government, or a revolutionary junta) has changed the land tenure system by fiat, he, she, or it has retained a substantial portion of the rights instead of yielding them to the peasant." John Powelson, The Story of Land, p. x.

The Zionist leadership concentrated energies and resources on the acquisition and settlement of land and the furtherance of agriculture. Much land was reclaimed from swamp or desert. Most of the lands acquired were purchased in large tracts from absentee private Arab proprietors. The mandatory administration itself controlled over a quarter of a million acres classed as state domain but it leased only a minute portion of this to Jewish agriculture. By the late 'thirties Jews held a little over a quarter of a million cultivable acres, approximately twice the area they had owned in 1920. In 1939, about five percent of the total land area of the country was in Jewish ownership.[268]

As regards the creation of Israel, the other elements of the ownership environment were considered from the outset. National identity and cohesiveness were considered by the British sponsors.

Underlying the British concept of the national home was the assumption that Jews and Arabs would become integrated within a broader Palestinian national identity. The British goal was to promote neither Jewish nor Arab sovereignty as such, but a polity of Palestinians. The Hebrew and Arabic languages, it was assumed, would afford the two peoples the means of separate cultural expression while the English language would provide a bridge for their political integration.[269]

The British understanding of the ownership possibilities was perhaps not well reasoned since Arab nationalism was inchoate while there existed an historical basis for a Palestinian identity among the Jews. The strength of a cohesive Jewish owner identity, associated

---

[268] Noah Lucas, The Modern History of Israel (New York: Praeger, 1975), pp. 111,112.
[269] Ibid., p. 114.

266

with the lands of Judea, in conjunction with the underdeveloped cohesiveness of Arab identities, led to the current condition of conflict--a conflict that is marked throughout by conspicuous property issues like homestead settlements on the West Bank of the Jordan, or autonomous rule in the Gaza Strip.[270]

The early Zionist strategy was a property strategy, but it is hard to fit it within the rubric of land reform. Nevertheless, misinterpretation of important elements of property ownership is a shared error in predicting effects. For instance, the concert of rights that constitutes land ownership includes the right to divest. This single characteristic of ownership can probably be blamed for half of the whole failure of land reforms in this century. If a peasant is given redistributed land, he will sell it unless he can afford to be the owner and wants to be. Therein lays the essential debility of a majority of land reform ideas. If a plan includes incentives for the peasant to stay on the land--seed credits, extension service advice, technical capitalization--the government is in effect entering the agricultural economy in a pervasive and very expensive way. Even with all necessary aid having been provided to the small farmer, there is little a government can do to assure the value of food staples. The next logical step is price support buying by the government, or other interventions into the market mechanism. Pressures build toward re-redistribution of ownership portions, either in new mortgages, resale to original owners, etc. In order to avoid the immediate frustration of the reapportionment, reform regulations tend to include tenure requirements such as residence during a fixed minimum number of harvests before the occupant receives title. In these cases, not only is part of the ownership retained by the government, the government has created a new form of serfdom. As with most government intrusions, the process is subject to corruption and to loopholes that allow the black market sale of quit claims, false appraisals, and so on.

---

[270] In 1997, Yasser Arafat publicly supported the death penalty for Arabs who sold land to Jews. See "Arafat defends death for sellers: Penalty for Arabs called response to Israeli land confiscation" 22 May 1997 Associated Press, <http://www.dallasnews.com/~dmnews/international-nf/int229.htm>.

In order to influence the lives of a large number of persons, agrarian reforms necessarily involve overarching central government control of prices and movement of labor. If successful on a large scale, agrarian reforms can slow a process of urbanization that, however painful, may be necessary to shift an economy away from subsistence farming. Having said the above, there have been occasions in which the forced reapportionment of rural terrain may be said to have supported strategic interests because of the changed property relationships. Accordingly, land reforms sometimes appear at the outset to be good ideas even to the anti-statist. A quote from the United States military governor of Korea in 1945 says everything:

> The program of Military Government included taking over all Japanese properties as rapidly as possible for the benefit of the Korean people, relieving labor from the conditions of absolute servitude under which it has existed for the last forty years, returning to the farmers the land which had been wrested from them by Japanese guile and treachery, and giving to the farmer a fair and just proportion of the fruit of his sweat and labor, restoring the principals of a free market, giving to every man, woman and child within the country equal opportunity to enjoy his fair and just share of the great wealth with which this beautiful nation has been endowed.[271]

In post-WWII Korea, land reform measures were taken by a military occupation force that followed another foreign occupier. Probably the most important policy impetus was a desire to undermine the appeal of socialist and communist arguments within a large rural

---

[271] Gary L. Olson, U.S. Foreign Policy and the Third World Peasant: Land Reform in Asia and Latin America, (New York: Praeger Publishers, 1974), p.42.

population. In this case, large tracts of virtually ownerless properties were available for redistribution.

In the case of the American occupation of Japan, the number of pure owner-cultivators was increased from 52.8 percent of the total farming households in 1946 to 61.8 percent of the total in 1950. Pure tenant households dropped from 28.7 percent to 5 percent.[272] In the process, one million former landlords were dispossessed. Rights in land had been purchased by the central government by instruction of the Supreme Command Allied Powers. The plan had its roots partly in pre-war academic appreciations of a relationship between feudal tenure systems in Japan and the power of militarist elites. General Macarthur's directive to the Japanese government stated in part:

> In order that the Imperial Japanese Government shall remove economic obstacles to the revival and strengthening of democratic tendencies, establish respect for the dignity of man, and destroy the economic bondage which has enslaved the Japanese farmer for centuries of feudal oppression, the Japanese Imperial Government is directed to take measures to insure that those who till the soil shall have a more equal opportunity to enjoy the fruits of their labor.[273]

It is difficult to claim that these land reform efforts led to the economic successes of Korea or Japan. Many other factors weigh in. At least they did not prevent economic development, and perhaps the redistribution of wealth broadened the base of material expectations. The land programs in both countries seem to have had a direct effect on elections that favored pro-United States elements. One observation is essential: These reforms were imposed. In one case they were imposed on a defeated enemy. In the other they were imposed on a country that

---

[272] Ibid., p. 28.
[273] Ibid., p. 24.

had been previously occupied by a foreign army. The observation does not lead to a conclusion that such changes must be imposed, but it does discredit the offhand and often-heard pandering that changes must be indigenous or locally motivated, even while it might be preferable.

In the states of southern Mexican, imperfections in collectivist land reform (finding their spiritual and bureaucratic roots in the history of the Mexican Revolution) are now showing their consequences. "Amid indecisive efforts to achieve a solution to the political-military conflict in this state (Chiapas), the struggle for land is heating up."[274] For some peasants the fight is over communal *ejido* land that was could be parceled out under a reform begun in 1992. Others complain about *ejido* land that was taken out of agricultural use to make a wilderness preserve. Nearby coffee plantations owned by foreign absentee owners are the object of armed squatting. "And in response to eviction threats from the government and the ranchers--who are calling for Army intervention--the peasants claim that the land belongs to them and they will not abandon it, 'even at the price of death.'"[275] Land pressures can create a sense of desperation among rural residents who been encouraged to remain on the land and are unprepared to leave it. Add to this the contiguity of oil rich regions and hydroelectric infrastructure on which the greater Mexican economy depends. Add, too, the leadership energy of outsiders who know how to focus the peasants' desperation and leverage the threat of violence against the government. A formula for extensive organized violence is evident.

> Mexico's land reform has left an ironic legacy. Though intended to benefit the campesinos, the reform actually made the land of the beneficiaries less productive than that of the non-beneficiaries. To the Mexican nation, this is a serious setback. Half of the country's

---

[274] Alonso Urrutia, "Seized Estate's Mixed Population Cited" Mexico City La Jornada in Spanish as translated in FBIS-LAT-94-240, p.25; see also Jose Gil Olmos and Elio Henriquez, "German Owners Criticized" as translated in FBIS-LAT-94-240, p.27; Julio Cesar Lopez, "Local Links Indicated" as translated in FBIS-LAT-94-240, p.29.
[275] Ibid.

agricultural land, which is in *ejidatario* hands cannot improve its productive capacity because *ejidatarios* cannot efficiently utilize it and because productive *non-ejido* farmers cannot acquire it.[276]

The above quote comes from a 1974 study on the political effects of land reform. The difficulty of which the author speaks was precisely the reason for the 1992 neo-liberal reform of the socialist revolutionary land reform. What was seen at least partially by the proponents of the 1992 effort (not discounting the involvement of particularized greed in some cases) is that land, though it maintains special emotional attachments, is a commodity subject to market forces. In fact, it is the separable rights associated with the land. Every disregard, defiance and ignorance of those forces will eventually charge a price. That is what has been happening in Chiapas, and it is why strategies, whether government, personal, corporate, military, insurgent or otherwise, should be determined as best as possible in accordance with the details of the ownership environment.[277]

---

[276] Hung-Chao Tai, Land Reform and Politics: A Comparative Analysis (Berkeley: University of California Press, 1974), p. 475; For an apologetic survey from the same period see Peter Dorner, Land Reform & Economic Development(Kingsport, Tennessee: Kingsport Press Inc., 1972).

[277] A pair of relevant articles comes from a land disgraced by the 1930s land reforms of Joe Stalin. See, G. Nikolayev, "Why Can't Russia Feed Herself" and "Private land ownership is the pivotal problem of reform," New Times International no.18 April 1993. The author may be speaking only for a pro-western minority, but his message is on-point if not universally accepted. According to Nikolayev, the problem of production has been a problem of ownership by farmers. In the 1990s, most peasants still worked on communist collective and other state farms. A growing minority owned their farms, but mortgages and capitalization was still out of reach for most would-be family farmers. The Mexican land reform that created tens of thousands of communal *ejidos* began shortly after the revolutions in 1917. That the neo-liberal counter-revolution moving peasant parcels back into the market economy began shortly after the collapse of the Soviet Union is at least interesting. The scope and effects (both on individual lives and strategically) of the counter-revolution in Mexican land ownership is being carefully studied by a team from the University of Kansas led by five-time Fulbright scholar Dr. Peter Herlihy under the auspices of the

Developing a modern, formal land ownership regime is a larger, more challenging objective than that of obtaining property data. A modern property regime includes mechanisms for trust building and for market fluidity. These mechanisms include title insurance, a regulated brokerage profession, professional property inspectors and appraisers, statutorily specific "quiet title" actions, clearly delineated occasions for self-help in regaining possession, enforceable punishments for unlawful self-help, enforcement of restraining orders and eviction, transparency of ownership files, well-publicized statutes-of-fraud that require transactions in real estate to be in writing, signed, notarized and registered, requirement that mortgages and encumbrances of all kinds be recorded or be without state enforcement, and so on. This litany of needs is included to underline an important disclaimer: creating property data (even if is technically exact, judicially correct and accessible) is not equivalent to creating a property regime similar to that known in the United States.

Nevertheless, the quality and utility of the data is highly dependent on the level of development of the property regime. Numerous developmental agencies from a variety of countries have contributed to modernizing the property regime in Colombia. To the extent these efforts have failed, it is due in part to the aid organizations' not having insisted on their obtaining a product in the form of transparent, digital property data. Neither USAID nor the IADB (and this probably holds true for other aid organizations) can produce results of their efforts in the form of property data. This fact responds to the culture of the organizations and their core missions. No proof of result was demanded because these organizations deal in the construction of institutions, to include the creation of service bureaucracies, training of personnel, etc., but they are not equipped for or interested in gaining and analyzing information. To some extent, the strategic developmental goal of establishing a modern property regime must be

---

American Geographical Society and assisted by scholars from the University of San Luis Potosí.

272

prompted, accelerated and audited by insistence on the lesser goal of obtaining the data. Western civilization is no so hard to understand in these terms: Rejection of oral evidence eventually means that contracts must have permanent stable evidence. The 'rule of law', the creation of an effective legal regime, the establishment of an equitable system of property ownership – all these are impossible until permanent trustworthy evidence of contracts is the norm. Fortunately, the technologies now available to improve the quality of evidence include positioning satellites, geographic placement software and the Internet. But they must be applied. In this area (the formalization of property) durable information is the ultimate goal, and so in a place like Colombia the objectives of developmental aid organizations and of intelligence agencies must be unified. Aid organizations will continue to distance themselves from 'intelligence' work and from active use of cadastral, land registry or other data in forensic and military matters. But they must not distance themselves from being able to prove the precision, transparency and comprehensiveness of the social contract, since that is the goal. Correspondingly, intelligence organizations must learn to work in the unclassified realm in such a way as to not compromise the developmental agencies' cultures. They should assist developmental efforts financially in order that they formalize property in areas of greatest security interest, and technically to the extent of providing quality control and results back to the developmentalists. The question of property distribution is central to our American inheritance, to our Revolutionary understanding of the world. "…the most common and durable source of factions has been the various and unequal distribution of property."[278]

---

[278] James Madison, "'Publius,'The Federalist X," Daily Advertiser (New York), November 22, 1787 reprinted in Bernard Bailyn, ed., The Debate on the Constitution, Part 1 (The Viking Press, 1992), p. 406; Madison's importance as an intellectual contributor to the American ideological revolution regarding property and the role of government is well established: "Madison's resolution of the conflict, real or apparent, between Jefferson and Locke adds up to a political doctrine that is so radically revolutionary that I do not believe it is possible to go beyond it. Many revolutions since the American rebellion at the end of the eighteenth century have failed or feared to go so far. Even the Russian Revolution, no matter how far-reaching its

James Madison's venerable words are to be tempered by the reminder that his idea of 'property' was not equivalent to 'land.' Land became property in the context of a functioning liberal social contract.

Fixing Cuba

Impending changes in Cuba were discussed in the Chapter Two, but it was emphasized that Cuba is not a threat in any traditional sense. It is included again here as the nearest example of a place in which property is absolutely critical to satisfactory practical understanding of the challenge, to any rational design for future engagement or for the architecture of Cuba's success as a society and nation. The conditions brought to the Caribbean by the end of Castroite control on the Island of Cuba could be such that American national security resources will be diverted for one reason or another. Worse, if the processes of change in Cuba do not result in a property regime featuring comprehensive, precise, transparent evidence of ownership; along with mechanisms for effecting that evidence and a liberal understanding of who can own what, then an historic opportunity will be lost and a set of potential dangers invited. Cuba can be fixed -- quickly made free, safe and

---

social and economic reforms, failed to take the final step that Madison said was imperative for the United States, that it 'equally respect the rights of property and the property in rights.'

The Soviets, in this century, have turned the first kind of property upside down, giving it to those who had nothing, taking it from those who had everything. There is a kind of simple justice in that, although economically it is dreadfully misguided. But no man's, woman's, or child's rights have been secure in the Soviet Union during this century, as they are mostly secure in Madison's country today.

To succeed in their revolution, the Soviets believed they had to abolish all private property. Perhaps they meant to abolish only the private property that Locke had claimed governments are instituted to protect. But they also abolished that other property, property in rights. Their revolution has therefore so far failed. It can succeed only when they understand and rectify this view." Charles Van Doren, A History of Knowledge: Past Present, and Future (New York: Carol Publishing Group, 1991), p.227.

prosperous, but only if the United States and others outside Cuba plan to act on behalf of Cubans to ensure that the property regime there is transformed.

To forecast the details of the kind of political mess that people might enter and form in Cuba, we can begin by reducing Cuba's ownership environment into the three streams of inquiry suggested by the definition of property in the introductory chapter regarding the quality of the evidence (*clarity of allocation*); the capacity to act on conclusions logically drawn from the evidence (*ease of alienability* and *security from trespass*); and conduciveness to peace of the basic rules delimiting the contract (*liberality*).

clarity of allocation

It appears that records exist and that they are in a moderate technical condition, and that they are not yet comprehensive. A surprising number or records that approach the nature of real estate ownership records exist in countries having experienced communist governments. Block censuses, agricultural quotas, vacation awards, and many other records may be found on which to build a cadastre and registry of property rights on the island.

Related to real property titling are simple landlord-tenant disputes. These might be rated as exacerbating events of a relatively minor scale. However, change from a patron-communist system of tenancy rules, accompanied by an overturn of landlords and judges, will change the balance of perceived rights and duties. This will be especially true in Cuba as relatives from the United States bring with them different legal expectations and litigious energy. This is an area for which property disposition strategies can be prepared in advance--a preparation that could prove to be an important ameliorating effort.

The identities of claimants will be a more complicated math than a simple search for documents. Many claims will be based on failed pre-existing duties. For instance, Fidel Castro's environmental legacy may prove as dismal as that of the other failed communist

275

countries. [279] Potential clean-up sites like the Boyeros asbestos factory near Havana, the experimental nuclear waste reprocessing center at Arroyo Naranjo, or any of a number of fouled waterways suggest that a multitude of agencies and organizations will find a mission in a post-Castro Cuba. Their rights and duties will conflict with those of other property claimants, and while the rights of foreign environmentalists may seem tenuous in a context of ambiguous sovereignty and system collapse, those rights will seem more valid as they become matched to political power generated in the United States and elsewhere. For this reason, and for the long-term benefit to Cuba, property interests expressed by environmental protection groups should be assigned due weight ahead of time. Under many plausible scenarios, effective control of key government lands will be lost. These properties could include large landholdings of the Cuban military such as the Ignacio Agramonte training area near Camaguey or the Siguanea training area on the Isle of Pines. Even if all Cuban military units were to divorce themselves from organized participation in any internal violence, much of the military land could be exposed to looters and squatters. It may be in the best interests of any follow-on government to insure the maintenance or orderly disposition of this land, especially if ecological recovery operations are needed.

---

[279] For an overview of possible ecological problem areas see Jose R. Oro, The Poisoning of Paradise: Environmental Pollution in the Republic of Cuba, (The Endowment for Cuban American Studies, Cuban American National Foundation, ISBN: 0-918901-87-1, 1992).

<u>ease of alienability and security from trespass</u>

Neither the capacity of the current government to exclude persons from terrain is to be doubted, nor is the resolve to do so. The incapacity of the residents to act on evidence of existing records, on the other hand, may be fairly complete. Given the lack of even a rudimentary real estate profession, any informality of land titles will invite conflicting claims and all kinds of blatant fraud schemes. These registry problems could be a tremendous source of violence, whether the subject is return of titles to pre-revolution landlords, patenting common property formerly owned by the state, preferences in the privatization of industries, or even reassignment to new government entities. Any judicial mechanism will be awash with claims and counter-claims. In order to lessen the violence that can easily accompany these cases, a system of courts could be pre-established, ready to accept cases as soon as possible. In addition, the regulatory framework and market incentives for the healthy growth of a real estate profession could be initiated.

Internal political convulsion and the attendant inability to conduct sophisticated police investigations will invigorate organized crime.[280] Brigands understand the opportunities that under-supervised territory presents. They quickly impose ownership regimes, offer services to offended claimants, create loyalties and obligations, and sow fear. Legal political parties, rogue military units, and even traditional guerrilla bands don't display the same efficiency and ruthlessness as does a criminal gang--or some hybrid. These groups directly and immediately focus on property rights. They deny opposition access to their safe havens, monopolize markets and small industries, and isolate transportation means. They cultivate exclusive

---

[280] "Former Eastern European communist security personnel have created organizations suspected of coercive actions and terrorist planning (for example, Red Fist in the former German Democratic Republic); the prospect of former DGI [Cuban intelligence] free-lance activities in an unsettled region must at least be considered." Graham H. Turbiville, "The Cuban 'threat' in the southern hemisphere: Goodbye to all that?," <u>Military Review</u>, December 1991, p. 87.

territorial identities. Communist Cuba boasts an unattractive record of collaboration between state security organizations and transnational criminal enterprises. The formats, contacts and corruption ethic are in place, if not the criminal organizations themselves. When political changes do come to the island, key members of the failing Communist regime may already be under indictment in U.S. courts for narcotics trafficking and related charges.[281]

liberality

In this there is a great shortcoming. Most exiled Cubans cannot own in any way under the present system, and most Cubans not only cannot be owners of record, their rights are strictly delimited even as tenants. Life estates seem to be the norm for many agriculturalists, underground rights are not marketed to citizenry, and use rights even to include profit from farmland are closely controlled. Creation of a property regime in which everyday rights and duties are openly and formally expressed in comprehensive, detailed, precise, stable, transparent evidence is a good idea whatever the basic rules. Knowing in advance who is to be considered full owners and what divisibility of ownership will be allowed will be more critical to peace in the short run. This requires cognizance that the Cuban constitution must be changed to become a fundamental law securing the polity against any excessive concentration of power that would endanger the protection of property rights – not principally a formula for choosing leaders.

Castro's revolution may survive for many more years or Cuba may slip from its communist revolutionary experience with an anticlimactic whimper. The very first steps taken after the incapacity of Castro brothers will probably be some form of constitutional convention in order to reconfirm or adjust the basic ownership rules.

---

[281] A proposed indictment of Raul Castro and the Cuban government on narcotics trafficking charges is reported in Jeff Leen and Andres Oppenheimer, "Clinton caught off guard by proposed Cuba charges," Miami Herald, 9 April 1993, p. 1A.; For a broad accusation regarding Cuban narcotics dealings of the Castro government see Castro and the Narcotics Connection (Washington, D.C.: Cuban American National Foundation, 1983).

The results of such a convention are not likely to satisfy. The intensity of ill will by Cubans toward each other is difficult to measure, but some interested observers insist that a bloodbath is likely given the abuses of power and the personal atrocities committed by the communist regime. An environment of retribution could easily deteriorate into violence. Grave disorder is one anticipated result when the Castros and the repressive mechanisms of their personalist regime lose effective control. Many of the determinants of that disorder are already engaged, others await precipitating events. Whatever the scenario, however, the weave of Cuba's future social fabric can be envisioned in terms of who has what rights in what property, beginning with obvious property such as choice real estate and infrastructure, and membership in organizational bodies that control the rules of ownership.

Perhaps most important, such a conceptualization can guide policy planning. In the face of property-rooted violence, it behooves planners to determine exactly who the owner-claimants are and what specific rights they might wish to defend in relation to exactly what locations. This will go a long way to finding hidden sponsors of violence, to finding areas of reconciliation and hidden wealth that can finance growth, or to deciding who might best pay for security measures. Without a complete appreciation of land ownership claims and of the competing systems in which the claims might be stabilized, there can be little practical expectation of long-term success in subduing potential armed conflict in Cuba. There can also be no reasonable expectation that the government of the United States would be able to retain strategic initiative in competition with non-state entities able and willing to identify and service the wide variety of owner-claimant identities.

Political changes coming to Cuba may pose a threat of deleterious and unpredictable impact on US domestic electioneering, and of anti-American opportunism in the international ambit. The most important reason for highlighting Cuba's transition, however, has nothing to do with threats, but rather the historic opportunity that the end of the Castro era presents to the American nation. It is in simplest terms a chance to revalidate America -- an opportunity to showcase and re-inspect the relative merits of the United States as a polity. Cuba's transition can rebuild the image and substance of American exceptionalism currently being expended in the war against terrorism. Cuba offers, in short, a big test, one the United States as a nation should take -- should revel in taking. To pass the test, the United States, as a nation, may need to review its understanding of its own revolution, and consider how central to its success the concept of property is. Of all places on earth, Cuba; and among all predictable crises, Cuba's transition, deserve to be framed as questions not of electoral democracy, but of protected property, of a social contract in which individuals and groups deal freely and confidently. If the development of answers to the problem of contested property becomes the basis for deriving correct political, developmental and diplomatic decisions associated with the Cuban people and the future of the island, it will be a positive milestone. Better still would be to design American politics, diplomacy and developmental programs in the service of creating a successful Cuban property regime.

Knowledge Strategy

If Marx were alive today, he might fairly call education the means of production.[282]

Walter B. Wriston

The relevant things worth knowing

The objectives, methods and resources of the overall intelligence apparatus of the United States government are hard to describe, and would remain so even without the veil of secrecy. Late in 2005, to commemorate the six-month anniversary of the establishment of the office of the Director of National Intelligence, that office published a document titled The National Intelligence Strategy of the United States.[283] The publication is a general call to service stressing institutional relationships and individual qualification. It is understandably short on specific threats or methods of collection. To a degree, however, any intelligence strategy is going to orient on a set of

[282] Walter B. Wriston, The Twilight of Sovereignty: How the Information Revolution is Transforming Our World (New York: Charles Scribner's Sons, 1992) p. 108. Wriston identified technology as a culprit in the dispersion of power as well as a key to maintaining national wealth. "If we are to compete in the global marketplace, we must constantly build and renew our intellectual capital. We have little or no control over the natural resources within our borders, but we do have control over our educational and cultural environment." Wriston was optimistic, however, saying that the information revolution gives advantage to superior ideas, and that freedom has proved over and over to be a superior idea. When placed in an unrestricted open market by new technologies, good ideas hard are to restrict. Wriston also pointed out the competitive importance of encoding and decoding. A state that does not master codes in the information age is highly vulnerable. Wriston called this the single advantage in an information age that cannot be sacrificed.
[283] John D. Negroponte, The National Intelligence Strategy of the United States of America, (Washington, D.C.: Office of the Director of National Intelligence, 2005), http://www.dni.gov/NISOctober2005.pdf

prioritized security concerns with the effort of investigation and analysis guided by some logic regarding geographic areas to be studied (Lake Victoria, France, the Great Outback, etc.) or bothersome phenomena (money laundering, terrorism, proliferation, beer, etc.) The major agencies (CIA, DIA, FBI, NSA, NGA...) grew in a particular manner and under special historic conditions. After WWII and especially with implementation of the National Security Act of 1947, American intelligence took a course that guided it away from academe and the community of America's scholars. This schism is still reflected between the lines of the National Intelligence Strategy, which is an institutional strategy aimed at the intelligence agencies and its members. It is not a national strategy to the extent that it barely mentions and does not engage the considerable information-gathering parts of the United States government outside the intelligence community, the data-thirsty American foreign business enterprise or the vast knowledge-creating universe of American academe and its foreign partners.

The observation made just above about the new capstone document of US Intelligence -- that it is inward looking -- is pertinent to the assertions of this book because most property knowledge is necessarily unclassified and publicly available, or should be. The best access to that information is by way of development programs, business information and most of all, independent scholarship. This brings us back to the nature of an intelligence strategy, something that a science professor might recognize as a research methodology, only sized-up and dumbed-down. A rationalized intelligence strategy or research methodology (or criminal investigation or business model) requires a sensible collection plan. That plan considers where useful information resides and can best be obtained, determines the various persons or agencies that might have the most practicable access, considers how those with access can be engaged to acquire the information, and determines how the information can be most practicably delivered to who need it most. As simple as that sounds, it is not what US government intelligence does. The US intelligence community has not discovered (or at least has not admitted discovering) that vast amounts of useable data reside in public administration, business, non-governmental and academic information files all over the world. It has not estimated who has access to the information, who can turn it in to relevant knowledge or how it might be delivered. Little proof of this ugly criticism is necessary, and not because the intelligence community muffed the weapons of mass destruction question as to Iraq. Almost any informed observer (in or out of the intelligence business, American or otherwise, enemy or not) would agree that the whole quantity of relevant knowledge in the world is greater by quantum leaps than that which is drawn by way of classified means into government decision-making processes. Disdain for a universe of knowledge seems to have become a hallmark of the intelligence apparatus. There exists almost no statement of national effort to describe the body of openly available knowledge for the purpose of converting relevant parts of it in service of national security.

On December 7, 2004, the Congress of the United States passed and the President then signed the Intelligence Reform and Terrorism Prevention Act of 2004. The law states in relevant part the following:

(a) Sense of Congress.--It is the sense of Congress that--
(1) the Director of National Intelligence should establish an intelligence center for the purpose of coordinating the collection, analysis, production, and dissemination of open source intelligence to elements of the intelligence community;
(2) open source intelligence is a valuable source that must be integrated into the intelligence cycle to ensure that United States policymakers are fully and completely informed; and
(3) the intelligence center should ensure that each element of the intelligence community uses open source intelligence consistent with the mission of such element.
(b) Requirement for Efficient Use by Intelligence Community of Open-source Intelligence.--The Director of

National Intelligence shall ensure that the intelligence community makes efficient and effective use of open-source information and analysis.[284]

As part of the response to this statement of the sense of the Congress, a new office opened called the Open Source Center to collect and study information that's publicly available around the world.[285] Unfortunately, the tenor, focus, and more importantly, funding, has so far been limited to the low-hanging fruit of the Internet, which is the centerpiece of current attention.[286] This is followed by renewed efforts at scouring foreign public news media, a forte of the Foreign Broadcast Information Service since before the founding of the CIA.

Another section of the same intelligence reform law changes the official definition of intelligence:

Paragraph (5) of section 3 of the National Security Act of 1947 (50 U.S.C. 401a) is amended to read as follows:
``(5) The terms `national intelligence' and `intelligence related to national security' refer to all intelligence, regardless of the source from which derived and including information gathered within or outside the United States, that--
``(A) pertains, as determined consistent with any guidance issued by the President, to more than one United States Government agency;

---

[284] Government Printing Office, Section 1052 Open-Source Intelligence, Intelligence Reform and Terrorism Prevention Act of 2004, Washington, D.C., House Reports Online via GPO Access, 2004 online at < whole text http://www.gpoaccess.gov/serialset/creports/pdf/108-796/108-796_intel_reform.html.
[285] Katherine Shrader, "New U.S. intel center studies free secrets," Associated Press and SeattlePI.com, November 8, 2005 online at <http://seattlepi.nwsource.com/national/1155AP_Open_Secrets_Center.html.
[286] The latest public estimate regarding the size of the overall annual intelligence budget of the United States holds it to be over forty billion dollars. Katherine Shrader, Ibid. The author would be surprised to find that the amount spent on open-source intelligence exceeded one-tenth of one percent of the total.

and
    ``(B) that involves--
        ``(i) threats to the United States,
its people, property, or interests;
        ``(ii) the development,
proliferation, or use of weapons of
mass destruction; or
        ``(iii) any other matter bearing on
United States national or homeland
security."

This is no small semantics. The older definition, while not explicitly excluding any type of source, gave room for an interpretation of the word satisfactory to those who would have 'intelligence' be only classified knowledge created and used behind the veil. Everything else was something else, and not the business of the intelligence community, and that was part of the cultural problem that the sense of Congress recognized.

If one were to check the Internet for Leavenworth County, to use our Kansas example one more time, the county websites would reveal more information than had ever before been available so inexpensively or from a distance. Still, by clicking the link to the county GIS office, you can read,

GIS has a growing archive of many map 'layers'. Aerial
photos, (ranging from 1941 to current), property
boundaries, land use, roads, hydrology, flood zones,
elevation, municipal boundaries, water districts, school
districts, tax districts, to name a few. They create and
maintain new layers as projects develop. They sell hard
copy paper maps of any layers separate or in any
combination. ... A person can contact this department
and get an aerial photo of any property that shows right-
of-ways, property lines, creeks and ponds, buildings,
flood zones, elevation, soil types, land use, etc. Since

this office was created, the information is all kept up-to-date. If they don't have the type of map you need, they can direct you to who does.

So if you were to visit the county courthouse and plop down about $2,500 you would get thousands of times more data about the county than if you limited yourself to the teaser on the Internet. While you were in town you could also go to the library and search through a number of historical files and, if you had an agreeable reason, go to any number of businesses and public offices for more information. The information is not hidden because it is tied to public decision-making processes -- taxation formulae, zoning, construction and many other activities that cannot otherwise function democratically. If you want an analysis of what it all means, you'll probably need to make friends with someone who has been dealing with the data in conjunction with the county's problems -- maybe the mayor, senior officers in the police department, school board members, or, of course, real estate agents. Foreign geographies are not so different, and to the extent they do not have as much information as Leavenworth to give or sell, it can be developed. The point is this: Most of the most useable information for finding people, their wealth, and their habits is in some sort of public form. Those forms have not been considered.

There exists today a growing worldwide movement, having nothing to do whatever with security intelligence, to promote transparency of wealth, the central purposes being to expose corruption and create the conditions for broad economic development.[287] Open bank accounts and real estate records are foremost on the list for exposure. Formalizing land records not only promotes the creation of development capital, it establishes a criminal deterrent. The threat of asset forfeiture is a powerful argument for law abidance among those who have something to lose. Creating formal, open land records shapes geographies for effective intelligence. As land databases dovetail with

---

[287] See, for instance, Transparency International: the coalition against corruption, transparency.org online at <http://www.transparency.org/.

286

other records, it becomes increasingly difficult for anyone with an appreciable level of wealth to act anti-socially without their wealth being subject to forfeiture, and without their family, friends, passport numbers, telephone numbers, etc. being exposed to law enforcement. The potentially negative consequences for personal liberty and privacy are obvious. Tyrannical governments seek the same control, but the expansion and formalization of ownership regimes is without doubt the long-term option for the control of dangerous behaviors, including government behaviors.[288]

Indiana Jones and direct sensing

The section just above stated that in the process of deriving a sensible information collection plan one would want to determine where the most relevant information resides, who has access and then seek to engage them in the process of creating useable knowledge. In the twentieth-century evolution of the American intelligence agencies, the problem of access took on tremendous weight, faced as the country had been by a powerful and threatening opponent with a closed society and paranoid government. Sending people to fish around for publicly available information in the Soviet Union was not reasonable as a mainstay strategy. As a result, technically-based remote sensing (something that could feed off a technical fascination anyway) seemed to solve many problems, especially when combined with sophisticated analytical and search techniques. In the process of mastering and re-mastering remote sensing, other methods simply withered away from the internal institutional culture. Geophysical characteristics of foreign places absorbed the lion's share of attention because they could be remotely sensed. The flashlight was on. Any captured cultural and event data would be limited to that which could be heard or overheard at a distance that obviated the problems of personal access. If something were broadcast, wittingly or unwittingly, it might get in.

---

[288] See Geoffrey B. Demarest, <u>Feasibility of Creating a Real Property Database for Colombia</u>, Foreign Military Studies Office, available online at

Something more obscure, such as legal characteristics, didn't have much chance of entering the intelligence holdings. Within the agencies charged with creating knowledge in support of government decisions this has meant that the culture of collection, and therefore the collection plan, was based on what persons *inside* the intelligence apparatus could safely learn based on the access *they* might have. Of course there have been spy-managers, but these are particularly expensive assets and so their application is in the direction of information that is specifically hidden, not the vast bulk of stuff.

The effect of a remotely-sensing knowledge culture is still evident in the National Intelligence Strategy. It is concerned with what the members of the intelligence community can find out on their own, and so the Internet becomes but another remote sensor. It is 'open-source' because it is the product of that vast world of knowledge not created by a securitized machine and from within the agencies. To the intelligence insider the Internet is almost synonymous with the open-source world of knowledge (we can add in foreign media emanations) because they can go to it 'directly' without access problems. It may be a difficult psychological step for that insider to admit that the Internet is but a small window into a huge world of knowledge to which, by the nature of his institution, he has little access. Due to his identity, he cannot go into that world efficiently. In other words, because they do not have practicable asset into the limitless world of knowledge about which the Internet hints, intelligence professionals tend to deny *institutionally* the size and value of the 'unclassified' knowledge-creating world.[289] For the cause of property this is very not good. Property information is dull in incremental form, and not subject to much remote acquisition, even while more and more information appears on the web. As I hope I have argued forcefully enough, property information and the strength of a society's social contract are so intimately tied that to not interpret that information is tantamount to not understanding the society. Besides, property information renders

---

[289] See, for instance, William M. Nolte, Rethinking War and Intelligence, in Anthony D. Mc Ivor, ed., <u>Rethinking the Principles of War</u> (Annapolis; Naval Institute Press, 2005), pp. 419-439.

its greatest probative value when considered in the context of other cultural information. Geophysical characteristics of the world are less than half the puzzle.

To limit the number and power of outlaw criminal organizations in the world, the wealth of those entities must be exposed. Movements that promote the elimination of anonymity of wealth are therefore helpful. If individuals and organizations are to achieve any level of power sufficient to threaten on a transnational level, they must necessarily amass wealth, and that wealth they must preserve and convert in one way or another if they are to implement their own strategies. The first purpose of brigandage is to amass wealth. The most stable and desirable form of wealth for the brigand is real estate, especially real estate located in geographies where the rules of ownership have been brought under the sway of the brigand. For this reason, the call for transparency of wealth should become one of the centerpieces of United States' defense diplomacy in every part of the world. Wealth records, such as land registries, aircraft registries, bank accounts, or insurance policies can be made transparent.

As a useful historical note, tying together the evolution of civilization and the purposes of mundane records, another look at England is in order. The Domesday Book was a property record compiled beginning in1086 by order of William the Conqueror to assess the land and other wealth owned in England. "'*there was no single hide nor a yard of land, nor indeed one ox nor one cow nor one pig which was left out'*. The grand and comprehensive scale on which the Domesday survey took place...and the irreversible nature of the information collected led people to compare it to the Last Judgement, or 'Doomsday', described in the Bible....'"[290] The book, now over 900 years old, is still in the British national archives. A website on the subject states;

---

[290] See, domesdaybook.co.uk, "The Domesday Book Online," domesdaybook.co.uk, online at <http://www.domesdaybook.co.uk/faqs.html#8.

The Domesday Book provides extensive records of landholders, their tenants, the amount of land they owned, how many people occupied the land (villagers, smallholders, free men, slaves, etc.), the amounts of woodland, meadow, animals, fish and ploughs on the land (if there were any) and other resources, any buildings present (churches, castles, mills, salthouses, etc.), and the whole purpose of the survey - the value of the land and its assets, before the Norman Conquest, after it, and at the time of Domesday. Some entries also chronicle disputes over who held land, some mention customary dues that had to be paid to the king, and entries for major towns include records of traders and number of houses.[291]

William knew what he was doing, but he was hardly the first to emphasize the importance of wealth records. Cuneiform in clay, one of the earliest forms of writing, dating from the 4th century BC, was invented exactly for the purpose of recording wealth, including real and chattel property.[292] The title of this book alludes to the application of technology to good governance as evident in the statutes of fraud. Need being the mother of invention, writing itself seems to have come about with the need for orderly records of wealth. The lesson of human history regarding the basics of civilization and effective governance will hopefully be consulted in order to judge today's projects and programs aimed at "governance." If such a project or program is not based on precise, comprehensive and transparent records of wealth, it not only misses the time-proven opportunity to apply technology to the challenge of human conflict, it ignores the human cultural record.

---

[291] Ibid.
[292] See C.B.F. Hooker, "Cuneiform," in Trustees of the British Museum, Reading the Past, (London: The British Museum Press, 1990), pp.15-74.

GIS stands for Geographic Information Systems, or perhaps Geographic Information Science. Sometimes the 'G' turns up as *georeferenced* or *geospatial* and the 'I' as *intelligence* but the overall meaning remains intact regardless. The term is thrown around freely to encompass the physical and organizational technologies that together allow data on every kind of phenomenon to be organized in database form, perhaps to be visualized in accurate spatial and temporal ratios on a computer screen, and made subject to calculations and analyses otherwise unavailable to the human mind. The GIS technological revolution is as important to academics and to intelligence as is the Internet. Tens of thousands of licenses for commercial GIS software are sold all around the world to academic, governmental and non-governmental organizations, which are using the technology in combination with GPS-derived data to create massive files of precise information on everything from endangered species to real property ownership.

GIS is the certain future of intelligence, as well as the technological/ methodological key to a universe of information in the files of foreign public administrative units, non-governmental organizations, foreign agencies and enterprises, and in the best-practice research efforts of university scholars. This universe of information, almost wholly unclassified, has within it the material needed to name foreign malefactors, tie one to another, and to trace their wealth. It is the same tool, and the same body of knowledge that allows checks on tax equity, specifies the effects of and responsibility for environmental harm, allows optimal traffic design and so on. GIS is raising standards of social science research, making the research of disparate disciplines compatible for comparison and enrichment, and allowing research to be more easily tested for veracity and scholarly care. GIS is the technical dimension of a revolution in public knowledge that the US federal government has not yet applied to questions of national security. As yet, almost all of the extensive investment in GIS by the various government agencies involved in US national security still revolves around the precise location and representation of geophysical phenomena.

A consolidating set of analytical and presentation protocols is also emerging in the wake of recognition of the suite of technologies associated with the term GIS. Consensus as to what constitutes a best-practice in GIS methodological science to some degree depends on the specific practical application or on theoretical preferences and traditions within a given academic discipline. Perhaps because the explosion of GIS is occurring within and as part of the accelerating pace of globalization, the currents of GIS knowledge and method are highly internationalized.

For decades now, the US military has taught as doctrine a process of information management, visualization and analysis known as Intelligence Preparation of the Battlefield (IPB). Its purpose is to define the battle environment, describe the effects of that environment, describe threats within it, and predict the likely courses of action of those threats. GIS is applied to a much greater an more complex set of variables and endeavors, many not associated with a threat, but, in the end, GIS is the way civilians spell IPB.

Are the goals, resources and methods applied by the United States and its allies to conflictive or unstable foreign countries reconciled? No, because the goals of conflict resolution are not matched to the resources and methods used to achieve them. Very little has been done by the United States to create, perfect or protect formal property around the world. Are the military efforts applied by the United States in internal warfare situations (insurgency, "low intensity conflict" guerrilla war, etc) in consonance with the essence of strategy - - to block the enemy leaders' lines of communication? To some degree no doubt, but this could be greatly improved by incorporation of police and academic information cultures on a military scale. Property information that paints in detail the relationship between persons, places and times is wholly inadequate, but could be radically improved.

Property Strategy

> *"Individual liberty is individual power,*
> *and as the power of a community*
> *is a mass compounded of individual powers,*
> *the nation which enjoys the most freedom*
> *must necessarily be in proportion*
> *to its numbers the most powerful nation."*[293]
>
> John Quincy Adams

> *"Strategic culture...is very much the product of*
> *geopolitical factors as they are locally interpreted."*[294]
>
> Colin S. Gray

If foreign powers were to occupy a place like Bosnia with military force to gain basic possession of terrain, then turn that possession over to whom it felt were rightful owners, could the occupying powers then leave without possession reverting to the unworthy? The answer is maybe. Occupying missions might wish to give ownership of land to a favored group, but can they establish a stable system of rules regarding that ownership, and a stable psychological environment regarding who has what rights in what land? In the case of Bosnia the results were not all negative, the good part relating directly to a real estate strategy:

> "This situation has significantly improved since 2000,
> however. The Property Implementation Plan, which
> featured a more vigorous implementation of established

---

[293] In a letter to James Lloyd, 1 October 1822, as reported online at
http://quotes.telemanage.ca/quotes.nsf/quotes/63377956d94ac5ef85256df8001c816d
[294] Colin S. Gray, The Geopolitics of Superpower (Lexington: The University of Kentucky Press, 1988) p. 51.

property laws, greatly facilitated the return process between 2000 and 2002. The coordinated work of OHR, SFOR, the UN Mission in Bosnia and Herzegovina, the OSCE, and UNHCR has been the key element in creating an environment conducive to returns."[295]

Neither Mackinder nor Spykman wrote of geographic areas as property with divisible rights. They mentioned cultural data as entries on lists of factors--like population or strategic materials, but their geopolitics assumed that whole geographies were lost or gained in gulps. Strategic materials and populations were obtained or subdued through territorial control. It is a whole-fee approach to property inspired by litmus test sovereign entities. Perhaps the threat posed by the Soviet Heartland is not gone forever, and anyway, more states exist that seem interested in gobbling up other lands. This fact demands respect. Geopolitics is not dead. However, it is the world of diffuse ownership and particularized power that promises to occupy the majority of spies and diplomats day to day. Most places demand a strategy whose theoretical roots show all the knotty twists of property relationships. In fact, the United States has at times formulated property-oriented strategies, usually a version of land reform. Land reform has been embraced in one form or another by the contenders in many conflicts throughout the world. We can ascribe unevenness of results to incomplete understanding of the ownership environment. Geopolitics does not analyze geography in terms of its basic human value of rights and duties, and it can fail miserably when a conflict involves multiple, divided and shared rights, or fractured and overlapping owner identities and partially competing ideologies. These complicated ownership environments are the rule, rather than the exception, in the 21st century, globalized world.

---

[295] James Dobbins, et. al. America's Role in Nation-Building: From Germany to Iraq. Santa Monica: Rand, 2003, p. 99.

On occasion, development of the property regime has been a military mission. The military has not only had to secure basic possession of territory against a hostile opponent, it has been asked to establish the social conditions that would allow itself to withdraw. Occupations of Japan, Korea, Taiwan, and part of Germany are the largest US examples in the twentieth century. The U.S. military held possession, but at least in Korea and Japan, also restructured the ownership regime, changing ideology and creating owners. In the Japanese case, the goal was not stabilizing ownership claims among competing ethnicities as might be the case in an area such as Bosnia. Instead, the question was one of making the population of Japan more owner and less owned; in other words, democratizing.

Newtonian logic--internalized by Clausewitz and applied to military strategy--still rules over a wide range of military math, but the new, beyond-Newton science of chaos and swarms requires something beyond Clausewitz, something that responds to non-linear, temporal, non-state and partially state challenges. Seen as a changing concert of rights and duties associated with parcels of geography at the local level, property appears as a first key toward understanding the new strategic geography. In The Geopolitics of Super Power, quoted at the beginning of this section, Gray favorably invokes the influence on America security policy of Mackinder's heartland and Nicholas Spykman's rimland theories. Reading his book a decade and a half later makes one strain to remember the strategic context in which Gray's advice was so plausible. "Even without a great statesman at the helm--though with policy makers who are, one hopes, familiar with the ideas of Halford Mackinder and Nicholas Spykman--Americans should be able to remember that the Soviet Union is going to be an enemy for a long time to come; that Soviet power needs to be distracted by major military tasks on the ground in Eurasia; and that Soviet seapower should be denied access at will to the world's oceans."[296] There may yet be a ring of truth there, but the inertia of this thinking created a

---

[296] Gray, supra note 294, p. 199.

mismatch between the theoretical underpinnings of American strategic policy and the kinds of challenges that the United States most often takes up.

One can see the powerful effect of entrenched military thinking. Environments where complicated owner relationships need adjustment simply do not lend themselves to blitzkriegs. Police work means suspects and trespasses, rather than enemies and invasions. The United States can easily expand its efforts to deny terrorists, brigands and subversives anonymity and impunity. This can be done by reconciliation of police, military and academic investigative cultures, and as part of that reconciliation the creation and sharing of databases that maintain non-geophysical information at a much greater resolution of detail than is the case today. Global security and world peace now depend upon, and United States foreign policy can promote, the transparency of wealth worldwide. Bank accounts, corporate interests, real estate, resource licenses and concessions, etc. can be made visible. As the threat to civilization becomes increasingly complex, we are obliged to use advanced technologies to expose concentrations of wealth that can be transmuted into instruments of hate.

Hohfeldian analysis of conflicts is not complicated. It requires:
Identification of all important rights and duties potentially at issue;
Naming all the possibly interested identities related to each right and each duty;
Determination of or assumption regarding the preferred and acceptable goals of each interested identity;
Measuring the resources that each of the identities could bring to bear on the issue;
Anticipating likely outcomes under a variety of circumstances; and
Estimating the costs and risks of distinct courses of action.

Each step requires knowledge about the rules of the relevant social contracts, details regarding the rights and duties, and the cultural habits and expectations of the potential identities. It, like big geopolitical analysis, seeks measurement of the relative power of potential contenders. This process of measuring power is also tied to property theory.

Measuring Property

At one place or another throughout the text of this book, the explanations, examples or quotations decorating the sections allude to the close association among the terms 'property,' 'power,' 'wealth' and 'ownership.' Since the immediately foregoing paragraphs reject mainstream strategic analysis and power measurement, and at the same time accept the idea that measurement of power is a good idea, then there arises a responsibility to state a better method. That better method, like Hohfeldian analysis, is based on property, and it necessarily has two aspects. The first is a method for measuring the quality of the property regime within a country or other geographical area. Included in this measurement falls the degree to which a given people participates in property world-wide -- perhaps meaning its level of globalization. The second is the measurement of power of individual identities that our Hohfeldian analyisis identifies as potentially mixed up in a specific conflict over specific rights and duties.

Beginning with the measurement of the quality of a property regime, we can apply an assessment methodology, an instrument applicable across societies and geographies that could compare the developmental status of property regimes -- not just as they concern the exposure of capital, but as they relate to security and freedom. Such an index would include elements recognizable to the geographer, cadastral bureaucrat, real estate agent, county sheriff and property lawyer -- and to the economist or military strategist. Recalling the definition of property asserted in Chapter One, that...

Property is a contract between society and owners that recognizes preferential rights and correlated duties; the strength of the social contract judged by the quality of its observance, which depends on the quality of the evidence of ownership and on the capacity of both owners and the society (usually by way of some government) to act on conclusions logically drawn from the evidence...

We can derive a universal instrument to measure of the quality of a property system as a vehicle for prosperity, freedom and peace. (measurement of the total value of a polity's ownership is a separate challenge that will be considered further below). The measurement will follow the three streams suggested by the definition:

1., the quality of the evidence delineating rights, duties and the identity of owners (this is sometimes referred to as *clarity of allocation*);

2., the capacity of owners (or claimants) and the government to act on conclusions logically drawn from the evidence (this is in some contexts referred to as *ease of alienability* or as *security from trespass* depending on the mix of owner rights and government duties involved); and

3., the conduciveness to peace of the basic rules delimiting the contract (this we at times refer to as *liberality*).

A detailed version of the instrument is included as an Appendix. The method does not support a mathematical comparison of one property regime to another, but it will allow researchers to build toward an objective comparison of property regimes.

The quality of the property regime internal to a polity will have a strong relationship to the nature of personal and business dealings that a people have with the rest of the world. A property-focused set of power elements can be used to measure the relative strength of entities

298

not contiguous to or synonymous with country-identity or of the overall power of a country as it deals with the outside world. This is what leads us to the second kind of power measurement that supports Hohfeldian analysis of conflicts. The following components are proposed for the calculation of power of namable identities using a property lens: *cohesiveness of owner identity, internal system of ownership rules, leadership, wealth, and technology.*

The first component, and the starting point for calculating power in a given circumstance, is cohesiveness of owner identity. When the United States citizenry is powerfully committed *as citizens of the United States* to do something, the power of the U.S. government is very great. This is the national morale listed by Spanier and it is the upshot of Ray Cline's politectonic essay. Resolve is the start point for application of any wealth that might be brought to bear on a problem, and cohesiveness of owner identity is the source of common resolve.[297] Resolve of the Venezuelan population to support the socialist revolutionary pretensions of their president Hugo Chavez may be falter, but apparently remains quite high in comparison with revolutionary movements in other countries in the past. How much communal resolve might be available to a post- Fidel Cuban leader is a great unknown on which sets much of the speculative distance between predictions regarding the future of that polity.

---

[297] *Resolve, morale, will,* and *cohesiveness* are closely related. The author has chosen to distinguish *cohesiveness* as the strength of a common identity as owners. The connotation is one of breadth and depth of emotion regarding a shared identity. A powerful feeling of solidarity as Americans gives an American president as a national leader, great potential power. *Resolve* and *will* carry a connotation more closely related to perseverance and willingness to sacrifice to achieve an end. They are less closely associated with strength of identity and solidarity. The meaning of *morale,* used especially by military people, seems to reside somewhere in between. One might say that the leader must translate cohesiveness into resolve in the face of a given project. If his organization, group, unit, or nation has high morale, the task is easy. The semantic differences are of secondary importance, and any overlap or lack of discipline in their use is of little harm to the principal points about national power.

Next on the component list for a property-based measurement of power is the system of ownership rules (which in broadest terms can be termed ideology). If the rules of ownership, the ideology that guides the corporate will in a given circumstance are deeply and broadly held, such legitimacy lends power. The United States enters most international competitions from a position of advantage because its basic values are broadly acceptable. However, the government of the United States can distance itself from this source of national power in two ways. First, even if Americans begin with great national cohesiveness regarding an international issue, cohesiveness and resolve will diminish if the United States government appears to promote rules that are not clear or not fair. In other words, resolve will collapse to the extent that the ownership environments produced (or to be produced) by the government's objective does not satisfy Americans' beliefs. Second, the United States government must appear to act within the system of American ownership rules. The government must appear to act according to the laws of the United States, the customs and mores of the nation, and to some degree international law. In other words, one way the government can undermine national power is related to its objectives, the other is related to the manner in which it proceeds.[298]

---

[298] Large-scale American involvement in Vietnam began in front of the force of great national will. The Tonkin Gulf Resolution evidenced national resolve, but the resolution was perhaps achieved by dissemblance on the part of President Lyndon Johnson as to the details of the Tonkin Gulf incident.[298] At any rate, national cohesiveness began to dissolve, albeit several years later, in two broad ways. Policy objectives (the ownership environment that was to be gained or preserved) were not sufficiently legitimate according to the perceptions of a growing number of Americans. The authoritarian regime of South Vietnam did not appear sufficiently noble to deserve American sacrifice, and the importance of Vietnam to other aspects of American ownership was seemingly insubstantial. In addition, the manner in which the United States prosecuted the war was increasingly portrayed as in violation of American moral standards. The My Lai massacre became emblematic of the perceived military behavior that determined this portrayal. In retrospect, the quantity of public resolve to wage the Vietnam War was great considering the limited direct U.S. property interests. Geopolitical arguments were laid that control of Vietnam would lead to Soviet control of Southeast Asia, threaten the United States' ASEAN allies and finally result in loss of open passage through the Straits of Molucca, a key ocean choke point. Oil resources of Indonesia and throughout the region would also

For Americans, national identity and the basic system of fairness (manifested in concepts like due process and equal protection) are probably overlapped more than for other national identities that might be glued together much less by ideology than by other cultural factors. The owner identity of a group such as Al Queda may be all but indistinguishable from its internal system of ownership rules (a set of Islamic-cult precepts). Comparing the two identities, American vice Al Qaeda jihadist, the United States holds immensely more power. Its ownership rules bind in common enterprises a broad range of humans and human experiences, while the narrow interpretation of Islam holding Al Qaeda together in jihad is ridged and not broadly attractive.

A third component of power is leadership. Whatever the identity of a group of owners, whatever the cohesiveness of their identity, and however compelling the system of ownership rules, leadership initiative and vision must be present in order for power to have any active meaning. Effective leadership builds cohesiveness, translates cohesiveness into resolve, and preserves resolve by ensuring that goals and actions are in consonance with the accepted system of ownership. Adolf Hitler was an effective leader in this sense--he identified the keys to building German cohesiveness and to turning it into aggressive resolve. His property enterprise was not subtle or complex. Aryans were rightful owners, others were not, and some, like the Jews, were not fit even as property. Germans, according to Nazi vision, had a right to more land, and had a right to own other peoples as part of it. Hitler worked to maintain cohesiveness, constructed a system of ownership rules that fed on and satisfied a national mindset, and translated German resolve into specific territorial goals. His

---

be lost to communist exploitation. Another Communist victory would embolden Communist radicals in other parts of the world, and would embolden the Soviets to support them. But these arguments, to the extent they were credible, lost importance to the American public. The United States fought for over a decade expending more than fifty-four thousand lives. Attempted strategies did not produce a favorable conclusion within the time made available by the existing quantity of American resolve. The North Vietnamese strategies did.

system of ownership rules was fueled by an arrogance that misjudged the resolve of the rest of the world. Hitler's leadership might have been sustainable if Nazi pretensions regarding ownership had not been so exaggerated. In the Ukraine, for instance, German domination might have been accepted as a favorable alternative to the enslaving Soviet rule. The Germans seized a lot of ground, but they could not incorporate enough demography into the shared ownership identity. They increased the amount of land but not the number of owners. They therefore could not increase the amount of potential resolve favoring the national project. German failure to understand the dynamics of ownership doomed the Third Reich.

Wealth is obviously a component of power. Wealth is determined to an extent by physical geography, which is to say, basic factors such as territorial space, location, minerals, water, or population – the preoccupation of geopoliticians. A geoproperty understanding of wealth goes beyond the natural bounty to include results of entrepreneurial skill, conquest, work habit and innovation. Wealth is power only when it is applied to some project. The United States enjoys so much national wealth that it can be led into endeavors even when the national will is limited and divided. With great national wealth, average leaders can successfully undertake projects that do not enjoy a high degree of resolve. Great leadership can make up for a lack of basic geographic wealth. Genghis Khan, with limited geographical resources, determined to conquer all of Asia. Wealth alone is not power, but it *is* property. Wealth as an element of power is both means and end. It is also the most important clue regarding the holders of power since wealth, more than cohesiveness, resolve, leadership skill or ideology, can be pinpointed, traced, counted, followed, ruined and confiscated.

Technological capacity is well recognized as a primary element in a society's ability to compete strategically. The author lists it separately as a component of power because it translates basic geographic factors into wealth, but does not fit well as basic geography. Technology is an aspect of culture that, in property competitions between societies, invites comparisons of relative advancement or primitiveness. A society with a changing technology tends to be dominant, other factors of power being more or less equal. Technology could be absorbed, in another reduction of the components of national power, into economic or military capacity or into wealth. Inventions not only impinge on the value of property, and on the ability to gain or protect property, they also at times create or constitute property. An important invention creates not just new, fungible wealth; it creates new sets of rights and duties, as well as new competitions and new owner relationships. Weapons are specialized technologies that help physically coerce, capture or kill people, and they are used to gain and protect property. Weapons technologies will be considered separately below because they are centrally important to the development of military strategies. Technology of all kinds paces the relative competition of modern states and yet, aside from weaponry, little scholarly work has been done on the effects or meaning of uneven technological progress as it relates to international conflict. As for entities apart from the nation states, technologies are more often organizational than physical, and often second-hand, but consider again Al Qaeda. The use of airliners as bombs, of individual suicide bombers or improvisation of remotely detonated bombs has been a hallmark of that organization's enterprise.

Military might, like diplomacy, is an instrument (as opposed to a basic element or component) of national power.[299] The military

---

[299] Some explanations of national power list the military as a basic element rather than as an instrument. When confronted by an international event or situation that requires or could benefit by the application or threat of physical force, the nation must arguably have some force on-hand. The technology, physical and organizational, of modern military force demands a development and procurement time so great that it is not feasible to wait for an enemy before determining to acquire a military instrument with which to respond. Also, the status of a nation-state seems so closely tied to the existence of a national military that the two concepts, state and military, often seem inseparable. The designation of military capacity as a basic element of power causes a new range of semantic problems, and twists arguments back in the loop of tautologies. For instance, does military power include police power? It is more than a word problem. Institutionally, many nations have national police or

instrument is a product of demographics, wealth, technology and leadership, and its formation is a manifestation of resolve on the part of the collective identity to defend or arrogate property.

Military technology is more than weaponry or intelligence and communication hardware. It includes organizational and doctrinal innovation. Organizational change seems often to lag behind significant changes in weapons technology and behind the environment of threats. Historical examples are legion, the tank being one of the most cited twentieth century example. The French, unable to comprehend the nexus between the machine and its best method of employment, suffered rapid defeat in WWII as a result. Even today, with a United States military that prides itself on technological transformation, the importance of some innovations is hard to digest. While the civilian world races to employ GIS to map in detail every aspect of culture from the varied pronunciation of words to political opinions, purchase habits and of course all manner of property rights and duties, the military to this point has only seen GIS as tool to precisely catalog physical features. An especially curious and debilitating phenomenon, it seems to ride hand in hand with a predisposition for thinking of intelligence capability as a separate entity of power apart from military power

Before leaving the measurement of power, the most presently relevant aspect of a property understanding of power deserves to be highlighted, repeated and underlined. Property pertains equally and with little adjustment to transnational, international, multinational, supranational or un-national entities of any kind that might wield power in any way for good or evil. This is of ultimate significance because

---

paramilitary forces under their defense departments. More important still is the question of intelligence. The capacity to know, under the rubric that knowledge is power, has fallen more and more to separate, civilian intelligence organizations. In many countries these apparatuses may be more significant than the military as supporting columns of the state. Some nations, meanwhile, have their entire intelligence apparatus under military control.

the measurement of power according to property theory supposes the search for data pertaining especially to wealth and to the names and interrelationships that define ownership and claimant groups. To better find these signs of power, related or unrelated to the nation states as generally understood by the power-balance practitioners, the implementation of laws and social expectations that lead to the creation of transparent records constitutes shaping of the environment for useful intelligence. This intelligence is born almost entirely of cultural processes, and is perfected through creation of georeferenced databases of phenomena that rarely present a physical signature detectable by remote sensors.

Chapter Five: What is to be Done?

Chapter Five: What is to be Done?

*"You can always count on Americans to do the right
thing - after they've tried everything else."*

Winston Churchill

Improvement of foreign property systems is a 'right thing' to do, and could usefully be made a principal column of plans for a peaceful world. As such, the promotion of formal property deserves mental, emotional and practical commitment equivalent to that assigned to human rights prosecutions or the mounting of fair elections. Foreign diplomacy, security strategy, intelligence planning and developmental efforts will profit by incorporating, if not founding themselves on, the spread and growth of formal property regimes. To the extent this formalization of property has been achieved in Iraq, the social contract there will have been readied to succeed on its own. To the extent this is accomplished during Cuba's transition away from the Castro tyranny, Cuba will transition toward being a member of the 'First World.

Chapter One introduced property as an evolved economic-jurisprudential-technological institution that has ameliorated and resolved conflict inside Western societies. It asserted formal property as a necessary precondition for peaceful society elsewhere. Chapter Two generalized global threats in property terms, and stated why development of property everywhere, and especially in the most troubled lands, translates into greater security for the United States. Chapter Three described Colombia, where the property regime has been stunted and malformed by competing ideological streams regarding how to distribute wealth and power, but where improvements of the property regime immediately and permanently contribute to prospects of peace. Chapter Four presented a way by which US national security strategy, including military strategy could more effectively respond to the changed nature of the global security environment, fully incorporating property rights concepts. In this final chapter the arguments are recapped and some related prescriptions drawn. First among these prescriptions is that the United States take a more energetic lead in promoting and demanding the creation of formal property systems, a recommendation that is followed immediately by a second --that foreign affairs decisions of all kinds be informed by complete and accurate property intelligence.

Create property

"As the farmers planted their barbed-wire quadrangles across the range, they came into ferocious conflict with the range cowboy. Such a battle could only have one outcome. The entire edifice of the law -- and with it every sheriff and U.S. marshal who ever became a white-hatted movie hero -- was on the side of property; in other words, of those whose land was measured and entered on a plat."[300]

Andro Linklater in <u>Measuring America</u>

It is one thing to assert that a property line between two farms -- mapped, monumented and properly registered at the county courthouse -- can serve the cause of peace between the two farmers. It is another to say that a legal and technical system generalizing formal property will help secure internal peace for a society; and it is yet another thing to claim that formalizing property around the world will make the United States and the world at large more secure. Nevertheless, that is the point. Within a democratic society, the precise comprehensive and transparent expression of everyday rights and duties is indispensable if trespass is to be controlled. By logical extension the same careful, explicit delineation of rights and duties is a necessary precondition for peace in an ever more 'globalizing' society. The security strategy of the United States should feature the creation and formalization of property as a central component. Military, diplomatic, intelligence and developmental sub-strategies should each explicitly commend and aggressively implement the improvement of property regimes, especially in those parts of the world most prone to the spawning of incivility.

---

[300] Andro Linklater. <u>Measuring America: How and Untamed Wilderness Shaped the United States and Fulfilled the Promise of Democracy</u>. New York: Walker & Company, 2002, p. 235.

Hernando De Soto and his team of researchers exhaustively documented that for the poor of the third world to advance materially, they need to be able to create capital, and that in most under-developed countries they cannot. The reason for this inability to create capital can be found in a lack of formalized property regimes. De Soto's perspective is a powerful, seemingly unavoidable challenge to any developmental strategy or project that does not embrace the question of broad-based capital formation. Furthermore, it is fast creating an intellectual assumption that availability of reliable land ownership data (transparency) is a necessary condition for the success of economic development projects.[301] As a result of a growing acceptance of the cadastre as an indispensable institution and organizational technology, some new money is being aimed at extending and modernizing cadastral systems as well as the extension of formal ownership. The scale of the effort in most places, however, is ridiculously inadequate and far out of proportion with the size of investment in other projects whose failure is all but predestined by the incomplete reaches of the property regime.

As the importance of formalized property for capital formation and economic opportunity becomes, properly, a conventional wisdom, so should the formalization of property become a pillar of practical theory in the areas of conflict avoidance and resolution. In this vein, a USAID initiative stemming from the Summit of the Americas, the Inter-Summit Property Systems Initiative (IPSI), calls for the governments of the Americas to incorporate alternative dispute resolution mechanisms into their plans. It is understood that successful local judicial and non-judicial resolution of property conflicts is dependent on reliable, open information regarding ownership. Assuring the fidelity and permanence of public records is an obvious

---

[301] On the subject of public information transparency, see Luz Estella Nagle, The Search for Accountability and Transparency in Plan Colombia: Reforming Judicial Institutions - Again, (Carlisle, Pennsylvania: Strategic Studies Institute, U.S. Army War College, 2002). "Transparency and accountability are essential to good governance. They will discourage nepotism and curb the bestowing of favors on family and friends." Ibid. p. 8.

start-point for building systems for quieting title (ending dispute over ownership by court decision).[302] However, while USAID is greatly to be credited with some of the most forward-looking efforts in property formalization, many efforts are predicated on building a tax base for local government and almost none of the programs demand a proof of product in the form of transparent information about owner rights and duties. A justifying argument may be that the agency must work through local national governments, and that improving tax bases is naturally attractive to these governments. It is unfortunate that the tax hook has become a driver of what should be an engine for ensuring government responsibility and accountability. Hopefully American programs to build property rights will move toward an impulse to impose obligation on government and protect the rights of owners, rather than the reverse. The AID programs also appear oblivious to or even disdainful of the powerful law enforcement utilities potentially derived from the process of formalization -- this in spite of the fact that creating a greater level of overall community security is a supposed centerpiece goal of assistance efforts, and in spite of the fact that greater security would have a positive effect on land values and, in turn, the tax base. Often lost in the analysis of land formalization economic assistance efforts is the essential fact that it is exactly the exposure of ownership slices (the defeat of impunity through the reduction of anonymity) that gives ' transparency' its worth in the social contract.

Creation of formalized and maintained land records offers a variety of forensic possibilities related to the illicit use of terrain by large criminal enterprises and to smaller, but well funded, terrorist organizations. To obtain this forensic benefit, foreign records must above all be transparent, and transparency of records has not been a principal goal or requirement of US development programs, or of US diplomacy. Since transparency of ownership records is what, in the final analysis, gives the social contract its long-term strength, this

---

[302] See "Virtual Office for the Inter-Summit Property Systems Initiative" <http://www.property-registration.org/Documents/IPSI.htm.

failure to emphasize transparency is an essential error. Real property and real property records have also not been a subject of US foreign intelligence except in the most anecdotal manner, in spite of the immense quantity of information available and its obvious utility. The logic flow bears repeating:

-- There is a positive correlation between formal land ownership and material progress;
-- There exists a complementary relationship between formal land ownership and social peace;
-- Informally owned and unregulated land ownership favors illicit land use and violence;
-- Property manipulation is a dimension of outlaw political and military strategies that has been overlooked by America's foreign intelligence;
-- Collection of property information on a strategic scale is practicable because of new technologies; and
-- Property information powerfully supports police, military, developmental, economic, and diplomatic decisions and programs.

The best human and financial capital that the developed countries can expend on less-developed countries will be on the creation of property, that is, to impel the entire process of establishing and solidifying an agreement about agreements regarding rights and duties associated with places and resources. As a practical matter, creating property means interviewing, surveying, monumenting, mapping, registering, filing, digitizing and web-mounting data, as well as parallel efforts to draft and pass laws conducive to the creation of stable reliable evidence, and to consequential enforcement of decisions derived from the evidence. The utility of this process of systematically building and using evidence of the exercise of rights related to places is not limited to dry civil law cases involving some plaintiff arguing over a road easement to a parking garage. It is also applicable to the identification and location of organized criminals, terrorists insurgents, etc. Creating property means building a foundation for social peace

312

and prosperity. It also and simultaneously means preparing the battlefield for intelligence.

Learn geography

> *"War is God's way of teaching geography"*
> Variously attributed

Among the sub-themes urged in this book is the return of Geography to a position of prominence as an academic discipline for guiding foreign affairs and international studies. It is a bandwagon observation really, since the new technologies conglomerated under techno-abbreviations like GIS, GPS or ESRI are forcing the ascendance of geography in universities all over the world.[303] Institutions closest to questions of security and defense, however, may find themselves a generation behind the curve if they do not react appropriately to the new math. The United States military, for instance, has for decades encouraged its officers to seek masters' degrees in business administration, or perhaps education or sometimes history, but almost never foreign languages or geography. How this happened is food for its own essay, but the effect is evident: few books on military geography have been written in the past thirty years. This may be about to change. As Jerry Dobson, President of the American Geographical Society, puts it, "Society cannot afford to continue "business as usual" with regard to geography and GIS, but remedies will require corrective actions as dramatic as those accorded to physics

---

[303] GIS stands for Geographic Information System, Geographic Information Science, or sometimes Geo-referenced Information System. GPS stands for Global Positioning Satellite or Global Positioning Satellite System. ESRI, which stands for Environmental Systems Research Institute, is not itself a system or innovation, but the name of the leading commercial firm dealing in GIS software and science promotion. The brand name is becoming synonymous with its software family of "Arc" products, such as ArcView® and ArcGIS®, which are the standard software platforms for practical GIS work.

313

and nuclear engineering after World War II."[304]

Once at the forefront of both strategy and US foreign intelligence, geography is making a silent, ineluctable comeback. The American Geographical Society, in particular, is cognizant not only of the implications of the new technologies, but of the pressing need to guide the healthy reemergence of the discipline, and for the US government to correctly exploit that re-emergence.[305] The position of the Society, if not misinterpreted by this author, is to reclaim the lost presence of geography as a practical and theoretical discipline by responding to the current need not just of the United States government, but of the nation, to improve its understanding of foreign lands and peoples. The Society's method is to engage civilian scholars from universities all over the United States in a rediscovery of the world, promoting the global presence of accomplished social scientists leading small expeditions of students and scholars in the creation of a new, continuously updated, unclassified body of geographical knowledge -- one that would invite participation and comment, would train a new generation of military and government officials, and would herald a better visibility of the world for Americans generally. Significantly, this would be done in a manner informed by and reconciled with the new world of GIS technologies, and by the highest standards of academic rigor. As a modest policy prescription, the author suggests that the US government add the position of Geographic Attaché to its diplomatic missions around the world, and that this

---

[304] J. E. Dobson. "The GIS Revolution in Science and Society," Chapter 24 in Stanley D. Brunn, et.al., editors. Geography and Technology. New York: Kluwer Academic Publishers, 2003, p. 573. Professor Dobson is a research professor at the University of Kansas in the Applied Remote Sensing Program of the Kansas Biological Survey and in the Department of Geography.

[305] See generally, Brunn, Geography and Technology. supra. Note 1. The AGS is an appropriate beacon for change given its organizational history. The United States government contracted with the AGS heavily in the early in half of the 20th century through the Second World War to provide mature intelligence before the modern national intelligence organizations existed. On the influential history of the AGS, see The American Geographical Society online at <http://www.amergeog.org/history.htm.

attaché should have working for him or her a group of technically competent GIS liaisons who could provide unclassified GIS support to all facets of the US embassies' missions. They not only could link themselves directly to the vast and growing GIS industry in government bureaucracies and NGOs around the globe, they could be the government's host in each country to visiting professors of the Society's worldwide network of muliti-discipline scholars. Geography is growing away from being a cute middle-school contest of who-knows-the-capitals and into its own as the multidiscipline integrator of place-based social science.

Why the emphasis on geographers and GIS? Because, as hopefully has been made clear in preceding chapters, property lies between law and land, land and economics and between military strategy and human rights. Property is the agreement about agreements, the basic conflict resolution mechanism, the social contract, the most successful of civilizing institutions, and the indispensable secret that permits liberty and long-term peace to flow as one. Like so many things, property as a term or concept or practical tool can only be fully understood and shaped against the context of other geographic knowledge.

> GIS is the medium through which most people know and practice the methods and techniques traditionally claimed by geographers. It is profoundly changing society, yet it may well be the most underutilized, relative to its proven capability, of any technology in existence. It is one of the most promising and, simultaneously, one of the most dangerous technologies emerging today.[306]

GIS is one vector of a convergence of phenomena that makes property and land use intelligence at a strategic level practicable. Only in the

---

[306] J. E. Dobson. "The GIS Revolution in Science and Society," supra. Note 1. at 537.

past decade or so has it been reasonable to expect cadastral records to be turned into mathematical digits, mounted on a computer database and transmitted over the Internet. All the theoretical assertions of Chapter One, or the forensic promise made in the following chapters, would be gratuitous if it were not for the GIS revolution. Furthermore, property records, while valuable of themselves, are immensely more useful to planners and scholars when their information is placed in the geographic context of other computer-mapped data. Environmental changes, engineering projects, biological and agricultural modeling, urban planning – all have been accelerated a thousand-fold by GIS technology. As such, the theories and preparations of Geography are newly ascendant. Geographers are now better equipped, and as a result, will probably be both more daring in application of their discipline and more docile in their assertions.

Ray Cline, geographer and maybe geopolitician mentioned in Chapter Four, named his formula for measuring national power after plate tectonics. His liberal allusion to plate theory was an artistic flourish suggesting that big answers are valid and that problems of international conflict can be mapped on a global scale. What might a global property map look like? Freedom House, a Washington based human rights NGO, produces a map that shows the status of human freedom by country.[307] Freedom House displays in an atlas-type composition what is an admittedly subjective comparison of a mixed bag of human liberties. The map shows countries as free, partly free, and not-free. With a little imagination, one can see that where not-free countries are close to free ones there is potential for conflict, or at least a lot of migration. A geostrategic message is delivered bell-clear by the

---

[307] In addition to an annual world map, Freedom House publishes a monthly journal, Freedom Review, and an annual survey of political rights entitled Freedom in the World; See also Michael Kidron & Ronald Segal, The New State of the World Atlas (New York: Simon and Schuster, 1987). The New State of the World Atlas places attention in graphic form on many of the kinds of relationships alluded to in this book. Map titles include "Urban Blight," "The Longer Reach"(international mail receipts and radio ownership), "The First Slice of the Cake," "Religions of Rule," etc. The atlas is an attempt to display

Freedom House world map. Color-coding on the Freedom House map does not display rimlands, shatterbelts, heartlands or other spatial relationships, but instead shows differentials in rights. Because the value of global lands is not generated only by location and shape, but by the way places are owned, geostrategists can see on the Freedom House map what is invisible on those of the Spykmans and Mackinders.

Other indices have been fabricated to trace a connection between visible societal conditions and the prospects of peace and prosperity. One is the Index of Economic Freedom.[308] Another is the Human Development Index, created by the United Nations.[309] Another is the Failed States Index and yet another the Oxford Analytica Risk Assessment.[310] That they differ in methodology, scope and purpose is clear from some of the differences in results. For instance, Cuba, mentioned often in this book, rates very poorly on the Economic Freedom index, but does moderately well on the UN's Human Development Index. Among this author's favorites are the Globalization Index and the Corruption Perceptions Index.[311] Since the writing of most of this text, the Property Rights Alliance published its

---

[308] See Edwin Feulner Jr. et al., 2005 Index of Economic Freedom, Washington, D.C.: The Wall Street Journal and the Heritage Foundation, 2005); The index has been published since1994. The methodology contains in it a superficial measure of property regimes, but looking at the country rankings, one would expect that, given a thorough comparison of property systems, that the countries at the top of the rankings will fare far better than those at the bottom. The rankings can be found online at < http://www.heritage.org/research/features/index/countries.cfm
[309] United Nations Develpment Programme, "Human Development Index," www.undp.org online at
<http://hdr.undp.org/statistics/data/hdi_rank_map.cfm.
[310] Aon Political Risk Services & Oxford Analytica "2007 Political and Economic Risk Map"; The Fund for Peace, "Failed States Index," online at www.fundforpeace.org <
http://www.fundforpeace.org/programs/fsi/fsindex.php?column=rank&.>;
[311] ATKearney Globalization Index at
<http://www.atkearney.com/main.taf?p=5,4,1,116>; Transparency International, Corruption Perceptions Index at
http://www.transparency.org/policy_research/surveys_indices/cpi.

International Property Rights Index (IPRI).[312] FMSO has for some time proposed a world index showing comparing property regimes, and the IPRI goes a long way in that direction. Although the Property Rights Alliance work is focused on economic advancement of the poor, rather than on avoidance and resolution of internal violence, it is probably a point of theoretical consensus that the two are intimately related in many places. Certain property rights, such as minority access to public and semi-public places, corporate ownership participation, water court operations, eligibility for leadership in cooperative ownership schemes, passport and visa requirements, or child illegitimacy might all be more revealing of potential conflict than some current measures of human rights status. For example, if we were to rate one place as less humane than another because of the existence of a death penalty, that measure may not be reflective of greater political instability or potential violence. Extreme differentials in ownership rights, combined with a lack of formal records, however, probably predict violence. Being able to anticipate war on the basis of geographic knowledge is a higher achievement than learning Geography as a result of war. In many parts of the world the most important geographic knowledge concerns rights related to land.

Very recently, the principle unit of employment of the American military has been shifting away from what had been the division, an organization of blessed with its own armor, artillery, engineers and other support units, of about sixteen thousand soldiers. As a result of the Global War on Terror, the main organizational unit seems now to be a special forces team, comprised perhaps of a dozen people. The difference is reflective of the nature of the threat, characteristics of globalization and the particularization of power discussed earlier. The basic elements of geography that guide our operational intelligence view of the world needs to be changed as well. Instead of the country, we need to focus on the county and its international cousins. Almost everywhere in the world the best property intelligence is at that level of territoriality and below.

---

[312] See footnote 56, infra.

Produce Property Knowledge

> *"You cannot convert the absence of information into a conclusion."*[313]
>
> Tom Clancy in <u>Sum of All Fears</u>

When a country invades another militarily, both face a set calculus regarding the amount of force they can bring to bear within specifiable amounts of time in given places. These decisions regarding where, when and how much force might be applied, though difficult and consequential, are relatively simple. The physical threat of a nation-state military can be roughly understood in relation to the characteristics of physical technologies--the range and speed of a missile, the march rate of a tank division. Trade-offs in terms of speed to the objective and risk to lines of communication can be clearly understood, even if not precisely calculated. Given unchallenged precision bombing, and other preparations, the US military was able to race to Baghdad in weeks. Other challenges to ownership are more confusing in terms of resources to be committed and time available. Cross-border migrations, transnational crime, acts of terror, environmental degradation, harmful trade barriers, or the proliferation of threatening technologies gestate at unknown rates and manifest themselves in seemingly unpredictable places. The application of physical force (or as is said these days, 'kinetic' weaponry) in support of policy initiatives aimed at such threats is therefore likely to be sporadic, erratic, inconsistent and imprecise. Today, the power to influence behavior (or to kill people) on a global scale has become more and more diffuse, is by no means monopolized by the nation-states. Successful strategies may even be the aggregate result of thousands of disparate, independent actions orchestrated by no more than a popular idea. One path toward understanding this complex environment is to identify the various owner and claimant identities as

---

[313] Tom Clancy, <u>Sum of all fears</u>, p. 935.

319

they relate to each potential slice of the ownership related to a place. That is to say, consider with precision the individual rights and duties in play, name all of the competitor identities and all of the rules and authority that might bear on the mix. Some contentions may be revealed that cannot be peaceably reconciled, but even in these cases many of the owner identities and claimed rights might be peaceably cleared from the mix.

To take this analytical approach at all, however, requires knowledge regarding the specific rights in question. To consider the panoply of rights and claims from which a stable resolution might be drawn requires written records of the most basic ownership interests. We know almost nothing about what people really fight over in the places where we have inserted ourselves. We can name the most obvious claimant identities, which are generally the most radical, but we have barely a clue about the specific ownership interests of the many contending identities. We can talk to the political parties through their leaders, but are usually oblivious to what those leaders own or with whom they own it, or what they would own if they could, or how they might peaceably go about owning it if a peaceable path were made available. In our enthusiasm for electoral democracy, we may even encourage the formation of claimant groups that confound the stability of the rule of law and the peaceable consideration of property rights. How can we presume to be peacemakers while we remain without any notion of the most basic objects of conflict? This is a truly odd condition to consider once one realizes how dependent on property intelligence a city council or county commission is when faced with major decisions regarding their communities.

In the United States, dozens of federal organizations add, in semi- or wholly independent ways, to the mountain of information national decision-makers might digest in regard to events n foreign lands. In addition to the traditional intelligence bureaucracies (such as the CIA, DIA, or NSA) the Department of State, the Drug Enforcement Agency, the Commerce Department, the Environmental Protection Agency, and myriad of others have informational responsibilities.

However massive or efficient a system of policy intelligence (not that the two characteristics are known to coincide), there is a fixed amount of information that can go into a decision maker's head in a given amount of time. For one thing, it is difficult to block some information in favor of others or even to decide the priority of sources. As a result, some of the wielders of the bits of particularized power that are partly or wholly at odds with American policy, whether they are within the government or not, are bound to have intelligence as good as, or better than that of the relevant American leader. Significantly, no US national intelligence agency produces property intelligence on any scale – there is no foreign property intelligence office. Meanwhile, opposition organizations, such as the Colombian FARC, are in possession of detailed ownership information on which they base many decisions. Groups like the FARC, with almost no capacity to mount technical collection means using remote sensors and the like, are able to mount specifically targeted agile campaigns of extortion and kidnapping or of illicit drug market penetration and delivery because they can identify with precision the amount and location of their mark's wealth and personal relationships. Our agility to mark them, meanwhile, is handicapped because we have lost sight of the relationships people have with places and things we disparage as property. The globalized enemy prizes information about the logistics of his targets and enemies, but the United States government has yet to see the same geography regarding these same lines of communication.

The traditional American intelligence organizations are large mainly because of the imperatives of the Cold War. Secrecy of sources and methods of collection has been seen within these organizations as paramount to maintaining a full flow of correct information. When dealing with the world of particularized power, secrecy becomes a legal and practical burden. In reference to a criminal organization or a violent political movement, secrecy of sources and methods is still critical to successful pursuit. Most other power-wielding identities depend heavily on open communication and on the creation of solidarity around ideas. They cannot afford too much secrecy of communications. Since the power being exerted by non-governmental groups and individuals often depends on mobilizing adherents, there almost always appears an openly publicized manifestation of effort. Correspondingly, open source intelligence on political matters is growing in importance, even within the intelligence community, to gain insight about the many particles of power that are being exercised today.[314] Whether this information is considered a part of the national wealth, a function of leadership, or a basic element of power is unimportant. It *is* important that the open source information is newly appreciated as a contributor to the fluid application of national power. Property information is by its nature almost entirely open-source, and while property intelligence is not yet being produced to any degree by any agency of the government, new acceptance of unclassified intelligence and security-relevant scholarship is a positive sign.

It is common to consider information itself as valuable private and common property.[315] It is likewise easy to understand the increased value of preferentially held information--proprietary information. More emphasis is being placed on unclassified

---

[314] The *Internet* is the realization of an old dream about universally shared global information. H.G. Wells, in one of his less well-known works, promoted the idea of a universal encyclopedia of knowledge and a world-wide common educational curriculum as an engine of world peace. Herbert George Wells, World Brain (London: Methuen & Co. Limited, 1938). Wells wasn't very optimistic about human nature or the use of information, however. "Man reflects before he acts, but not very much; he is still by nature intellectually impatient. No sooner does he apprehend, in whole or in part, the need of a new world, than, without further plans or estimates, he gets into a state of passionate aggressiveness and suspicion and sets about trying to change the present order. There and then, he sets about it, with anything that comes handy, violently, disastrously, making the discordances worse instead of better, and quarrelling bitterly with anyone who is not in complete accordance with his particular spasmodic conception of the change needful. He is unable to realize that when the time comes to act, that also is the time to think fast and hard. He will not think enough." Ibid., p. xi.

[315] See Anne Wells Branscomb, Who Owns Information?, (New York: Harper Collins, 1994). Branscomb correctly treats information in terms both of power and property. She asks, Who Owns Your Name and Address?, Who Owns Your Electronic Messages?, Who Owns Computer Software?, Who Owns Government Information?, and other questions that have direct bearing on the pace of the diffusion of ownership and the particularization of power.

information gathering and processing to avoid legal and practical pitfalls of government secrecy, and because it is so valuable in its own right.[316] Regardless of the growth of open-source information in support of national policy, the most dangerous threats to a state's sovereignty will continue to require monitoring by secret and expensive means. Particularization of power includes bad groups and individuals as well as good. The bad tend to be more liberal in their willingness to enforce their property pretensions through the use of violence. They are also more likely to understand and manage the value of closely held information. For this reason, national governments, and even large non-governmental organizations, will probably invest more in information security and in attempts to gain the closely held information of others. The size and utility of general purpose armed forces may continue to decrease, but investment in intelligence gathering and information protection will increase.

Build national security law, international law

> *"No State shall make or enforce any law which shall abridge the privileges or immunities of citizens of the United States; nor shall any State deprive any person of life, liberty, or property, without due process of law; nor deny any person within its jurisdiction the equal protection of the laws."*
> From Section 1, Amendment XIV of the United States Constitution

---

[316] An oddly relevant historical analogy can be found in Hagen Schulze, The Course of German Nationalism (New York: Cambridge University Press, 1985). In one section, Schulze describes the energy generated in 1848 Berlin over news of the revolution in Paris. A Public opinion immediately entered a stage familiar to the early history of all revolutions: that of widespread excitement and general exasperation, when opportunities for general outbursts are cultivated, without giving the police occasion for effective counter-attacks. The public places=, wrote a contemporary observer, the reading-booths...presented an unusual appearance as overcrowded political meeting places.... Ibid., p. 7. The dawn of new communication technologies and the widespread, poorly censored or monitored use of public communications gives hint to the importance of the Internet.

The United States military has been a bit slow to recognize the revolutionary implications of GIS beyond the realm of precision in the guidance of munitions. It has been more complete in its response to the slower onslaught of the law into all dimensions of military operations and life. Americans have by and large agreed that "we the people" has to include more than one status--that the cohesiveness of national identity (by force of arguments about the nature of rights, and the pragmatics of an immigrant culture) demand inclusive interpretations of constitutional principles, even in the post 9/11 world of security consciousness, and in spite of decisions related to the sui generis captivities of Al Qaeda suspects.

A 'US Person' is defined by executive order to be "a United States citizen, an alien known by the intelligence agency concerned to be a permanent resident alien, an unincorporated association substantially composed of United States citizens or permanent resident aliens, or a corporation directed and controlled by a foreign government or governments."[317] US Person status engages a range of constitutional protections including those relating to illegal government searches, invasion of privacy, and warrantless arrests. It is an example of a self-imposed dilution of sovereignty. For many law enforcement purposes, the rights accruing to United States citizens have been extended beyond citizenship and beyond US borders. For instance, units along the border US-Mexico border have long taken a broad interpretation of the executive order defining the US Person. In that spirit, and guided by the intent of the Posse Comitatus Act, they are normally cautious, presuming anyone within the United States, but outside a certain distance from the border, to be a US Person. They may also presume that anyone heading toward Mexico from the interior of the United States is a US Person. Whether or not operational intelligence overlays and briefings detail the legal limitations on government forces is of

---

[317] Ronald Reagan, Executive Order No. 12333, December 4, 1981, "Presidents Oversight Intelligence Board." Can be found in Compilation of Intelligence Laws and Related Laws and Executive Orders of Interest to the National Intelligence Community (Washington, D.C.: U.S. Gov't. Printing Office, 1993), 645.

secondary importance. The greater point is that along the Mexican-US border the traditional intelligence fodder of enemy, weather, and terrain gave way to worries about illegal impositions on the concert of civil and property rights. These worries can even be translated into graphically illustrated planning factors. In almost every military mission that occurs under within the confines of some domestic legal system, the parameters of property laws can be mapped (mapped in the most traditional sense of lines, shapes and colors on paper or on a computer screen). The social consequence of property law has a geographical shape important to planning, and so should be fully incorporated into security doctrine, including national security law, its subordinate, military operational law, and operational planning.

The upshot of these assertions for scholarly analysis or for strategic intelligence is obvious. However, the possibility of making a continuous weave from the global scale to the local or tactical is especially intriguing. Property struggles can be mapped down to the life estate rights of tenant farmers, the right to carry a concealed weapon, the right to keep a dog off a leash, to vote on a school bond, or to carry away fallen wood. Every one of these things influences political contests, and every armed political contest will contain a mixture of these kinds of issues. Even the potentially big wars of the future are sure to be cluttered with extortion and parasitic enemy strategies. To win against these, any country must be able to target discreetly with the correct amount of force and informed by the correct kinds of intelligence. Notably, to describe the objectives, determine success and prepare strategies for the confused conflicts of the future, the relevant competitions can best be described in property terms.

Keying on property reminds that the job of protecting diffuse rights and duties is as often a police job as it is a military one. The force structure necessary for a successful application of the rule of law will not only lend the physical strength to take and keep possession, but to create and protect property rights until such a time that conflicts over rights and duties can be satisfactorily resolved without the immediate presence of armed force. As Robert Ardrey noted in <u>Territorial Imperative,</u>

> "We may also say that in all territorial species, without exception, possession of a territory lends enhanced energy to the proprietor. Students of animal behavior cannot agree as to why this should be, but the challenger is almost invariably defeated, the intruder expelled. In part, there seems some mysterious flow of energy and resolve which invests a proprietor on his home grounds. But likewise, so marked is the inhibition lying on the intruder, so evident his sense of trespass, we may be permitted to wonder if in all territorial species there does not exist, more profound than simple learning, some universal recognition of territorial rights."[318]

However noble a foreign presence and however welcome among even a majority of the local population, there is something innately and universally understood about territoriality that gives a foreign force only so much time to set a society on a peaceable course. That is to say, time cannot be wasted waiting on a secure moment before establishing the evidentiary basis for a stable social contract. Foreign armed forces will enjoy a diminishing welcome over time, wherever they are posted. To secure a lasting and positive result, to give substance to a veneer of 'democracy,' it will nowhere be enough to teach elections, or to have a 'mandate.' A property regime must be established that is likely to service human flourishing.

What should not be done

> *"Land...cannot be treated as an ordinary asset, controlled by individuals and subject to the pressures*

---

[318] Robert Ardrey, <u>The Territorial Imperative: A Personal Inquiry into the Animal Origins of Property and Nations</u>. New York: Antheneum, 1966, p. 3.

and inefficiencies of the market. Private land ownership
is also a principal instrument of accumulation and
concentration of wealth and therefore contributes to
social injustice; if unchecked, it may become a major
obstacle in the planning and implementation of
development schemes....."[319]

UN Policy statement, 1976

The official policy of the United Nations has evolved considerably since the above policy statement was written. Nevertheless, in 2004 the United Nations published a report, with principal sponsorship from the European Union, on the condition of democracy, or of the concept of democracy, in Latin America.[320] The report was presented in Spanish from the UNDP website in PDF format, allowing the reader to download reasonably sized portions of the lengthy document and its appendices. The electronic format also permitted quick word search and content analyses. One might suppose that Hernando De Soto's writings would figure in the report, since the report highlights unrealized material prosperity in the region as a determinant of flagging faith in democracy.

The report mentions De Soto's work only once, however, in the bibliography, and this reference to his 1984 work, The Other Path. The Mystery of Capital did not make it into the body of works that the preparers of the report considered worth mentioning. (The report was printed in Peru and several of the text contributors are, like Mr. De Soto, Peruvian.) This dismissal of De Soto's thesis was cause enough to search a bit deeper into the contents of the report. Looking for

---

[319] "Report of Habitat: United Nations Conference on Human Settlements," Vancouver, 31 May - 11 June, 1976, (A/Conf.70/15) found online at The UN and property rights <http://www.sovereignty.net/p/land/unproprts.htm.
[320] The United Nations Development Programme. La Democracia en América Latina: Hacia una democracia de ciudadanas y ciudadanos. (Democracy in Latin America: Toward a democracy of the citizenry). Buenos Aires: Aguilar, Altea, Taurus, Alfaguara, S.A., 2004; online at
<http://www.undp.org/dpa/pressrelease/releases/2004/april/0421prodal.html.

'cadastre' (*catastro*) was perhaps a frivolity, but absence of the word at least determined that the researchers had made no intellectual incursion into the vocabulary of land value or tax equity. Of the 12 times the word 'property' (*propiedad*) appears in the text, four are in the sense of a statistical characteristic, not ownership. Two other appearances of *property* are in a pair of repetitive footnote references to a 1965 work by T.H. Marshal.[321] The report writers state a preference for Marshal's division of citizens' rights into three general types: civil, political, and social. Both citations embrace Marshal's inclusion within civil rights of the "right to property" or the "right to possess property." In these instances, the report writers, like Marshal, employ the word in terms of the thing, rights not being embedded in the concept. Thus, along with the absence of the word 'land' (*tierra*) or its near synonyms, the failure to address the question property could be forgiven as a simple decision not to direct the report in the overly vocational direction of land or money. Another use of the word *property* is given in reference to an index of the favorability of business climates, another related to an individual's right to governmental information, in this case about his or her property ownership data.[322] The next use betrays the distance between the authors' concept of property and other rights.

> "Missing is a State able to guide the general direction of the society, manage conflicts according to democratic principles, effectively guarantee the functioning of the legal system (property rights and citizens' rights simultaneously,…)"[323]

The next reference is a minor note about crimes against persons and property[324], and the last an inert reference of large holdings and private enterprise.[325] The word *rights*, meanwhile, appears more than 500

---

[321] Ibid., p. 58, note 25 and p. 60, note 32.
[322] Ibid., p. 109.
[323] Ibid., p. 187.
[324] Ibid., p. 189.
[325] Ibid., p. 195.

times. Potentially, reconciliation is available between those who see property as a body of rights and those who see it as theft. The Pipes, Bethels, and De Sotos of the world understand formal property as a set of asserted, affirmed, evidenced, represented, respected and enforced rights – the object of ownership being of less significance. One can suppose that a body of thinkers, such as those authoring this UNDP document, who clearly place rights at the center of their concerns, could be shown common ground in the De Soto argument. Perusal of the various rights discussed or promulgated in the UN report -- and of the assumptions regarding the nature of society, the role of the State, and the prescriptions offered -- suggest that the United Nations writers cannot embrace the De Soto message. For most of them it seems, Latin American development is detained by insufficient democratic political participation at all levels. Their general prescription, to the extent there is a consensus, calls for more broad-based forms of mass democracy that go beyond simple elections, involve *civil society* organizations, and common ownership. Almost no favorable mention is made of private property. As for the creation of capital, or any relationship between security and the development of a property regime, the report is absolutely oblivious. Capital itself is mentioned almost exclusively in the context of the injustices of capitalism. Meanwhile, much of the report and accompanying 'debate' is hard to follow in that so many paragraphs are admixtures of abstractions and apparent code words. The debate seems to welcome class struggle analysis and bemoans limitations on the powers of elected executives to exercise sovereign authority.

The report, written from an intellectual world-view able to so completely exclude De Soto and his thesis should exasperate the reader looking for insight into conflict resolution, the suppression of violence or the spread of prosperity. While the report gives worried attention to enclaves of State militarism, and to a constant threat of arrogation by the regions' national armed forces, there is almost no mention of insurgents, subversives, terrorists, narcotraffickers or illegal organized groups of any kind, much less the impact their actions have had on the prospects of democracy or development. The Latin American universe of organized malefactors is reduced in the report to indirect reference, and blamed on general conditions of the economy and weakness of the state.[326]

The weekend after the UNDP report was released, the Miami Herald ran an article by Frances Robles titled, "Lead vs. Machete" about land-related violence in Venezuela. The abstract stated,

> Bloody disputes erupt between those who had property and those letting [sic] their first taste of ownership. Nowhere are these battles currently claiming more lives than in Venezuela. [327]

In his 1,200 word article, Robles brings us far closer to the central question weighing on peace, prosperity and freedom in Latin America, and in most of the world, than the UNDP did in hundreds of pages. (It is appropriate that it ran in the Miami Herald, too, from a community intellectually and emotionally close to the coming Cuba crisis. Cuban property will be a centerpiece of all practicable and intelligent consideration of that great impending change.)

This book's Chapter Three discussion of the property regime in Colombia mentioned a 2003 United Nations report that was also produced by the UN Development Programme.[328] That report barely considered property, and passed on the notion of defeating the armed enemies of the Colombian State. The intellectual consistency between the two UN reports cannot be coincidental. The vision of the United Nations, at least as manifested by the vanguard of its developmental and conflict resolution thinkers, appeared to be moving on an azimuth 180 degrees removed from what this book proposes as the necessary

---

[326] Ibid., p. 167.

[327] Frances Robles. "Lead vs. Machete." Miami Herald April 25, 2004. Online at <http://www.miami.com/mld/miamiherald/news/8504687.htm?1c.

[328] The United Nations Development Programme. El Conflicto, callejón con salida: Informe Nacional de Desarrollo Humano Colombia – 2003. Bogotá: Panamericana Formas e Impresos, S.A., 2003.

330

path. Chapter Three suggested there have been four historical strains of intellectual influence on conflict in Colombia – conquest & evangelism; federalism vice anti-federalism; social revolution; and unbridled gangster capitalism. The United Nations reports embody and exaggerate the third strain and gave a blind eye to the forth. However we might characterize the intellectual underpinnings of the United Nations vision for peace and prosperity, the practical result can be unfortunate. The United Nations, to the extent it is guided by the same thinking that produces it's literature on the subject, seemed to disqualify itself, in the face of history, evidence and logic, from being a useful partner in promoting human flourishing. It appeared that the United Nations was stuck in the same theoretical world as that of the pre-World War II geopoliticians, in which whole-fee nation-states and indivisible sovereignties rule the mind and guide program goals and methods. The real world is just not that way. It is a world of divisible and diffuse ownership, ephemeral ownership identities, and particularized power. The corporate understanding of the United Nations, expressed in its publications and internalized to its programs, has not been the right path, not what is to be done. It is an error of concept that doubly insults the lofty purposes of the United Nations because in this one thing, formalized property, material development and human security coincide. The original reason of property was and remains conflict resolution. This is a proposition seemingly rejected by the corporate intellect of the United Nations, a rejection that will ultimately disqualify the United Nations in development as in security.

The good news at the United Nations is a fresh counter-current. In 2006, Hernando De Soto was made co-chair, along with former secretary of State Madeleine Albright, of the UNDP Commission on Legal Empowerment of the Poor, a non-governmental cooperation. Dr. Karol Boudreaux, another accomplished advocate of formalizing property as a developmental necessity, is a member of the commission's 'Working Group on Property Rights.' Dr. Boudreaux is an expert on international property systems at the Mercatus Center, George Mason University and has studied the insufficiencies of property regimes in Africa, especially Sudan. We can hope that this recognition of the importance of property rights spreads from an understanding connected only to the economic progress of the desperately poor to one connected to the internal peace of societies in general.

Unfortunately, the predispositions noted in the United Nations reports have also been present, if to a lesser degree, in the developmental thinking of US missions abroad. For instance, the word property does not appear in the widely successful 1966 textbook titled Nation Building, which was published as a collaboration of some of the leading political science scholars in the United States at the time. Land reform does not appear and even agriculture is barely mentioned. To be fair, the book was not so much focused on the practical problems of development as it was political party organization, identity, and the relationship of economic progress on the consolidation of democratic electoral forms in emerging states. Still, it appears that the notion of property, and its central place in Western heritage, held no space at all in the minds of a significant slice of the political science elite at the time. In 2003, Rand published an anthology titled America's Role in Nation-Building: From Germany to Iraq. In this effort, several of an equally qualified group of scholars do address the role of property and property development.

> " In Japan, SCAP pushed through a land reform that destroyed the power of the landholding classes and made the peasantry property owners. SCAP also greatly expanded workers' rights and forced through the dissolution of the large business combines (*zaibatsu*) that had dominated the economy."[329]

> "The damage resulting from generations of communist mismanagement followed by a decade of Serbian looting proved difficult to repair. Facing disagreement within

---

[329] James Dobbins, et. al. America's Role in Nation-Building: From Germany to Iraq. Santa Monica: Rand, 2003, p. 55.

the international community on how to tackle these
challenges, the UN administration delayed many of its
decisions. By the end of 2000, Kosovo had a much-
improved commercial code, the outcome of international
development efforts. Nearly a year passed after the
conflict before a criminal and civil code was put in
place, and then it was the Yugoslav code dating
from1989, which had the virtue of being pre-Milosevic
but the disadvantage of also being pre-post-communist.
A number of property disputes therefore remain
unresolved even today."[330]

The writers also briefly touted success of a private property
formalization program in Bosnia. Curiously, there is no mention of
property in the 'lessons learned' section, which is not that surprising, in
a sense. Ambassador James Dobbins, one of the lead authors and a
respected developmental planner, served, *inter-alia*, as Special Advisor
on Haiti to the U S State Department during the Carter administration.
In 1995, Ambassador Dobbins delivered a presentation extolling US
and international peacekeeping efforts in Haiti.[331] It was
understandably upbeat, recanting the relatively peaceful
reestablishment of Bertrand Aristide as President, as well as a number
of developmental and democratizing programs and projects. At the
time, some 200 million dollars per year was being spent on Haiti, most
of it from the United States -- but almost no money was spent toward
establishing a modern property regime.

Contemporaneously, Hernando De Soto's team of economists
completed a brief survey of the country. According to that
investigation, only one/third of urban dwellings in Haiti fell within
some formal framework of ownership, and in rural areas only three
percent of the land was formally owned. The evidence of "dead

---

[330] Ibid. p. 125.
[331] James F. Dobbins. "Haiti: A Case Study in Post-Cold War Peacekeeping,"
remarks at the ISD Conference on Diplomacy and the Use of Force, September 21,
1995. <http://sfswww.georgetown.edu/sfs/programs/isd/files/haiti.htm.

capital" indicated "the total assets of the poor are more than one hundred fifty times greater than all the foreign investment received since Haiti's independence from France in 1804."[332] De Soto clearly expressed the need to perfect Haiti's property system and to streamline the quagmire of requirements for the legalization of property. The role of property development as an engine of economic prosperity and freedom was well-explained. Nevertheless, property did not figure as more than a minor, tangential subject of international programs there. Regardless, U.S. plans for Iraq have been similar to those applied in Haiti, only times 200. In March of 2004, Mr. Dobbins testified before congress, giving recommendations as to Haiti's future.[333] He did not mention property. Also outspoken regarding Iraq, he stated in 2003 "We don't seem to have learned much."[334] He is doubtless right, but he still had not mentioned property, and it is this oversight on the part of our leading developmentalists that must be addressed and reversed. De Soto asks, "How could something so important have slipped our minds?"[335] Perhaps against an un-sensed educational and ideological background that disdains the word. Seeing after less than a decade how international efforts in Haiti have been unrewarded by conditions there, it is sobering to think what the result will be in Iraq. Just as the now obvious missing component of property development was identified and ignored as to Haiti, it has been identified and dutifully ignored as to Iraq. American thinking regarding the significance of property progressed only slightly from Nation-Building to America's Role in Nation-Building.

---

[332] Hernando De Soto, p.5.
[333] James Dobbins. "A Fresh Start for Haiti?: Charting Future U.S. Haitian Relations." Testimony presented to the Senate Committee on Foreign Relations Subcommittee on Western Hemisphere, Peace Corps, and Narcotic Affairs, March 10, 2004. online at
<http://foreign.senate.gov/testimony/2004/DobbinsTestimony040310.pdf.
[334] George Gedda. "President Bush's Ex-Envoy for Afghanistan Criticizes U.S. Effort in Iraq." Associated Press July 16, 2003 online at the Common Dreams News Center, <http://www.commondreams.org/headlines03/0716-03.htm.
[335] Hernando de Soto, , p. 8.

The United States committed to spending a lot of money in Iraq, but most of it will have been wasted if the institutions that underpin trust and accountability are not created. These are the social qualities that make trade in real estate possible. Collateral is created and capital made representable for commerce when property, and especially rights in land, are made transparent and protected. When real estate in Iraq is bought and sold freely and confidently, peace will not have been a bi-product; it will have been the essential product.

> "most people cannot participate in an expanded market because they do not have access to a legal property rights system that represents their assets in a manner that makes them widely transferable and fungible, that allows them to be encumbered and permits their owners to be held accountable. So long as the assets of the majority are not properly documented and tracked by a property bureaucracy, they are invisible and sterile in the marketplace."[336]

This will continue to be true in Haiti and Iraq regardless of other programs. Worse, without property formalization, Haiti will never enjoy both electoral democracy and internal calm. It will be condemned to possessions by force or tyranny regardless of the amount of money spent there by international aid organizations or the United States. So it is with Iraq. So what is not to be done is to continue to place property development on a secondary plane of goals.

Colombia, Cuba, Mexico and other places

An aside of this book is an observation that the geographic focus of United States security concerns might better be made closer to home, that the near abroad and the security problems in our own neighborhood of worthy of precedent. The challenges in our own

---

[336] Ibid. p. 211.

hemisphere are multi-faceted, mixing uncontrolled migration, organized crime, violent rebellion and changes of leadership, corruption and the aggressive misapplication of natural resources. Physical proximity is no insignificant variable in the calculus that turns these ugly things into a threat to the United States. The incomplete nature of the property regimes in the Western Hemisphere underlies the causes, and improving property regimes is the most effective solution for the long term. This is not to say that the same prescription of improved, formalized property does not apply to all the places around the world where the United States and its allies have security interests and concerns. It does, but starting close to home is not a bad idea, in light of the facts of time and space.

Of five countries chosen for mention, Colombia, with a generally liberal system of ownership, is in the midst of violent internal challenge from powerful brigands. Colombia has a stunted property regime, which it is trying to improve while defeating its internal enemies. Mexico has a property regime that is only slightly further along than that of Colombia. Major changes in the Mexican property regime are underway and understanding them is critical to confronting the challenges that the United States and Mexico will overcome together or not at all. Haiti, already considered in the previous section, is a country that aspires just to join the third world, but which regularly re-enters political and economic crisis despite massive international assistance, especially from the United States. Unfortunately, little of the aid has gone to fixing the Haitian property regime. Cuba is a country about to face the death of a king. It has a completely illiberal social contract and a significant portion of disaffected citizens that will demand something better or leave. Finally, Venezuela is another country with an insufficient property system, and it is quickly turning into another Cuba in spite of considerable oil income.

Colombia

It does not take much of an education in Geography to see why

336

Colombia might become a place where the United States spends a lot of its defense capital. Almost any theory pointing up an element of physical geography as a determinant of relative strategic importance could find Colombia near the top of the list. Colombian history has been one in which globalized supply and demand for a changing variety of valuable natural resources has constantly re-coded the value of Colombian places. In this context Colombian's have fought over rights related to those resources – rights to extraction, access and control of labor, transport routes, taxation, processing. Colombians will continue to debate the traditional questions of territorial autonomy and taxing power, continually revisit the practical nature of taxation authority in light of physical and social realities. Eventually they will overtake and subdue amoral, violent entrepreneurs. As for social revolution and class struggle, that intellectual current is alive and well, and while it contributes positively at some level, one of its ill effects has been to close mental space about the nature of property. Disdain for 'private' property has crippled understanding of property generally, as well as property's role in economic prosperity, liberty and social peace. In turn, space has been closed to practical international assistance programs that would build a precise, comprehensive and transparent property regime. The first thing that must be done, then, in Colombia and elsewhere, is to check anti-property ideology and resulting prescriptions that reject property as a building block of socio-economic development and peace.

The United States has been slow to settle on a unified interpretation of the problem that could allow either effective advice or assistance. Even if all players in the design and implementation of US policy were to willingly concentrate on defeat of the illegal armed forces, the resulting victory could be short-lived. Military victory, though achievable, will not leave a Colombian polity organized to resolve and obviate territorial competitions before they grow again into organized armed arrogations. Another recent document that has been a stimulus for academic debate in and about Colombia is titled 'Andes 2020: A New Strategy for the Challenges of Colombia and the

Region.'[337] Among the document's key recommendations, "the imposition and enforcement of property tax; acceleration of land titling and registry; and the enactment of strategic, market-assisted land reform in an accountable and transparent fashion." That emphasis is put on the formalization of property is great; that the first thought understanding of property is the imposition of a tax is a shame -- in a country the violent history of which so often turns on questions of who will tax what.

United States government decisions regarding Colombia, whether related to counter-narcotics, counter-terrorism, economic development, military operations, long-term peace or otherwise, are not well-taken unless fully informed regarding the ownership of real property. Only a few years ago such an assertion not only would have been curious, but unreasonable -- not so much because property ownership did not influence political actors in Colombia, since they undoubtedly have, but rather because such intelligence could rarely be had. Even if US decision-makers would like to have had better information about who owned what and with whom, the intelligence challenge was generally insurmountable, at least beyond immediate and anecdotal investigation. Today, property data can be collected, organized, analyzed and presented in ways that can support foreign policy and strategy. A convergence of new technologies, including global positioning satellites, and expanding technical protocols such as the National Spatial Data Infrastructure, makes provision of detailed foreign property information to United States decision-makers practicable.

Colombia's governments can do more to make land ownership precise and transparent, and therefore to control corruption and reduce disillusionment. Part of the problem in recent decades may have been an unfortunate set of signals from the United States regarding the importance of formalized land ownership as a fundamental mechanism

---

[337] Council on Foreign Relations, Andes 2020: A New Strategy for the Challenges of Colombia and the Region, New York: Council on Foreign Relations Center for Preventive Action, 2004.

for social peace and honest government. United States aid programs have only recently addressed the question of formal property, and then usually on a 'micro-pilot' scale chasing secondary purposes such as building a local government tax base or giving titles as a quid in some 'alternative crop' scheme. Meanwhile a great deal of emphasis has been expended on prosecuting the perpetrators of violent felonies. There has never been a correspondingly energetic campaign to establish civil law that might resolve the conditions that led to the abuses in question. There has been little attention to building the social contract, to building the property regime -- even while real estate has always been at the absolute center of Colombian violence.

The shortcoming isn't just what we try to do in Colombia, but what we don't know. In face of US desire to assist Colombia in ridding itself of brigands, and to curb corruption, the United States needs more detailed information -- strategically relevant, comprehensive data about whose ox is gored and whose pocket lined with every major political decision made.

Success for Colombia in dealing with its internal enemies, and in establishing the conditions for long-term peace, depends on gaining a better understanding of the details of ownership. In order to influence the course of Colombian change, the United States needs a better grasp on who specifically benefits from the redistribution of interests in land, who is involved in land-based money laundering, land extortions and organized squatting. To succeed at counter-narcotics, the US must know more about who owns illicit cultivations, and about geographic value beyond the crop areas themselves. US foreign policy need not veer away from human rights discipline, but could focus on the erosion of liberty and property that precede gross violations. A complete map of Colombia is needed, one that comprehends ownership and land-use, that shows the quality of rights and progress (or lack of it) against the underlying causes of gross human rights violations there.[338] The US can assist in its creation and should demand its transparency.

The measures of effectiveness applied in determining the success or failure of US policies and those of the Colombian government also need to be improved. It might be useful to keep track of quantities of illicit drugs grown, shipped or sprayed, but the value, in detail, of Colombian land is more significant by far.[339] When Colombia begins to enjoy widespread, regular increases in rural property values, it will be the surest indicator that their war is being won. As well, Colombian and US government policies to pacify the country will by necessity correlate both to the success of the legal regime and to the implementation of environmental regulations and standards that allow for rational, sustainable exploitation of natural resources.[340] Here again, development of formal property is a prerequisite for success.

The upshot of these observations about the nature and significance of property and property mapping in Colombia is clear. The government of Colombia is attempting to improve its property system to support long term security, remediate rights violations

---

[338] Violations of human rights most decried by our government, and by private citizens working through non-governmental organizations include lack of habeas corpus, torture, organized rape, extrajudicial execution, forced exile, disenfranchisement, and genocide. Any situation involving the violation of human rights could be expressed in ownership terms, but with reference to these most serious violations, the use of property terminology might sterilize or routinize descriptions. At that point, the relative utility of a property-based description of events and conflicts would be exceeded. Most important in defending broad attention to property rights in the analysis of national and international security affairs is observation of the close linkage between denied property rights and evolution of basic human rights abuses.

[339] Colombia has a sufficiently competent and knowledgeable quantity of land appraisers, organized into a national professional federation, that it is feasible to implement a methodology for determining market values of land in most areas of the country.

[340] A description of US aid to Colombia is provided by Center for International Policy, Internet, online at <www.ciponline.org/.

340

already suffered and to combat violent illegal organizations. US assistance can help Colombia formalize land ownership, make land ownership and value information complete and readily available, challenge concentrations of ownership in the hands of outlaws and more fully incorporate real property purchases and distribution into its own counter-narcotics and counter-terrorist strategies. This will contribute to a State with a visible commitment not just to security, but also to civil rights and open government.

Precisely enunciating and evidencing (that is mapping, monumenting, titling, registering, digitizing and publishing) the various rights associated with the object of conflict (land in most rural contexts) is an indispensable action for peace. Creating an open, fluid market for real estate rights will further identify relative worth, who actually has control of it, and how the overall worth of Colombia's social contract is progressing, or not. Colombia's is a history of territorial competition, land grabs and failed reforms. It needs to become one of property development if as a nation it is ever to join the community of prosperous and peaceful countries that is generally considered as the "First World." That said, as with so many aspects of development, Colombia is uneven in its property. It is by no means underdeveloped in all places or in regard to all real estate. The differentials in the development of formal property themselves have an influence on the geography of social conflict. Colombia is the example used here of a country suffering violent organized internal conflict, but the lessons apply to other countries in the same straits.

More immediately, in the context of the still virulent and on-going war that Colombia has to wage against a mix of dangerous home-grown enemies, the following news item is revealing:

> "*Las autoridades intervinieron 18 bienes inmuebles, propiedad de un jefe de frente de la guerrilla de las FARC, informaron en Bogotá fuentes judiciales. ... [S]e trata de seis fincas, cuatro campamentos, dos tiendas de*

341

*víveres, una gallera, una joyería, una farmacia, un local
de billares, dos discotecas y un hotel...*"[341]

(Judicial authorities inform that they have confiscated 18
pieces of real estate, property of a FARC Front leader.
Involved are six farms, four camps, two food stores, a
cock fighting ring, a jewelry store, a pharmacy, a
billiards parlor, two discotheques and a hotel.)

To put the above news item into its best perspective, we recall
the words of T. Miller Maguire quoted in Chapter 2 on the essence of
military strategy – *"a general whose road homeward or to his base is
threatened or cut by a superior force must, if he loses a decisive battle,
be ruined as well as defeated."* The Colombian authorities did not just
confiscate some real estate from an outlaw, they smashed his line of
communication, making it impossible for that unit of the FARC to
operate at any where near the level it had, because its logistics network
was severely damaged and the boss's 'route homeward' badly
impaired. The insurgent's ability to hide among the population was all
but ruined. The real estate itself is but a part of the story, but therein
lies the essential military importance of property, property records and
property intelligence in the context of internal warfare.

Cuba

Cuba is nothing like Colombia. No violent anti-government

---

[341] EFE, "Incautan propiedades de un jefe de las FARC,"14 de diciembre de 2006;
Ths blow was delivered against a unit of the FARC. For a similar case, but against
the Autodefensas Unidas de Colombia (AUC) see Fiscalia de la Nación (Attorney
General's Office), "Propiedades de alias 'don Antonio' pasarán al Estado
Colombiano," (Properties of AKA 'don Antonio' pass to the Colombian State) at
http://www.fiscalia.gov.co/PAG/DIVULGA/noticias2007/lavado/LavaAntonioAbr12.
htm

outlaws are marching around extorting, stealing, smuggling, kidnapping and murdering. It is, in a depressing, submissive sense, peaceful. The Castros' rebels won decades ago, but soon the time of their governance may run out. Whatever the prospects for a post-Raul survival of the regime, loss of control by the Castro brothers will attract global attention to the island. Although 'human rights' may crowd headlines, no subject will be more critical to the prospects of human flourishing than that of property rights.

We will witness a disaster of nearsightedness if the Cuban property puzzle is treated as one revolving around claims that must be resolved in order to facilitate a transition to democracy, or as set of disputes that must be rectified in order to re-establish normal diplomatic or economic relations. That is not what is to be done. Instead, the transition must be *of* property. Property cannot be taken as a stumbling block, a step to be taken, or as a matter to be resolved *enroute* to the goal of a successful transition, but must instead *be* the transition. Changing the system, the property regime, must be the centerpiece of design and action. How Cubans account for the day-to-day rights that Cubans have in relationship to Cuban places – that is the heart of the social contract. One way to protect the social contract is by way of balancing and limiting political power. Democratic political processes must be established, of course, to help peaceably protect the social contract, but why bother if the social contract itself is not the object of careful design? If Cuba is to succeed, and particularly if it is to succeed beyond the inconsistent and haphazard levels of other Latin American countries, it must underpin a liberal social contract on formal property.

The reasons for such a property-based strategy are pragmatic. US goals for Cuba should include that it not be a locus of military or criminal threat to its neighbors, that it not be the source of unwelcome human migration, and that it contribute to regional economic well-being. Cuba becoming a democracy is presupposed, but that term begs definition of form and quality. Outsiders can lead Cuba to become a place where liberty and property is protected, and where the value of that property is consistently improved for all Cubans. All this, in shorthand, means making Cuba successful.

There will be a number of problems at which the US will probably have to throw money, perhaps in quantity not dissimilar to that expended on Iraq. Claims in the Property Claims Commission claims can be paid by the US government outright, as they are a needless distraction. A similar commission and court apparatus can be pre- established, perhaps in a third country for quieting title to expatriate and exile claims. Real property possession, including the exact identity and quality of ownership must be mapped and publicly exposed as soon as possible an integral part of a comprehensive GIS mapping effort. Continuous public update of this information should be a central requirement of the transition effort. Along with the ownership information, the process of changing ownership must also be transparent. A strict statute of frauds is a must, requiring that all contracts for an interest in real property be signed, notarized, registered, digitized and quickly made publicly transparent; all contracts of over some fixed amount should have a reasonable challenge period from the time of registry in order to diminish land frauds and weaken insider trading; no government offices dealing with real property registration should be allowed to close for more than one day per week; no offshore or secret banking should be allowed; no contracting companies should be allowed to maintain confidential accounts of Cuban dealings; no confidential banking activities should be allowed on the island, etc. These are the kinds of things that will steward Cuba during a difficult period of change -- far more than elections, which might best be postponed. The above list of property items presuppose that the current Cuban constitution will be voided. Initial wording of the constitution regarding alienation of property, and initial laws regarding registration and frauds will more than likely have to be provided from outside the Island.

Some limitations on real estate assignment and alienation may be necessary at the outset and should immediately negotiated. For instance, at least at the beginning of the transition, interests in land should be under Cuban or Cuban-majority ownership. This point is of central importance as an assurance to Cubans and to the world that the transition is not a free-for-all land rush, or worse, an inside-trader land rush that would simply shove out Cubans. 'Cuban' should be clearly defined from the outset, and as part of the transition agreement, to mean, perhaps, born on the Island or the genetic son or daughter of at least one Island-born parent.[342]

The kinds of things mentioned above, and others like them, amount to a property-based strategy as opposed to a principally diplomatic or political one. It is a strategy intended to give certain property advantages within a fixed and transparent set of rules. It establishes a rule of law for a period of transition and anticipates an end-state of formal property in which stable, precise, comprehensive evidence of ownership is the norm and the basis of conflict resolution. Engaging such a strategy, far more than stewarding fair elections, will ensure that Cuba, unlike its Latin American neighbors, will successfully enter the First World, the West, where it belongs. There is an international market for property regimes. Past and current residents of the Island of Cuba under the Castro system of property have tried to leave the island because the value of rights there is not high. We can help improve the value of Cuban rights.

Mexico

Setting aside hyperbole regarding the rate and structure of undocumented migration to the United States across the Mexican border, suffice it to say that as a nation the United States does not know to any appreciable degree of precision the who, where or how many. Whatever the potential threat to the security of the United States, the

---

[342] In order to deter over-concentration of ownership, a rule might be pre-emplaced that no single individual or corporate entity be allowed to aggregate ownership of more than some small percent of real property by value or by surface area during a fixed period of transition. This could help to force investors to include a broader range of Cubans as owner participants.

345

dangers of human contraband are palpable both to the migrants involved and to the communities and populations whose land is being crossed. The tight relationship of the property system in Mexico to questions of migration and criminal enterprise was noted in Chapter Two, but a prescription was not made. That prescription needs to be made, in the opinion of the author, not in terms of property rights, but in terms of civil and human rights. This is not to abandon in the last chapter the entire thrust of this book regarding the importance of the social contract expressed in property regimes, but the argument is dull in the face of some phenomena the poignancy of which deserve a more direct expression. The lives of hundreds of thousands of undocumented aliens in the United States is one of para-citizenship in which property rights are suspect, civil rights are incomplete and human rights correspondingly vulnerable. As noted in Chapter Two, the strength of the United States rests ultimately on the way in which we conceive of property -- not how we divide the pie, but the strength of our own common agreement about who can be owners of what, an agreement supported by the best evidence. The United States can remain a place where people prefer to go.

In Tancanhuitz, Mexico, the people can catch a weekly bus to the United States. Many of their lives and livelihoods depend on safe passage. Defense against gangs such as the Mara Salvatrucha or terrorists from other parts of the world depends on the participation of hundreds of thousands of people such as those from Tancanhuitz. When their passage is dignified and welcomed and their rights honored best in the United States, the honor will be repaid. It is not a flowery concept but a pragmatic one. When the bulk of Mexican migration is legalized and made easy, illegal migration will expose itself. The geography and associations of illegal migration will be separated from the legal, and the legal migrants whose families and livelihoods depend on cross-border economics and societal links will participate freely in protection of the system and the exposure of its enemies. Protection of the US-Mexican border depends on recognition that the geography of the border and of migrant populations is not a line, but a vast puzzle of ownership identities, rights and duties. We can map that puzzle.

346

Mexican cooperation in the battle to protect ourselves is but a grace away, and that grace is to define 'ourselves' and 'border' intelligently, inclusively. When Americans go to Tancanhuitz they cannot be indifferent, and it is not an engagement born of sympathy. It is engagement born of the realization that the mayor of a town that speaks Tenic (into which a little Spanish and English is mixed) knows the rate and origination of foreign remittances, box scores of professional sports teams, tuition rates at various major universities, routes and itineraries of at major transportation hubs…. He is intensely interested in Mexican *and* American success. That success is the success of his *ejido* and his family, of his personal leadership, of his neighbors' math whizzes; it is not a distant or foreign dream of opportunity. When US law furthers the structure of life in Tancanhuitz, the right path to national security along the Mexican border will be found. The insecurity America senses is due to omissions, not to the activities called globalization. The United States implicitly invites the people of Tancanhuitz to migrate. They need to be made owners, perhaps or perhaps not citizens, but not fugitives.

The formal condition of property within the United States is the most important existing defense against internal violence. US national cohesiveness, and public cooperation to help government limit violence, is born of a faith in government's role of protecting public and private property rights, especially in land. Constricting illegal migration is important as an act of solidarity with current owners, even if legal migration is liberalized. The actual buying and selling of real estate to encourage specific land uses and population shifts can also an important strategy option. Finally, the regulated privatization of law enforcement activities, (especially those related to property protection) can anticipate and undercut vigilantism.

Other places

The countries chosen above are all nearby the United States. It makes sense to begin close to home to describe how property bears on

347

questions of national security, how property issues in one country bear on the security of another. The author believes that for the United States, the space within a few thousand miles to the south is of utmost security importance, but the near abroad is used as an example in this book, not as the subject. The argument applies to all parts of the world, especially those parts where governance is far from perfected and where violence is more the norm than the exception. At the time this book is being written, Iraq and Afghanistan are the preoccupation of American military leaders. Hopefully it is not too late to lay the groundwork of social and administrative intelligence, of censuses, personal identification systems and cadastres necessary to build a foundation for just, durable and productive property regimes in those countries. It will not be too late because it is ever past being a good idea, but perhaps because American national will to remain may have been expended, or because local power has grown sufficient to block transparency measures. It might also be that other interests will occupy developmental funding that might have been made available for the creation of property and property records. So this book is probably for the next place. In that next place, money will be wasted until a formal, liberal property regime is in the making. For the next place, property is what is to be done.

Restatement

> *"You cannot divorce property from power. You can only make them change hands."*
> John Randolph Roanoke

The rule of law starts with law against trespass, not murder. Our reverence of constitutions and elections has put them almost everywhere, and human rights are for Americans a permanent crusade, but somehow the central role of property in building a peaceful society slipped our minds. The essential victory of the American experiment, and the foundation of the success of Western polities, is not the way we choose or unseat our leaders. If by the success of a society we mean

348

parallel improvement in freedom, material prosperity and social peace -
- a trio which together might fairly be called human flourishing -- then
construction of formal, liberal property regimes is as important toward
achieving success as is the writing of constitutions, the holding of
elections or the prosecution of human rights violations. The
Constitution of the United States of America looked to protect life,
liberty and property from the machinations of government, and the
three values were seen to travel together. The founding fathers were
interested in electoral democracy as a way to peacefully change those
to whom the privilege of service was to be temporarily lent; but the
exercise was not essentially one of creating democracy, which many of
the fathers also feared as a potential tyranny. The goal was to build and
protect an equitable social contract, a property regime that was likely to
resolve conflict and induce prosperity. At some point we forgot that,
fell in love with the competition for leadership and forgot the meat of
the design. Accordingly we push the democracy part and overlook the
social contract.

There is no camouflaging the sanctimony of American human
rights policies once it becomes obvious that they are uninformed of, or
oblivious to, the basic rights and duties that lead to abuses. Doggedly
prosecuting a murder appears as a gratuitous moral huff if the jury
realizes that the State has had no interest in the habitual disregard of
rights and obligations that led to the crime. If we have no grasp of or
interest in who has what and who took what from whom, then we
deserve to suffer not only be the lightened weight of our moral suasion,
but the harsh backlash accorded to hypocrisy. The West, if it is to
proceed to improve the observance of human rights standards in the
world, must improve property rights in the world, and to do that it must
develop the information necessary to know who has what, and where.

The inhumanities that energize American foreign policy are the
violent consequences of underlying conditions, conditions that by
themselves failed to generate emotional energy. Violent symptoms
rather than underlying causes seem to become the focal point of policy.
By better appreciating property we can consider a broader range of

those contested rights and duties that lead to violence. If, in all the lands where the United States regularly cites grave human rights inadequacies, one were to ask simple questions about landlord-tenant laws, title registry systems, zoning ordinances, mining stakes, paving contracts, street gang territories, paternity laws or water courts, two judgments would be reached: First, that powerful linkages exist between violent abuses of human rights and contested property. Second, that U.S. intelligence collectors, analysts, and policy makers have been indifferent to details of the ownership environment. Ask everyone in the Defense Intelligence Agency what they know about the details of taxation in Iraq and the answers will underwhelm.

It is not just that the United States and other Western countries waste billions of development dollars every year on programs that have not been built on firm property systems, but that they also fail constantly to learn about who owns what in the world. As power in the world has become more and more diffuse, threats to physical security are decreasingly well described by the name of a country. Many of the worst threats are better identified by the names of individual humans (the Pablo Escobars and Bin Ladens) and by the trouble they can personally bring to bear with the wealth they amass. Yet we have been caught unaware regarding who has what wealth in the world. We set our categories and definitions according to geopolitics, rather than according to the much finer and detailed view of power that the county sheriff or property judge would take. While not long ago the argument might have existed that such a detailed understanding of the world of power was out-of-reach technically, that argument is no longer valid. Strategic knowledge of personal, family, party or corporate power is very possible today, and it is especially possible to know the nature of power as it is reflected in real property.

One typical reaction to the list of Western property details (easements, zoning, deed restrictions, etc.) is that so many societies do not have such fine developments. But that reaction is always bred of near total ignorance of the facts. To be sure, where the indoor toilet is unknown the sewer easement is absent, but it is in those same places that solid evidence regarding the division of those rights and duties that *do* exist is needed and can be created. If we say that valid evidence of ownership rights cannot be found or created…what can such an assertion mean? -- that we don't know with any confidence who is in charge of what resources, who has what power, who can do and who cannot? How do we deal with such a place? One would hope the answer is not simply to hold elections and deal with whoever wins.

We in the West confuse electoral democracy with the condition of our success, which we have come to label democracy. The secret to that condition, which includes electoral democracy, is something else, however. It is an application of physical and organizational innovations that protect the social contract. That social contract is an agreement about agreements. It is an agreement to enforce agreements about the division and exercise of everyday rights and duties. The social contract, agreement about agreements, enforcement of quotidian rights and duties, is the West's fundamental mechanism for conflict resolution. The West is successful because its property regimes are simultaneously advantageous to the three prongs of human flourishing – freedom, material prosperity and social peace -- in measure appropriate to the particulars of local culture. The West's property regimes are successful because of the high quality of the evidence of everyday rights, the capacity of the citizenry and governments to implement the meaning of that evidence, and because the basic rules which determine what can be owned and who can be owners are liberal in measure appropriate to the common understanding of justice.

Formalizing property serves peace in at least five ways. Formalized property information feeds conflict resolution mechanisms by clearly identifying owners, claimants, rights and duties so that disagreements can be more peaceably reconciled. Formalizing property creates confident stakeholders willing to support the rule of law. Formal property regimes create and expose capital, which ameliorates negative socio-economic conditions that fuel internal conflict. Landowners are less likely to engage in illegal behavior when they risk forfeiture if they involve themselves in outlawry. Finally, the records

351

associated with formal property provide a powerful forensic tool with which to support peaceful conflict resolution processes, combat illegal activities and bring violators of basic human rights to justice. It is no exaggeration to say that to formalize property is to build the peaceful rule of law. In addition, the condition in which humans are secure in their possessions is in-and-of-itself a happiness. Nevertheless, the principle assertion of this book is not that building property systems will lead to peace. The assertion has been in the negative. In countries where informal property regimes are allowed to continue, there will not be peace. Outside the lines of formal property lies possession by force. The gamut of societal choices is actually very narrow, the choices few – formal property, internal violence, or tyranny. It is unfortunate that peoples often choose tyranny over violence because the first choice, formal property, has not been offered.

The security challenge of the United States can be summed as follows: The march of technology has brought us to a point in history wherein the problems of our neighbors are quickly our own, where the peace and prosperity of foreign places is undeniably tied to ours. Fortunately, the march of technology has also provided us with the ability to create nearly perfect evidence regarding the peaceable assignment of rights and duties. In terms of human temperament we are in no better shape than the English Parliament in 1677 when it recognized the opportunity to put technology in the service of improving man's commitments. We do, however, have better technology with which to support modern statutes of fraud. To the extent that writing is civilization, our writing instruments have improved, but we have to use them. The soldier may ask what this bloodless, tiresome subject of social contracts and documentation has to do with his job, with warfare. The answer is 'nothing' -- unless he wants to find and fix an illusive enemy; unless it is important to the soldier to establish conditions after combat that will allow him to go home; unless he thinks it important to keep insurgencies from forming so that his presence in those difficult environments is not necessary; or unless he would prefer there to be fewer places where terrorists were bred an sponsored. Otherwise, property should not be important to the soldier.

Places that are not at peace within themselves are a danger to the globe, and places that do not develop their property regimes cannot be at peace within themselves. Therefore, and with little room for exceptions, it is directly in the interest of American and global security to promote the development of formal property regimes everywhere. Furthermore, it is not possible to proceed in the improvement of property systems without knowledge regarding the details of ownership, knowledge we do not now have.

What, then, is to be done?

1. Vigorously create and formalize property everywhere.

2. Encourage governments to make ownership records precise, comprehensive and transparent, so that the world knows who owns what, and who claims what.

3. Precondition assistance programs on the formalization property regimes, not just electoral democracy.

4. Prosecute the violation of human rights, but promote observance of everyday rights and duties called property.

5. Teach leaders to demand complete information about who owns what and where.

6. Teach the philosophical principles of the liberal social contract.

7. Apply property strategies that place stakeholders of a beneficial social contract where they can best defend it, and that deny anonymity to those who offend it.

Appendix: Instrument to measure the quality of a property regime

Subjoined is a taxonomy of questions that the author proposes be used as a research instrument as part of a methodology for determining the relative quality of a real property regime. The definition of 'real property' presented on page 4 of the text is the basis of the investigative framework. That definition reads:

> Property is a contract between society and owners that recognizes preferential rights and correlated duties. The strength of the social contract is judged by the quality of its observance, which depends on the quality of the evidence of ownership and on the capacity of both owners and the society (usually by way of some government) to act on conclusions logically drawn from the evidence.

The relative quality of property regimes can be measured by following three streams of inquiry into 1., the quality of the evidence delineating rights, duties and the identity of owners (this is sometimes referred to as *clarity of allocation*); 2., the capacity of owners (or claimants) and the government to act on conclusions logically drawn from the evidence (this is in some contexts referred to as *ease of alienability* or as *security from trespass* depending on the mix of owner rights and government duties involved); and 3., the conduciveness to peace of the basic rules delimiting the contract, especially who is allowed to own what. (At times this is denominated *liberality*).

Consequent field research (implementation of a methodology for determining the quality of a property regime) would include collection of data elements more-or-less according to the three streams of inquiry suggested above and detailed below. The third of the three streams -- that related to liberality, is not as clearly announced in the definition as the first two. It may be a more complex question than it seems, as it is possible to subtly exclude groups from equal ownership possibilities.

Three streams of inquiry:

1. The quality of the evidence delineating rights, duties and the identity of owners (sometimes *clarity of allocation*). Quality of this evidence is determined by three characteristics: accuracy (or precision. How accurate technically is the geographic description, and how accurate legally in terms of owners and rights, and perhaps how accurate in terms of value); comprehensiveness (what is the coverage both geographically and in terms of the percentage of owners and the possible rights involved); and transparency (the visibility and availability of the data and its resistance to corruption and fraud).

A. accuracy
B. comprehensiveness
C. transparency

A. accuracy
   1. Extent to which ownership registry and cadastral descriptions are unified.
   2. Existence of a statute of frauds and related statutory requirements.
   3. Availability and use of title insurance;
   4. Accuracy of surveying technologies;
   5. Monument quality and density;
   6. Age of records;
   7. Capacity of cadastral and registry bureaucracy;
   8. Appraisal cost and availability;
   9. Relationship of tax assessments to market value appraisals if applicable.

B. comprehensiveness

   1. Percentage of the geographic surface represented in cadastral maps;
   2. Percentage of owners whose properties are represented in cadastral maps;
   3. Difficulty of registration;
   4. Percentage of properties with tax appraisals;
   5. Percentage of properties with market appraisals.

C. transparency

   1. Access to cadastral information on;
   2. Access to land-use data on-line;
   3. Are paper records available for public;
   4. Where records are kept;
   5. Are registries and cadastral records digitized;
   6. Are cadastral maps digitized and vectorized;
   7. If government development projects are advertised on-line and GISed;
   8. What records cost;

2. Capacity of owners (or claimants) and the government to act on conclusions logically drawn from the evidence (sometimes *ease of alienability* or *security from trespass* depending on the mix of owner rights and government duties involved). It also can be reduced to three parts: marketability, protection from invasion, and protection of the social contract generally.

    A. Marketability
    B. Protection from invasion
    C. Protection of the social contract

    A. Marketability
        1. Ratio of properties bought and sold to total properties in a given time;
        2. Existence of a professional real estate industry and its measures of professionalism;
        3. Regulatory limitations on sale commissions, and their effect;
        4. Real estate price controls and what is the effect;
        5. Where zoning laws exist;
        6. If deed restrictions and other controls on alienation are used, where and for what;
        7. Existence of a MLS;
        8. What collateral is accepted for loans and what are standard rates across types of real estate.

    B. Protection from invasion
        1. How long it takes to file a quiet-title claim;
        2. If there is a grievance mechanism against real estate professionals;
        3. How much it costs to conduct a quiet-title action.

    C. Protection of the social contract
        1. How often the statue of frauds is applied;
        2. If agency contracts are used;
        3. If sales contracts are used;
        4. Whether or not the police use formal records to resolve property disputes;

5. Professional standards of real property sales force;
6. Professional standards for appraisals;
7. Prenuptial requirements (is there a statutory requirement, what are the choices, what is the intention, how do they limit alienability).

3. Conduciveness to peace of the basic rules delimiting the contract (at times called *liberality*). The two general determinants of liberality are inclusiveness (who can effectively be owners) and divisibility & alienation (how thoroughly can real estate be divided, and what rights do supposed owners have as to disposal of real property.

   A. Inclusiveness
   B. Divisibility and Alienation

   A. Inclusiveness
      1. If women can own property;
      2. If foreigners can own property and to what extent, where, etc.;
      3. Are other religious or ethnic identities excluded;

   B. Divisibility and Alienation
      1. If subsurface rights can be bought and sold;
      2. The ratio of registered names in relation to geography and population;
      3. Can real property be freely bequeathed by testators;
      4. How intestate estate property is disposed by statute;
      5. If life estates are used;
      6. What other divisions are used (time shares, condominiums, joint, common, partnership, corporate etc and is there data on geographic distribution and percentage of types);
      7. Standard tenancy patterns (leases, sharecrop arrangements, *ejidos*, communes, family corporations, etc.);
      8. If land is otherwise fully alienatable (can be bequeathed, leased sold rented, etc.);
      9. Do any studies relate ownership and tenancy forms to violence migration or illicit narcotics production or trafficking?

Bibliography

Abel, Annie Heloise. The American Indian as American Slaveholder and Secessionist. Cleveland: The Arthur H. Clarke Company, 1914.

Agenda Ciudadana. Las claves territoriales de la guerra y la paz, desarrollo regional, participación ciudadana y agenda de paz (Territorial keys to war and peace, regional development and citizen participation and peace agenda). Bogotá: Agenda Ciudadana y Cátedra para la Paz, 2000.

Alexander, Gregory S. Commodity & Property: Competing Visions of Property in American Legal Thought 1776-1970, Chicago: The University of Chicago Press, 1997.

Anderson, Malcolm. Territory and State Formation in the Modern World. Cambridge: Polity Press and Blackwell, 1995.

Ardrey, Robert. The Territorial Imperative: A Personal Inquiry into the Animal Origins of Property and Nations. New York: Antheneum, 1966.

Aricada, Ricardo, Comuna 13: crónica de una guerra urbana (Borough 13: Cronicle of an Urban War). Medellín: Editorial Universidad de Antioquia, 2005.

Ashworth, G.J. War and the City. New York: Routledge, 1991.

Aspin, Les. Report on the Bottom-Up Review. Washington: U.S. Department of Defense, 1993.

Augustine of Hippo. City of God. Edited by Vernon J. Bourke and translated by Gerald G. Walsh, Demetrius B. Zema, Grace Monahan, and Daniel J. Honan. Garden City, New York: Doubleday, 1958.

Ayittey, George B.N., Indigenous African Institutions. New York: Transnational Publishers, 1991.

Bailyn, Bernard. The Ideological Origins of the American Revolution. Cambridge, Massachusetts: Harvard University Press, 1967.

Bailyn, Bernard, ed. The Debate on the Constitution, Part 1. New York: The Viking Press, 1992.

Bauer, Peter. The Development Frontier: Essays in Applied Economics. Cambridge, Massachusetts: Harvard University Press, 1991.

Barzel, Yoram. Economic Analysis of Property Rights. Cambridge: Cambridge University Press, 1989.

Beaglehole, Ernest. Property, A Study in Social Psychology. London: Unwin Brothers Ltd., 1932.

359

Beard, Charles A. The Idea of the National Interest. New York: Macmillan, 1934.

Beckett, Ian F. W. Modern Insurgencies and Counter-Insurgencies: Guerrillas and their Opponents since 1750. London: Routledge, 2001.

Bejarano Ávila, Jesús Antonio (Director of Research). Colombia: inseguridad, violencia y desempeño económico en las áreas rurales. Bogotá: Universidad Externado de Colombia 1997.

Bell, Morag, et al, eds. Geography and Imperialism 1820-1940. New York: Manchester University Press, 1995.

Bergquist, Charles, Ricardo Peñaranda and Gonzalo Sánchez. Violence in Colombia 1990-2000. Wilmington, Delaware: Scholarly Resources, 2001.

Bergquist, Charles: Café y conflicto en Colombia, 1886-1910. (Coffee and conflict in Colombia, 1886-1910). Medellin: Faes, 1981.

Bethell, Tom. The Noblest Triumph: Property and Prosperity Through the Ages. New York: St. Martin's Press, 1998.

Blainey, Geoffrey. The Causes of War. New York: Macmillan, 1973.

Blumenfeld, Samuel L. Property in a Humane Economy. LaSalle, Illinois, Open Court Publishing, 1974.

Bowen, Catherine Drinker. Miracle at Philadelphia: The Story of the Constitutional Convention May to September 1787. Boston: Little, Brown, 1986.

Brierly, J.L. The Law of Nations: An Introduction to the International law of Peace.Sixth Edition. Edited by Sir Humphrey Waldock. Oxford: Oxford University Press, 1963.

Brooks, Noah. Abraham Lincoln and the Downfall of American Slavery. New York: G.P. Putnam's Sons, 1898.

Brunn, Stanley D., et. al., editors. Geography and Technology. New York: Kluwer Academic Publishers, 2003.

Buchanan, James M. Property as a Guarantor of Liberty. Cambridge, University Press, 1993.

Bucholz, Arden. Hans Delbruck and The German Military Establishment: War Images in Conflict. Iowa City: University of Iowa Press, 1985.

Burch, Kurt "Property" and the making of the international system (Boulder: Lynne Rienner Publishers, Inc., 1998)

Bush, George M. National Security Strategy of the United States. Washington, D.C.: The White House, 1993.

Bush, George W. National Security Strategy of the United States. Washington, D.C.: The White House, 2005.

Bush, Vannevar. Modern Arms and Free Men. New York: Simon ans Schuster, 1949.

Cahn, Edgar S. and Hearne, David W., eds. Our Brother's Keeper: The Indian in White America. New York: New American Library, 1970.

Carter, Frank W. and Norris, Harold T., eds. The Changing Shape of the Balkans. Boulder: Westview, 1996.

Castaneda, Jorge G. Utopia Unarmed: The Latin American Left After the Cold War. New York: Alfred Knopf, 1993.

CEHOPU (Centro de Estudios Historicos de Obras Publicas y Urbanismo) (Historical Study Center of Public Works and Urbanism). La Ciudad Hispanoamericana: El Sueno de un Orden (The Hispanoamerican City: The Dream of Order). Madrid: Ministerio de Obras Publicas y Urbanismo, 1989.

Cervantes, Miguel. The Story of That Ingenious Gentleman Don Quijote De la Mancha translated from the Spanish by Burton Raffel. New York: W.W. Norton & Company, 1995.

Chairman, Joint Chiefs of Staff. Joint Publication 1, Joint Warfare of the U.S. Armed Forces. Washington, D.C.: Joint Chiefs of Staff, 1991.

Chaliand, Gerard and Rageau, Jean-Pierre. A Strategic Atlas of

Human Rights (Edited by Thomas Draper) New York: H.W. Wilson Company, 1982.

Chaliand, Gerard and Rageau, Jean-Pierre. A Strategic Atlas. Second Edition. Translated from the French by Tony Berrett. New York: Harper and Row, 1983.

Chaliand, Gerard, ed. Guerrilla Strategies: An Historical Anthology from the Long March to Afghanistan. Berkeley: University of California Press, 1982.

Chertikhin, V.Y.,et al. The Revolutionary Movement of Our Time and Nationalism. Translated by Vic Schneierson. Moscow: Progress Publishers, 1975.

Cline, Ray S. World Power Assessment. Boulder: Westview, 1975.

Clinton, William J. A National Security Strategy of Engagement and Enlargement. Washington: The White House, 1994.

Clinton, William J. National Security Strategy of Engagement and Enlargement. Washington: 1997.

Coate, Roger A., ed. U.S. Policy and the Future of the United Nations. New York: The Twentieth Century Fund, 1994.

361

Commission on Integrated Long-Term Strategy. Discriminate Deterrence. Washington, D.C.: U.S. Government Printing Office, 1988.

Cooper, Jeffrey R. Another View of the Revolution in Military Affairs. Carlisle, Pennsylvania: Strategic Studies Institute, 1994.

Corbridge, Stuart. Mastering Space: Hegemony, Territory & International Economy. New York: Routledge, 1997.

Council on Foreign Relations. Andes 2020: A New Strategy for the Challenges of Colombia and the Region. New York: Council on Foreign Relations Center for Preventive Action, 2004.

Cuban Research Institute of the Latin America and Caribbean Center. Transition in Cuba: New Challenges for U.S. Policy. Miami: Florida International University and The Office of Research, U.S. Department of State Bureau for Latin America & the Caribbean and The U.S. Agency for International Development, 1995.

Davis, Mike. Planet of Slums. New York: Verso, 206.

Davis, Mike. Urban Control: The Ecology of Fear. Westfield, New Jersey: The Open Magazine Pamphlet Series, 1994.

Davis, Mike. L.A. Was Just the Beginning--Urban Revolt in the United States: A Thousand Points of Light. Westfield, New Jersey: The Open Magazine Pamphlet Series, 1992.

Demarest, Geoffrey. Geoproperty: Foreign Affairs, National Security and Property Rights. London: Frank Cass, 1998.

Demarest, Geoffrey. Mapping Colombia: The Correlation Between Land Data and Strategy. Carlisle, Pennsylvania: Strategic Studies Institute and University of Miami North South Center, 2003.

De Soto, Hernando. The Mystery of Capital: Why Capitalism Triumphs in the West and Fails Everywhere Else. New York,: Basic Books, 2000.

Department of the Army. Field Manual 3-24, Counterinsurgency. Washington, D.C.: Department of the Army, 2006.

Department of the Army. Field Manual 100-20, Internal Defense and Development. Washington, D.C.: Department of the Army, 1974.

Department of the Army. Field Manual 100-5, Operations. Washington: U.S. Government Printing Office, 1993.

Department of the Army. Field Manual 100-20, Low Intensity Conflict. Washington, D.C.: Department of the Army, 1981.

Department of the Army. Field Manual 7-98, Operations in a Low Intensity Conflict. Washington, D.C.: Department of the Army, 1992.

Department of the Army. Field Manual 100-20, Military Operations in Low Intensity Conflict. Washington, D.C.: Department of the Army, 1990.

Department of State. Post-Conflict Reconstruction Essential Tasks. Washington, D.C.: Headquarters, Office of the Coordinator for Stabilization and Reconstruction, 2005.

Deutsch, Karl and Foltz, William J., eds. Nation-Building. New York: Atherton Press, 1966.

Dietze, Gottfried. In Defense of Property. Chicago: Henry Regnery Company, 1963.

Dijkink, Gertjan. National Identity and Geopolitical Visions: Maps of Pride and Pain. New York: Routledge, 1997.

Dobbins, James, et. al. America's Role in Nation-Building: From Germany to Iraq. Santa Monica: Rand, 2003.

Dodge, Toby. Inventing Iraq: The Failure of Nation Building and a History of Denial. New York: Columbia University Press, 2003.

Dorner, Peter. Land Reform & Economic Development. Kingsport, Tennessee: Kingsport Press, 1972.

Downs, Anthony. New Visions for Metropolitan America. Washington, D.C.: The Brookings Institute, 1994.

Duchacek, Ivo D. The Territorial Dimension of Politics Within, Among, and Across Nations. Boulder: Westview, 1986.

Efimenco, N. Marbury, ed. World Political Geography: Second Edition. New York: Thomas Y. Crowell Company, 1957.

Ellickson, Robert C. Order Without Law: How Neighbors Settle Disputes. Cambridge, MA: Harvard University Press, 1991.

Eshleman, J. Ross and Cashion, Barbara G. Sociology, An Introduction. Boston: Little, Brown & Company, 1983.

Fals Borda, Orlando. Región e historia: elementos sobre ordenamiento y equilibrio regional en Colombia. (Region and history: basics of regional planning and equilibrium in Colombia.). Bogotá: Tercer Mundo, 1996.

Fals Borda, Orlando. Historia de la cuestión agraria en Colombia (History of the agrarian question in Colombia). Bogotá: Carlos Valencia Editores, 1982.

Fowler, Michael Ross and Bunck, Julie Marie. Law, Power, and the Sovereign State: The Evolution and Application of the Concept of Sovereignty. University Park: Pennsylvania State University Press, 1995.

Freedman, Lawrence. Atlas of Global Strategy. New York: Facts on File, Inc., 1985.

Freedom House. Cuba in the Nineties. Washington, D.C.: Freedom House, 1990.

Furubotn, Eirik G. and Pejovich, Svetozar, eds. The Economics of Property Rights. Cambridge, Mass.: Ballinger, 1974.

Gardeazábal, Mauricio Rengifo. Los Derechos de Propiedad en Colombia: Una Interpretación Comprensiva (Property Rights in Colombia: A Comprehensive Interpretation). Bogotá: Ediciones Uniandes, 2003.

George Mason University. Rethinking Institutional Analysis: Interviews with Vincent and Elinor Ostrom. Vienna, Virginia, 2003.

Gonzalez, Edward and Ronfeldt, David. Storm Warnings Over Cuba. Santa Monica, California: RAND, 1994.

González, Margarita. El resguardo en el nuevo reino de Granada (The reservation in the new kingdom of Granada). Bogotá: El Áncora Editores, 1992

Gray de Cerdan, Nelly Amalia. Territorio y Urbanismo: Bases de Geografía Prospectiva (Territory and Urbanism: Bases of a predictive geography). Mendoza, Argentina: Consejo Nacional de Investigaciones Científicas y Técnicas, 1987.

Gray, Colin S. The Geopolitics of Superpower. Lexington: The University of Kentucky Press, 1988.

Greenfield, Gerald Michael, ed. Latin American Urbanization. Westport, Connecticut: Greenwood Publishing Group, 1994.

González, Manuel et. al. Una Mirada Argentina sobre Colombia. Buenos Aires: Instituto de Investigación sobre Seguridad y Crimen Oranizado (ISCO), 1999.

Harris, J. W. Property and Justice, Oxford: Clarendon Press, 1996

Harris, Richard L. Marxism Socialism and Democracy in Latin America. Boulder: Westview, 1992.

Harrison, Lawrence E. Under-Development is a State of Mind. Lanham, MD: Madison Books, 1985.

Hilberg, Raul. The Destruction of the European Jews. New York: Holmes & Meier, 1985.

Hobsbawm, E. J. Primitive Rebels: Studies of Archaic Forms of Social Movement in the 19th and 20th Centuries. New York: W. W. Norton & Company, Inc., 1959.

Hohfeld, Wesley Newcomb. Fundamental Legal Conceptions as Applied to Judicial Reasoning. New Haven: Yale University Press, 1919 (reissued 1964).

Holt-Jensen, Arild. Geography: History and Concepts. Totowa, New Jersey: Barnes and Noble Books, 1988.

Howard, Michael, The Invention of Peace: Reflections on War and International Order. New Haven: Yale University Press, 2000.

Instituto Colombiano de la Reforma Agraria (INCORA) (Colombian Agrarian Reform Institute). Colombia tierra y paz: experiencias y caminos para la reforma agraria, alternativas para el siglo XXI, 1961-2001 (Colombia peace and land: experiences and pathways for agrarian reform, alternatives for the 21st century, 1961-2001). Bogotá: Incora, 2002.

Instituto Geográfico Agustín Codazzi. Atlas de Colombia Quinta Edición (Atlas of Colombia, Fifth Edition). Bogotá: Instituto Geográfico Agustín Codazzi (IGAC), 2002.

Instituto Panamericano de Geografía e Historia. Manual de Métodos Geográficos Para el Análisis Urbano, Chile (Manual of Geographical Methods of Analysis, Chile). (Mexico City: Comisión de Geografía, Comité de Geografiía Urbana, 1988.

Joes, Anthony James. Resisting Rebellion: The History and Politics of Counterinsurgency. Lexington, KY, The University Press of Kentucky, 2004.

Kelly, Phillip. Checkerboards and Shatterbelts: The Geopolitics of South America. Austin: University of Texas Press, 1997.

Kent, Edward Allen, ed. Law and Philosophy. New York: Meredith Corporation, 1970.

Ibañez Sánchez, José Roberto. Teoría del Estado, Geopolítica y Geoestrategia (Theory of the State, Geopolitics and Geostrategy). Bogotá: Imprenta y Publicaciones de las Fuerzas Militares, 1985.

International and Operational Law Division. Operational Law Handbook. Charlottesville, Virginia: The Judge Advocate General's School, 1994.

Jacobson, Harold K. Networks of Interdependence: International Organizations and the Global Political System. New York: Alfred A. Knopf, 1979.

Jenkins, Brian Michael. An Urban Strategy for Guerrillas and Governments. Santa Monica, California: The Rand Corporation, 1972.

Johannsen, Robert W. Lincoln, the South, and Slavery: The Political Dimension. Baton Rouge, Louisiana: Louisiana State University Press, 1991.

Kasarda, John H. Third World Cities: Problems, Policies and Prospects. Newbury Park, California, Sage Publications, 1993.

Keegan, John. Intelligence in War. New York: Vintage Books, 2004.

Kennedy, Paul. The Rise and Fall of the Great Powers: Economic Changes and Military Conflict from 1500 to 2000. New York: Random House, 1987.

365

Kent, Edward Allen, ed. Law and Philosophy: Readings in Legal Philosophy. New York: Meredith Corporation, 1970.

Kidron, Michael and Segal, Ronald. The New State of the World Atlas. New York: Simon and Schuster, 1987.

Kipling, Rudyard. The Portable Kipling (Edited and with an Introduction by Irving Howe). New York: The Viking Press, 1982.

Klare, Michael T. Resource Wars: The New Landscape of Global Conflict. New York: Metropolitan Books, 2001.

Knox, Paul L. Urbanization: An Introduction to Urban Geography. Englewood Cliffs, New Jersey: Center for Urban & Regional Studies, Virginia Polytechnic Institute & State University, Prentice Hall, 1994.

Kohl, James and Litt, John. Urban Guerrilla Warfare in Latin America. Cambridge: The MIT Press, 1974.

Kopel, David B. The Samurai, the Mountie, and the Cowboy: Should America Adopt the Gun Controls of Other Democracies? Buffalo, NewYork: Prometheus Books, 1992.

Laqueur, Walter. The Guerrilla Reader: A Historical Anthology. Philadelphia: Temple University Press, 1977.

La Rotta, Jesus E., Las finanzas de la subversión Colombiana. Bogotá: INCISE, 1996.

Larzelere, Alex. The 1980 Cuban Boatlift. Washington, D.C.: National Defense University Press, U.S. Government Printing Office, 1988.

Latell, Brian. After Fidel: The Inside Story of Castro's regime and Cuba's Next Leader. New York: Palgrave MacMillan, 2005.

Laveleye, Emile de (translated from the French by G.R.L. Marriott), Primitive Property. London: Macmillan and Co., 1878.

LeGrand, Catherine, Frontier expansion and peasant protest in Colombia, 1850-1936. Albuquerque: The University of New Mexico Press, 1986.

Libecap, Gary D. Contracting for Property Rights. Cambridge: Cambridge University Press, 1989.

Leiberman, Benjamin. Terrible Fate: Ethnic Cleansing in the Making of Modern Europe. Chicago: Ivan R. Dee, 2006.

Linklater, Andro. Measuring America: How and Untamed Wilderness Shaped the United States and Fulfilled the Promise of Democracy. New York: Walker & Company, 2002.

Lipschutz, Ronnie D. When Nations Clash: Raw Materials, Ideology, and Foreign Policy. New York: Harper & Row, 1989.

Locke, John. Two Treatises of Government. Second Edition. Peter Laslett, ed. Cambridge: Cambridge University Press, 1967.

Lomov, N.A., ed. Scientific-Technical Progress and the Revolution in Militray Affairs: A Soviet View (Translated by the United States Air Force). Washington, D.C.: U.S. Government Printing Office, 1979.

Lowe, James Trapier. Geopolitics and War: Mackinder's Philosophy of Power. Washington, D.C.: University Press of America, 1981.

Lucas, Noah. The Modern History of Israel. New York: Praeger, 1975.

Lykke, Arthur F. Jr., ed. Military Strategy: Theory and Application. Carlisle Barracks, Pennsylvania, U.S. Army War College, 1989.

Mackinder, Halford J. Democratic Ideals and Reality. New York: W. W. Norton & Company, 1962.

Marcella, Gabriel. Haiti Strategy: Control, Legitimacy, Sovereignty, Rule of Law, Handoffs, and Exit. Carlisle Barracks, Pennsylvania: U.S. Army War College, 1994.

Maguire, T. Miller. Outlines of Military Geography. Cambridge: University Press, 1899.

Marcella, Gabriel and Schulz, Donald. Colombia's Three Wars: U.S. Strategy at the Crossroads. Carlisle, PA: Strategic Studies Institute, 1999.

Mazaar, Michael J., et. al. The Military Technical Revolution. Washington, D. C.: Center for Strategic and International Studies, 1993.

Mazarr, Michael J. The Revolution in Military Affairs: A Framework for Defense Planning. Carlisle, Pennsylvania: Strategic Studies Institute, 1994.

McIvor, Anthony D., editor. Rethinking the Principles of War. Annapolis; Naval Institute Press, 2005.

Medina Gallego, Carlos. ELN: una historia de los orígenes (Bogotá: Rodríguez Quito, 2001).

Melville, Thomas. Guatemala: The Politics of Land Ownership. New York: Free Press, 1971.

Metz, Steven and Kievit, James. The Revolution in Military Affairs and Conflict Short of War. Carlisle, Pennsylvania: Strategic Studies Institute, 1994.

Moen, Matthew C. and Gustaffson, Lowell F., eds. The Religious Challenge to the State. Philadelphia: Temple University Press, 1992.

367

Molano, Alfredo. Desterrados: crónicas del desarraigo. Bogotá: El Áncora Editores 2001.

Molano, Alfredo. Aguas Arriba: Entre la coca y el oro. Bogotá: El Áncora Editores, 1998.

Monmonier, Mark. How to Lie with Maps, second edition. Chicago: University of Chicago Press, 1991.

Moore, John Norton, et. al. National Security Law. Durham, North Carolina: Carolina Academic Press, 1990.

Morgenthau, Hans J. and Thompson, Kenneth W. Politics Among Nations: the Struggle for Power and Peace, Sixth Edition. New York: Alfred Knopf, 1973.

Morrison Taw, Jennifer and Hoffman, Bruce. The Urbanization of Insurgency. Santa Monica, California: RAND Arroyo Center, 1994.

Mosquera, Rodrigo Villalba. Colombia Tierra y Paz (Colombia Land and Peace). Bogotá: Ministry of Agriculture and Rural Development, 2003.

Muller, Jerry Z. Adam Smith in His Time and Ours. New York: The Free Press, 1993.

Murphy, David T. The Heroic Earth: Geopolitical Thought in Weimar Germany, 1918-1933. Kent, Ohio: Kent State University Press, 1997.

Myles, Marc A., et. al. 2004 Index of Economic Freedom: Establishing the Link Between Economic Freedom and Prosperity. Washington, D.C.: The Heritage Foundation, 2004.

Nagle, Luz Estela. Plan Colombia: Reality of the Colombian Crisis and Implications for Hemispheric Security. Carlisle, Pennsylvania: Strategic Studies Institute and University of Miami North South Center, 2002.

Negroponte, John D. The National Intelligence Strategy of the United States of America. Washington, D.C.: Office of the Director of National Intelligence, 2005.

North, Douglass C. & Thomas, Robert Paul. The Rise of the Western World, A New Economic History. Cambridge: Cambridge University Press, 1973.

Noyes, Reinold. The Institution of Property. New York: Longmans, Green and Co., 1936.

Olson, Gary L. U.S. Foreign Policy and the Third World Peasant: Land Reform in Asia and Latin America. New York: Praeger Publishers, 1974.

Olson, William C. and Groom, A.J.R. International Relations Then and Now: Origins and Trends in Interpretation. London: Harper Collins Academic, 1991.

368

Center for Army Lessons Learned. <u>Operation Restore Hope: Lessons Learned Report, Operations Other Than War</u>. Ft. Leavenworth, Kansas: U.S. Army Combined Arms Command, 1993.

Observatorio del Programa Presidencial de Derechos Humanos y DIH. <u>Colombia: Conflicto armado, regions, derechos humanos y DIH 1998-2002</u>. Bogotá Vicepresidencia de la República, 2002.

Office of Information Systems--OEIPS/TAF Program. <u>Patent Counts By Country/State and Year, Utility Patents, January 1993--June 1992</u>. Washington, D.C.: U.S. Patent and Trademark Office, 1992).

O'Neill, Bard E. <u>Insurgency & Terrorism</u>. Washington, D.C.: Potomac Books, 2005.

Oppenheimer, Andres. <u>Castro's Final Hour: The Secret Story Behind the Coming Downfall of Communist Cuba</u>. New York: Simon and Schuster, 1992.

Oro, Jose R. <u>The Poisoning of Paradise: Environmental Pollution in the Republic of Cuba</u>. Miami: The Endowment for Cuban American Studies, Cuban American National Foundation, 1992.

Orsolini, Mario. <u>Montoneros: Sus Proyectos y Sus Planes</u>. Buenos Aires: Círculo Militar, 1989.

Pardo Rueda, Rafael. <u>La Historia de las Guerras</u> (The History of Wars). Bogotá: Ediciones B Colombia S. A., 2004.

Paret, Peter, ed. <u>Makers of Modern Strategy: from Machiavelli to the Nuclear Age</u>. Princeton, New Jersey: Princeton University Press, 1986.

Parra Lleras, Ernesto. Apuntes de Catastro (Notes about the Cadastre). Bogotá: Universidad Externado de Colombia, 2002.

Patent and Trademark Office. <u>Technology Assessment and Forecast Program Brochure</u>. (Washington, D.C.: U.S. Department of Commerce, 1992).

Payne, James L. <u>Labor and Politics in Peru: The System of Political Bargaining</u>. New Haven: Yale University Press, 1965.

Pejovich, Svetozar. The <u>Economic Foundations of Property Rights: Selected Readings</u>. Northhampton, MA: Edward Elgar, 1997.

Pejovich, Svetozar. <u>The Economics of Property Rights</u>. Boston: Kluwer Academic Publishers, 1990.

Penner, J.E. <u>The Idea of Property in Law.</u> Oxford: Clarendon Press, 1997.

Pipes, Richard. <u>Property and Freedom</u>. New York: Vintage Books, 2000.

Pizarro Leongómez, Eduardo. <u>Las FARC: 1949-1966.</u> Bogotá: Tercer Mundo, 1992.

Powelson, John P. The Story of Land: A World History of Land Tenure and Agrarian Reform. Cambridge, Massachusetts: Lincoln Institute of Land Policy, 1988.

Proudhon, P.J. (1840). What is Property? An Inquiry Into the Principle of Right and Government. trans. B.R. Tucker, 1876. New York: Humbold, 1890; New York: Dover, 1970; Cambridge, Cambridge University Press, 1994.

Rabasa, Angel and Peter Chalk. Colombian Labyrinth: The synergy of Drugs and Insurgency and Its Implications for Regional Stability. Santa Monica, CA: RAND, 2001.

Ramírez, María Clemencia. Entre el estado y la guerrilla: identidad y ciudadanía en el movimiento de los campesinos del Putumayo (Between the state and the guerrilla: identity and citizenship in the campesino movement in Putumayo). Bogotá: Instituto Colombiano de Antropología e Historia, 2002.

Ramsey, Russell W. Guerrilleros y Soldados. Bogotá: Ediciones Tercer Mundo, 1981.

Riding, Alan. Distant Neighbors: A Portrait of the Mexicans. New York: Vintage Books, 1986.

Rojas, Marta, editor. Tierra, Economia, y Sociedad. Bogota: Incora ,1993.

Rose, Carol M. Property and Persuasion: Essays on the History, Theory, and Rhetoric of Ownership. Boulder: Westview Press, 1994.

Rosenberg, Nathan and Birdzell, L.E., Jr. How the West Grew Rich: The Economic Transformation of the Industrial World. New York: Basic Books, 1986.

Ryan, Alan. Property. Minneapolis: University of Minnesota Press, 1987.

Ryan, Alan. Property and Political Theory. Oxford: Basil Blackwell, 1984.

Sloan, Geoffrey R. Geopolitics in United States Strategic Policy, 1890-1987. New York: St. Martin's Press, 1988.

Smith Adam. Edited by Edwin Cannan. Lectures on Justice, Police, Revenue and Arms. Oxford: Clarendon Press, 1896.

Smith, David Drakakis. The Third World City. New York: Routledge, 1990.

Spanier, John. Games Nations Play Eighth Edition. Washington: Congressional Quarterly, Inc., 1993.

Spykman, Nicholas J. The Geography of the Peace. Edited by Helen R. Nicholl. New York: Harcourt, Brace, 1944.

Spykman, N. J. American Strategy in World Politics. 1942.

Seton-Watson, Hugh. Nations and States. Boulder: Westview, 1977.

370

Sreenivasan, Gopal. The Limits of Lockean Rights in Property. New York: Oxford University Press, 1995.

Summers, Harry G. Jr. On Strategy: The Vietnam War in Context. Carlisle, Pennslyvania: Strategic Studies Institute, 1981.

Superior War School. Basic Manual. Brazil: Escola Superior de Guerra, 1992.

Svechin, Alexandr Andreevich. Strategy edited by Kent D. Lee. Minneapolis: East View Press, 1992.

Tai, Hung-Chao. Land Reform and Politics: A Comparative Analysis. Berkeley: University of California Press, 1974.

Taylor, Peter J., ed. World Government. New York: Oxford University Press, 1990.

Tennyson, Alfred. Alfred Tennyson Selected Poetry: Edited, with an Introduction by Douglas Smith. New York: Random House, 1951.

The Arms Project of Human Rights Watch & Physicians for Human Rights. Landmines: A Deadly Legacy. New York: Human Rights Watch and Physicians for Human Rights, 1993.

The CIA and the Media: Hearings Before the House Subcommittee on Oversight, Permanent Select Committee on Intelligence, 95th Cong., 1st. and 2nd. Sess. (1978)

Trinquier, Roger. Modern Warfare: A French View of Counterinsurgency. New York: Praeger, 1964.

Trustees of the British Museum. Reading the Past. London: The British Museum Press, 1990.

Tuan, Yi-Fu. Landscapes of Fear. Oxford: Blackwell, 1979.

Tunkin, G. I. Theory of International Law. Translated by William E. Butler. Cambridge, Massachusettes: Harvard University Press, 1974.

Umbeck, John R. A Theory of Property Rights: With Application to the California Gold Rush. Ames, Iowa: The Iowa State University Press, 1981.

United Nations Development Programme. El Conflicto, callejón con salida: Informe Nacional de Desarrollo Humano Colombia – 2003. Bogotá: Panamericana Formas e Impresas, 2003.

United Nations Development Programme. La Democracia en América Latina: Hacia una democracia de ciudadanas y ciudadanos. Buenos Aires: Aguilar, Altea, Taurus, Alfaguara, S.A., 2004.

United Nations Development Programme, et. al. Tierra, Economia y Sociedad (Land, Economics and Society). Bogotá: Pnud-Incora-Fao, 1993.

U.S. Patent and Trademark Office. All Technologies Report, January 1963--June 1992, Washington D.C.: U.S. Patent and Trademark Office, 1992.

United States Congress, Goldwater-Nichols Department of Defense Reorganization Act of 1986, PL 99-433, 1 October 1986, Section 104.

Valencia Tovar, Alvaro. Inseguridad y Violencia en Colombia. Bogotá: Universidad Sergio Arboleda, 1997.

Van Doren, Charles. A History of Knowledge: Past Present, and Future. New York: Carol Publishing Group, 1991.

Vattel, Emerich de. The Law of Nations. Edited by Joseph Chitty. Philadelphia: T. and J. W. Johnson & Co., 1883.

Von Clausewitz, Carl. On War. Edited and translated by Michael Howard and Peter Paret. Princeton. N.J.: Princeton University Press, 1989.

Waldman, Carl. Atlas of the North American Indian. New York: Facts on File, Inc., 1985.

Walter, Angela Tejada de and Bidó, Soraya Peralta. Mercados de Tierras Rurales en la República Dominicana. Santiago de Chile, United Nation, Red de Desarrollo Agropecuario, 2000.

Weiner, Myron, ed. International Migration and Security. Boulder: Westview, 1993.

Wells, Herbert George. World Brain. London: Methuen & Co. Limited, 1938.

Wriston, Walter B. The Twilight of Sovereignty: How the Information Revolution is Transforming Our World. New York: Charles Scribner's Sons, 1992.

Xuanming, Wang. Secret Art of War: Thirty –Six Strategems. Singapore: Asiapac Books, 1996.

Zoppo, Ciro and Zorgbibe, Charles, eds. On Geopolitics: Classical and Nuclear. Boston: Martinus Nijhoff, 1985.

Index

373

About the Author

Geoffrey Demarest has been an analyst at the Foreign Military Studies Office at Ft. Leavenworth, Kansas since 2000. He is a retired US Army officer and also practiced law as a civilian. He earned his undergraduate degree in Economics at the University of Colorado in 1970, a law degree at the Denver University School of Law in 1980 and PhD at the Denver University Graduate School of International Studies in 1989.

www.ingramcontent.com/pod-product-compliance
Lightning Source LLC
Chambersburg PA
CBHW060959280326
41935CB00009B/766